Working with
The Study of.
Economics
Principles, Concepts & Applications

Sixth Edition

Turley Mings Matthew Marlin

CONNE**CTEXT**

Prepared by

Cynthia Lay Harter	*Eastern Kentucky University*
Matthew Marlin	*Duquesne University*
Turley Mings	*formerly of San Jose State University*

Dushkin/McGraw-Hill
A Division of The McGraw-Hill Companies

Dushkin/McGraw-Hill &

A Division of The McGraw-Hill Companies

Working with The Study of Economics: Principles, Concepts & Applications, Sixth Edition

1 2 3 4 5 6 7 8 9 QPD/QPD 4 3 2 1 0

ISBN 0-07-366244-5

http://www.dushkin.com

To the Student

This workbook is intended to help you get the most out of your text, *The Study of Economics: Principles, Concepts & Applications,* 6th edition. It contains summaries of the text chapters, schematic outlines of each section of the chapters, review exercises in accordance with the learning objectives, additional Case Applications, practice tests, crossword puzzles to test your understanding of the economic terms, and, at the end of the book, answers to the review exercises, workbook Case Application questions, practice tests, and crossword puzzles.

As you study economics you will encounter many concepts that are new to you. Your first objective should be to understand what each of these concepts means. Being able to explain a concept is the first step in being able to make use of it. The second step is recognizing how the concept applies to a particular situation. This entails moving from the ability to explain a concept to the ability to use it in analyzing a situation and reaching logical conclusions with the help of the concept. The final step is making the concept a part of your intellectual resources, so that whenever a situation arises in the future that can be better understood with the use of the concept, it will come to mind.

The ability to make use of economic concepts in reasoning about personal, national, and world economic problems is termed economic literacy. The importance of economic literacy has been widely recognized in recent years. There has been a great increase in the amount of attention given in the media to economic matters. The vocabulary of economics has spread from the confines of classrooms, textbooks, and specialized journals to newspapers, magazines, and the evening news on television. Each national network and many a local station has its own economics reporter appearing with an important story almost every day. Economic terms such as cost-of-living index, Gross Domestic Product, budget deficit, and balance of payments regularly appear in news stories. To understand what the news is about, you have to be economically literate. When you have completed *The Study of Economics* you will be more literate in economics than most people; and if you make a diligent attempt to incorporate the economic principles and concepts into your intellectual equipment, you can contribute to the nation's ability to deal with its economic problems.

This supplement, *Working with The Study of Economics,* includes a variety of aids to increase your economic literacy. Each chapter begins with a *Chapter Outline* of the contents in the text and a *Summary of Economic Analysis* of the chapter. The summary is more succinct than the Putting It Together sections at the end of the textbook chapters. It briefly states the main principles in the chapter.

The text chapters are divided into three to four sections headed by organizing questions, and this workbook is organized similarly. We have included a *Schematic Outline* at the beginning of each section that shows the concept organization of that section. These schematic outlines can be very helpful in your studying. The best way to make use of them is explained as follows, in a format similar to that of the schematic outlines themselves.

In the outline on the next page there are two sequential concepts under the topic of schematic outlines. The first concept is the use of schematic outlines as a preview of the material in the text. It is a well-established principle in learning that you can read a selection with better understanding if you first skim it for content. But skimming complex material is difficult. The schematic outlines provide an easier and more certain way of previewing the reading material. In using the outlines as a preview, focus on the relationships of the different concepts. Note which ones are sequential (listed one after the other, as they are in this case), which ones are parallel (listed side by side, such as the three functions of money--see workbook page 123), and which ones are main and which subordinate concepts. The leading concepts are shown in all capital letters in bold typeface, while secondary concepts are in lowercase letters in bold type. Subordinate concepts appear in boxes within main concept boxes. For example, the attributes of a good medium of exchange are listed in a box contained within the main concept box of "medium of

How Can You Use Your Study Time Most Efficiently?

SCHEMATIC OUTLINES

The schematic outlines at the beginning of each chapter section in this workbook show the relationships between the different concepts and give a brief explanation of their meaning. These outlines can increase the efficiency of your study time when used as follows:

As a Preview

Studies of how people learn show that you get more out of reading something if you have an idea in advance of what the reading is about. Before you read a section in the textbook, look over the schematic outline of that section. Do not try to understand everything in the outline. Concentrate on the headings and observe how the different concepts relate to each other— which ones are parallel concepts, which are sequential, and which are subordinate concepts of others.

As a Review

After reading the section in the textbook chapter, go over the schematic outline again. This time study it more carefully to reinforce your learning of the concepts and better retain what you read in the text.

exchange" as one of the functions of money in the example on page 123. When using the schematic outlines as a preview, do not try to master the concepts. Just observe their relationships and skip the fine print.

The second function of the schematic outlines is their use as a review after reading the material. Again, it is an accepted principle--one taught in the study methods seminars that have become popular in recent years--that understanding and retention are improved by reviewing material that you have just read. The schematic outlines provide a convenient means for doing this. Study them more carefully this time. Do read the fine print. If you find that you are not certain of the meaning of a concept, go over it again in the text. For longer retention of the material, it would be helpful for you to review the schematic outlines again the next day.

We have provided a new *Case Application* for each chapter section to give you additional experience in applying the economic concepts to real-world situations. The old adage "Practice makes perfect" is particularly true for economic literacy. Repeated experience in applying economics will give you the ability to make use of economic reasoning in the future. The value of the Case Applications is enhanced by answering the *Economic Reasoning* questions following each one. As in the text, the Case Applications all have three questions. Answering the first of the three should be relatively easy if you have understood the explanation of the concepts in the text. The second question is generally more difficult, requiring you to use economic analysis in answering it. The third question calls for your opinion and involves value judgments as well as economic reasoning. Suggested answers to the Economic Reasoning questions in the workbook are also to be found in the back of this book.

Each chapter then concludes with a *Practice Test* consisting of 15 multiple-choice and 5 true/false questions. These questions have been prepared with the same objectives in mind as those provided to teachers for use in testing. The answers to these questions are also in the back part of the book.

Following the last chapter in each of the four units into which the book is divided is a *Crossword Puzzle* that can be solved by using the key ideas introduced in the unit. The solutions to the crossword puzzles are at the end of the book.

Best wishes with your study of economics! We hope this workbook will make it easier and more rewarding.

Turley Mings
Matthew Marlin

Contents Summary

Contents

CHAPTER 3 ECONOMIC SYSTEMS 29

CHAPTER 4 MARKET PRICING 40

UNIT II. MICROECONOMICS

CHAPTER 5   EARNING AND SPENDING: THE CONSUMER   57

CHAPTER 6   THE BUSINESS FIRM AND MARKET STRUCTURE   68

CHAPTER 7   INDUSTRIAL PERFORMANCE   80

CHAPTER 8 GOVERNMENT AND BUSINESS 92

CHAPTER 9 GOVERNMENT AND HOUSEHOLDS 105

CHAPTER 13 PUBLIC FINANCE 164

CHAPTER 14 POLICIES FOR ECONOMIC STABILITY AND GROWTH 177

Crossword Puzzle for Chapters 10–14   195

UNIT IV.   WORLD ECONOMICS

CHAPTER 15   INTERNATIONAL TRADE   196

CHAPTER 16   INTERNATIONAL FINANCE AND THE NATIONAL ECONOMY   212

Chapter 1
Economic Methods

I. Chapter Outline

The study of economics is the study of how society deals with the existence of **scarcity**—the fact that we cannot produce enough goods and services for everybody to have everything that he or she wants. Economists study this problem with a variety of factual and theoretical tools; charts and graphs are especially useful.

Introductory Article: An Apple a Day

Small business owners face many economic choices that often involve conflicting interests. They must be aware of factors that affect consumers' demand and their own costs of production. They must also abide by government regulations and adapt production to changes occurring in society. Richard and Maria Hernandez encounter these types of decisions in growing apples and raising bees.

Economic Analysis

This chapter introduces what the study of economics is about and the tools that economists use by addressing the three following questions:

1. **What Is Economics?**

   Important Concepts: Scarcity, The scientific method, Economic reasoning

   Case Application: Who Needs the Rain Forests?

2. **What Are the Tools of Economics?**

   Important Concepts: Factual tools, Theoretical tools

   Case Application: Something in the Air

3. **What Are the Uses of Graphs?**

   Important Concepts: Descriptive charts, Variables, Analytical diagrams

   Comparative Case Application: The Energy Gluttons

Perspective: The Master Model Builder

   Biography—Paul Samuelson

II. Summary of Economic Analysis

1. The basic problem that economics is concerned with is **scarcity**.
2. Anything that is scarce is an **economic good**.
3. Producing economic goods requires the use of **resources**, or **factors of production**, which are also scarce.
4. Economics, like other sciences, makes use of the **scientific method** to analyze facts and draw conclusions. **Economic reasoning** consists of using factual and theoretical tools in a logical manner.
5. Simplified representations of the real world called **economic models** are the most important analytical economic tool.
6. Economists often present descriptive information in **charts** and the relationship between variables in **diagrams**.

III. Review of the Learning Objectives *(Answers begin on p. 256.)*

What Is Economics?

SCARCITY

Economics is the social science concerned with how resources are used to satisfy people's wants. Since there are not sufficient resources to satisfy all wants, economics must overcome the problem of scarcity.

RESOURCES

Land	Labor	Capital
Includes all natural resources—minerals, forests, air, and so forth	Includes workers, managers, and professionals	Generally refers to real capital—the machinery, factories, and office buildings used in production

Entrepreneurs
Individuals who organize resources to produce a good or service

Financial Capital
The funds to purchase the resources used in production

SCIENTIFIC METHOD

The scientific method consists of:

1. observing an event.
2. devising an explanation (hypothesis) accounting for the event.
3. testing the hypothesis.
4. tentatively accepting, rejecting, or revising the hypothesis.

ECONOMIC REASONING

Economic reasoning is the process of applying the tools of economics to a problem in order to understand it and analyze the effects of alternative solutions.

(See page iii in the foreword "To the Student" for how to make the best use of this schematic outline.)

1.1 Explain scarcity as an economic term. *(Write in answers below.)*

(The code 1.1 means chapter 1, Learning Objective 1, in the textbook. You will find this code used throughout this workbook.)

A. The basic problem that economics is concerned with is _scarcity_.

B. Any good that is scarce is called a(n) _economic good_.

C. A rare good or resource is only scarce if someone _wants_ it.

D. Place a check next to the items listed below that are scarce.

1. _✓_ Pure air
2. ____ Radioactive waste
3. ____ Termites
4. _✓_ Time
5. _✓_ Money
6. ____ Flu germs
7. _✓_ Economics instructors

1.2 List the factors of production.

A. Indicate the appropriate resource category of each of the following:

1. Water

   Land

2. Small business owners

   Entrepreneurs / Labor

3. Truck driver

   Labor

4. Technology

   Capital

5. Automobile assembly plant

   Capital

6. Sunshine

   Land

7. Classrooms

   Capital

B. List five specific resources used to produce an economics student.

1. *food*
2. *housing*
3.
4.
5.

1.3 Describe the steps in the scientific method.

A. According to the scientific method, a theory should be accepted if it can accurately

predict

B. The most difficult step in the scientific method for economists is

testing hypothesis

C. Which step in the scientific method is indicated by each of the following:

I cough when I stand behind an idling car.

observation

I hold a bottle over an exhaust pipe, close the bottle, and then examine the contents of the bottle.

gathering data

I make an educated guess that car exhaust makes me cough.

hypothesis

I stand behind another idling car and start coughing again.

accepting the hypothesis

1.4 Give three definitions of economics.

A. Economics is the social science that is concerned with how ___resources___ are used to satisfy ___wants___.

B. Economics is the science of ___choice___

C. The application of theoretical and factual tools of economic analysis to explain economic developments or solve economic problems is ___economic reasoning___

Case Application: The Vanishing Land

In the United States land is disappearing at a rapid rate. Millions of acres have disappeared in the last decade. In Western Europe 1% disappears every 4 or 5 years. Land is disappearing at an even faster rate in much of the less developed areas of the world.

The vanishing land has not ceased to exist, of course. It is disappearing because it is being covered over by expanding cities, highways, and reservoirs, or it is being stripped away for mining. Many of these activities serve a useful purpose, but much of the land that is disappearing is farmland, and the production of food is a basic necessity.

Every year the United States loses about 1.4 million acres of agricultural land to development, and the rate is increasing. Unless the situation changes, urban development in this country over the next 25 years will consume a land area equivalent to that of New Hampshire, Vermont, Massachusetts, and Rhode Island combined.

Additional croplands are being lost to erosion because of farming methods that do not practice conservation. According to a report by the Department of Agriculture, about 3 billion tons of topsoil are being eroded from U.S. croplands every year. For every ton of grain produced, 6 tons of soil are lost to erosion. In Iowa, before the land was cultivated, there was a layer of topsoil that averaged about 16 inches. Today that layer is down to 8 inches, and it continues to diminish.

The conversion of cropland to urban uses and the erosion of topsoil is happening in countries around the globe. Worldwide, erosion is destroying 23 million acres of cropland every year. India may be losing its topsoil at four times the U.S. rate and China even faster: the Yellow River carries 1.6 billion tons of sediment to the sea each year. Some population experts predict that the Earth's population will double in the next generation. If world food output is barely adequate for present needs, what will happen in the future when more food will have to be produced on less available agricultural land?

Economic Reasoning *(Write your responses on a separate sheet. Answers begin on p. 256.)*

1. Which factor of production is becoming more scarce as a result of urban development and wasteful farming practices?
2. Present a hypothesis that explains the reduction in cropland around the world. Can your hypothesis be tested? How?
3. Do you think that the government should force farmers to use farming methods that reduce soil erosion, even though those methods might lower farmers' income? Why or why not?

What Are the Tools of Economics?

FACTUAL TOOLS	THEORETICAL TOOLS

FACTUAL TOOLS

Statistics

Data	Methods

History

Economic history

Institutions

Organizations
Customs
Patterns of behavior

THEORETICAL TOOLS

Economic Concepts

Words or phrases that convey a specific meaning in economics

Economic Models

Simplified representations of the real world

Words	Mathematical equations	Graphs

1.5 Describe three types of factual tools used in economics.

A. What are the three types of factual tools used by economists?

1. _Statistics_
2. _History_
3. _Institutions_

B. Indicate which factual tool of economics is demonstrated by each of the following:

1. The levels of U.S. and Mexican imports and exports
   Statistics

2. Free trade agreements
   Institutions

3. The effects of free trade with other countries
   history

4. Tariffs and quotas
   institutions

5. The effects of free trade on Mexican unemployment rates
   Statistics

C. Two uses of statistics are to _describe_ data and to _analyze_ data.

1.6 Describe the theoretical tools used in economics.

A. Economic _Concepts_ are ideas that convey specific meanings in economics, and economic _Models_ are simplified representations of the real world.

B. Indicate whether the following are concepts (C) or models (M).

1. _C_ Unemployment
2. _C_ Scarcity
3. _M_ Cost-benefit analysis
4. _C_ Equity
5. _M_ Diagrams

6. _M_ $Y = a + b(X)$ (the equation of a line)

7. _M_ Weight increases with height

C. In what three ways can models be presented?

1. _words_

2. _equations_

3. _graphs_

Case Application: Hot or Cold? Cost-Benefit Analysis

A small publishing company was having trouble controlling the temperature in its editorial offices. Because of poor insulation and the exposed location of the building, the offices were difficult and expensive to heat on winter mornings. During the summer, they were equally difficult to cool. The company engaged an engineer to study the situation. He recommended the following improvements and estimated their costs:

Additional air conditioning	$1,200
Additional insulation	2,500
Storm windows and screens	700
Total cost of improvements	$4,400

The engineer also estimated the dollar value of the benefits these improvements would provide. The benefits consisted of the following:

Reduced heating costs from storm windows, screens, insulation	$600 per year
Minus: Increased electric costs for new air conditioning	−175 per year
Net expected savings (benefits)	$425 per year

The company's controller analyzed these costs and benefits and calculated that the cost of the investment would be fully recovered only after 11 years, ignoring future increases in utility costs. With utility costs expected to increase 10% a year, based on past experience, the investment would be recovered in 8 years. But the company's goal was to recover its investment of capital within 5 years. The controller, therefore, could not justify this investment strictly on financial grounds. In fact, several other investment proposals were likely to pay back their investments in periods of 5 years or less.

But the president of the company felt that other benefits had to be considered, some of which could not be measured in dollars and cents. He felt the company should provide its employees with reasonably good working conditions. If necessary, the company would have to accept reduced profitability. Actually, he doubted profits would suffer from this investment, because he was confident that improved office facilities would generate less-obvious cost benefits to the company that the controller had not uncovered, such as increased productivity among its employees.

Economic Reasoning (Write your responses on a separate sheet. Answers begin on p. 256.)

1. What type of economic tool is a cost-benefit analysis?
2. Are there examples of three types of factual tools in this analysis? What are they?
3. Should the president of the company make the improvements even if it results in reducing profits? Why or why not?

What Are the Uses of Graphs?

DESCRIPTIVE CHARTS

Type of Chart	Use
Pie chart	To show the relative size of the components of a whole
Line graph	To show the statistical relation of two or more variables
Column chart	To compare the discrete values of one variable with another or the values of a single variable over time
Bar chart	Similiar to column chart
Area chart	To show the way in which the relative components of a variable change over time

Variable—an item whose value changes in relation to changes in the value of another item

Time series—a graph with years measured on the horizontal axis

ANALYTICAL DIAGRAMS

These graphic models show the relationship between two or more variables. They are based on observation and economic reasoning.

Direct Relationship	Inverse Relationship
When two related variables change in the same direction, they have a direct relationship.	When two related variables change in opposite directions, they have an inverse relationship.

1.7 Give four examples of different types of charts.

A. Present the following (hypothetical) data in a *line graph:*

Year	Population (100 thousands)
1991	2.0
1992	2.1
1993	2.3
1994	2.2
1995	2.5
1996	2.8
1997	2.2
1998	2.5

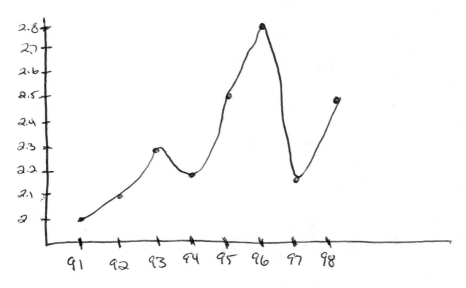

B. Present the following (hypothetical) data showing the tons of pollution in the air in a *stacked column chart:*

Year	Pollution from CFCs	Pollution from Energy Production	Other	Total Pollution
1993	0.6	1.2	0.2	2.0
1994	0.6	2.3	0.3	3.2
1995	0.7	3.5	0.0	4.2
1996	0.5	6.1	0.7	7.3
1997	0.7	3.4	0.1	4.2
1998	0.5	3.4	0.2	4.1

C. Present the following (hypothetical) data comparing the 1990 and 1998 average incomes of high school dropouts, high school graduates, and college graduates in a *column chart:*

	1990	1998
Dropouts	$12,000	$14,000
High school graduates	18,000	22,000
College graduates	27,000	32,000

D. Present in a *pie chart* the following (hypothetical) data describing students' spending patterns.

Spending Category	Percent of Budget
Food	10
Clothing	20
Housing	5
Entertainment	35
Transportation	10
Medical Care	5
Other	15

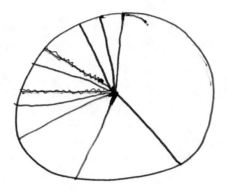

1.8 Explain what an analytical diagram is used for.

A. Diagrams are used to show the relationship between two _____.

B. A diagram that shows a line sloping down and to the right is showing a(n) _____ relationship.

C. A diagram that shows a line sloping up and to the right is showing a(n) _____ relationship.

D. Whereas _____ are generally used to describe data, _____ are generally used to show relationships.

1.9 Draw and label an analytical diagram showing the relationship between two variables.

A. Agnes can read 5 pages of economics in an hour, Bob can read 8 pages in an hour, and Carlos can read 10 pages in an hour. Construct and label a diagram that shows how much each can read in 1, 2, 3, or 4 hours. (Put pages on the vertical axis and hours on the horizontal axis.)

B. The following table shows the number of baby buggies Boris made per week in his first 6 weeks on the job. Construct and label a diagram that shows this "learning curve" by graphing weeks on the horizontal axis and the number of buggies on the vertical axis.

Week	Number
1	5
2	9
3	15
4	23
5	25
6	26

What does the diagram tell you about learning curves?

_____

C. The Military Industrial Company (MIC) made 10 cannons this past year and had no olive trees. MIC can trade cannons to Dove Industries at a rate of 1 cannon for 2 olive trees. Construct and label a diagram that shows how MIC's number of cannons (on the vertical axis) declines and its number of olive trees increases (on the horizontal axis), as it trades more and more cannons for trees. Indicate on the diagram the number of cannons and trees MIC will have if it trades 2, 5, or 10 cannons.

D. Jerome has a part-time job and earns $8/hour. He can work up to 20 hours per week. Draw and label a diagram that shows the number of hours worked on the horizontal axis and Jerome's total earnings on the vertical axis. Use the diagram to show how much Jerome will earn if he works 8 hours in a given week.

E. One molecule of CFC will destroy 2,500 molecules of ozone, and with each percentage point drop in the amount of ozone, the strength of ultraviolet radiation increases by 2 percentage points.

1. Construct an analytical diagram that shows the relationship between the level of CFCs and the level of ozone in the atmosphere. (Put CFCs on the horizontal axis.)

2. Construct an analytical diagram that shows the relationship between ozone levels and the level of ultraviolet rays. (Put ozone levels on the horizontal axis.)

3. Construct an analytical diagram that shows the relationship between the level of CFCs and the level of ultraviolet rays. (Put CFCs on the horizontal axis.)

Case Application: Air Quality in the United States

The threat of global warming is only one aspect of the problem of air pollution. Another is the quality of the air we breathe. The government's efforts to upgrade our air quality, which began with the passing of the Clean Air Act in 1970, have made some progress.

As the table below illustrates, particulate matter has decreased significantly. This reduction is largely due to less reliance on coal, especially soft coal, as a source of heat and energy and to the regulations imposed on smokestack emissions. While the emissions of nitrogen dioxide have remained fairly steady since 1970, the emissions of other gases such as sulfur dioxide and carbon monoxide have declined. Again, this can be attributed to regulations imposed on these emissions.

The most progress has been made in reducing the amount of lead in the air. The amount of lead in the air in 1995 was only 2% of 1970 levels, and this is credited for the most part to the use of unleaded gasoline. It is a very important victory in the clean air battle because of the great health hazards of lead.

Altogether, U.S. industry releases a rather significant amount of toxic substances into the air each year. Add to this the air pollution from vehicles and households, and you have to consider whether breathing isn't hazardous to your health.

National Air Pollution Emissions, 1970–1995

(In thousands of tons except where noted)

Year	Particles*	Sulfur Dioxide	Nitrogen Dioxide	Carbon Monoxide	Lead (tons)
1970	13,044	31,161	20,625	128,079	219,471
1975	7,617	28,011	21,889	115,110	158,541
1980	7,050	25,905	23,281	115,625	74,956
1985	4,094	23,230	22,860	114,690	21,124
1990	3,195	22,433	23,038	100,650	5,666
1995	3,050	18,319	21,779	92,099	4,986

*less than 10 microns

Source: *Statistical Abstract of the United States.*

Economic Reasoning *(Write your responses on a separate sheet. Answers begin on p. 258.)*

1. What type of chart would be best for showing the data in the table? Make a rough sketch of the chart, labeling the vertical and horizontal axes and showing the measurement scales.
2. How would you diagram the relationship between the quantity of gaseous emissions and air quality? Is it a direct relationship or an inverse relationship? Sketch such a diagram, labeling the axes but not including any measurement scales.
3. Should air quality standards be tightened even further, despite the costs to producers and consumers? Why or why not?

IV. Practice Test *(Answers begin on p. 258.)*

Multiple-Choice Questions *(Circle the correct answer.)*

(1.1) 1. Economics is the study of which one of the following?
    a. how to operate a business
    b. how to turn resources into economic goods
    c. how to satisfy human wants with limited resources
    d. how to eliminate scarcity

(1.1) 2. Which one of the following best summarizes the economic problem of scarcity?
    a. rarity
    b. economic reasoning
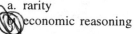

    c. factors of production
    d. limited resources and unlimited wants

(1.2) 3. The development and use of a Web site to accompany this textbook is considered what type of resource?
    a. land
    b. labor
    c. capital
    d. entrepreneurship

(1.2) 4. What do entrepreneurs do?
    a. They eliminate (or try to eliminate) scarcity.
    b. They combine resources to make economic goods.
    c. They produce and sell the factors of production.
    d. They work according to the scientific method.

(1.3) 5. The scientific method includes each of the following steps *except*
    a. assuming the correct conclusion.
    b. gathering data.
    c. rejecting or accepting a hypothesis.
    d. observing an event.

(1.3) 6. Economic reasoning includes each of the following *except*
    a. logical reasoning.
    b. assumptions about human behavior.
    c. critical thinking.
    d. value judgments.

(1.4) 7. Which one of the following best summarizes the concept of economic reasoning?
    a. observation of an event and formulation of an economic hypothesis
    b. body of skills and knowledge that makes up the processes used in production
    c. limited resources for production relative to the demand for goods and services
    d. application of tools of economic analysis to explaining economic developments

(1.4) 8. Which one of the following is a definition of economics?
    a. the science of choice
    b. the study of abundant resources
    c. the science that is concerned with how pollution affects society
    d. the application of experimental results to modifying human behavior

(1.5) 9. Which one of the following is considered to be an economic institution?
    a. private property
    b. the unemployment rate
    c. the greenhouse effect
    d. pollution

(1.6) 10. Which one of the following is the best one-word definition of an economic concept?
    a. an institution
    b. a model
    c. an idea
    d. a relationship
    e. a definition

(1.6) 11. Economic models can be presented in which one of the following forms?
    a. mathematical equations
    b. analytical diagrams
    c. words (verbal descriptions)
    d. all of the above
    e. none of the above

(1.7) 12. The relative sizes of the parts that make up a whole are best shown in which one of the following?
    a. an analytical diagram
    b. a bar chart
    c. a pie chart
    d. a time series
    e. a line chart

(1.7) 13. Time series are best shown by using which kind of charts?
    a. analytical diagrams
    b. pie charts
    c. column charts
    d. line charts
    e. area charts

(1.8) 14. Analytical diagrams are usually used to show the relationship between two
    a. concepts.
    b. models.
    c. charts or graphs.
    d. variables.

(1.8) 15. Which one of the statements below is *true* concerning the following graph?
    a. As P increases, so does Q.
    b. The variables P and Q are directly related.
    c. The variables P and Q are inversely related.
    d. There is no systematic relationship between the variables P and Q.

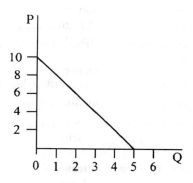

True/False Questions *(Circle T or F.)*

(1.1) 16. In economics, a resource is said to be scarce when the amount available is less than the amount needed to satisfy our wants. T or F

(1.2) 17. The three factors of production are land, labor, and technology. T or F

(1.3) 18. The first step in the scientific method is to devise a hypothesis. T or F

(1.6) 19. The two principal theoretical tools of economics are concepts and models. T or F

(1.8) 20. We use analytical diagrams to help us understand how two or more variables relate to one another. T or F

Chapter 2
Economic Choices

I. Chapter Outline

We cannot have everything we want (because of *scarcity*), so we are forced to make choices. An unfortunate reality is that when we make a *choice* to have one thing, we are at the same time choosing to give up (*trade off*) something else. What we give up is a very real *cost* associated with every choice we make. This relationship—scarcity implies choice implies cost—is the heart and soul of the study of economics. Or, as we economists like to say, "There's no such thing as a free lunch!"

Introductory Article: Steeling Away

What is your impression of the city of Pittsburgh? It was formerly the world's leading producer of steel, and the environment in the city was grimy and dirty. However, recent changes have decreased the importance of steel production to the economy of Pittsburgh. Today the city is a leader in industries such as robotics and organ transplants. The choices Pittsburgh's citizens have made concerning the use of their economic resources have changed during the twentieth century.

Economic Analysis

This chapter introduces the heart of the economic problem: the fact that choices always must be made and that everything has a cost. The chapter addresses the problem by asking the following three questions:

1. **What Are the Consequences of Economic Choices?**

   Important Concepts: Trade-offs, Opportunity costs, Increasing costs

   Important Model: Production possibility frontier

   Case Application: Tough Choices

2. **What Are the Basic Economic Questions?**

   Important Concepts: Infrastructure

   Case Application: To Nuclear or Not to Nuclear

3. **What Are Society's Economic Goals?**

   Important Concepts: Efficiency, Full employment, Price stability, Economic growth, Socioeconomic goals

   Case Application: The Computer Craze

   Perspective: The Affluent Society

   Biography—John Kenneth Galbraith

II. Summary of Economic Analysis

1. Because of **scarcity** we must make **choices** about how to use our scarce resources.
2. Choices involve **trade-offs**.
3. That which is given up in a trade-off is the **opportunity cost**—or cost—associated with the choice. Every choice results in a cost.
4. In a general sense, we must make choices about **what** we are going to produce, **how** we are going to produce it, and **for whom** we are producing.

5. In order to make our choices wisely, and to get the most from our scarce resources, we must know what we are trying to achieve: we must agree on certain **economic goals**.

6. Most economists agree on the desirability of these economic goals: **economic growth**, **efficiency**, **full employment**, and **price stability**.

7. In contrast to their agreement about economic goals, economists have different values and therefore different attitudes toward **socioeconomic goals** such as equity, environmental pollution, and income security.

III. Review of the Learning Objectives *(Answers begin on p. 258.)*

What Are the Consequences of Economic Choices?

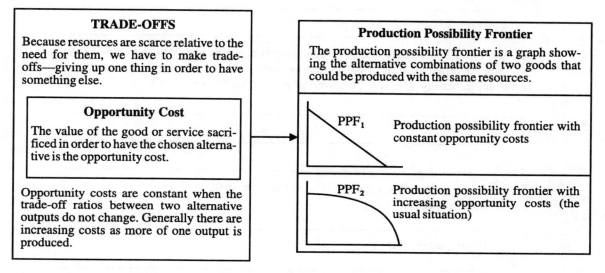

TRADE-OFFS

Because resources are scarce relative to the need for them, we have to make trade-offs—giving up one thing in order to have something else.

Opportunity Cost

The value of the good or service sacrificed in order to have the chosen alternative is the opportunity cost.

Opportunity costs are constant when the trade-off ratios between two alternative outputs do not change. Generally there are increasing costs as more of one output is produced.

Production Possibility Frontier

The production possibility frontier is a graph showing the alternative combinations of two goods that could be produced with the same resources.

PPF₁ — Production possibility frontier with constant opportunity costs

PPF₂ — Production possibility frontier with increasing opportunity costs (the usual situation)

(See page iii in the foreword "To the Student" for how to make the best use of this schematic outline.)

2.1 Define and give examples of economic trade-offs. *(Write in answers below.)*

A. Having to trade off one thing to get another is sometimes an unpleasant experience. Nonetheless we are forced to make trade-offs because of

_____

B. Indicate three things that U.S. citizens have "traded off" in return for their military strength.

_____

_____

_____

C. Give three examples of trade-offs that you make with one of your truly scarce resources—your time.

_____

_____

_____

D. Indicate one possible cost of each of the following:
   1. Increased public infrastructure investment

_____

2. Constructing a new shopping mall

_____

3. Sleeping late in the morning

_____

4. Going to a movie

_____

2.2 Apply the concept of opportunity cost to any economic choice.

A. What is the economic meaning of the expression, "There's no such thing as a free lunch"?

_____

_____

B. Mr. Jones is a teacher and Ms. Applegate is a pharmacist. Would they have the same or different ideas about the opportunity cost of increased health care? Explain, indicating who will perceive the costs to be higher.

_____

_____

_____

C. Indicate your possible opportunity cost for each of the following:
1. Baking a cake

_____

2. Buying a new CD

_____

3. Planting an apple tree in your yard

_____

4. Going to college

_____

5. Attending economics class

_____

6. Paying taxes

_____

D. What is the opportunity cost of eating a big piece of hot apple pie with ice cream?

_____

2.3 Use a production possibility frontier to demonstrate increasing costs, trade-offs, opportunity cost, and economic growth.

A. The country of Utopia has the following production possibilities:

Item	A	B	C	D	E	F	G
CD Players	0	20	40	60	80	100	120
Cellular Telephones	180	170	155	135	100	60	0

Use the grid below to plot each of the these points and draw the economy's production possibility frontier. Label each point (A, B, C, etc.) on your graph.

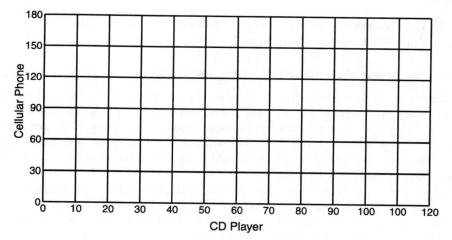

1.
   a. Starting at Point A on your graph, what is the opportunity cost of 20 CD players?
   b. Starting at Point B on your graph, what is the opportunity cost of 20 CD players?
   c. Starting at Point C on your graph, what is the opportunity cost of 20 CD players?
   d. Starting at Point D on your graph, what is the opportunity cost of 20 CD players?
2. The trade-off between CD players and cellular telephones is an example of
_____ opportunity costs.

B. The country of Nirvana has the following production possibilities:

Item	A	B	C	D	E	F	G
CD Players	0	20	40	60	80	100	120
Cellular Telephones	180	150	120	90	60	30	0

Use the grid below to plot each of the these points and draw the economy's production possibility frontier. Label each point (A, B, C, etc.) on your graph.

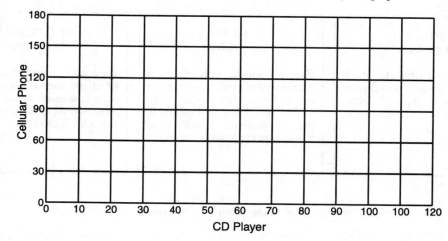

1.
   a. Starting at Point A on your graph, what is the opportunity cost of 20 CD players?
   b. Starting at Point B on your graph, what is the opportunity cost of 20 CD players?
   c. Starting at Point C on your graph, what is the opportunity cost of 20 CD players?
   d. Starting at Point D on your graph, what is the opportunity cost of 20 CD players?
2. The trade-off between CD players and cellular telephones is an example of
_____ opportunity costs.

C. Compare the production possibility frontiers in A and B above. What do the shapes (slopes) of the frontiers imply about the substitutability of productive resources between the production processes for each country?

D. The production possibility curve is an example of an economic _____.
(Hint: the answer is from chapter 1.)

Case Application: Spotted Owls vs. Loggers

In the northwestern United States, there is an ongoing battle between environmentalists and the logging industry. The survival of northern spotted owls is threatened as their habitat disappears when trees are cut for timber production. The owls are protected by the Endangered Species Act of 1973, and policymakers have concluded that protecting the owls means preserving the forests in which they live. The central question now is how much of the forests to preserve.

Towns such as Forks, Washington, and Sweet Home, Oregon, have been hit hard by restrictions on logging that are intended to protect the habitat of the spotted owl. Unemployment has soared, businesses are failing, and tax revenues are declining in these towns. Some are asking whether it is better to save an owl or save a logger.

While the residents of many of these cities are dealing with loss of jobs and incomes, citizens in other areas of the United States are not really incurring costs for preserving the owls. At most, they may experience slightly higher prices for lumber, furniture, homes, or other wood products.

Economic Reasoning *(Write your responses on a separate sheet. Answers begin on p. 259.)*

1. What are the trade-offs involved in this situation?
2. What is the opportunity cost of saving the habitat of the spotted owl? Sketch a diagram showing the trade-offs between owls and loggers. Are there increasing opportunity costs?
3. What, if anything, should the government do about this issue?

What Are the Basic Economic Questions?

WHAT to produce	**HOW** to produce	**FOR WHOM** to produce
The economic system must decide what goods and services to produce with its land, labor, and capital.	The economic system must decide how to produce each good or service—determining what mix of land, labor, and capital to use in production and what production methods to employ.	The economic system must decide which members of society will receive how much of the goods and services produced—the process of allocating income.

2.4 Give examples of the three basic economic questions.

A. Each of the following economic situations presents an example of resolving one of the three basic economic questions. Indicate the correct question (or questions) in each case.

1. Congress debates what to do with the budget surplus. _____ and _____

2. The recreation department of Brownsville, U.S.A., is considering buying automated garbage trucks. _____

3. An automobile manufacturer is contemplating installing robots on the assembly line. _____

4. Consumers become more health conscious and start to eat foods that they think are better for them._____

B. An economy's selection of either point A or point B on the production possibility frontier shown below involves answering which of the three basic economic questions?

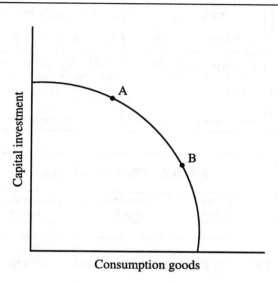

Case Application: **Is Coal the Heir to the Energy Throne?**

Coal, the presumptive heir to the energy throne as petroleum supplies give out in the future and nuclear power becomes more costly and dangerous, doesn't look the part right now. The industry's profits are rather small, often as low as 5 cents a ton after taxes. And despite the fact that coal costs only about one-fourth as much as petroleum per unit of energy produced, utility companies have been slow to embrace coal as a substitute for oil in generating electricity. The air pollution and acid rainwater from burning coal violate environmental standards and are expensive to clean up.

However, coal is regaining some of the respect it had. Long-closed mines are being reopened and new mines are being dug. A lot of the new activity is in underground mines rather than on the surface strip mines. The underground mines of Appalachia produce a higher quality of coal, lower in sulphur content, than the coal from the strip mines of the western states. And the Appalachian coal is closer to eastern industrial centers and to seaports for shipment to European customers.

We should be able to supply European coal needs as well as our own for some time to come. It is estimated that the United States has a 200-year supply of coal reserves. The obstacles to coal regaining its throne as the king of energy are the costs of extracting it and the environmental costs of burning it.

Economic Reasoning *(Write your responses on a separate sheet. Answers begin on p. 259.)*

1. The decision about whether to produce coal by underground tunneling or surface strip mining illustrates which type of basic economic decision?
2. What considerations enter into the "what" decision regarding the production of coal?
3. Should coal be substituted for nuclear power in the production of electricity, even if it results in an increase in air and water pollution? Why or why not?

What Are Society's Economic Goals?

PRINCIPALLY ECONOMIC GOALS			
Growth	**Efficiency**	**Price Stability**	**Full Employment**
Economic growth comes from an increase in the production capacity of the economy.	Obtaining the largest possible amount of output per unit of input helps to overcome scarcity.	It is important to have the overall level of prices for goods and services remain relatively constant.	It is best to have an unemployment level of not more than 4% or 5%, considered full employment.

SOCIOECONOMIC GOALS				
Environmental Protection	**Financial Security**	**Economic Equity**	**Economic Justice**	**Economic Freedom**

2.5 Understand the four primary economic goals of society.

A. List the four economic goals.

1. _____

2. _____

3. _____

4. _____

B. Using the numbers to your answers in exercise A, indicate which goal each of the following statements reflects.

1. ____ Congress passes a tax act designed to stimulate investment in new capital equipment.

2. ____ The Federal Reserve bank announces plans to fight inflation.

3. ____ Mega Motors Corporation announces plans to install robots on all assembly lines in order to increase productivity.

4. ____ The president announces a new program designed to find jobs for workers who are replaced by robots.

2.6 Explain the effect on output of increasing employment to full employment.

A. Reducing unemployment is an economic goal for two reasons. What are they?

1. _____

2. _____

B. Reducing unemployment also contributes to achieving the economic goal of _____ .

C. The production possibility frontier below shows the trade-offs involved in producing peanut butter and jelly. Indicate points that correspond to the following:

1. Unemployment (point A)
2. Full employment (point B)
3. An unattainable level of output (point C)

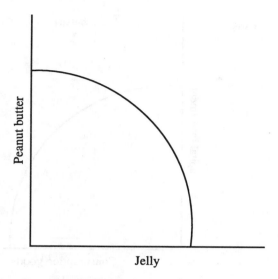

2.7 Explain the effect on output of improving economic efficiency.

A. The production possibility frontier below shows an economy's trade-off between M-16 tanks and automobiles.

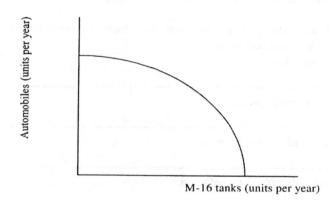

1. Label a point A that corresponds to efficient production.
2. Label a point B that corresponds to inefficient production.

B. Which of the following is (are) consistent with efficient production?
1. unemployment rate of 15%
2. fully using all available resources
3. giving employees 30-minute breaks twice a day
4. producing a specific quantity of output at the lowest possible cost

2.8 Explain the effect on economic growth of producing and using technologically sophisticated capital goods.

A. The production possibility frontier (PPF) below shows an economy's trade-off between consumption goods and capital goods.

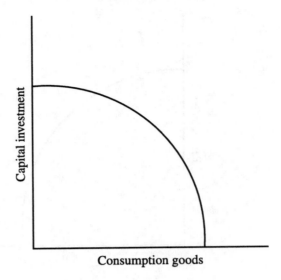

1. Indicate a point on the curve (point A) that reflects more capital investment than consumption spending.
2. Add two new PPFs to the graph: one that shows more current consumption and one that shows less current consumption.

B. Give an example of a productive investment in capital that might be carried out by each of the following:

1. Your school

_____

2. Your local government

_____

3. The federal government

_____

4. An automobile manufacturer

_____

5. A law office

_____

2.9 Give examples of trade-offs between economic and socioeconomic goals.

A. In each of the following situations, indicate an economic goal (or goals) that will be promoted and a socioeconomic goal that will *not* be promoted.

1. A farmer uses insecticides to produce more apples.
   Economic goal:

_____

   Socioeconomic goal:

_____

2. A manufacturer installs robots to produce more goods at lower costs.
   Economic goal:

_____

   Socioeconomic goal:

_____

3. The government places price controls on the sellers of gasoline (your local gas station).

Economic goal:

_____

Socioeconomic goal:

_____

4. Congress passes an act that reduces aid for social programs and increases subsidies for capital investment.

Economic goal:

_____

Socioeconomic goal:

_____

B. Cite three examples of conflicts between economic and socioeconomic goals that have been in the news recently.

1. _____

2. _____

3. _____

2.10 Understand the connection between choices in consumption and choices in production.

A. Consumers affect decisions about how resources are allocated when they _____.

B. Cite two examples of consumer decisions that you have observed that have affected what is produced in the United States.

Case Application: **A Plastic World**

Plastics, along with computers and robotics, have become ubiquitous in the modern world. The growth of the plastics industry in the past two decades has been three times that of manufacturing in general.

Part of the growth of plastics has been at the expense of other, more traditional materials—steel in automobile production, wood in furniture production, and natural fibers in clothing—depriving workers in those older industries of a livelihood. But some of the growth in the use of plastics has been in entirely new products made possible by this material: foam for flotation and packaging and artificial-turf football fields, for example.

One of the useful characteristics of plastics, their durability, has also turned out to be one of their drawbacks, a drawback which some environmentalists fear poses a danger to the planet's life-forms and ecosystem. Plastic garbage is collecting in the oceans in astonishing quantities. Underwater explorers have come across great "rivers" of plastic garbage carried by currents in the middle of the Atlantic and other oceans. Four biologists who went to study the seabirds on Laysan, a small island in a remote area of the Pacific about 1,000 miles northwest of Hawaii, were startled to find the beaches strewn with all sorts of plastic trash that had washed ashore.

Other types of garbage tend to decompose under the corrosive action of air, sun, and water. But many plastics are virtually indestructible in the natural environment. They not only despoil nature, but are taking a heavy toll on marine life that ingest or become entangled in them—especially seals, sea lions, turtles, and various species of seabirds, such as the albatross.

Chemists at a U.S. Department of Agriculture research center and in private laboratories are attempting to develop plastics that will decompose after a period of time in water or under sunlight. But, perversely, plastics that will decompose tend to be more expensive to produce than those that will last indefinitely.

Economic Reasoning *(Write your responses on a separate sheet. Answers begin on p. 260.)*

1. What economic goals has the plastics industry helped in achieving?
2. How has the growth of the plastics industry also resulted in a trade-off of some economic or socioeconomic goals that are not being satisfied?
3. Should growth of the plastics industry be retarded by restricting the use of plastics that are not biodegradable? Why or why not?

IV. Practice Test *(Answers begin on p. 260.)*

Multiple-Choice Questions *(Circle the correct answer.)*

(2.1) 1. Why are trade-offs necessary?
   a. because resources are scarce
   b. because of increasing costs
   c. because economic goals sometimes conflict with each other
   d. because of different production possibilities

(2.2) 2. Which one of the following best describes the concept "opportunity cost"?
   a. the money spent to produce goods and services
   b. the monetary (dollar) value of goods and services
   c. the value of what must be given up to get something
   d. the cost of eliminating scarcity

(2.2) 3. Which one of the following is an opportunity cost of a clean and safe environment?
   a. colder houses in the winter because of less heating
   b. more expensive fruit because of fewer pesticides
   c. colder food due to less use of heat-insulating foam containers
   d. all of the above

(2.3) 4. Production possibility frontiers are usually curved (rather than being straight lines) because of
   a. economies of scale.
   b. increasing costs.
   c. opportunity costs.
   d. less-than-full employment.

(2.3) 5. A point lying *outside* of the production possibility frontier represents which one of the following?
   a. unemployment
   b. high prices
   c. increasing costs
   d. an unattainable combination of two goods

(2.4) 6. Which one of the following is an example of the "how" question?
   a. determining the mix of public and private goods people will get
   b. determining whether to use labor-intensive or capital-intensive production techniques
   c. determining how to divide public goods among different groups
   d. determining how to price different resources for different uses

(2.5) 7. Which one of the following is *not* an economic goal?
   a. equity
   b. efficiency
   c. price stability
   d. full employment

(2.5) 8. What is the importance (significance) of economic goals?
- a. Each goal provides the answer to one of the basic economic questions.
- b. Economic goals provide a moral or ethical basis for creating an economically fair society.
- c. Economic goals are necessary to help guide us when we make economic choices.
- d. Achieving these economic goals is the only way to overcome the problem of scarcity.

(2.6) 9. Which one of the following is the best description of "full employment"?
- a. Everyone who wants a job has a job.
- b. Everyone who is not retired or in school has a job.
- c. Every household has at least one person with a job.
- d. The level of employment necessary to overcome scarcity has been reached.

(2.7) 10. The graph below shows a production possibility frontier for a hypothetical country. Which point on the graph represents efficient production?
- a. A
- b. B
- c. C
- d. D

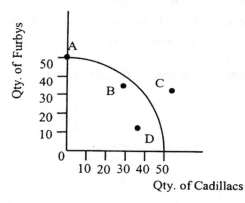

(2.7) 11. Efficiency means
- a. an economy's entire stock of capital.
- b. the real economic cost of a good or service.
- c. maximizing the amount of output obtained from a given amount of resources.
- d. choosing between alternative uses for a given quantity of productive resources.

(2.7) 12. Which one of the following is a *true* statement?
- a. Economic growth cannot be influenced by society's choices about what to produce.
- b. A society's choice to produce consumption goods has no effect on its ability to produce capital goods.
- c. Choosing to produce more capital goods today will result in greater economic growth in the future.
- d. An economy can make choices about which consumption goods to produce, but there are no choices that can influence the level of capital investment.

(2.7) 13. Investment in new plants and equipment creates which of the following?
- a. more capital
- b. greater productive capacity
- c. economic growth
- d. all of the above

(2.9) 14. Cleaning up our environment and keeping it pollution-free will more than likely *directly* conflict with which of the following?
   a. the goal of equity
   b. the goal of economic growth
   c. the goal of price stability
   d. the goal of economic freedom

(2.10) 15. Which one of the following situations is *not* an example of consumption choices affecting production choices?
   a. Americans increasingly prefer automobiles with leather interiors.
   b. A vaccine for cancer is discovered and Americans flock to their doctors' offices to get the shot.
   c. Farmers plant more wheat because the government offers to purchase any surpluses at prices above market-determined levels.
   d. Medical reports emphasizing the importance of good nutrition cause consumers to purchase more healthy snacks and fewer snacks that are high in fat.

True/False Questions *(Circle T or F.)*

(2.2) 16. Because of scarcity, everything has an opportunity cost. T or F

(2.3) 17. The PPF is curved because of trade-offs. T or F

(2.5) 18. Achieving an equitable distribution of income is an economic goal. T or F

(2.6) 19. The goal of "full employment" helps an economy reach the goal of "economic growth." T or F

(2.8) 20. Because capital is a resource, investing in more of it leads to economic growth. T or F

Chapter 3
Economic Systems

I. Chapter Outline

Every society must resolve the three basic economic questions of what, how, and for whom to produce. Finding satisfactory answers requires the use of some type of economic **system** of organizing and coordinating economic activities. The more advanced and more complex societies become, the more they depend on such systems and the more important the systems become. Like most other industrialized countries, the United States depends primarily on the free-market economic system.

Introductory Article: That Old Time Rock and Roll

What kind of music is your favorite? Regardless of your preferences, the way music and musical instruments are produced today differs greatly from the way they were produced 100 years ago because of technological advancements.While this discussion focuses on such developments in the area of rock and roll music, societies in general are continually evolving and finding new ways to answer the three basic economic questions.

Economic Analysis

This chapter introduces economic systems and examines the way that they work by addressing the following three questions:

  1. **Why Are Economic Systems Needed?**

     Important Concepts: Specialization, Absolute and comparative advantage, Interdependence

     Case Application: The Efficiency Burger

  2. **What Are the Principal Types of Economic Systems?**

     Important Concepts: Market economies, Centrally directed economies, Traditional economies, Mixed economies

     Case Application: Islamic Economics

  3. **How Does a Market System Resolve the Three Basic Economic Questions?**

     Important Concepts: Markets, Incentives, Product and factor markets, Rent, Interest, Households, Businesses

     Important Model: The circular flow diagram

     Case Application: The Burger Wars

Perspective: The Industrial Revolution

II. Summary of Economic Analysis

1. **Specialization** in production increases economic efficiency.
2. Specialization should be based on **comparative advantage,** where one producer can produce a good or service at a lower opportunity cost than the other. If two producers have **absolute advantages** in different production methods (that is, each one can produce more of one good or service than the other with the same amount of resources), then each producer also has a comparative advantage in the production method in which he or she has an absolute advantage.
3. Specialization leads to **interdependence**.
4. Because of interdependence, modern societies need some type of **economic system** to organize and coordinate production and distribution, and thereby find answers to the three basic questions (what, how, and for whom to produce).
5. Three types of economic systems that have been used in the past and continue to be used today are **free-market, centrally directed,** and **traditional** economic systems.
6. To a greater or lesser extent, all modern economies are **mixed economies**—they contain aspects of all three types of economic systems.
7. **Markets** are either real or abstract places where buyers and sellers meet to buy and sell goods and services.
8. In market economies, the **profit motive** is the incentive for businesses to buy resources and sell finished products.
9. **Factor markets** are where the different factors of production (resources) are bought and sold. These markets represent the inputs into the production process.
10. **Product markets** are where finished goods and services (consumption goods) are sold to their final users. These markets represent the outputs of the production process.
11. The term **households** is used to represent those parts of the economy that own and sell resources and buy finished goods.
12. The term **businesses** is used to represent those parts of the economy that buy resources, undertake production, and sell finished goods.
13. The **circular flow diagram** is an important model that shows the circular nature of a market economy. Households sell resources to businesses and buy finished goods from businesses. Businesses buy resources from households and sell finished goods to households.
14. Two competing systems—free-market and centrally directed—contended for some six decades, but they have now become less distinct.

III. Review of the Learning Objectives *(Answers begin on p. 260.)*

Why Are Economic Systems Needed?

SPECIALIZATION

Productive resources, such as labor, can produce more efficiently if they specialize their activities—concentrating on what they do best according to their:

Absolute Advantage	**or**	**Comparative Advantage**
When one producer can produce a product more efficiently than a second producer and the second producer can produce a different product more efficiently than the first, the two producers benefit when each produces the product in which he or she has an absolute advantage and trades part of his or her output for the other product.		When one producer can produce two or more products more efficiently than a second producer, but the ratio of advantage is greater in one of the products than in the other, both producers benefit by the efficient producer's producing the product in which he or she has the greatest comparative advantage and by the inefficient producer's producing the product in which he or she has the smallest disadvantage. Each trades for the product he or she doesn't produce.

INTERDEPENDENCE

Specialization according to absolute or comparative advantage results in interdependence, each producing unit depending on the other, necessitating an economic system to coordinate their activities.

3.1 Distinguish between absolute and comparative advantage. *(Write in answers below.)*

A. A producer who can produce a good or service at a lower relative cost than another producer has a(n) _____ advantage in the production of that good or service.

B. A producer who can produce both widgets *and* doodads more efficiently than another producer is said to have a(n) _____ advantage in the production of both.

C. If Japan can produce both autos and stereos more efficiently than New Zealand, then New Zealand should specialize in the good in which it has the greatest _____ advantage.

D. Necessary household chores are generally divided up among family members. List three chores that you (or your family members) are responsible for and explain how they reflect on the absolute and/or comparative advantages of different family members.

1. _____

2. _____

3. _____

3.2 Explain why specialization based on comparative advantage results in greater economic growth and interdependence.

A. A fast-food company advertises that they do only one thing and that they do it well. An economist would say that they _____ in the production of that good and that this leads to greater _____ and _____ costs in producing it.

B. List three things that people in the United States at one time did for themselves but depend on specialists for today.

    1. _____

    2. _____

    3. _____

C. Doing one thing and doing it well has certain advantages for society, but it also involves one major problem. Can you think of what this problem is?

    _____

D. Lisa is an auto mechanic but she is also the best housecleaner in town. She can tune up a car's engine or clean an average-sized house in 2 hours. Bart is a housecleaner. He can clean an average house in 3 hours and he can tune up his car in 4 hours. Lisa earns $35 per hour tuning up cars and Bart earns $20 an hour cleaning houses.

    1. In terms of lost income from tuning up cars, how much would it cost Lisa to clean her own house? _____

    2. How much would Lisa have to pay Bart to clean her house? _____

    3. Who should clean Lisa's house? Why?

    _____

    4. In terms of lost income from housecleaning, how much would it cost Bart to tune up his own car? _____

    5. How much would Bart have to pay Lisa to tune up his car? _____

    6. Who should tune up Bart's car? Why? _____

    7. Does either Bart or Lisa have an absolute advantage? _____

    8. What does each have a comparative advantage in doing?
Bart:_____ Lisa:_____

    9. What activities should each specialize in? Bart:_____
Lisa:_____

    10. What are the net benefits of specialization and exchange versus cleaning their own houses and tuning up their own cars (in dollars)? _____

    _____

3.3 Explain why specialization creates the coordination problem.

A. If every person does only one thing (and does it well, of course), then people will be _____ on each other in order to get all the different things that they want.

B. As the degree of _____ increases in our society, we become more and more _____.

C. The problem of how we make sure that all the specialized activities of people will be brought together by an economic system to answer the basic economic questions is the _____.

D. Place a check next to the situations below that describe coordination problems.

    1. _____ Striking airline pilots

    2. _____ Suppliers who break delivery contracts

3. ____ Doctors who are on call for 12-hour shifts

4. ____ Men and women leaving the labor force to stay home and be homemakers

5. ____ Flooding in the midwestern United States that causes towboats to be unable to navigate inland waterways to get shipments to their final destinations

Case Application: **From Farm to City**

At the time of our first census in 1790, the population of the United States was 3.9 million people. Of this number, only 5% was urban—that is, resided in towns or cities of at least 2,500 people. The rural population made up 95% of the total. By 1998 the population had grown to 270 million and three-quarters of it was urban, while only one-quarter was rural.

The dramatic shift of population to the cities implies an enormous rise in the productiveness of agriculture. Formerly, 95 of every 100 Americans were in families whose farms fed themselves plus the urban 5% of the population. Today, the less than 2% of the population that is directly engaged in agriculture is so productive that it can feed the domestic population as well as export a great quantity of agricultural commodities.

The concentration of people in cities has resulted in massive urban sprawl in some areas such as BoWash, the nearly uninterrupted urban corridor from Massachusetts to Virginia; ChiPitts, the stretch from Chicago to Pittsburgh; and SoCal, between San Diego and Santa Barbara. The cities continue to grow despite overcrowding, pollution, crime, and other social problems. They grow because they are economically efficient.

Economic Reasoning *(Write your responses on a separate sheet. Answers begin on p. 261.)*

1. Are people more interdependent now than they were in 1790? Why?
2. How does the growth of large metropolitan areas like BoWash, ChiPitts, and SoCal illustrate the principle of comparative advantage?
3. Would the United States be better off if it were still predominantly rural? Why or why not?

What Are the Principal Types of Economic Systems?

MARKET ECONOMIES	**CENTRALLY DIRECTED ECONOMIES**	**TRADITIONAL ECONOMIES**
are economic systems in which the basic questions of what, how, and for whom to produce are resolved primarily by buyers and sellers interacting in markets.	are economic systems in which the basic questions of what, how, and for whom to produce are resolved primarily by governmental authority.	are economic systems in which the basic questions of what, how, and for whom to produce are resolved primarily by custom and tradition.

MIXED ECONOMIES

are economic systems in which the basic questions of what, how, and for whom to produce are resolved by a mixture of market forces with government direction and/or custom and tradition.

3.4 Identify the three major types of economic systems, and explain how they differ.

A. Indicate whether the following are examples of how market (M), centrally directed (C), or traditional (T) economies answer the three basic economic questions.

1. _____ A pharaoh in ancient Egypt demands that a pyramid be built.

2. _____ A son takes over his father's business when the father retires.

3. _____ A person goes to the movies to see a new movie.

4. _____ Your community provides public schools.

5. _____ Most nurses in the United States are women and most doctors are men.

6. _____ Nintendo develops a new game.

B. List three ways that the government influences the production and sale of beef in the United States.

1. _____

2. _____

3. _____

C. When the government determines how the three basic questions are answered, the economy is referred to as a _____.

D. When the government interferes in a primarily market economy, the resulting type of economy is called a _____.

E. Can you think of one industry or production in the United States that is *not* influenced in some way by government activity?

Case Application: Digging a Subway in Calcutta

Calcutta is a city with overwhelming problems, even by the standards of other cities in India. A large percentage of its more than 10 million citizens are poor and unemployed, and many are homeless. Its public facilities are totally inadequate for the size of the population. The roads are in very poor condition, and there are not nearly enough of them to accommodate the hordes of pedestrians, carts, rickshaws, ancient and overcrowded buses, and sacred cows that wander the streets. Whereas large American cities have as much as 40% of their surface allocated to streets (and the other major cities of India about 15%), Calcutta's streets cover only 6% of its area. As a result of the congestion, the city is virtually immobilized during peak hours of traffic.

In order to alleviate the traffic problem, work began on a subway in December 1972, the first on the Indian subcontinent. It was scheduled to be completed in 1979. Due to the slow progress of construction, it was not completed until 1990, by which time the population of the city had reached 13.5 million, with the subway accommodating approximately only 13% of the transportation needs of the city's people.

Reasons for the delays in construction included flooding and other geologic difficulties, cost overruns, and shortages of funds. These are familiar problems for subway projects in the United States as well, but there is one major difference between the way the Calcutta subway was constructed and the way subways are built in most developed countries. In Calcutta there were initially no bulldozers, excavators, or other large earthmoving equipment used. Instead, 3,000 workers, dressed in the traditional garb of the Indian laborer, toiled away with shovels, filling straw baskets with mud from 40-foot-deep trenches. The baskets were carried out of the ditches on the heads of young Indian women to waiting trucks that then carried the mud away to dump sites. In this fashion, 2.25 million cubic feet of earth was removed from the trenches for the subway tunnels. Because the minimum wage was about $1.30 a day, the government planners calculated that digging the subway with Calcutta's hordes of unskilled laborers was cheaper, if slower, than using mechanized equipment. Furthermore, it helped alleviate the unemployment problem.

Economic Reasoning *(Write your responses on a separate sheet. Answers begin on p. 261.)*

1. The use of manual labor rather than mechanized equipment to dig the Calcutta subway is characteristic of what type of economic system?
2. Manual labor is frequently used in place of machinery by private enterprise in India as well as by government. Why would private enterprise, which is not concerned about the unemployment problem, use manual labor?
3. Do you think that the Calcutta government should have used unskilled workers to build the subway even if it slowed down construction and eventually cost more than using mechanized equipment? Why or why not?

How Does a Market System Resolve the Three Basic Economic Questions?

MARKETS
In a market economy the what, how, and for whom questions are resolved by the interchanges of buyers and sellers in markets.

Factor Markets	Product Markets
Resources and semifinished products are exchanged in factor markets for the production of final goods.	Finished goods and services are exchanged in product markets where they are supplied to consumers.

INCENTIVES
In a market economy, the principal incentive that motivates production is profits.

3.5 Explain how a market system resolves the three basic economic questions.

A. Market economies rely on the _____ motive of individuals to answer the three basic economic questions.

B. Higher prices provide incentives for producers to sell _____ and for consumers to buy _____.

C. Lower prices provide incentives for producers to sell _____ and for consumers to buy _____.

D. The owners of resources (households) provide business firms with _____, _____, and _____ in return for income in the form of _____, _____, and _____.

E. Businesses provide households with _____ in return for _____.

3.6 Distinguish between goods and services sold in product markets and those that are sold in factor markets.

A. Indicate which of the following are *usually* sold in product markets (P) and which are *usually* sold in factor markets (F).

1. _____ Tractors

2. _____ Automobiles

3. _____ Microwave pizzas

4. ____ Computer games

5. ____ Farmland

6. ____ Refrigerators

7. ____ Coal

8. ____ Televisions

B. For each of the following items, give one example of when it would be sold in a factor market and one example of when it would be sold in a product market.

1. A microwave oven:

Factor market _____

Product market _____

2. A computer:

Factor market _____

Product market _____

3. A plumber's services:

Factor market _____

Product market _____

3.7 Understand the two complementary flows in the circular flow diagram of a market economy.

A. Label the circular flow diagram shown below.

CIRCULAR FLOW DIAGRAM

B. Consumers _____ (buy/sell) resources _____ (to/from) businesses in _____ (product/factor) markets.

C. Businesses _____ (buy/sell) final goods and services _____ (to/from) consumers in _____ (product/factor) markets.

D. Explain who the buyers are and who the sellers are in a market economy.

E. For each item listed below, indicate whether it is bought and sold in factor markets (F) or product markets (P).

1. A television_____

2. An office building_____

3. An economics textbook_____

4. The services of a television repairperson_____

5. A loaf of bread for sale at a grocery store_____

6. A loaf of bread for sale from a bakery to local restaurants_____

Case Application: The Shale Age—Not Yet

Under a 16,000-square-mile area in Colorado, Utah, and Wyoming there lie 2 trillion barrels of oil—three times as much as the rest of the world's petroleum reserves. The problem is that the oil is locked up in shale, a laminated rock structure permeated with oil.

Oil from shale rock was actually in use before the discovery and drilling of oil wells in Pennsylvania in 1859. But since petroleum was much easier and cheaper to pump from wells than to extract from the shale, the shale oil deposits remained undeveloped. There were efforts at times to exploit the shale oil fields. In fact, a 1953 headline in the *Denver Post* announced, "The Shale Age Has Begun." But the announcement was premature. It was not until the oil price hikes of the 1970s that the large oil companies took a serious interest in shale oil and significant activity began. The deposits are almost entirely on federal government land, and a number of oil companies took leases on various pieces of this property to obtain control of the resources.

A few of the companies undertook experimental processes for extracting the oil from the shale. Exxon, in partnership with Tosco Corporation, invested $5 billion in its Colony Shale Oil Project near Rifle, Colorado, before shutting down the project in May 1982 due to rising costs and falling oil prices. That project employed a process called "retorting," heating the rock to release the oil after the shale has been brought to the surface. Occidental Petroleum and its partner, Tenneco, experimented with a process that ignites the shale underground, causing the heat to free the oil from the rock so that it can be pumped to the surface.

Progress on these and other experimental shale oil projects has been intermittent. The companies have closed down their projects for the present, waiting for increased petroleum shortages and higher prices in the future to justify the high development costs of shale oil technology. In addition to the high costs, there are problems of obtaining adequate water supplies for processing the shale—two to four barrels of water are required for each barrel of oil produced—and disposing of the rock residue from retorting in a way that will not harm the environment. Delayed by high costs and environmental problems, the age of shale has not yet arrived.

Economic Reasoning *(Write your responses on a separate sheet. Answers begin on p. 261.)*

1. Would shale oil be sold in a product market or a factor market? How can you determine which type of market it would be sold in?
2. If the problems of adequate water supplies and rock waste disposal could be solved, would the oil companies go ahead with their shale oil projects? What would cause them to do so?
3. In view of the dependence of the United States on imported oil, much of it from the politically unstable Middle East, should the government step in to speed up the development of shale oil production on government lands? Why or why not?

IV. Practice Test *(Answers begin on p. 262.)*

Multiple-Choice Questions *(Circle the correct answer.)*

(3.1) 1. Joe Superman is a better plumber *and* a better carpenter than Harry Helpless. This means that Joe has a(n) _____ advantage over Harry in both types of work.
   a. specialized
   b. interdependent
   c. absolute
   d. comparative

(3.1) 2. Based on the information in question 1, which one of the following is *true* if Joe and Harry are on the same construction team?

    a. Joe should do all the carpentry and plumbing.

    b. Harry will still have a comparative advantage in one of the jobs and therefore should do that one.

    c. Harry will have an absolute advantage in one of the two jobs and therefore should do that one.

    d. Specialization cannot occur in this situation because Joe is better at both jobs.

(3.2) 3. Specialization can lead directly to each of the following *except*

    a. improved equity.

    b. improved efficiency.

    c. increased interdependence.

    d. lower costs.

(3.2) 4. Specialization deals directly with which one of the basic economic questions?

    a. For whom to produce?

    b. How to produce?

    c. What to produce?

    d. How much to produce?

(3.3) 5. Which one of the following best summarizes the coordination problem that results from specialization?

    a. the problem of McDonald's simplifying the processes by which hamburgers are made

    b. the problem of one person having an exclusive right to use a scarce resource in whatever he chooses

    c. the problem of how specialized activities of people will be brought together by an economic system

    d. the problem of one producer having the ability to produce more of a good than another with the same amount of resources

(3.4) 6. An economy that relies on customs to answer the three basic economic questions is best characterized as a

    a. mixed economy.

    b. market economy.

    c. command economy.

    d. traditional economy.

(3.4) 7. Which one of the following is the major difference between a market economy and a centrally directed economy?

    a. A market economy relies more on the use of money.

    b. Prices are important in a market economy, but they are not used in a centrally directed economy.

    c. Market economies rely on self-interest and profit incentives to answer the basic economic questions; centrally directed economies rely on agency decisions.

    d. Market economies must find answers to the three basic economic questions; the three questions do not matter in centrally directed economies.

(3.5) 8. Which one of the following socioeconomic goals is most important to the proper working of a market economy?

    a. price stability

    b. job security

    c. economic freedom

    d. equity

(3.6) 9. Which one of the following is most likely to be bought and sold in a factor market?

    a. a television set
    b. a truck
    c. a can of tuna
    d. a carpet

(3.6) 10. Which one of the following is most likely to be bought and sold in a product market?

    a. a 40-pound tuna
    b. 100 acres of farmland
    c. a dozen eggs
    d. 1,000 feet of copper pipe

(3.7) 11. In the circular flow diagram, households do each of the following *except*

    a. buy finished goods.
    b. sell resources.
    c. receive wages.
    d. pay interest.

(3.7) 12. Which one of the following is *not* shown in the circular flow model of the economy?

    a. Interest is the payment for use of capital.
    b. Entrepreneurs earn the largest share of income.
    c. Everyone's income is someone else's expenditure.
    d. Businesses transform resources into final goods and services.

(3.4) 13. The U.S. economy is best described as being a

    a. command economy.
    b. traditional economy.
    c. market economy.
    d. mixed economy.

(3.5) 14. Market economies rely *most* on which of the following?

    a. accurate planning by the government
    b. the self-interest of individuals
    c. the interaction between government and individuals
    d. lessons learned from past economic experiences

(3.6) 15. Which one of the following occurs in factor markets?

    a. Businesses earn their profits.
    b. Individuals earn their incomes.
    c. Households obtain their desired goods and services.
    d. Consumption spending takes place.

True/False Questions *(Circle T or F.)*

(3.1) 16. If one producer has an absolute advantage over another, there can be no gains from specialization and trade. T or F

(3.3) 17. Specialization increases total output and decreases the complexity of the co-ordination problem. T or F

(3.4) 18. Most economies are either purely market, purely command, or purely traditional, with little mixing of the three. T or F

(3.5) 19. In a market economy, the profit motive is most important in determining what gets produced. T or F

(3.6) 20. Consumers are the sellers in factor markets. T or F

Chapter 4

Market Pricing

I. Chapter Outline

In a market economy, prices are determined by the demand for and supply of goods and services. Prices increase to eliminate shortages and decrease to eliminate surpluses. Through this process, the price of each good or service moves to an equilibrium price. Once the market arrives at an equilibrium price, the price will not change unless demand or supply changes. If that should happen, the market will move to a new equilibrium price and the quantity of goods bought and sold will change.

Introductory Article: The Peanut Butter Crunch

Market prices are the result of many influences, including consumer demand, available supplies, and government actions. The prices of agricultural products are especially sensitive to these influences. On the supply side, they are affected by weather conditions, damage from insects and diseases, and government price supports. On the demand side, they are affected by changes in income, changes in taste, changes in the prices of related goods, and (of course) government regulation.

Economic Analysis

This chapter examines market pricing by addressing the following four questions:

1. What Forces Determine Prices in the Marketplace?

Important Concepts: Demand, Substitution effect, Income effect, Supply, Equilibrium, Shortage, Surplus

Important Model: Demand and supply curves

Case Application: Price-Gouging

2. What Determines Demand?

Important Concepts: Consumer tastes and preferences, Income, Substitutes, Complements, Population

Case Application: Pedal Power

3. What Determines Supply?

Important Concepts: Prices of Resources, Technology, Short run, Long run

Case Application: Jojoba: A Desert Weed That Smells Like Money

4. Why Do Prices Change?

Important Concepts: Shifts in demand, Shifts in supply, Change in quantity demanded, Change in quantity supplied

Comparative Case Application: Oiled and Ready

Perspective: Adam Smith's Marketplace

Biography—Adam Smith

II. Summary of Economic Analysis

1. **Demand** is the amount of a product that consumers are willing (and able) to buy at different prices.
2. According to the **law of demand**, a greater quantity of a product is demanded at lower prices (and a smaller quantity is demanded at higher prices).
3. Because of the law of demand, there is an inverse relationship between quantity demanded and price. Consequently, the **demand curve** slopes down and to the right when prices are on the vertical axis and quantities are on the horizontal axis.
4. **Supply** is the amount of a product that sellers are willing to offer for sale at different prices.
5. According to the **law of supply**, a greater quantity of a good is supplied at higher prices (and a smaller quantity is supplied at lower prices).
6. Because of the law of supply, there is a direct relationship between quantity supplied and price. Consequently, the **supply curve** slopes up and to the right.
7. The price of a good and the quantity of it bought and sold are in **equilibrium** when the quantity supplied just equals the quantity demanded.
8. **Shortages** result when market prices are lower than the equilibrium price.
9. **Surpluses** result when market prices are higher than the equilibrium price.
10. The **determinants of demand** are **consumer tastes and preferences, consumers' income**, the prices of **substitutes** and **complements**, and the size of the **market population**.
11. The most important **determinant of supply** is the cost of production. This is affected by the prices of resources and technology. Suppliers must also take into account the time period being considered—short run or long run.
12. In the **short run**, output can be varied only by changing the amounts of labor or material inputs; the capacity of production (capital) is fixed at some level. In the **long run**, output can be varied by changing the capacity of production as well.
13. A **shift in demand** results from a change in one or more of the determinants of demand and is shown by a shift of the entire demand curve.
14. A **shift in supply** results from a change in one or more of the determinants of supply and is shown by a shift of the entire supply curve.
15. A change in demand changes the price of a good, resulting in a **change in the quantity supplied**. This is shown as a shift of the entire demand curve and *a movement along the supply curve*.
16. A change in supply changes the price of a good, resulting in a **change in the quantity demanded**. This is shown as a shift of the entire supply curve and *a movement along the demand curve*.

III. Review of the Learning Objectives *(Answers begin on p. 262.)*

What Forces Determine Prices in the Marketplace?

DEMAND

On one side of the market are the buyers. Demand is the schedule of quantities that they would purchase at different prices.

Law of Demand

The lower the price, the larger the quantity that will be demanded; the higher the price, the smaller the quantity that will be demanded.

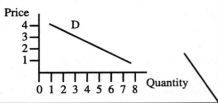

SUPPLY

On the other side of the market are the sellers. Supply is the schedule of quantities that they would offer at different prices.

Law of Supply

The lower the price, the smaller the quantity that will be supplied; the higher the price, the larger the quantity that will be supplied.

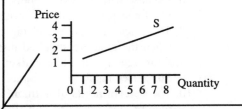

EQUILIBRIUM

When the buyers and sellers come together in a market, the price at which the quantity of the good or service demanded by the buyers is exactly equal to the quantity that is offered by the sellers is the equilibrium price (E).

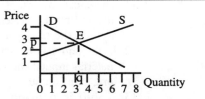

4.1 Explain the laws of demand and supply. *(Write in answers below.)*

A. 1. The law of demand states that lower prices cause a(n) _____ in the quantity of a good demanded and higher prices cause a(n) _____ in the quantity demanded.

2. The law of supply states that lower prices cause a(n) _____ in the quantity of a good supplied and higher prices cause a(n) _____ in quantity supplied.

B. Indicate whether each of the following is an example of the income (I) or substitution (S) effect on demand:

1. _____ Because of higher gasoline prices, Ms. Octane cannot afford to drive as much as she once did.

2. _____ Because of higher pork prices, Ms. Pullet buys more chicken.

3. _____ When coffee prices increase, Maria drinks tea.

4. _____ When the price of electricity doubled, Mr. Watt had to give up watching television all Saturday night.

C. 1. Demand curves show the relationship between the two variables, _____ and _____. Demand curves slope down and to the right, indicating that there is a(n) _____ relationship between the variables.

2. Supply curves show the relationship between the two variables, _____ and _____. Supply curves slope up and to the right, indicating that there is a(n) _____ relationship between the variables.

D. When the price of chicken, salami, or Krazy Kola increases, people buy a lot less of these products. On the other hand, when the price of electricity, medicine, or salt increases, people still buy about the same amount. Why?

———————————————————

E. Using the schedules provided, construct a demand curve and a supply curve in the space provided. The schedules show the supply of and demand for cups of cappuccino. Also, determine the equilibrium price and quantity.

Price	Quantity Demanded	Price	Quantity Supplied
2	5	2	1
4	4	4	2
6	3	6	3
8	2	8	4
10	1	10	5

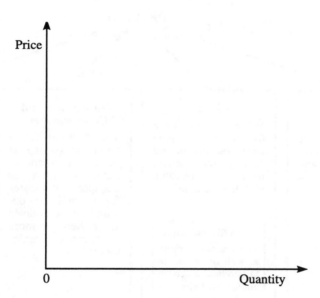

Case Application: Are You an Oat Burner?

In racetrack jargon, horses were referred to as "oat burners" because their diet consisted mainly of oats. More recently oats, particularly the bran part of oat kernels, have been recommended as a heart-healthy diet for us humans. When oats were used principally as animal feed, they were not as profitable a crop as wheat, corn, or soybeans, which receive higher federal subsidies.

Attitudes toward the cereal changed when an article in the American Medical Association journal reported test results showing that oat bran included in a person's diet reduced cholesterol, a cause of heart attacks. As a result of this report, and other articles and books praising the health benefits of oat bran, the sales of oat bran cereals jumped 240%. Grocers' shelves were cleared of oat bran. A name brand of hot oat bran cereal, which cost 99 cents for a one-pound box before the health reports, disappeared from stores for a while. When it reappeared, the price had doubled to $1.98 a box. In the meantime, the scarcity gave rise to numerous off-brands, available in health food stores at premium prices.

Because of the boom in oat bran popularity, coming at the time of an unusually small oat crop, the price received by farmers for their oats reached as high as $4.25 a bushel. To meet the demand, cereal companies actively encouraged farmers to plant oats, guaranteeing to buy their oat harvest and offering them prize incentives in addition. With favorable weather, the oat crop harvest the following year rose 92%. This expansion of production caused the price of oats to fall to $1.15 a bushel.

Follow-up studies on the health benefits of oat bran consumption suggest that, while oats do not have any magical health properties, substituting cereals for foods containing saturated fats in your diet does reduce cholesterol. We should all be oat burners.

Economic Reasoning (*Write your responses on a separate sheet. Answers begin on p. 262.*)

1. What market curves—the demand for oats, the supply of oats, or both—were affected by the incidents described in this case?
2. What happened to the equilibrium price received by farmers for the oat crop as a result of these incidents?
3. Was the doubling of the price of oat bran cereal after reports of its health benefits a good thing or a bad thing? Why?

What Determines Demand?

```
                    ┌──────────────┐
                    │   DEMAND     │
                    └──────────────┘
         ↗        ↗        ↖        ↖
```

Tastes and Preferences	**Income**	**Substitutes and Complements**	**Population**
The desire on the part of consumers for specific goods and services creates a demand for them.	When people have the income to purchase the goods and services they desire, their wants become effective demand.	The demand for a good or service is decreased whenever there are more or cheaper substitutes for it, and the demand is increased when there are more or cheaper complements for it.	The larger the population size of the market, the larger will be the demand for the various goods and services.
	Effective Demand The financial ability as well as the desire to purchase a certain number of units of a good or service at a given price.		

4.2 List and understand the determinants of demand.

A. Indicate the determinant of demand associated with each of the following:

1. Bicycle sales are up. _____

2. Jelly sales decreased when peanut butter prices increased._____
_____

3. Baloney sales increased when peanut butter prices increased._____
_____

4. The demand for retirement homes will increase when the "baby boomers" retire._____

5. Because of a recession, people buy fewer cars. _____
_____

6. Tickets for Pearl Jam concerts sell out overnight. _____
_____

B. Indicate whether the following will cause an increase (I) or a decrease (D) in the demand for ketchup in Atlanta.

1. ____ The price of hamburgers decreases.

2. ____ The price of mustard decreases.

3. ____ Incomes increase.

4. ____ A medical report says that ketchup causes baldness.

5. ____ More people move to Atlanta.

6. ____ The price of french fries decreases.

Case Application: Upscale Munching

The sales of superquality munchies—from ice cream to cookies to popcorn to muffins—have exploded in recent years.

The popularity of so-called superpremium ice creams, containing natural ingredients and an abundance of butterfat, has made familiar names of such brands as Häagen-Dazs (Pillsbury) and Ben & Jerry's (manufactured in Vermont). Famous Amos and Mrs. Fields have made speciality cookie stores almost as common as ice cream shops. Orville Redenbacher and the producers of flavored popcorns have elevated the lowly popcorn kernel to the status of a gourmet item. Both the new (to American palates) croissant and the old-fashioned muffin have caught on as upscale snack foods.

What explains this upswing in the sales of expensive goodies? It is not always obvious what creates a particular trend, but some of the factors in this trend can be identified.

One of the causes of the surge in snack-food sales in general is the size of the age group that tends to consume such products—teenagers and young adults. The baby boom generation born in the years after World War II has created a large market for snack foods. And as the baby boomers have obtained jobs and more disposable income, they have indulged their taste for snack foods at a higher level of quality and cost.

The popularity of gourmet munchies may also be a reaction to counterbalance the ascetic diets that many baby boomers have put themselves on, avoiding meals consisting of fatty, rich foods. They consider a fancy chocolate chip cookie to be a fair reward for sticking to their salad-only lunch diet.

Whatever the causes, the market for upscale munchies has taken off, and the next millionaire is likely to be someone who triples the price of an old snack item and sells it as a new gourmet delicacy.

Economic Reasoning (*Write your responses on a separate sheet. Answers begin on p. 262.*)

1. What determinants of demand have caused the popularity of gourmet snack products?
2. What has caused a change in the effective demand of the baby boom generation, and how has it affected the market for snack foods?
3. Are the superpremium ice creams worth their extra cost? What factors need to be considered in answering this?

What Determines Supply?

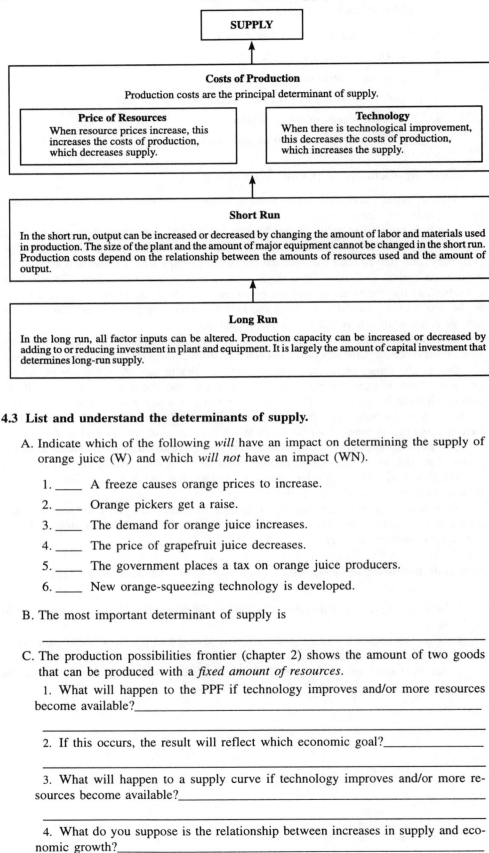

SUPPLY

Costs of Production
Production costs are the principal determinant of supply.

Price of Resources
When resource prices increase, this increases the costs of production, which decreases supply.

Technology
When there is technological improvement, this decreases the costs of production, which increases the supply.

Short Run
In the short run, output can be increased or decreased by changing the amount of labor and materials used in production. The size of the plant and the amount of major equipment cannot be changed in the short run. Production costs depend on the relationship between the amounts of resources used and the amount of output.

Long Run
In the long run, all factor inputs can be altered. Production capacity can be increased or decreased by adding to or reducing investment in plant and equipment. It is largely the amount of capital investment that determines long-run supply.

4.3 List and understand the determinants of supply.

A. Indicate which of the following *will* have an impact on determining the supply of orange juice (W) and which *will not* have an impact (WN).

1. _____ A freeze causes orange prices to increase.

2. _____ Orange pickers get a raise.

3. _____ The demand for orange juice increases.

4. _____ The price of grapefruit juice decreases.

5. _____ The government places a tax on orange juice producers.

6. _____ New orange-squeezing technology is developed.

B. The most important determinant of supply is

_____

C. The production possibilities frontier (chapter 2) shows the amount of two goods that can be produced with a *fixed amount of resources*.

1. What will happen to the PPF if technology improves and/or more resources become available?_____

_____

2. If this occurs, the result will reflect which economic goal?_____

_____

3. What will happen to a supply curve if technology improves and/or more resources become available?_____

_____

4. What do you suppose is the relationship between increases in supply and economic growth?_____

_____

4.4 Distinguish between short-run and long-run supply.

   A. The difference between the short and long runs depends on how long it takes to expand a firm's_____.

   B. Increasing production in the short run is usually associated with higher costs because each worker has less _____ to work with.

   C. For each of the following industries, indicate what you think is the short-run "constraint" that can be changed only in the long run.
      1. A fast-food restaurant_____
      2. A hair stylist_____
      3. A school_____
      4. An automobile manufacturer_____

Case Application: Black Walnut Worth Gold

Two rustlers pulled their truck up to the M. W. Leitner house in a comfortable, middle-class section of Des Moines. The family was out of town. The rustlers chopped down the century-old black walnut tree that shaded the house.

The rustlers would get up to $1,000 for the black walnut from a lumber company. Walnut is prized by producers of veneers, thin exterior sheets of wood used for facings on fine furniture. Cut by "shavers" into paper-thinness sometimes only one thirty-sixth of an inch thick, each sheet of veneer brings $25 to $50 at the retail level.

Black walnut trees grow throughout the Midwest. A tree generally takes 60 to 80 years to reach maturity, but with fertilizing and special care, a tree may be brought to maturity in 30 years. Nevertheless, because of growing demand, many conservationists are worried about preserving the species. Competition for wood is fierce—with buyers from the United States, Germany, Sweden, and Japan bidding up to $1,000 per thousand board feet or higher. In the mid-1960s, the price was about $350 per thousand board feet.

The high demand has more than doubled the value of the wood marketed since the 1960s, while supplies have dwindled. A spokesman for a conservation group said, "In the mid-1960s, nearly half the hardwood veneers from domestic firms were black walnut. But that figure is way down now."

Missouri is the only state requiring the log buyer to know where the wood was cut, but that regulation is rarely enforced. A town marshall commented, "Some buyers don't know the wood is stolen. Some don't care. But the law produces few convictions. The stuff is so valuable they're even stealing it from the national parks."

Economic Reasoning (*Write your responses on a separate sheet. Answers begin on p. 262.*)

   1. How does the rustling of black walnut trees affect the short-run supply of black walnut veneer?
   2. What effect does the length of time required for black walnut trees to mature have on the long-run supply of black walnut veneer?
   3. Should laws be enacted in other states to prosecute log buyers who purchase black walnut without knowing where it came from?

Why Do Prices Change?

SHIFTS IN DEMAND

If there is a change in any one or more of the four determinants of demand—tastes, incomes, price and availability of substitutes and complements, and population size—there will be a shift in the demand schedule. A decrease in demand means that at each and every price less would be purchased than previously.

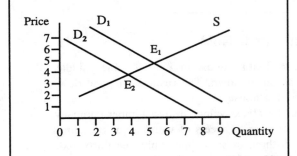

SHIFTS IN SUPPLY

A change in production costs results in a shift in the supply schedule. If production costs increase, less will be supplied at each and every price.

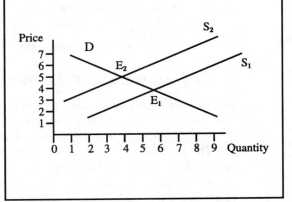

4.5 Identify the causes of shifts in demand and explain how they affect market equilibrium.

A. List the five things that can cause a shift in the demand curve.

1. _____

2. _____

3. _____

4. _____

5. _____

B. Circle the correct answer within the parentheses.

1. Other things being the same, an increase in the price of Nike sneakers will cause (a decrease/an increase) in the equilibrium price of Reebok sneakers and (a decrease/an increase) in the equilibrium quantity of Reebok sneakers.

2. Other things being the same, an increase in the price of bacon will cause (a decrease/an increase) in the equilibrium price of eggs and (a decrease/an increase) in the equilibrium quantity of eggs.

3. Suppose the government releases a report stating that drinking orange juice will prevent wrinkles. Other things being the same, this will cause (a decrease/an increase) in the equilibrium price of orange juice and (a decrease/an increase) in the equilibrium quantity of orange juice.

4. Suppose the government relaxes immigration laws and the population increases by 10%. Other things being the same, this will cause (a decrease/an increase) in the equilibrium price of houses and (a decrease/an increase) in the equilibrium quantity of houses.

5. Macaroni and cheese is sometimes referred to as being an *inferior* good because when people's incomes go up, they buy less of it, and when their incomes go down, they buy more of it. This being the case, an increase in incomes will cause (a decrease/an increase) in the equilibrum price of macaroni and cheese and (a decrease/an increase) in the equilibrium quantity of macaroni and cheese sold.

C. The demand and supply graphs below represent the market for pepperoni pizza. Graphically show what will happen if:

1. the prices of hamburgers and fries increase.
2. the price of pepperoni increases.

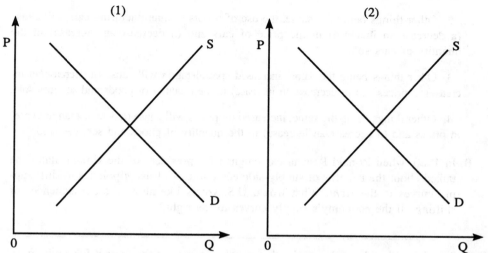

(1)   (2)

D. For each of the above cases, indicate what happens to the equilibrium price and quantity of pepperoni pizzas.

   1. Price _____ Quantity _____

   2. Price _____ Quantity _____

E. Using the schedules provided, construct the two demand curves indicated in the space provided and indicate which one represents the greater level of demand.

Price	Quantity Demanded	Price	Quantity Supplied
$1	5	$1	7
$2	4	$2	6
$3	3	$3	5
$4	2	$4	4
$5	1	$5	3

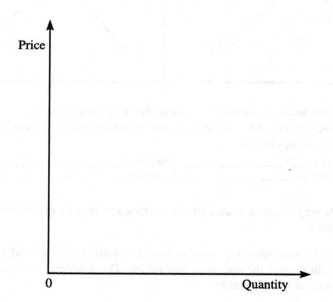

4.6 Identify the causes of shifts in supply and explain how they affect market equilibrium.

A. Circle the correct answer within the parentheses.

1. Other things being the same, an increase in pilots' wages will cause (a decrease/an increase) in the price of flying and (a decrease/an increase) in the quantity of airplane trips taken.

2. Other things being the same, the use of robots in manufacturing cars will cause (a decrease/an increase) in the price of cars and (a decrease/an increase) in the quantity of cars sold.

3. Other things being the same, increased specialization will cause (a decrease/an increase) in prices and (a decrease/an increase) in the quantity of goods and services sold.

4. Other things being the same, increased oil prices will cause (a decrease/an increase) in prices and (a decrease/an increase) in the quantity of goods and services sold.

B. In 1980, when Ronald Reagan campaigned for president of the United States, he talked about the benefits of supply-side economics—of using policies to shift supply curves to the *right*. What would U.S. voters like about the consequences of shifting all the economy's supply curves to the right?

_____

C. The demand and supply graphs shown below represent the market for apple juice. Graphically depict what happens if:

1. environmentalists force apple growers to use fewer chemical fertilizers and insecticides.

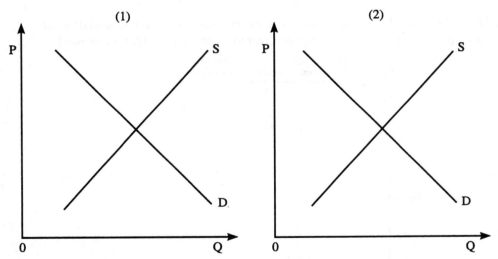

2. good weather results in an especially good apple harvest.
D. For each of the above cases, indicate what happens to the equilibrium price and quantity of apple juice.

1. Price _____ Quantity _____
2. Price _____ Quantity _____

4.7 Explain why shortages and surpluses cause prices to move toward an equilibrium price.

A. Using the schedules and space provided, construct demand and supply schedules, and then answer the questions that follow. The schedules show the supply of and demand for cheese pizzas.

Price	Quantity Demanded	Price	Quantity Supplied
$10	5	$10	25
$8	10	$8	20
$6	15	$6	15
$4	20	$4	10

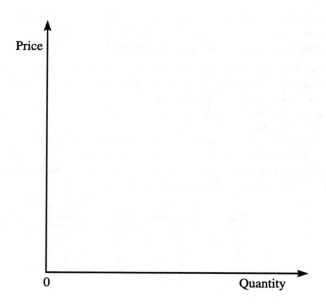

1. If the price of a pizza is $10, there will be a _____ of _____ pizzas on the market.

2. If the price of a pizza is $4, there will be a _____ of _____ pizzas on the market.

3. The equilibrium price and quantity of pizzas are _____ and _____.

4. Show your answers to questions 1, 2, and 3 on the graph that you constructed. Make sure you label everything.

B. Suppose the price of a good is *above* its equilibrium price. Complete the sentences that follow:

1. A _____ will exist.
2. The price will _____.
3. As a result of the price change, the quantity demanded will _____ and the quantity supplied will _____.
4. Based on your answers in question 3, the _____ caused by the high price will _____.

C. Suppose the price of a good is *below* its equilibrium price. Complete the sentences that follow:

1. A _____ will exist.
2. The price will _____.
3. As a result of the price change, the quantity demanded will _____ and the quantity supplied will _____.
4. Based on your answers in question 3, the _____ caused by the low price will _____.

D. Only at the _____ price will the quantity demanded be equal to the quantity supplied, so that there are no _____ and no _____.

4.8 Distinguish between a change in demand and a change in quantity demanded.

A. Every year during the holiday shopping season, there seems to be at least one toy that is hugely popular. This change in tastes causes a(n) _____ (increase/decrease) in _____ (demand, quantity demanded) in the market for the popular toy.

B. Suppose the government increases the minimum wage. This change in the price of labor causes a(n) _____ (increase/decrease) in _____ (demand, quantity demanded) in the market for the labor.

C. For each of the following, indicate whether it will cause a change in demand (D) or a change in quantity demanded (QD) in the market for CDs:

1. The price of CD players increases. _____
2. Consumer incomes decrease. _____
3. The price of CDs falls. _____
4. The price of audio cassette tapes increases. _____

D. Using the demand schedules given below, construct the two demand curves in the space provided and indicate which one represents an increase in demand. Also show on the graph a change in quantity demanded.

Price	Quantity Demanded	Price	Quantity Supplied
$1	5	$1	10
$2	4	$2	8
$3	3	$3	6
$4	2	$4	4
$5	1	$5	2

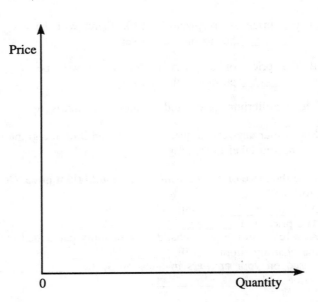

4.9 Distinguish between a change in supply and a change in quantity supplied.

A. Suppose the government increases the minimum wage. This change in the price of labor causes a(n) _____ (increase/decrease) in _____ (supply, quantity supplied) in the market for labor.

B. If the government increases the minimum wage, this change in the price of labor will cause a(n) _____ (increase/decrease) in _____ (supply, quantity supplied) in the market for the McDonald's hamburgers (produced by minimum wage workers).

C. For each of the following, indicate whether it will cause a change in supply (S) or a change in quantity supplied (QS) in the market for pizza:

1. The price of pizza increases. _____
2. The price of mozzarella cheese increases. _____

3. New technology makes the production of pizzas cheaper. _____
4. Flooding destroys the tomato crop. _____

D. Suppose that tomorrow morning's newspaper reports that hamburgers, fries, and milkshakes are actually good for you and represent the perfectly balanced meal. Select the correct answer for the following sequence of events:

1. The demand for burgers (increases/decreases).
2. The quantity of burgers supplied (increases/decreases).
3. In the short run, the price of burgers (increases/decreases).
4. In the long run, more people open hamburger restaurants and the supply of burgers (increases/decreases).
5. As a result of the increased supply, the price of burgers (increases/decreases).
6. As a result of the lower prices, the quantity of burgers demanded (increases/decreases).
7. In the end, the economy will have (more/less) burgers at a (lower/higher) price.

Case Application: Do Boycotts Work?

Some years ago consumers in the United States were faced with very rapid increases in beef prices. Homemakers, restaurant owners, and fast-food operators were outraged. Many organized spontaneous consumer boycotts aimed at supermarkets. People refused to buy or eat beef.

Meanwhile, back in the feedlots, cattlemen complained bitterly about the high cost of grain, the primary food for cattle. They wondered why they should be blamed for high retail prices. After all, cattlemen were not responsible for the high costs of feed for their cattle.

Do consumer boycotts really have an impact on prices? Most consumers do not boycott—they merely reduce quantities purchased as prices rise. They do not change their demand schedules. If the boycotts actually grow large enough to change market demand (to move the whole curve), there may be a reduction in market prices.

Economic Reasoning (Write your responses on a separate sheet. Answers begin on p. 264.)

1. Does a boycott cause a shift in the demand curve or a movement along the demand curve?
2. Does a boycott result in lower prices? Why or why not?
3. Are boycotts such as the one described in this application fair? Why or why not?

IV. Practice Test (Answers begin on p. 264.)

Multiple-Choice Questions (Circle the correct answer.)

(4.1) 1. The law of supply indicates that as prices increase
    a. the quantity supplied increases.
    b. the quantity supplied decreases.
    c. surpluses increase.
    d. shortages increase.

(4.1) 2. Which one of the following is an example of the *substitution effect* on demand?
    a. Advertising by a cola company causes you to switch to their brand.
    b. Higher tuition causes you to work longer hours.
    c. An increase in the price of movie theater tickets causes you to rent more home videos.
    d. If the price of corn increases, more farmers will grow corn instead of wheat.

(4.2) 3. Which one of the following will cause the demand curve for jeans to increase?
   a. a decrease in the price of denim
   b. a decrease in consumer incomes
   c. an increase in the cost of producing jeans
   d. a decrease in the price of T-shirts, a complement good

(4.2) 4. Good Y is a "substitute" for Good X if
   a. the demand for Y increases when the price of X increases.
   b. the demand for Y increases when the supply of X decreases.
   c. the supply of Y increases when the demand for X increases.
   d. the supply of Y increases when the supply of X increases.

(4.3) 5. The most important determinant of supply is
   a. demand.
   b. income.
   c. costs of production.
   d. the equilibrium price.

(4.4) 6. Which one of the following best describes the "short run"?
   a. the time period during which demand is fixed
   b. one accounting period
   c. the time it takes demand changes to adjust to supply changes
   d. the time period in which at least one factor of production cannot be changed

(4.4) 7. As output levels increase in the short run, workers will be less and less productive because
   a. demand always increases faster than output.
   b. the amount of the fixed factor changes when output changes.
   c. each worker has less capital to work with.
   d. the equilibrium price is higher in the short run.

(4.5) 8. Which one of the following will *not* cause the demand curve for product A to shift?
   a. a change in the price of A
   b. an increase in the population
   c. an increase in the price of B, a substitute
   d. a decrease in the price of C, a complement

(4.5) 9. Other things being the same, what will happen if consumer incomes decrease?
   a. Demand and prices will decrease.
   b. Demand and prices will increase.
   c. Demand will decrease and prices will increase.
   d. Demand will increase and prices will increase.

(4.6) 10. Which one of the following will *not* cause the supply curve to shift?
   a. a change in demand
   b. a change in taxes
   c. a change in wage rates
   d. a change in interest rates

(4.6) 11. A decrease in supply will result in which one of the following?
   a. increased prices and equilibrium quantities
   b. decreased prices and equilibrium quantities
   c. increased prices and decreased equilibrium quantities
   d. decreased prices and increased equilibrium quantities

(4.7) 12. If the current price is above the equilibrium price, then the _____ exceeds the _____, and there is a _____ in the market.
   a. quantity demanded, quantity supplied, surplus
   b. quantity supplied, quantity demanded, surplus
   c. quantity demanded, quantity supplied, shortage
   d. quantity supplied, quantity demanded, shortage

(4.7) 13. An equilibrium price will not change *unless*
    a. demand changes.
    b. supply changes.
    c. both demand and supply change.
    d. either demand or supply changes (or both).

(4.8) 14. Which one of the following describes a "decrease in quantity demanded"?
    a. a leftward shift of the demand curve
    b. a rightward shift of the demand curve
    c. a leftward movement along a given demand curve
    d. a rightward movement along a given demand curve

(4.9) 15. An increase in production costs results in which of the following?
    a. a decrease in supply and a decrease in quantity supplied
    b. an increase in supply and a decrease in quantity supplied
    c. a decrease in supply and a decrease in quantity demanded
    d. a decrease in supply and an increase in quantity demanded

True/False Questions *(Circle T or F.)*

(4.1) 16. Demand represents the buyers' side of the market, and supply represents the sellers' side of the market. T or F

(4.3) 17. Supply depends upon demand. T or F

(4.6) 18. An improvement in the technology to produce automobiles will cause a decrease in the price of automobiles. T or F

(4.7) 19. In market economies, surpluses are usually eliminated by an increase in prices. T or F

(4.8) 20. An increase in demand is the same as an increase in quantity demanded. T or F

Foundations Crossword Puzzle (Chapters 1–4)

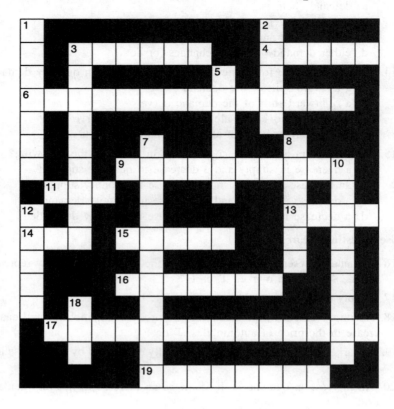

Across

3. An increase in _____ causes an increase in the demand for normal goods.
4. A description of the type of economy that is prevalent throughout the world
6. The highways, bridges, airports, and public transportation facilities of an economy
9. What salsa is to tortilla chips
11. The type of chart used to show the relative size of the components of a whole
13. Smith who wrote *The Wealth of Nations*
14. Increasing output in the short _____ generally increases the cost of producing each unit.
15. Human resources
16. These "tools" for an economist are statistics, history, and how institutions operate.
17. When nations produce those goods and services that their resources are best suited to produce, this is called _____.
19. "What to produce?" is this type of question.

Down

1. Refers to the machinery, factories, and office buildings used in production for an economy
2. Associated with the "invisible hand"
3. The continual rise of the general price level
5. This curve shows the relationship between the price of Bif peanut butter and the number of jars that the Bif company would like to sell.
7. If Ben must give up producing 2 mailboxes for each birdhouse he produces while Jim gives up producing only 1 mailbox for each birdhouse he produces, we conclude that Jim has a _____ advantage in producing birdhouses.
8. This curve represents the relationship between the price of a product and the quantity demanded.
10. An economy that produces and distributes goods without the function of a market or the command of a centralized authority usually does so by _____.
12. A _____ -off usually must occur when choosing between allocating a nation's production to military use or to civilian use.
18. The type of graph showing the different maximum output combinations of goods or services that can be obtained from a fixed amount of resources

Chapter 5

Earning and Spending: The Consumer

I. Chapter Outline

In a market economy, producers supply what consumers demand: the consumer is sovereign. Understanding more about how consumers act, and react, as they attempt to get the most from their limited incomes is therefore important if we are to understand the workings of a market economy better.

Introductory Article: Blowing Smoke Rings

Consumers of cigarettes, like the consumers of any product, make use of any available information when making their decisions about how they will spend their money. Sometimes the information comes from the government in the form of required product labeling, but mostly it comes from advertisers who have a vested interest in selling their products. Sometimes, as in the case of cigarettes, information alone cannot influence consumer choice because consumers find that they have no substitute product to turn to.

Economic Analysis

This chapter examines the issue of consumer choice by addressing the following three questions:

1. **What Determines Incomes?**

    Important Concepts: Functional income distribution, Derived demand, Rent, Interest, Profits

    Case Application: Five Strikes and You're Out

2. **What Choices Do Consumers Make?**

    Important Concepts: Consumption, Price elasticity of demand, Consumer sovereignty, Average propensity to consume, Average propensity to save

    Case Application: The Channel Race

3. **How Can Consumers Make Better Choices?**

    Important Concepts: Utility, Advertising

    Comparative Case Application: Intellectual Property Rights

Perspective: Conspicuous Consumption

    Biography—Thorstein Veblen

II. Summary of Economic Analysis

1. The **functional distribution of income** shows the distribution of household incomes according to the factor of production used to earn the income—wages and salaries for labor, rent for land, interest for capital, and profits for entrepreneurship.
2. The demand for resources such as labor is a **derived demand.** It is derived from the demand for goods and services that are produced by the resource.
3. People divide their after-tax income between **consumption spending** (on **necessities** and **luxuries**) and **savings**.

4. The law of demand states that price and quantity demanded are inversely related; **price elasticity of demand** indicates *how much* quantity changes when the price changes.

5. If demand is **elastic**, quantity demanded is sensitive to price changes and it changes proportionately more than the change in prices. The demand for luxury items tends to be elastic.

6. If demand is **inelastic**, quantity demanded is insensitive to price changes and it changes proportionately less than the change in prices. The demand for necessities tends to be inelastic.

7. The **elasticity ratio** is equal to the percentage change in quantity demanded divided by the percentage change in the price of the good or service. If the ratio is less than one, demand is inelastic; if it is greater than one, demand is elastic; and if it is equal to one, elasticity is unitary.

8. The principle of **consumer sovereignty** implies that consumer demand determines what is produced.

9. The **average propensity to consume** is the percentage of after-tax income that is spent on consumer goods and the **average propensity to save** is the percentage that is saved. The two propensities must add up to 100%, indicating that after-tax income is either spent or saved.

10. The amount of satisfaction obtained from consuming or saving is called **utility**. The objective of consumers is to maximize their **total utility**.

11. Making the best consumption and savings decisions requires adequate **information**.

12. Although **advertising** is the major source of consumer information, it adds to product prices and sometimes is deceptive.

III. Review of the Learning Objectives *(Answers begin on p. 264.)*

What Determines Income?

> **SPENDING CHOICES**
>
> Consumers earn income by selling factors of production to businesses. The functional distribution of income shows the distribution of household incomes according to the factor of production used to earn the income.
>
> | **Wages and Salaries**
Payment for labor | **Rent**
Payment for land | **Interest**
Payment for financial capital | **Profits**
Payment for entrepreneurship |
> | --- | --- | --- | --- |

5.1 Define and describe the different income sources that make up the functional distribution of income.

A. The shares of total income distributed according to the type of resource for which they are paid is the _____.

B. According to the functional distribution of income, the payment for labor is_____, the payment for land is _____, the payment for financial capital is _____, and the payment for entrepreneurship is_____.

C. Indicate whether each of the following refers to interest (I), profits (P), rent (R), or wages (W).

   1. ____ Money received for sale of a vacant lot

   2. ____ Interest earned on a checking account

3. _____ Weekly paycheck for a minimum wage worker

4. _____ Corporate dividends

5. _____ Money received for use of your tropical island by vacationers

6. _____ CEO's salary

5.2 Explain how the use of capital influences the demand for labor.

A. If labor and capital are_____, then increasing the amount of capital will decrease the demand for labor.

B. If, as is commonly the case, an increase in the amount of capital requires an increase in the demand for labor, then labor and capital are _____.

C.

1. The making of widgets requires 50 workers to operate each widget-making machine. Therefore, if the owner of the firm purchases an additional machine, he will need to hire 50 more workers. In this case, capital and labor are _____.

2. If a ski resort replaces its ski instructors with televisions, VCRs, and instructive videos, capital and labor at the resort are_____.

5.3 Understand the special characteristics of rent and its relationship to limited supply.

A. Because the supply of land is_____, the level of rent depends almost entirely on demand.

B.

1. Suppose there is an increase in demand for a resource that has perfectly inelastic supply. In this case, the change in demand has more of an effect on _____ (price or quantity).

2. Suppose there is an increase in demand for a resource that has perfectly elastic supply. In this case, the change in demand has more of an effect on _____ (price or quantity).

Case Application: Karl Marx's Prediction

Karl Marx was an economic philosopher who wrote during the 1800s. He predicted that a capitalistic economy would fail because the business owners, or "capitalists," would accumulate wealth, power, and income while the workers would remain poor. This would presumably happen because, in a market economy, one's income depends on the quantity and quality of inputs owned. Since the business owners command more inputs, Marx believed that the average worker would be unable to accumulate wealth and power in such an economy. The functional distribution of income shows that Marx was wrong. The table below illustrates the functional distribution of income in the United States during the twentieth century.

Year	Wages & Salaries	Rental Income	Net Interest	Corporate Profits	Proprietors' Income
1929	60.0%	6.0%	6.0%	11.0%	17.0%
1939	67.0	4.0	5.0	8.0	16.0
1949	66.0	3.0	1.0	13.0	17.0
1959	68.6	3.6	2.5	12.8	12.6
1969	72.4	2.3	4.2	11.2	9.9
1979	73.4	0.1	7.4	9.9	8.9
1989	73.0	−0.3	10.7	8.5	8.2
1996	72.3	2.6	6.5	10.7	8.5

Source: *Economic Report of the President,* 1997 and earlier years.

Until the 1980s, labor's share of income continually increased. The distinction between workers and capitalists has changed through profit-sharing programs, employee ownership of businesses, and widespread corporate stock ownership. Although it appears that the increase in labor's share of income has leveled off in recent years, if U.S. production continues to shift toward services, labor's share of total income will continue to rise.

Economic Reasoning (*Write your responses on a separate sheet. Answers begin on p. 264.*)

1. What has happened to the share of income earned by each factor of production in the United States during the twentieth century?
2. Why would profit-sharing programs cause Marx's prediction to fail?
3. In what country might labor's share of income be higher than in the United States? Explain.

What Choices Do Consumers Make?

SPENDING CHOICES

People continuously make spending decisions in order to satisfy their consumption needs and desires for necessities and luxuries.

Price Elasticity of Demand

The extent to which the quantity demanded of a good varies with small changes in its price is its elasticity of demand.

Measurement of Elasticity

$$\text{Elasticity ratio} = \frac{\%\ \text{change in quantity}}{\%\ \text{change in price}}$$

Consumer sovereignty

means that the spending decisions of consumers dictate what producers make and how resources are allocated.

SAVINGS CHOICES

The alternative to spending for the after-tax income of consumers is savings.

Average Propensity to Consume

The amount we typically spend on goods and services out of a dollar of income is our average propensity to consume. In this country it tends to be around 95¢ of each dollar or 95%.

The other 5¢ we save. Consumers' average propensity to save is 5%.

5.4 Understand the concept elasticity of demand. (*Write in answers below.*)

A. Price elasticity of demand is a measure of how much _____ changes when the price of a product changes.

B. If goods are necessities their demand will tend to be _____. If they are luxuries their demand will tend to be _____.

C. What are the two most important things that influence the elasticity of demand for a product?

    1. _____

    2. _____

D. Indicate whether the demand for each of the following is elastic (E) or inelastic (I).

    1. ____ Gasoline

    2. ____ Texaco gasoline

    3. ____ Brand X paper towels

    4. ____ Yachts

    5. ____ Electricity

    6. ____ Soap

7. _____ Rubber bands

8. _____ Automobile batteries

9. _____ Pepperoni pizzas

10. _____ Chevrolets

5.5 Differentiate among perfectly elastic, relatively elastic, unitary elastic, relatively inelastic, and perfectly inelastic demand.

A. If the demand for good X is perfectly elastic, then what must be true about the substitutes for good X?

_____

B. If the demand for good Y is perfectly inelastic, then what must be true about the substitutes for good Y?

_____

C. Indicate whether the demand for the following goods is close to being perfectly elastic (PE), relatively elastic (RE), perfectly inelastic (PI), or relatively inelastic (RI).

1. _____ A life preserver for a drowning person

2. _____ Farmer Jones's wheat

3. _____ Water

4. _____ 3/4-inch bolts from Lundberg's Hardware Store

5. _____ Pizza

6. _____ Movie tickets

7. _____ Tickets for the Game of the Century when it is not televised

8. _____ Tickets for the Game of the Century when it is televised

D. On the graph provided below, draw the demand curve for insulin and label it D_1. Next, draw the demand curve for the insulin sold at a specific pharmacy and label it D_2.

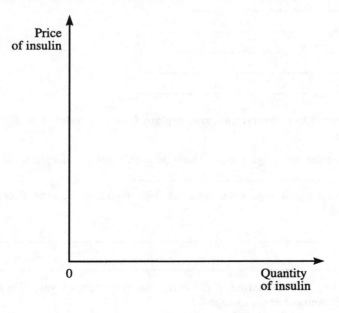

E.

1. Below, draw the *relatively inelastic* demand curve for car tires on the graph on the left and draw the *relatively elastic* demand curve (D) for car seat covers on the graph on the right. Draw a supply curve (S_1) on each graph and indicate the equilibrium quantity (Q_1) and price (P_1).

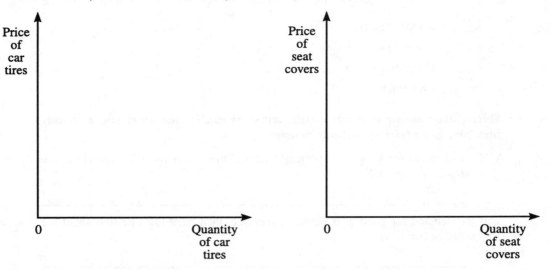

2. Draw new supply curves (S₂) on each of the above graphs that represent equal reductions in supply (the same vertical distance between the supply curves). Indicate the new equilibrium price (P₂) and quantity (Q₂). In which case does the price increase the most, and in which case does the quantity demanded decrease the most?

5.6 Compute a demand elasticity ratio.

A. Compute the elasticity ratio in each of following instances:
   1. Price increases 25% and quantity decreases 50%._____
   2. Price decreases 50% and quantity decreases 50%._____
   3. Price decreases 10% and quantity increases 1%._____
   4. Price increases 1% and quantity falls to zero._____
   5. Price decreases 15% and quantity does not change._____
B. For each of the above cases, indicate whether the demand is perfectly elastic (PE), relatively elastic (RE), unitary elastic (UE), relatively inelastic (RI), or perfectly inelastic (PI), and give an example for each.

   1. ____   _____
   2. ____   _____
   3. ____   _____
   4. ____   _____
   5. ____   _____

5.7 Define consumer sovereignty and explain how it is related to the allocation of resources.

A. If consumer sovereignty exists, how does an economy decide what goods to produce?_____

B. If consumer sovereignty did *not* exist, how would an economy decide what goods to make?

   _____

   _____

C. According to the doctrine of consumer sovereignty, does supply react to demand, or does demand react to supply?

   _____

5.8 Define average propensity to consume and average propensity to save.

A. What are the three things that people can do with their before-tax income?

1. _____

2. _____

3. _____

B. If a person's income is $10,000 a year and he or she saves $1,500, then what is that person's:

average propensity to save? _____
average propensity to consume? _____

C. Which of the following would be likely to increase a person's average propensity to consume (C), and which would be likely to increase a person's average propensity to save (S)?

1. _____ An increase in income

2. _____ A belief that the world will end next week

3. _____ A decision to go to college

4. _____ A decrease in the rate of return to savings

5. _____ A vote by Congress to end the Social Security system

6. _____ A vote by Congress to allow tax deductions for new savings accounts

D. Businesses will be both hurt and helped if there is an increase in the average propensity to save. How will they be hurt?_____

How will they be helped?_____

Case Application: Going to the Movies

Carol and Martin Gardner of Little Rock, Arkansas, were avid movie fans and usually saw at least one cinema movie a week. But recently they have had to make some changes in their choice of entertainment. With ticket prices at $7 or more per person, Carol and Martin have been taking more bicycle rides, having picnics, and watching more rental tapes and television than ever before.

Carol described the situation this way: "Who wants to pay $14 just for tickets? That doesn't even include the price of gas, parking, or snacks. We didn't mind paying $5 or $6 for a ticket, but when the price went up to $7, that was too much. Now we consider more carefully whether we really want to see the film at the theater or whether we can pass it by and wait until it comes out on rental tape or see it on TV."

Movie customers expect certain satisfactions when they pay for their tickets. When admission prices increase to $7 or $8 a ticket, people begin to question whether their limited entertainment budgets can handle the higher prices. Many are concerned that as prices of many goods and services continue to rise, they will have to cut into their entertainment budget to buy necessities. As Martin put it, "If the price of food keeps going up the way it has been, pretty soon we'll have to substitute groceries for movies."

The young Arkansas couple, like most people, do not want to stop entertaining themselves, and they do want to see some cinema movies, even at higher prices. That means making choices—deciding how much they want to see a particular film or passing it up altogether in favor of other forms of recreation.

Economic Reasoning *(Write your responses on a separate sheet. Answers begin on p. 265.)*

1. Do the Gardners consider going to the movies a necessity or a luxury?
2. From the application, does it appear that the Gardners' demand for theater movies is perfectly elastic, relatively elastic, relatively inelastic, or perfectly inelastic?
3. Is $7 too much to pay for a ticket to the movies? What are your criteria for how much is too much?

How Can Consumers Make Better Choices?

INFORMATION

In order to allocate their incomes to obtain maximum utility, consumers need to have adequate and accurate information about the availability, characteristics, quality, sources, and prices of the goods and services that they might be interested in buying.

Advertising

The most common source of information about products and services is advertising. Advertising is beneficial when it provides consumers with better information for making choices and when it reduces production costs by expanding the market for a product. But it is detrimental when it is false or misleading and when it adds to costs.

Limits on Information

Ideally, consumers should have as much information as possible about available products, but there are costs to acquiring, disseminating, and evaluating information.

5.9 Explain how consumers get information about the products that they buy.

A. Where would you look for information before buying a new car?

_____

_____

B. List four products that you have purchased recently where some of your information about the product was provided by the producer because the government required it.

1. _____
2. _____
3. _____
4. _____

C. List four products that you have purchased recently based on information provided by advertisers.

1. _____
2. _____
3. _____
4. _____

D. Has increased use of the Internet affected consumer behavior? How?

_____

_____

5.10 Explain how information influences consumer choices.

A. An objective of advertising is to influence consumer behavior by making demand _____ (more or less) elastic.

B. Suppose *Consumer Reports* publishes the results of a test that shows that certain brands of smoke detectors do not sound an alarm during a fire. Would this affect the demand for these smoke detectors? How?

_____

_____

C. List any cases where false or misleading advertising caused you, or someone you know, to buy a product that might otherwise not have been purchased.

_____

_____

D. What are two sources of consumer information other than that which the government requires and that which is provided through advertisements?

1. _____

2. _____

E. Do you feel that the sources that you indicated in exercise D above are more or less reliable than advertisements as a source of information? Why?

_____

_____

Case Application: Do You Have Time for Your Possessions?

We consumers are hooked on laborsaving devices and convenience gadgets—coffeemakers, programmable VCRs, telephone answering machines, food processors, microwave ovens, remote-control TVs, ice makers, and electronic automobile controls that maintain a set speed, lock doors, and turn lights on and off, all automatically.

There seems to be a limitless market for products that make our lives easier. But the question is now being asked, Do all of these new gadgets really save us time, or are they in fact putting more demands on us? Acquiring them takes time. We must evaluate and shop for a new product. Then we must frequently assemble it and learn how to use it. But the problems that most occupy our time and nervous energy are those that arise in servicing, repairing, and replacing items that do not work properly or at all. Another set of problems arises in protecting all of our possessions—VCRs are the favorite target of burglars. Devices to protect the house from burglaries frequently malfunction, sometimes triggering false alarms to the police or private security agencies.

Are our concerns with possessions and our need to own the latest and newest of everything actually adding to our burdens rather than lightening them? By loading ourselves up with gadgets, are we cutting into our leisure time and leaving less time for enjoyment?

Our higher incomes have given us the ability to acquire many more material possessions than were available to previous generations. As a consequence, studies show that we spend a lot more time shopping. And when something goes wrong with one of our personal, household, or automobile convenience devices, we generally have to find someone to fix it and either take it in to be repaired or arrange to be at home for a service call. Even when appliances work properly, many of them require periodic servicing. We have become dependent on the availability and skill of a variety of service technicians to keep our gadget-filled lives functioning smoothly. Every time we buy an additional appliance we assume a new responsibility.

How many more "laborsaving" products do we have time for?

Economic Reasoning (*Write your responses on a separate sheet. Answers begin on p. 265.*)

1. How do consumers normally find out about the availability of new products?
2. What information do consumers need that they do not generally have when purchasing convenience products, which would help them make better choices?

3. Should producers be required to provide customers with information about the average number of repairs required on their appliances and the average cost of maintaining them? Why or why not?

IV. Practice Test (Answers begin on p. 266.)

Multiple-Choice Questions (*Circle the correct answer.*)

(5.1) 1. The functional distribution of income shows that most income in the United States is earned through which of the productive resources?
    a. land
    b. labor
    c. capital
    d. entrepreneurship

(5.1) 2. Which one of the following is the payment for capital?
    a. rent
    b. wages
    c. profits
    d. interest

(5.2) 3. If capital and labor are complements, then
    a. a decrease in the quantity of capital will have no effect on the demand for labor.
    b. a decrease in the quantity of capital will be accompanied by an increase in the demand for labor.
    c. an increase in the quantity of capital will be accompanied by a decrease in the demand for labor.
    d. an increase in the quantity of capital will be accompanied by an increase in the demand for labor.

(5.3) 4. Which one of the following productive resources often has a fixed supply?
    a. land
    b. labor
    c. capital
    d. entrepreneurship

(5.4) 5. Which one of the following most likely has elastic demand?
    a. Good A, which is a necessity
    b. Good B, which teachers require their students to purchase
    c. Good C, which does not have any suitable substitutes currently available
    d. Good D, which has a similar substitute that is sold at convenient locations near you

(5.4) 6. Which of one the following are the most important in determining the elasticity of demand for a product?
    a. its cost of production and the number of complements
    b. its price relative to one's income and the number of substitutes
    c. its price and cost of production
    d. the number of available substitutes and complements

(5.5) 7. If there are very few substitutes for a product, then the demand for the product is likely to be
    a. relatively inelastic.
    b. relatively elastic.
    c. perfectly elastic.
    d. perfectly inelastic.
    e. unitary elastic.

(5.5) 8. The demand for which one of the following types of labor is likely to be the most *elastic*?
    a. heart transplant surgeons
    b. airline pilots

    c. basketball players who score 30 points a game

    d. economics teachers

(5.6) 9. If the elasticity ratio for a good is 0.1 and its seller wants to make as much money as possible, he or she should

    a. raise the price.

    b. lower the price.

    c. advertise more.

    d. provide more information.

(5.6) 10. If a 10% price increase leads to a 4% reduction in the quantity of a good sold, then the elasticity ratio is equal to

    a. 0.40.

    b. 4.00.

    c. 0.25.

    d. 2.50.

(5.7) 11. Which one of the following best describes the doctrine of consumer sovereignty?

    a. The average propensity to save plus the average propensity to consume equals 100%.

    b. Demand creates supply.

    c. Marginal utility diminishes with additional units of a good.

    d. Consumers respond more to price changes when demand is elastic.

(5.8) 12. The average propensity to save is the

    a. average number of people in the economy who are net savers.

    b. percentage change in saving divided by the percentage change in income.

    c. percentage of after-tax income that is saved.

    d. quantity of a good not bought when price increases and demand is elastic.

(5.8) 13. Changing the average propensity to consume will result in a change in which of the following?

    a. the position of the demand curve for at least some goods

    b. the average propensity to save

    c. the amount of consumer goods and services sold in the economy

    d. all of the above

(5.9) 14. In which of the following transactions does the government require the seller to provide information to the consumer?

    a. A bank makes a car loan.

    b. A car dealer sells a new car to a customer.

    c. A person buys a new mattress.

    d. all of the above

(5.10) 15. Which one of the following is a result of government programs that provide information to consumers?

    a. lower information costs for consumers

    b. lower selling prices for producers

    c. the preservation of firms' reputations

    d. diminished need for product labeling

True/False Questions (*Circle T or F.*)

(5.3) 16. The exorbitant incomes paid to entertainers is more like rent than a salary. T or F

(5.4) 17. The demand for gasoline will be more elastic than the demand for different brands of gasoline. T or F

(5.5) 18. A good that has a perfectly elastic demand has perfect substitutes. T or F

(5.6) 19. If the government wants to increase the amount of revenue collected from taxes, it should tax goods that have elastic demand. T or F

(5.8) 20. The average propensity to save is always less than 100%. T or F

Chapter 6

The Business Firm and Market Structure

I. Chapter Outline

While consumer demand tells businesses *what* consumers want, it is the role of private firms to figure out how to go about producing, pricing, and delivering the goods. In particular, they must determine the best way to organize their firms, how much to produce, and what prices to charge. The answers to these questions depend a great deal on the structure of the industry that the firms are in.

Introductory Article: Farm Aid

In a freely competitive market, firms sometimes make a profit and sometimes fail to make a profit. In a free-market system, those who do not make efficient use of an economy's scarce resources will soon be out of business. In the past few decades, American farmers have discovered this as technological advances in farm equipment and methods have led to many small farmers going out of business. However, the outlook for the future for American farmers is more optimistic. Since the United States is the world's most efficient producer of food, increases in international trade should provide opportunities for increased production.

Economic Analysis

This chapter examines the issue of the business firm and market (industry) structure by addressing the following three questions:

1. **What Are the Forms and Economic Functions of Business Firms?**

   Important Concepts: Proprietorships, Partnerships, Corporations, Cooperatives, Limited liability, Real capital investment

   Case Application: Running with the Bulls

2. **What Determines a Firm's Profits?**

   Important Concepts: Total costs, Variable costs, Fixed costs, Diminishing returns, Total revenue, Normal rate of return, Economic profits

   Important Model: Total revenue and total cost

   Case Application: Aging Rockers Hit the Road One More Time

3. **How Does Industry Market Structure Affect Price and Output Decisions?**

   Important Concepts: Pure competition, Pure monopoly, Shared monopoly, Differentiated competition

   Important Model: Maximizing profit when marginal revenue equals marginal cost

   Case Application: Crashing the PC Market

Perspective: The Evolution of the Modern Corporation

II. Summary of Economic Analysis

1. The three main types of business organization are **proprietorships**, **partnerships**, and **corporations**.

2. Each type of organization has its advantages. **Proprietorships** are inexpensive to start and the owner manages the business carefully because he or she gets all the profit. **Partnerships** can take advantage of the human and financial resources of two or more individuals. The main advantages of **corporations** are their **limited liability** and status as legal entities, which enable them to raise large amounts of financial resources.

3. Each type of business organization also has its disadvantages. **Proprietorships** have limited resources and the owner is personally liable for the business's debts. Each partner in a **partnership** is legally liable for the actions of the firm (and the other partner), and the firm must be dissolved if one partner dies. Problems with **corporations** include double taxation, extra regulations, and dispersed ownership that cannot carefully monitor the firm.

4. The principal functions of business firms are to **identify consumer wants, organize production, allocate revenues (or purchasing power)**, and **increase the amount of real capital**.

5. Production costs consist of **fixed costs** (overhead), such as the depreciation of capital, and **variable costs**, such as labor, raw materials, and other inputs. **Total costs** are the sum of fixed plus variable costs.

6. When additional units of a variable input are added to one or more fixed inputs to produce additional units of output, **diminishing returns** will eventually occur. This is observed when additional units of the variable input yield successively smaller increases in output.

7. **Total revenue** is the price times the number of units sold ($P \times Q$).

8. **Profits** are total revenue minus total cost.

9. **Accounting profits** are total revenue minus **explicit** or direct costs of production.

10. **Economic profits** are total revenue minus total cost where total cost includes *both* explicit (or accounting) costs and implicit (or opportunity) costs.

11. **Implicit costs** include the opportunity cost of a proprietor's labor and the **normal rate of return** on capital invested in a business. Thus, economic profits are earnings on invested capital that are in excess of the normal rate of return.

12. There are four types of **market** (or **industry**) **structure: pure competition, differentiated competition, shared monopoly**, and **pure monopoly**.

13. A market is **purely competitive** when it has a large number of firms producing a standardized product and in which there is ease of entry into and out of the industry. As a result of ease of entry, long-run economic profits in purely competitive industries tend to zero.

14. An industry with **differentiated competition** has a large number of sellers, but they produce a nonstandardized product. Production costs are higher because of packaging and advertising, but ease of entry again results in the disappearance of economic profits.

15. A **pure monopoly** is an industry in which there is only one producer—the firm and the industry are one and the same. Pure monopolies are rare, with the best example being regulated **public utilities**.

16. A **shared monopoly** is an industry in which there are only a few firms producing either a standardized or nonstandardized product. Because of barriers to entry, economic profits may persist in the long run.

III. Review of the Learning Objectives *(Answers begin on p. 266.)*

What Are the Forms and Economic Functions of Business Firms?

FORMS OF BUSINESS ORGANIZATION

Proprietorships are owned and operated by one individual or one family.	**Partnerships** are the pooling of the capital and the business efforts of two or more people.	**Corporations** are businesses owned by the stockholders and managed by officers of the company.	**Cooperatives** are business associations of producers or consumers.

FUNCTIONS OF BUSINESS FIRMS

Identifying Consumer Wants Business firms determine what to produce on the basis of consumer wants.	**Organizing Production** Firms decide what mix of the factors of production will best achieve the desired output.	**Allocating Revenues** Firms allocate their revenues to pay company employees, suppliers, and the investors.	**Real Capital Investment** Firms increase the stock of real capital by investing in plant and equipment.

6.1 List the three main forms of business organization and cite the advantages and disadvantages of each. *(Write in answers below.)*

A. Indicate whether the following are most likely to be proprietorships (PR), partnerships (PA), or corporations (C).

    1. _____ The family farm

    2. _____ A car manufacturer

    3. _____ A corner grocery

    4. _____ A supermarket chain

    5. _____ A local real estate development firm

B. Indicate whether the following are *advantages* of proprietorships (PR), partnerships (PA), or corporations (C).

    1. _____ Ability to raise financial capital

    2. _____ Knowledge about actual costs and revenues

    3. _____ Combined resources without higher taxes

    4. _____ Ease of start-up

    5. _____ Limited liability of owners

    6. _____ "Immortality" in the eyes of the law

C. Indicate whether the following are *disadvantages* of proprietorships (PR), partnerships (PA), or corporations (C).

    1. _____ Double taxation

    2. _____ Liability for someone else's actions

3. ____ Difficulty in raising financial capital

4. ____ Regulations

5. ____ Dissolution of the firm when an owner dies

D. The owners of a corporation are its stockholders, who want the firm to make as much money as possible. These owners, however, usually never see or visit the firm that they "own" or have a chance to find out what the firm's managers do all day. What problem can occur in this case that will not occur in a proprietorship? [Hint: What kind of incentives does the corporate management face?]

_____

_____

_____

6.2 Describe the four functions of business firms.

A. When a firm makes a decision about how to _____, at the same time they will be making a decision as to how they _____ because *what* they buy directly impacts the income of *whom* they buy from.

B. In the two examples below, indicate how each of the following economic functions is represented: identifying consumer wants (I), organizing production (O), allocating resources (A), and real capital investment (C).

1. A soft-drink company buys new bottling equipment that is designed for using recyclable glass bottles rather than plastic bottles.

(I)_____

(O)_____

(A)_____

(C)_____

2. A concert promoter buys a new sound and light system.

(I)_____

(O)_____

(A)_____

(C)_____

Case Application: **The Progressive Bike Shop**

Pat and Jeff, a struggling young married couple attending college on a part-time basis, planned to enter the retail business on a small scale, but they were having difficulty deciding exactly what type of shop to open.

Pat learned in a marketing course that the percentage of family income spent on recreation and related goods and services had risen from 8% 30 years ago to approximately 13% today. Considering these statistics, the couple concluded that as society gets more prosperous, people will continue to spend additional money for recreational products. They decided to open a bicycle shop, because bicycles are a product in the recreational category and Jeff had some knowledge of their construction and repair.

After taking a survey at their college to determine what types and brand names of bicycles people demanded most, they formulated an initial purchasing list. Pat's parents agreed to invest $14,000 in the shop for a share of the profits, but running the business was left entirely to Pat and Jeff. The choice of a site was influenced by their limited funds. Rent downtown was unaffordable, so they decided to rent a storefront on the fringe of a decaying inner-city neighborhood near the campus. Here the rent would fall within their budget, and the population of young people was the greatest.

Their chosen site, although affordable and convenient to their target population, needed some renovation. Jeff, who was handy at such endeavors, turned the drab-looking storefront into an attractive, eye-catching shop.

Young and old flocked to the shop on opening day. Nearby community residents praised the couple's attempt to restore retail life to a once-thriving area of proprietorship. Pat and Jeff named their store the "Progressive Bike Shop." To find out what happened to Pat and Jeff's bike shop, see the next Case Application.

Economic Reasoning *(Write your responses on a separate sheet. Answers begin on p. 266.)*

1. What form of business organization was the Progressive Bike Shop?
2. What economic functions did the Progressive Bike Shop perform?
3. Do you think locating the shop in a deteriorated neighborhood was a good idea? Why or why not?

What Determines a Firm's Profits?

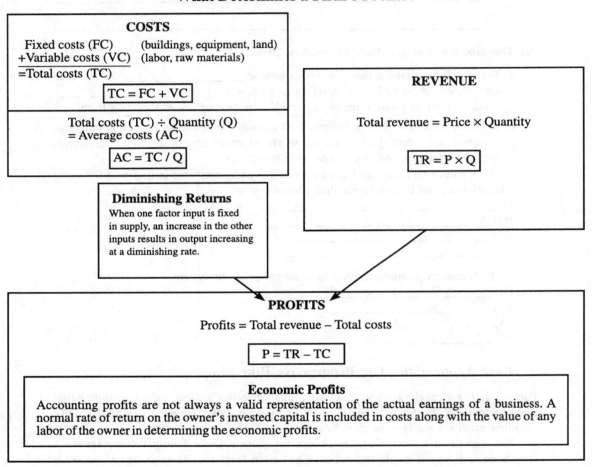

COSTS

Fixed costs (FC)   (buildings, equipment, land)
+Variable costs (VC)   (labor, raw materials)
=Total costs (TC)

$$TC = FC + VC$$

Total costs (TC) ÷ Quantity (Q)
= Average costs (AC)

$$AC = TC / Q$$

REVENUE

Total revenue = Price × Quantity

$$TR = P \times Q$$

Diminishing Returns
When one factor input is fixed in supply, an increase in the other inputs results in output increasing at a diminishing rate.

PROFITS

Profits = Total revenue – Total costs

$$P = TR - TC$$

Economic Profits
Accounting profits are not always a valid representation of the actual earnings of a business. A normal rate of return on the owner's invested capital is included in costs along with the value of any labor of the owner in determining the economic profits.

6.3 Distinguish between fixed costs and variable costs.

A. Do fixed costs exist in the *short run* or in the *long run*? Explain. (You may want to review the discussion of short and long runs in chapter 4.)

_____

_____

B. Indicate which of the following are fixed costs (F) and which are variable costs (V).

1. ___ Mortgage payments on a fast-food restaurant building

2. ___ Wages for labor

3. ___ Sesame-seed buns

4. ___ Electricity to heat the fry kettles

5. ___ $30,000 of the owner's money invested in the restaurant

6. ___ Depreciation on the grill

7. ___ Monthly payments on the delivery truck

C. The annual fixed costs of capital goods are called _____. The dollar value of these annual costs depends on the original cost of the capital and its _____. During periods of rapid technological change, capital equipment may need to be replaced earlier because it becomes _____.

6.4 Show the relationship between total cost and total revenue to profit.

A. Total revenue minus total cost is _____.

B. A firm is earning profit when _____ is greater than _____. A firm is breaking even when _____ is equal to _____.

C. Complete the following table by entering values for total cost, total revenue, and profit.

Quantity	Price	Fixed Cost	Variable Cost	Total Cost	Total Revenue	Profit
0	$10	$2	$0	$	$	$
1	9	2	5			
2	8	2	9			
3	7	2	12			
4	6	2	14			
5	5	1	15			
6	4	2	16			
7	3	2	18			
8	2	2	21			
9	1	2	25			
10	0	2	30			

D. Use the table in exercise C to answer the following questions:

1. At output levels greater than _____ and less than _____, the firm earns a profit.

2. The output level that maximizes profit is _____.

E.

1. A price increase has both positive and negative impacts on total revenue. A greater price is paid for each unit, but fewer units are sold. If demand is *inelastic*, the quantity demanded will decrease relatively less than the increase in price. Accordingly, what will happen to total revenue if the price increases? Explain.

_____

_____

2. If demand is *elastic*, the quantity demanded will decrease relatively more than the increase in price. Accordingly, what will happen to total revenue if the price increases?

_____

_____

6.5 Distinguish between normal rate of return and economic profit.

A. The rate of earnings on invested capital that is normal for a given degree of risk is called the _____ while earnings that are in excess of this amount are _____.

B. In order for the owner of a firm to stay in business he or she must be earning at least _____.

C. Suppose Juanita takes $200,000 from her own bank account, where it was earning 10% per year, and uses the money to start a business. She quits her job, where she was earning $25,000 a year, in order to work the same number of hours in her business. At the end of the first year, her total revenues were $100,000, but she had paid $40,000 in wages to her employees and another $20,000 for rent, supplies, and so on.

   1. How much economic profit did Juanita make?_____
   2. Should she stay in business for another year? Explain._____

Case Application: **The Fortunes of the Progressive Bike Shop**

During their first year of operation, Pat and Jeff sold 144 bicycles at an average price of $310 per bicycle. They sold an additional $9,620 worth of accessories and parts and took in $6,800 for repair work on bicycles brought into the shop for service. Their total revenue during that first year amounted to $61,060. The cost to them for the bicycles and other merchandise they sold was $26,400. Their rent, utilities, and other overhead costs were $16,800. Their total direct costs were thus $43,200 ($26,400 + $16,800).

After subtracting their costs from their revenues, Pat and Jeff were left with a net income of $17,860. According to their agreement with Pat's parents, they paid 20% of this amount to the parents as a return on the money they had invested in the business. This left Pat and Jeff with earnings of $14,288 for the year. Considering all the time they had put into running the shop and the $6,000 of their own money they had invested in it, this did not seem like much. However, business had steadily improved during the year as the Progressive Bike Shop's reputation for charging reasonable prices and standing behind its merchandise spread around the area. Pat and Jeff were confident they would do better during the second year of operations.

Economic Reasoning *(Write your responses on a separate sheet. Answers begin on p. 266.)*

1. Was the $26,400 cost of the merchandise a fixed cost or a variable cost?
2. What economic costs of operating the Progressive Bike Shop were not included in the $43,200 given as the total cost?
3. Was it fair for Pat's parents to get 20% of the net receipts for their $14,000 investment in the business? Why or why not?

How Does Industry Market Structure Affect Price and Output Decisions?

PURE COMPETITION	PURE MONOPOLY	SHARED MONOPOLY	DIFFERENTIATED COMPETITION
An industry in which there are so many producers of a single standardized product that no one firm can affect the market price	An industry in which there is only one producer	An industry in which there are only a few producers of a single standardized product or a differentiated product	An industry in which there are very many producers of a single differentiated product

PURE COMPETITION

An industry in which there are so many producers of a single standardized product that no one firm can affect the market price

Firms in the industry produce at a minimum cost and sell at the lowest possible price.

In the long run, economic profits in pure competition tend toward zero due to ease of entry into the industry.

PURE MONOPOLY

An industry in which there is only one producer

Maximum Profit Output

A monopolist will produce the output at which the revenue from the marginal unit produced just equals the cost of producing it; that is, Marginal Revenue (MR) equals Marginal Cost (MC).

$$MR = MC$$

Monopolistic firms restrict their output in order to keep the price at the level which will maximize profits.

SHARED MONOPOLY

An industry in which there are only a few producers of a single standardized product or a differentiated product

Price Leadership

When there are only a few firms in a single industry, each one of them is affected by the pricing policies of the other firms. A price cut by one firm to increase sales is likely to start a price war. Consequently, the firms stabilize prices in the industry by means of price leadership.

DIFFERENTIATED COMPETITION

An industry in which there are very many producers of a single differentiated product

Firms in the industry attempt to attract new customers by differentiating their product from those of their competitors. This frequently involves spending on advertising and packaging.

Ease of entry into the industry causes the profits to tend toward zero.

6.6 List the characteristics of a purely competitive industry.

A. Indicate by a check (√) which of the following are characteristics of purely competitive firms.

1. _____ Firms independently determine what prices to charge for their products.

2. _____ A firm's total revenue will increase at an increasing rate.

3. _____ There are many small firms in the industry.

4. _____ It is easy for new firms to enter the industry.

5. _____ One firm's product is a perfect substitute for any other firm's product.

6. _____ A firm's costs are subject to diminishing returns.

B. Indicate by a check (√) which of the following are close to being purely competitive industries.

1. _____ Farming

2. _____ The production of nails

3. _____ The fast-food industry

4. _____ Different vendors selling peanuts at an outdoor concert

5. _____ The snack bar at a movie theater

6. _____ The videotape rental industry

7. _____ Vegetable stands along a highway

6.7 Explain why consumers benefit when industries are purely competitive.

A. In a purely competitive industry, firms produce at _____ cost and sell at _____ prices.

B. What would happen to a single purely competitive firm if it raised its price on its own? _____

C. What would you do, as a consumer, if a purely competitive firm did not produce a product that was of satisfactory quality or provide adequate customer service?

_____

6.8 Explain why purely competitive firms cannot make economic profits in the long run.

A. If a purely competitive firm is earning economic profit, other firms will _____ this market.

B. Suppose that growing tomatoes is a purely competitive industry. Because of a discovery that eating tomatoes provides protection against developing various kinds of cancer, farmers in this market are currently earning economic profits. Check each of the following events that will occur in the short run in this purely competitive market.

1. ____ New farmers enter the industry.

2. ____ Farmers leave the industry.

3. ____ Market supply increases.

4. ____ Market supply decreases.

5. ____ The market price increases.

6. ____ The market price decreases.

7. ____ Economic profits increase.

8. ____ Economic profits decrease.

C. What if the situation in exercise B were reversed? In other words, suppose it has been discovered that eating tomatoes is harmful to one's health, and tomato farmers are currently incurring economic losses. Check each of the following events that will occur in the short run in this purely competitive market.

1. ____ New farmers enter the industry.

2. ____ Farmers leave the industry.

3. ____ Market supply increases.

4. ____ Market supply decreases.

5. ____ The market price increases.

6. ____ The market price decreases.

7. ____ Economic losses increase.

8. ____ Economic losses decrease.

D. The entry and exit that occurs in the tomato farming industry in exercises B and C will lead to long-term economic profits equal to _____ in this purely competitive industry.

6.9 Explain how differentiated competition, monopoly, and shared monopoly differ from pure competition in terms of number of firms, barriers to entry, homogeneous products, and long-term profits.

A. If an industry has no barriers to entry, long-term profits will be equal to _____.

B. Indicate whether each of the following industries is differentiated competition (DC), pure monopoly (PM), shared monopoly (SM), or pure competition (PC).

1. ____ Diamond mining

2. ____ Fast-food hamburgers

3. ____ Automobiles

4. ____ Breakfast cereals

5. ____ First-class mail delivery

6. ____ Cable television in your neighborhood

7. ____ Retail clothing stores

8. ____ Local bus service

9. ____ Airline companies

C. Which types of market structures have the following characteristics? (PC = pure competition, DC = differentiated competition, PM = pure monopoly, SM = shared monopoly)

1. ____ Above-normal profits in the long run

2. ____ The ability to set prices

3. ____ Efforts to differentiate products from rivals' products

4. ____ A large number of firms in the industry

5. ____ Existence of diminishing returns

6. ____ The ability to earn short-run economic profits

7. ____ Ease of entry into the industry

8. ____ Price leadership

9. ____ Cartels

Case Application: Wheat Farmers in Debt

Gus Bailey, a hardworking wheat farmer, raised his eyes to the hot Kansas sun. He feared that the blistering dry spell would reduce his harvest to the point where he could not sell it for enough cash to pay his bills.

The bills for additional seed, gasoline, and fertilizer flashed before him. How would he pay? When he had made the decision to plant more acres, it had seemed such a good idea. Now Gus had doubts. Back then he had reasoned: "I've got to pay taxes on my land whether I use it or not. The mortgage has to be paid, and the hired hand will be on the payroll. My planting and harvesting equipment is already costing me plenty and handling two more acres wouldn't change that." The only additional costs Gus could think of would be some extra wheat seed, the high-yield fertilizer, a few extra gallons of gasoline, and maybe another part-time field hand when harvest time came. "Surely the return on two extra acres will pay those costs," Gus had thought, "and leave some extra money."

Several days later the weather pattern shifted. Rains came in just the right quantities during the remaining growing season, and the warm sun performed its magic. Gus Bailey was blessed with a bountiful harvest, and he eagerly anticipated lucrative market results. His wheat crop was larger and better than Gus had ever obtained in 20 years of farming.

"Two-fifty a bushel," shouted the grain elevator operator. "I can't pay you any more than that." Gus was shocked and saddened by the response. At $2.50 a bushel, Gus could just barely meet his out-of-pocket expenses. He might even have to take out a bank loan to pay his taxes and buy seed for next year. Gus wondered if he should get out of farming altogether. Jake Wilson had offered to buy his land and turn it into house lots. Gus would have to think about the offer, but perhaps prices would be better next year.

Economic Reasoning (*Write your responses on a separate sheet. Answers begin on p. 267.*)

1. What was there in Gus Bailey's experience to show that he is in a purely competitive market?

2. How does the application illustrate that under purely competitive conditions, economic profits tend toward zero?

3. Do farmers deserve government subsidies or other special assistance not afforded to other industries? Why or why not?

IV. Practice Test (Answers begin on p. 267.)

Multiple-Choice Questions *(Circle the correct answer.)*

(6.1) 1. The concept of "limited liability" applies in which of the following type(s) of business organizations?
   a. proprietorships
   b. partnerships
   c. corporations
   d. all of the above

(6.1) 2. The firm has a legal identity separate from its owner or owners in which type(s) of business organizations?
   a. proprietorships
   b. partnerships
   c. corporations
   d. all of the above

(6.2) 3. The answers to which of the following basic economic questions will be influenced by business firms as they undertake their four economic functions?
   a. How to produce?
   b. What to produce?
   c. For whom to produce?
   d. all of the above

(6.3) 4. Which of the following is a fixed cost for a manufacturer of blue jeans?
   a. denim
   b. depreciation
   c. labor
   d. electricity for running sewing machines
   e. none of the above

(6.3) 5. Which of the following is a *true* statement?
   a. Fixed costs equal total costs when output equals zero.
   b. Fixed costs do not exist in the long run.
   c. Variable costs equal zero when output equals zero.
   d. Fixed costs do not change when output levels change.
   e. all of the above

(6.4) 6. Profit is equal to
   a. price times quantity.
   b. total revenue times total cost.
   c. total revenue minus total cost.
   d. fixed costs plus variable costs.

(6.4) 7. Total costs are calculated as the sum of
   a. marginal and average costs.
   b. marginal and fixed costs.
   c. average and variable costs.
   d. fixed and variable costs.

(6.5) 8. If Wayne made an accounting profit of $45,000 in his business last year, but he did not take into account the implicit or opportunity costs of his resources, he
   a. earned only the normal rate of return.
   b. definitely earned economic profit as well.
   c. earned economic profit if the implicit costs are less than $45,000.
   d. earned economic profit if the implicit costs are greater than $45,000.

(6.6) 9. Which one of the following is *not* a characteristic of a purely competitive industry?
   a. price-takers
   b. price wars
   c. many, small firms
   d. significant market power

(6.6) 10. In which one of the market structures listed below are firms forced to sell at the lowest possible price?
   a. pure monopoly
   b. pure competition
   c. shared monopoly
   d. differentiated competition

(6.8) 11. Which one of the following is a *true* statement about purely competitive firms?
   a. They can earn economic profits in the short run, but they are limited to a normal return in the long run.
   b. They can earn economic profits in the long run, but they are limited to a normal return in the short run.
   c. They can earn economic profits in both the long and short runs.
   d. They can never earn an economic profit.

(6.7) 12. Which one of the following is *not* typical of firms in a purely competitive industry?
   a. They produce a standardized product.
   b. They set the price that maximizes their profits.
   c. They do not need to worry about what the other firms in the industry are charging for the product.
   d. They can exit and enter the industry easily.

(6.8) 13. Which one of the characteristics of purely competitive firms listed below explains why firms in this industry earn zero long-term economic profits?
   a. price-takers
   b. many, small firms
   c. free entry and exit
   d. homogeneous products

(6.9) 14. A lot of money is spent on advertising and packaging in which type of market?
   a. pure monopoly
   b. pure competition
   c. shared monopoly
   d. differentiated competition

(6.9) 15. Price leadership is most often found in which type of industry?
   a. pure competition
   b. differentiated competition
   c. shared monopoly
   d. pure monopoly

True/False Questions *(Circle T or F.)*

(6.1) 16. Partnerships are subject to double taxation on their profits. T or F

(6.3) 17. Depreciation is a variable cost. T or F

(6.5) 18. Economic profit is another name for the normal rate of return. T or F

(6.8) 19. Purely competitive firms earn the normal rate of return in the long run. T or F

(6.9) 20. There are significant barriers to entry in industries that are pure monopolies. T or F

Chapter 7
Industrial Performance

I. Chapter Outline

It is easy, in theory, to discuss how economies need to answer the three basic economic questions as efficiently as possible. In practice, beginning in the last century, U.S. industry was the world leader in answering the "how to produce" question efficiently—up to the 1970s, that is. Then Japanese firms caught up with and surpassed American firms in production efficiency and quality in the auto industry and a number of others. In the 1990s, however, the competitiveness of U.S. industry has reasserted itself.

Introductory Article: The Industrial Phoenix

At one time, the expression "made in Japan" implied cheap, shoddy merchandise that was below the quality of goods produced in the United States. During the past two decades, however, the products imported from Japan generally became accepted as being of superior quality at a competitive price. By using business techniques developed in America (but ignored for years by American business leaders), the Japanese improved both their productivity and product quality to a point where they took markets from U.S. businesses and jobs from U.S. workers. The dramatic rise of the Japanese economy was not achieved without cost: the Japanese people worked hard, saved their money, and learned to live with fewer consumption goods for themselves in order to become one of the world's most productive societies. It has taken some time, but with increased emphasis on hard work and product quality, American businesses have fought back and are regaining market share in industry after industry. Perhaps we should be thankful to the Japanese for forcing us to refocus on quality, productivity, and putting the customer first. Without such a focus we will not be able to remain competitive in a global economy.

Economic Analysis

This chapter examines the relative decline of American industrial leadership by examining the following questions:

1. **What Determines Industry Performance?**

   Important Concepts: Productivity, Quality, Responsiveness to the market and to social concerns

   Comparative Case Application: Eyes Too Big in a Tantalizing Market

2. **How Can Industry Performance Be Improved?**

   Important Concepts: Investment in capital equipment, Real investment, Just-in-time manufacturing, Investment in human capital, Learning curve, Cross-training, Employee involvement programs, Employee empowerment, Total quality management (TQM), Business process re-engineering (BPR), Research and development

   Case Application: The New Industrial Revolution

3. **What Are the Effects of Market Structure on Industry Performance?**

   Important Concepts: Market concentration, Aggregate concentration, Barriers to entry, Predatory practices

   Case Application: Corporate Raiders, LBOs, and the Feeding Frenzy

Perspective: An Imperfect World

Biography—Joan Violet Robinson

II. Summary of Economic Analysis

1. **Industry performance** is generally measured according to the following criteria: **productivity, product quality, responsiveness to the market**, and **responsiveness to social concerns.**

2. In an effort to stimulate U.S. firms to pay closer attention to improving product quality, the U.S. Congress established the **Malcolm Baldrige National Quality Award** in 1988.

3. Perhaps the most important measure of performance, **productivity**, is measured as the amount of output per unit of input.

4. Increased **real investment in capital equipment** is one necessary condition for increased productivity. However, obtaining the necessary funds for this investment will require an increased **savings rate** in the United States.

5. Another important factor that leads to increased productivity is investment in **human capital**, that is, improvements in worker skills and motivation. Improvements in worker performance over time can be measured by the **learning curve**.

6. Employee involvement in decision-making processes can reduce costs and improve productivity even though it is often criticized by unions, middle managers, and foremen. More American businesses are practicing **employee empowerment** where workers are given the ability and responsibility to make decisions about how their work should best be done. Employee involvement is also fostered through **total quality management** and **business process re-engineering** programs in which employees contribute to company success.

7. Improvements in both capital and human inputs are the result of **research and development (R & D)** that results in new technologies, production techniques, and management techniques.

8. The structure of American markets may also have an impact on industrial performance. **Market concentration** describes whether an industry is characterized by a few businesses (high concentration) or many businesses (low concentration). A commonly used measure of market concentration is the **concentration ratio**.

9. **Aggregate concentration** describes the share of an economy's total output that is accounted for by the nation's largest firms.

10. Concentration can result from a number of factors, including **mergers, barriers to entry**, and **predatory business practices**.

11. The consequences of high concentration include **monopolistic pricing, economic instability**, and a general **misallocation of resources.**

III. Review of the Learning Objectives *(Answers begin on p. 267.)*

What Determines Industry Performance?

PRODUCTIVITY	QUALITY	RESPONSIVENESS TO THE MARKET	RESPONSIVENESS TO SOCIAL CONCERNS
The low productivity growth since 1973 has put industry competitiveness in the United States behind that in Japan and other countries.	The quality of a firm's output begins with the quality of the parts made by its suppliers.	Responding quickly to changes in consumer preferences and being able to target market niches puts producers in a position to better satisfy demand in the marketplace.	Industries are now held accountable for their environmental effects, resource conservation, product and worker safety, and providing equal opportunity in employment practices.

7.1 Describe four factors that determine industry performance. Define productivity and describe how it is measured. *(Write in answers below.)*

A. The four indicators of industry performance are:

1. _____

2. _____

3. _____

4. _____

B. Using the numbers from the above list, indicate which of the indicators of performance is at issue in each of the following:

1. ____ MegaMotors reports that it is recalling its new cars to repair defects in the steering wheels.

2. ____ The government fines KO Chemicals for dumping waste products that kill whales and dolphins.

3. ____ Employers reimburse workers for extra training that they receive on their own time.

4. ____ Canadian consumers buy more imported stereos because the imports have the features that they want.

5. ____ American consumers buy more imported personal computers because these computers break down less frequently than domestic computers.

6. ____ More corn can be cultivated with tractors than with hoes.

7. ____ A washing machine company advertises that its repairmen are lonely.

8. ____ A product is made with planned obsolescence.

9. ____ Workers and managers schedule weekly meetings to discuss how to improve output and working conditions.

C. Which measures of industry performance are directly related to the "what to produce" question?

1. _____

2. _____

D. An indication of improved productivity would be a _____ level of output from a given level of inputs, or a given level of output from a _____ level of inputs.

E. For each of the following, indicate a hypothetical increase in productivity. (For example, increased productivity in car manufacturing might be indicated by fewer labor hours per car.) Then indicate a possible source of the increased productivity.

1. A fast-food restaurant

_____

_____

_____

2. A lawyer's office

_____

_____

_____

3. Your local electric company

_____

_____

_____

7.2 Explain why product quality is important and how it can be improved.

A. Give an example of something that would indicate poor quality in each of the following:
   1. Nuclear electric plants_____
   2. Hot dogs_____
   3. Computer printers_____
   4. Television sets_____
   5. Bicycles_____
   6. A new building_____

B. List advertisements for three products that you have seen that indicate the seller is concerned about quality.

   1. _____

   2. _____

   3. _____

C. American producers are (rightfully) interested in making profits. Explain why they would also be interested in winning the Malcolm Baldrige Award.

_____

_____

_____

7.3 Describe why and how businesses respond to social concerns.

A. What are three things that a fast-food restaurant might do that would indicate a *disregard* for social concerns?

   1. _____

   2. _____

   3. _____

B. What are three things that a fast-food restaurant might do that would indicate a *regard* for social concerns?

   1. _____

   2. _____

   3. _____

C. What are two *costs* that could be associated with "antisocial" actions by private firms?

   1. _____

   2. _____

D. What are two economic or socioeconomic goals consistent with "responding to social concerns"? (See chapter 2.)

   1. _____

   2. _____

Case Application: Academic Theory Put into Practice

When Professor William P. Lyons of Yale, an adjunct professor in both the business and law schools, acquired control of the Duro-Test Corporation, he became chairman and president of the country's fourth-largest maker of light bulbs, with 5% of the market. It is the largest maker of specialty bulbs.

Before Lyons obtained control the company had been in decline, with output falling to half the level it had once produced. It was operating at only 30% of its production capacity.

To reverse the decline, Lyons concentrated on expanding the sales of the company's Vita-Lite bulb. The Vita-Lite bulb has a long life due to its special filament and design. It is said to produce a light closely resembling sunlight. This light is supposed to reduce worker fatigue and error on the job.

The sales force of Duro-Test was consolidated so that sales representatives from different divisions were not competing with each other for the same accounts. Lyons also offered the firm's 1,600 workers an employee stock ownership plan.

Economic Reasoning *(Write your responses on a separate sheet. Answers begin on p. 267.)*

1. Which of the factors determining industry performance do you find in the case of Duro-Test Corporation?
2. What did Professor Lyons hope to accomplish by establishing an employee stock ownership plan?
3. Do you think teachers are likely to make good company presidents? Why or why not?

How Can Industry Performance Be Improved?

INVESTMENT IN CAPITAL EQUIPMENT	INVESTMENT IN HUMAN CAPITAL	RESEARCH AND DEVELOPMENT	EMPLOYEE INVOLVEMENT (EI)
Productivity depends greatly on the amount of real investment per worker.	Investment by companies in worker training produces even larger returns than investment in machinery.	The spending on R & D for new products or new production technologies results in greater success for companies in their markets.	In order to reduce costs and improve quality, firms are empowering their employees by allowing them to make decisions about how their jobs should best be done.

INVESTMENT IN CAPITAL EQUIPMENT

Real investment in the United States is low because of:
1. a low savings rate and the high cost of financial capital.
2. the diversion of financial capital from real investment into speculative investment in existing assets.
3. short time horizons for corporate objectives.

INVESTMENT IN HUMAN CAPITAL

Learning Curve
The productivity rate with new equipment and new production processes rises more rapidly when workers are given more training.

EMPLOYEE INVOLVEMENT (EI)

1. Self-managing teams
2. Problem-solving teams
3. Special-purpose teams

The use of a relatively flat rather than vertical organizational structure results in more efficient communications between different departments.

7.4 Explain the importance of investment in capital equipment.

A. Circle the correct answer within the parentheses.

There is a (direct/inverse/constant) relationship between capital equipment per worker and productivity.

B. If the size of the labor force increases while investment in capital equipment declines, then productivity will _____.

C. Give an example of capital equipment investment that could increase (or has increased) productivity in each of the following industries:

    1. Grocery stores_____
    2. Education_____
    3. Auto manufacturing_____

7.5 Explain why capital investment is so low in the United States and how it can be increased.

A. What are the three reasons why U.S. investment in capital equipment has lagged behind Japanese investment?

    1. _____

    2. _____

    3. _____

B. Although the Japanese have been more successful than Americans in investing in capital equipment, they have paid a price. What is an *opportunity cost* of Japan's higher level of investment?

_____

7.6 Understand the importance of research and development.

A. R & D stands for_____.

B. R & D generally enhances the productivity of which factor of production?

_____

C. What are two important sources of R & D in the United States?

    1. _____

    2. _____

D. Will a perfectly competitive firm invest in R & D? Why or why not?

_____

_____

_____

7.7 Describe employee involvement and explain how it improves productivity.

A. Giving workers the ability and responsibility to make decisions about how their work should best be done is called _____.

B. Employee involvement changes the organizational structure of a company by making the system _____ (more or less) flat.

C. For each firm listed below, describe how employee involvement might increase productivity.

    1. Pizza parlor

_____

_____

    2. Automobile manufacturing factory

_____

3. Bank

_____

_____

7.8 List and give examples of three kinds of employee involvement teams.

A. EI stands for _____.

B. Indicate whether each of the following is an example of a self-managing team (SM), a problem-solving team (PS), or a special-purpose team (SP):

1. _____ Students and teachers work together to schedule class times, vacation times, and curriculum.

2. _____ A special committee of students and teachers is organized to study why some students have difficulty reading.

3. _____ A team of workers learns one anothers' tasks so that if one becomes ill, the rest can fill in.

4. _____ A group of students and teachers meets once a week to discuss mutual concerns about education.

C. The *idea* of using EI teams was first introduced in _____, but these teams were first used extensively in _____.

D. What are two interest groups that oppose EI groups?

1. _____

2. _____

Case Application: Dell Deals Direct

A bold concept—direct customer contact—has made Dell Computer Corporation one of the most successful companies of the 1990s. During the first quarter of 1999, Dell took a wide lead as the No. 1 computer systems vendor to U.S. businesses. The company is also the market share leader in total PC shipments within the overall U.S. workplace segment, according to a 1999 report from ZD Market Intelligence. Dell Computer Corporation's market share has increased in every quarter since the fourth quarter of 1997, while the company's competitors are falling further and further behind.

The company advertises that you can buy directly and have your system custom-built with exactly the features you desire. It appears that U.S. business customers are recognizing the value of Dell's direct model and the customized products and services the company offers.

Dell assists its customers through its factory-integration service called DellPlus. The factory has become highly automated, and the company has eliminated distributors by dealing directly with customers. Dell does not stock systems but builds them to order in the factory. This eliminates computers held in inventory by distributors and allows the company to introduce new components quickly and respond rapidly to price changes in components. Their own employees are trained to give customers direct attention rather than using dealers to maintain customer relationships.

Economic Reasoning (*Write your responses on a separate sheet. Answers begin on p. 268.*)

1. In which areas of performance do you think Dell has excelled (investment in capital equipment, investment in human capital, employee involvement, or research and development)?

2. How does Dell's system illustrate just-in-time manufacturing?

3. Which is a better method for computer companies—dealing directly with customers as Dell does or supplying systems to distributors who then deal with customers? Why?

What Are the Effects of Market Structure on Industry Performance?

MARKET CONCENTRATION	AGGREGATE CONCENTRATION
Market concentration refers to the number of firms in an industry that are competing for customers. It ranges from pure competition to pure monopoly.	Aggregate concentration refers to the percentage of the total sales of all industries together that is accounted for by the largest firms. There is no standard measurement for aggregate concentration, but concentration is increasing.

Concentration Ratio

The concentration ratio in an industry is measured by calculating the amount of sales by the largest four firms in the industry as a percentage of the total sales of the industry.

CONCENTRATION AND INDUSTRY PERFORMANCE

Causes of Concentration

1. Mergers
2. Barriers to entry
3. Predatory business practices
   a. Price discrimination
   b. Sales below cost
   c. Kickbacks

Results of Concentration

1. Monopolistic pricing—prices set above costs of production, resulting in monopoly profits
2. Misallocation of resources—supply limited to keep prices high, resulting in resource misallocation
3. Noninformational advertising expenses and nonutilitarian product differentiation
4. Greater economic instability in the business cycle

7.9 Describe market concentration and explain how it is measured by the concentration ratio.

A. Indicate whether each of the following industries is characterized by high (H) or low (L) market concentration.

1. _____ Automobile manufacturing

2. _____ Dairies

3. _____ Breakfast cereal producers

4. _____ Concentrated lemon juice

5. _____ Retail clothes

6. _____ Commercial airlines

7. _____ PC makers

8. _____ Banks

9. _____ Long-distance telephone companies

10. _____ Cable television companies in your town

11. _____ Taxi companies in your town

B. Which of the four *market structures* is (are) characterized by high market concentration?

_____

C. Calculate the concentration ratios for each of the following three industries:

1. Industry X has 10 firms, each with an equal market share.

2. Industry Y has one firm with 37% of the market and 63 firms with 1% each.

3. Industry Z has 20 firms with 3% of the market and 20 firms with 2% of the market.

D. Which of the above industries is a competitive industry?_____

7.10 Explain the difference between market and aggregate concentration.

A. The Fortune 500 list of America's largest firms gives an idea of the extent of _____ concentration.

B. Which of the following mergers would increase both aggregate and market concentration (AM), and which would increase only aggregate concentration (A)?

1. ____ General Motors merges with Ford Motor Company.

2. ____ Alcoa merges with Coca Cola.

3. ____ Kellogg's merges with Quaker Oats.

4. ____ CBS merges with Fox.

5. ____ IBM merges with Apple Computers.

7.11 Explain the consequences of high market concentration.

A. What are three *causes* of high industry concentration?

1. _____

2. _____

3. _____

B. Dutch Schultz, a famous gangster in the 1920s, monopolized the New York numbers game by killing his competitors. This is an example of increasing market concentration by

_____

C. The four *consequences* of high industry concentration are:

1. _____

2. _____

3. _____

4. _____

D. List three products that you use that represent examples of product differentiation by producers:

1. _____

2. _____

3. _____

Case Application: Rent-a-Kidney Business: Dialysis for Profit?

The rent-a-kidney business is an industry that provides dialysis—an artificial method of purifying the blood—for people with kidney failure. Those who need dialysis can get it from a dialysis center. If they want dialysis at home they can buy the machine and its associate supplies from firms like Eric, Inc., or National Medical Care.

When artificial kidneys first came into use, the units were only used in hospitals, and patients had to stay in the hospital for a very long period of intensive care. But when home dialysis units became affordable, patients were able to dialyze themselves. National Medical Care is the largest dialysis business in the United States. It sells all necessary supplies to almost 50% of all home dialysis patients.

Profit-seeking dialysis centers have been established outside hospitals in cities like New York and Boston. National Medical Care is also active in that branch of the rent-a-kidney business. It owns many dialysis centers, where it handles about 16% of those dialysis patients not dialyzing at home.

Congress has enacted legislation under which the government pays the costs for the treatment of kidneys. Even though the cost of dialysis in the centers is 49% higher than that of home dialysis, the percentage of patients in home dialysis has declined steadily since the government program began.

Economic Reasoning *(Write your responses on a separate sheet. Answers begin on p. 268.)*

1. How would you classify the home dialysis equipment industry with respect to the type of market structure in the industry?
2. Does the hospital-based dialysis service industry have the same market structure as the home dialysis equipment industry? How can you judge from the information in the application whether or not the two industries operate in the same type of market?
3. The government dialysis program has increased the profitability of firms such as National Medical Care. Is this justified? Why or why not?

IV. Practice Test (Answers begin on p. 269.)

Multiple-Choice Questions *(Circle the correct answer.)*

(7.1) 1. Which of the following is *not* one of the four factors that determine industry performance?
    a. responsiveness to markets
    b. product quality
    c. wages and salaries
    d. responsiveness to social concerns

(7.1) 2. Productivity is measured as the ratio of
    a. wages to outputs.
    b. quality to quantity.
    c. outputs to inputs.
    d. social to market responsiveness.

(7.2) 3. The Malcolm Baldrige Award is a prize awarded for improvements in
    a. productivity.
    b. product quality.
    c. environmental protection.
    d. R & D.

(7.3) 4. Why did StarKist insist that its tuna suppliers change their fishing techniques?
    a. Consumers threatened a boycott over a social concern.
    b. StarKist needed to become more productive in response to Japanese competition in the tuna market.
    c. Consumers were complaining about poor product quality.
    d. all of the above

(7.4) 5. One way to avoid diminishing returns (when additional units of a variable input yield successively smaller increases in output) is to increase
    a. total revenue.
    b. costs of production.
    c. the number of employees.
    d. investment in capital equipment.

(7.5) 6. Which one of the following is *not* a reason that capital investment has declined in the United States?
    a. high interest rates
    b. a relatively flat learning curve
    c. a short-term profit horizon
    d. use of available funds for speculation

(7.5) 7. The high level of interest rates in the United States is the result of
    a. low productivity.
    b. low savings rates.
    c. a short time horizon on the part of borrowers.
    d. low levels of capital investment.

(7.6) 8. R & D spending is important in order to improve
    a. education.
    b. process innovation.
    c. productivity.
    d. responsiveness to markets.

(7.7) 9. The flatter organizational structure that is characteristic of companies that practice employee involvement was first evident in which country?
    a. Japan
    b. Mexico
    c. Germany
    d. the United States

(7.7) 10. Which one of the following describes a program through which employees can contribute to company success?
    a. Boycott
    b. Just-in-time
    c. Real investment
    d. Total quality management

(7.8) 11. Which one of the following is an example of EI?
    a. self-managing teams
    b. investment in capital equipment
    c. responding to consumer wants
    d. eliminating excess labor

(7.9) 12. Which one of the following is a drawback of using the concentration ratio as a measure of competition in an industry?
    a. Many concentration ratios include only domestic firms.
    b. Concentration ratios are used to identify market structures.
    c. When the concentration ratio is less than 25%, industries are assumed to be competitive.
    d. All firms in a particular market are considered when calculating the concentration ratio for that market.

(7.9) 13. Which one of the following types of industries have the highest market concentration?
    a. pure competition
    b. differentiated competition
    c. shared monopoly
    d. pure monopoly

(7.10) 14. Which one of the following is a *true* statement?
  a. Aggregate concentration has increased in the United States since 1940.
  b. An industry characterized by high aggregate concentration is either a shared or a pure monopoly.
  c. Aggregate concentration refers to the use of capital-intensive production techniques.
  d. Increased aggregate concentration is a direct result of the introduction of process innovations.

(7.11) 15. The most important consequence of high market concentration is
  a. low profits.
  b. low productivity.
  c. high prices.
  d. flat learning curves.

True/False Questions *(Circle T or F.)*

(7.1) 16. Industry performance is measured by the concentration ratio. T or F

(7.1) 17. Productivity is measured by the ratio of outputs to inputs. T or F

(7.4) 18. A nation's productivity depends on investment in capital equipment. T or F

(7.5) 19. Just-in-time is a delivery system that increases a firm's inventory. T or F

(7.10) 20. The concentration ratio measures the level of aggregate concentration in industries. T or F

Chapter 8

Government and Business

I. Chapter Outline

Although market economies work well to provide answers to the three basic economic questions, there are instances when the market fails to allocate resources efficiently. These include situations such as a lack of competition (high market concentration), the existence of collective goods, or the existence of external economies or external costs. In these instances, there is a rationale for the government to interfere with the workings of the market in an effort to improve the allocation of resources.

Introductory Article: Who Is Building the Information Superhighway?

As the telecommunications industry has evolved from the telegraph to the telephone to the global connection of computers via e-mail and the Internet, the economic structure of the communications industry in the United States has also evolved. At one time AT&T held a monopoly over nearly all parts of the industry. However, U.S. antitrust policy discourages unregulated monopolization of any industry, and, as a result, the government ordered a break-up of "Ma Bell" in the 1980s. Since then the structure of the industry has varied between regulated monopoly in local telephone service (the "Baby Bells") and vigorous unregulated competition in the telephone hardware and long-distance service industries. New technologies that offer television, computer, satellite, and telephone services together are diminishing the importance of traditional telephone service. The Telecommunications Reform Act of 1996 has opened this industry to competition, so it remains to be seen which companies will control the information superhighway.

Economic Analysis

This chapter evaluates the roles played by government in the U.S. economy by examining the following questions:

1. **How Does the Government Limit Monopoly Power?**

   Important Concepts: Antitrust legislation, Industrial consortiums, Public utility regulation, Natural monopoly, Deregulation

   Case Application: Air Warfare

2. **Why Does the Government Produce Goods and Services?**

   Important Concepts: Collective goods, External economies, Merit goods

   Case Application: The New War between the States

3. **What Is the Role of Government in Protecting the Environment?**

   Important Concepts: External costs, Environmental protection, Command-and-control regulations, Emission permits, Eco-taxes

   Case Application: A Common Problem

Perspective: The Interstate Highway to Serfdom

   Biography—Friedrich August von Hayek

II. Summary of Economic Analysis

1. Concern over the market power of the great American trusts (monopolies) in the late 1800s led Congress to enact **antitrust legislation** in an effort to prevent collusion and monopoly abuses.

2. The most important antitrust acts include the **Interstate Commerce Commission Act** (1887), the **Sherman Act** (1890), the **Clayton Act** (1914), and the **Celler-Kefauver Act** (1950).

3. In an effort to help American businesses compete in the global marketplace, Congress now *encourages* collusion through the formation of **industry consortiums**, groups of firms working together in some areas of R & D.

4. The **National Co-operative Research Act of 1984** provides antitrust exemptions in some instances where firms collude in their R & D efforts.

5. When **natural monopolies** exist, the market is best served by a single firm. Many public utilities (water, electric, telephone, and gas service) are natural monopolies.

6. When a public utility is a natural monopoly, the firm is allowed to operate as a monopoly, but it is subject to **public utility regulation**, and the regulating agency is often called a **public utility commission**.

7. Growing dissatisfaction with the results of regulation of firms that are not natural monopolies has led to a movement toward **deregulation** in these industries.

8. **Collective goods** are goods that are useful and beneficial but are not feasible to produce and sell in a market system. If they are to be produced, they must be produced by the government and consumed "collectively."

9. Goods and services that benefit not only the purchaser and the seller but also third parties are goods that generate **external economies**.

10. **Collective goods** are sometimes provided by the government in order to achieve the socioeconomic goal of greater **economic equity.**

11. Goods and services that impose costs not only on the seller of a good but also on third parties are goods that generate **external costs**.

12. **Pollution** is an example of an external cost imposed on the environment.

13. **Environmental protection** laws are enacted and enforced by the government to reduce the external costs associated with pollution.

14. The government protects the environment by forcing firms to **internalize their externalities**. This is done through **command-and-control regulation, emission allowances**, or **eco-taxes**.

III. Review of the Learning Objectives *(Answers begin on p. 269.)*

How Does the Government Limit Monopoly Power?

ANTITRUST LEGISLATION

Interstate Commerce Act (1887)
This act established the Interstate Commerce Commission (ICC) to regulate the railroads; it abolished rate discrimination.

Sherman Antitrust Act (1890)
This act became the nation's basic antitrust legislation. It prohibited monopoly and outlawed attempts to monopolize an industry.

Clayton Antitrust Act (1914)
It reinforced the Sherman Act by specifying specific illegal practices. It exempted unions.

Celler-Kefauver Antimerger Act (1950)
This act prohibited mergers that would lessen competition. It reduced horizontal mergers.

> **Industrial Consortiums**
> Recently antitrust policy has been modified to meet foreign competition by permitting firms in an industry to form consortiums for joint R & D projects.

PUBLIC UTILITY REGULATION

If an industry is a natural monopoly because it is more efficient for one firm to serve all of the customers in an area, the government regulates the firm through establishing a public utility commission.

> **Deregulation**
> In recent years there has been a move to deregulate industries in order to increase competition.

8.1 Explain the purposes of the Interstate Commerce Act and the Sherman, Clayton, and Celler-Kefauver Acts.

A. Indicate which antitrust act—the Interstate Commerce Act (ICA), the Sherman Act (SA), the Clayton Act (CA), or the Celler-Kefauver Act (CKA)—would apply in each of the following cases:

1. _____ A railroad charges high prices to one group in order to subsidize low rates to another.

2. _____ A planned merger between Ford and General Motors would substantially lessen competition in the automobile industry.

3. _____ AT&T attempts to buy a controlling interest of MCI stock.

4. _____ MegaBucks, Inc., is accused of driving the Mom & Pop Company out of business by using price discrimination.

5. _____ Acme Dirtworks, Inc., is accused of attempting to monopolize the market for potting soil.

B. Antitrust laws are designed to limit what three types of activity?

1. _____

2. _____

3. _____

C. Why are firms in purely competitive and differentiated competitive industries not likely to be accused of violating antitrust laws?_____

_____

8.2 Explain the purpose of industry R & D consortiums and why they are exempt from the antitrust laws.

A. Why does the government grant antitrust exemptions to groups of firms that collude in certain R & D activities?

_____

_____

B. What law permits R & D collusion?

_____

_____

C. Suppose that firms are *not* allowed to collude in their research and development efforts. Give an example of a disadvantage of such policy in the area of automobile safety research.

_____

_____

D. General Motors and Toyota worked together to build the Saturn automobile in Tennessee. What is one possible *disadvantage* of allowing such cooperation?

_____

_____

8.3 List the causes of natural monopoly and explain why natural monopolies often do not remain natural monopolies.

A. The primary cause of natural monopoly is the existence of

_____

B. If there are economies of scale in production, why would it be a bad idea for the government to use antitrust laws to break up a natural monopoly?

_____

_____

C. List at least three firms that you know that are natural monopolies.

1. _____

2. _____

3. _____

D. What are two problems that could explain why an industry with a natural monopoly might become competitive?

_____

_____

8.4 Explain why it is often necessary for public utility commissions to regulate natural monopolies.

A. What is an alternative to government regulation of natural monopolies? (Hint: This is what is done in most Western European countries.)

_____

B. Public utility commissions are called different things in different states. What is the name of the public utility commission in your state?

_____

C. Suppose that you are a public utility commissioner. What kind of real-world problems can you foresee in trying to determine a "fair" price for a giant utility company?

    1. _____

    2. _____

D.

    1. Assume that you do not like high electric bills. Have you written to a public utility commissioner to complain? _____

    2. Your electric company likes high electric prices. Do you think that they have written to a public utility commissioner? _____

    3. Who do you suppose has more influence with public utility commissions, customers or the firms that they regulate? _____

E. According to economists' definitions of profit, what would constitute a "fair" profit for a regulated utility?

_____

8.5 Explain the reasons for and the consequences of deregulation.

A. Deregulation of an industry will be beneficial to *consumers* only if the industry structure is

_____

B. Indicate which of the following have been *harmed* by the deregulation of the airline industry:

    1. _____ Labor unions

    2. _____ Passengers who live in big cities

    3. _____ Passengers who live in small towns

    4. _____ Established airlines

    5. _____ Passengers worried about safety

C. One method used to regulate the trucking industry was the establishment of barriers to entry for potential new firms. After deregulation, what do you think happened to prices and profits in the trucking industry?

Case Application: Water, Water, Everywhere, and Not a Drop (That's Fit) to Drink

The stories are rampant in cities from Massachusetts to California and all over the country between—in New Jersey, Ohio, Oklahoma, Minnesota, Arizona, and at least 15 other states—about drinking water that is not fit to drink.

In the Boston suburbs of Dedham and Westwood, the water flowing from kitchen faucets was so bad—reddish-brown in color, with a sickening smell and taste—that residents of the two towns held a referendum on taking over the private water company by condemning it under the power of eminent domain.

Water companies, whether privately owned utilities or municipal utilities, have been confronted with increasing problems of underground water supplies polluted by the seepage of toxic waste dumps, and surface water supplies poisoned by industrial chemical discharges and runoffs of agricultural pesticides and fertilizers. The public's concern over impure drinking water supplies has resulted in stricter regulation of water systems.

The answer for the citizens of Dedham and Westwood was to acquire the local water company for a price of $17–20 million and contract with the previous owner, American Water Works Company, to manage it. A new water treatment facility was scheduled for construction. The costs of the new plant would have to be included in the customers' water bills, and rates were expected to increase 20–25% a year for at least 2 years. But the 40,000 residents of Dedham and Westwood hoped to have clear water running from their faucets at last, water that they could launder their clothes in without ruining them, water that they could drink.

Economic Reasoning *(Write your responses on a separate sheet. Answers begin on p. 269.)*

1. In what way is the move toward stricter regulation of water utilities contrary to the trend in government policies?
2. How did the fact that there was only one company supplying water to Dedham and Westwood result in the problems that they had in obtaining satisfactory water?
3. Should government intervene to ensure the purity of water supplies, whatever the cost? Why or why not?

Why Does the Government Produce Goods and Services?

COLLECTIVE GOODS

Some goods and services that are considered essential to society but are not adequately provided by the private sector are supplied by the government as collective goods (public goods).

External Economies

One reason for providing collective goods is the existence of external economies that arise when there are benefits from a good or service that accrue to the public, which are in addition to the benefits to the consumer of the good or service. Something that raises the cultural level of society is a merit good.

Collective Goods and Equity

Another reason for the government to provide goods and services is to achieve the goal of greater equity in real income by providing essential services, such as transportation and housing, to those who cannot afford them.

8.6 Identify the kinds of goods and services that are collective goods and explain why the government often provides them.

A. Which of the following goods or services are collective goods (CG), and which could *feasibly* be sold for a price by the private sector (PS) in a market economy?

1. ____ A fireworks display
2. ____ 200 firecrackers
3. ____ A lighthouse
4. ____ A streetlight
5. ____ Elementary school education
6. ____ Entry to a park
7. ____ Use of an interstate highway
8. ____ Use of a local street

B. List three goods provided by your local government that *could* be provided by a private company.

1. _____

2. _____

3. _____

C. Suppose you decided to make some extra money by buying some really great fireworks and charging people to see the fireworks show. Even if everybody loved fireworks displays, why would you have a problem making any money?

_____

D. An entrepreneur can determine whether or not to produce a certain good by comparing its cost of production to the amount people will pay for it. What problem does a government agency have in determining whether or not to produce a collective good?

_____

8.7 Explain the concepts of external economies and external costs.

A. Indicate which of the following activities generate external economies (EE) and which generate external costs (EC):

1. _____ Your neighbor's yard is a mess.

2. _____ Your neighbor plays loud music all night.

3. _____ Parents have their new baby vaccinated against smallpox.

4. _____ Everybody in your town learns to read and write.

5. _____ You pay to have a telephone installed in your home.

6. _____ MegaSlime, Inc., dumps waste products into the air and water.

7. _____ A commuter pulls his or her car onto a busy highway at rush hour.

8. _____ A full, satisfied diner at a nice restaurant lights up an after-dinner cigar.

B.

1. Total (social) costs are equal to a firm's private costs plus external costs. The following graph shows the demand and supply for a product and the private optimal (Q_{po}) level of production *based on the firm's private costs alone*. Draw a new supply curve that represents *total* costs of production and label it $S_{social\ costs}$. Also indicate the socially optimal (Q_{so}) level of output.

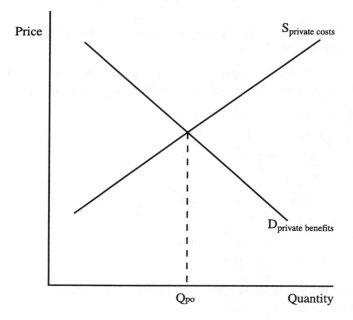

2. Is the socially optimal level of production higher or lower than the level that would be reached if the firm worried only about its private costs?

_____

C.

    1. Total (social) benefits are equal to private benefits plus external economies. The graph below shows the demand and supply for a product and the private optimal (Q_{po}) level of production *based on private benefits alone*. Draw a new demand curve that represents the *total* (social) benefits from the good and label it D_{social} benefits. Also indicate the socially optimal (Q_{so}) level of output.

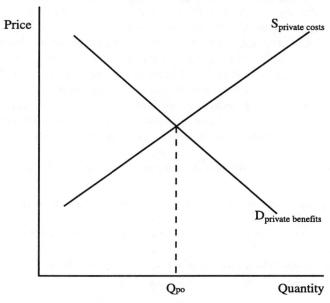

    2. Is the socially optimal level of output higher or lower than the level that would be reached if only private benefits were considered?

_____

D. Based on your answers to exercises B and C, what general statement can you make about the amount of goods and services provided by the market when external costs and external economies are present?

_____

_____

_____

E. What are two external economies associated with a mass transit system in an urban area?

    1. _____

    2. _____

Case Application: **Should the Government Be in the Railroad Business?**

Around the world, the railroads are run by the government—except in the United States, where railroads have traditionally been private enterprises. But two exceptions to the rule of private ownership of the railroads in this country emerged in the 1970s: Amtrak and Conrail.

    Amtrak was formed in 1970 as the National Railroad Passenger Corporation. It took over the faltering passenger rail services from the rail lines that no longer found them profitable due to competition from air and bus lines. In 1976 the Consolidated Rail

Corporation—Conrail for short—was put together as a government rescue operation from the wreckage of seven failed freight lines.

Conrail lost some $7 billion in its first 5 years of operation but then began to turn a profit. Amtrak continues to lose money, although less as time goes on and passenger traffic increases. One of the criticisms of the government's subsidizing Amtrak is that most of its passengers are middle- and upper-middle-income. A survey of riders in the Northeast, where more than half of Amtrak passenger traffic is, showed that the majority of riders had incomes over $30,000.

In 1987 Conrail, after becoming profitable under government operation, was transformed into a private corporation through the sale of shares. As part of its efforts to deregulate the economy, the Reagan administration also attempted to privatize Amtrak. That would have put an end to Amtrak's long-haul services, if not finish rail passenger service altogether. Congress successfully opposed getting rid of Amtrak because passenger rail service would virtually cease to exist in this country without government subsidy. In 1995, Amtrak reorganized itself by decentralizing management into three separate business units—Northeast, Intercity, and Western. The change was made in order to increase accountability and responsiveness, but cuts in service have been recommended because the company still suffers from financial problems. These cuts are controversial, and in order to postpone them, many states have increased payments to support Amtrak.

Economic Reasoning *(Write your responses on a separate sheet. Answers begin on p. 270.)*

1. Can the government subsidy of Amtrak be justified in terms of equity? Why or why not?
2. Are there external economies associated with passenger rail transportation? With freight rail transportation? If so, what are they?
3. Should the government dispose of Amtrak? Why or why not?

What Is the Role of Government in Protecting the Environment?

ENVIRONMENTAL PROTECTION

The principal government agency for protection of the environment is the Environmental Protection Agency (EPA).

External Costs

An economic justification for protecting the environment against pollution is the existence of external costs.

Efficiency of resources allocation is improved when producers internalize the external costs.

How Pollution is Controlled

Command-and-control regulation or direct regulation by the government has been used extensively in the past.

Emission permits allow the holder to emit a specified amount of pollution and can be sold in a market.

Eco-taxes are fees imposed per unit of pollution emitted.

Permits and fees are more efficient and provide incentives for firms to develop new pollution-control technology.

8.8 Explain why pollution exists.

A. Pollution occurs because our air and water are treated as _____ goods by producers.

B. Holidays Are Here, Inc. produces holiday wrapping paper, and the production process generates noxious fumes. What would be the cheapest way for Holidays Are Here, Inc. to handle these fumes?

_____

_____

C. Based on your answer in exercise B, who would pay the costs associated with the fumes?

_____

_____

D. What do you think should be done about the fumes generated by Holidays Are Here, Inc.?

_____

_____

8.9 Describe three alternative types of policies that the government can use to reduce pollution.

A. What are three ways that firms can be forced to internalize their external costs?

1. _____

2. _____

3. _____

B. Suppose that firm X and firm Y each produce 100 tons of hydrocarbons in their production processes. Firm X can reduce its emissions for $5 per ton, and firm Y can reduce its emissions for $10 per ton.

1. What will be the total amount of pollution eliminated and the total cleanup cost if both firms are required to reduce their pollution by half? _____ tons for $_____

2. What would be a less expensive way to remove the same amount of pollutants?

_____

_____

3. What would make Firm X willing to go along with the idea presented in question 2?

_____

_____

C.

1. If firms are not forced to internalize their external costs, who pays for the pollution they generate?

_____

2. If firms are forced to internalize their external costs, who pays for this internalization?

_____

D. Remember that higher costs usually lead to higher prices and a smaller quantity demanded. What are two *opportunity costs* of requiring electric utilities to internalize their externalities?

1. _____

2. _____

Case Application: **Declaration of Air Pollution Emergency**

In October 1948, a disaster occurred just 20 miles southeast of Pittsburgh, in Donora, Pennsylvania. Twenty people died. Nearly half of Donora's 14,000 residents became ill. What happened?

Air pollution struck. Some people became sick and others died because of poisonous smog. The huge black cloud was composed of sulphur dioxide, industrial gases, particles of iron oxide, zinc oxide, silicates, and carbon.

In November 1975, in a northeast suburb of Pittsburgh, 30 industrial plants in the Monongahela and Youghiogheny river valleys were forced to curtail operations. An air pollution emergency was declared by the Allegheny County commissioners. In 1974 the residents of Allegheny County had passed a stringent air-pollution law establishing a modern monitoring system. Under the law, the commissioners could take drastic measures. They could close schools and prohibit all commercial activities. As an alternative action, the commissioners decided to cut back the production level of steel output.

According to county public health officials, a pollution index of 15 to 35 is normal. When the index reaches 100, an alert is sent out. When the index reaches the 200 level, a health warning must be issued. One week in November the pollution index in the Allegheny County area was over 250.

The hospitals in the affected area were reporting increased numbers of pollution-related complaints, such as headaches, choking, and stinging eyes. People suffering from asthma, especially asthmatic children, were the most affected. Public health officials warned that the pollution from soot and sulphur dioxide could cause special problems for those with respiratory and heart ailments. The police department reported that the combination of fog and soot caused widespread traffic delays. The Pennsylvania Department of Environmental Resources, a statewide government agency for environmental protection, was also alerted in case the pollution started to spread due to changing weather conditions.

Right after the declaration of the pollution emergency, the U.S. Steel Corporation announced that because of the cutback in production in many of its plants, hundreds of workers would be laid off. The situation would be worse by December, when the production processes would be required to switch from coal to natural gas. To comply with pollution control requirements, the industry would need to install fabric filters for electric arcs, high-energy wet scrubbers for open-hearth and basic oxygen furnaces, and electrostatic precipitators for smokestacks.

Economic Reasoning *(Write your responses on a separate sheet. Answers begin on p. 270.)*

1. What external costs were associated with steel production in Allegheny County?
2. What would the U.S. Steel Corporation have to do to internalize the external costs of its steel production operations? What would happen to the price and quantity of steel production when external costs were internalized? Explain your answer by a graph of demand and supply.
3. Should U.S. Steel be forced to internalize its external costs even though that would result in increased unemployment in the Pittsburgh area? Why or why not?

IV. Practice Test *(Answers begin on p. 271.)*

Multiple-Choice Questions *(Circle the correct answer.)*

(8.1) 1. Which one of the following acts is designed to reduce the number of mergers that lessen competition?
    a. the Interstate Commerce Act
    b. the Sherman Act
    c. the Clayton Act
    d. the Celler-Kefauver Act

(8.1) 2. Abuses and monopolistic practices in which industry led Congress to pass the Interstate Commerce Act?
   a. trucking
   b. agriculture
   c. the production of military hardware
   d. railroad shipping

(8.2) 3. Industry consortiums engaged in R & D are often exempt from antitrust prosecutions as a result of which congressional act?
   a. the Interstate Commerce Act
   b. the Baker-Hatfield International Competition Act
   c. the National Co-operative Research Act
   d. the Industry Consortium Protection Act

(8.3) 4. Which one of the following is the closest to being a natural monopoly?
   a. the U.S. Postal Service
   b. your local cable television company
   c. long-distance telephone service
   d. public education

(8.3) 5. The primary economic cause of natural monopolies is
   a. diminishing returns.
   b. inelastic demand for a good or service.
   c. trade-offs between increased production and environmental damage.
   d. economies of scale.

(8.4) 6. Natural monopolies are usually limited in the prices they can charge by
   a. congressional acts.
   b. referendums conducted among all voters.
   c. public utility commissions.
   d. their own estimates of consumers' elasticity of demand.

(8.5) 7. Deregulation will work best when the deregulated industry
   a. is monopolistic.
   b. is a shared monopoly.
   c. is competitive.
   d. has high barriers to entry.

(8.5) 8. Certain industries such as airlines and trucking that were deregulated during the 1980s were originally regulated so as to
   a. prevent competition.
   b. keep consumer prices low.
   c. ensure consumer safety.
   d. reduce foreign competition in American markets.

(8.6) 9. Which one of the following is an example of a merit good?
   a. a public school
   b. a fireworks display
   c. a barbecue
   d. a bookstore

(8.6) 10. Which one of the following exists for private goods but does not exist in the case of collective goods?
   a. the ability to charge all those who use the good
   b. external costs
   c. a trade-off because of scarcity
   d. demand and supply

(8.7) 11. If external costs occur in the production of good X and firms are *not* required to internalize these costs, which of the following will result?
   a. There will be a shortage of good X.
   b. The demand for good X will become more elastic.
   c. Firms making good X will earn economic profits.
   d. There will be too much X produced and used.

(8.7) 12. A good that is provided by governments because it generates external economies is called a(n)
   a. collective good.
   b. external good.
   c. merit good.
   d. positive good.

(8.8) 13. If firms are forced to internalize their external costs, who will pay the resulting
higher price for the firms' products?
   a. everybody who bears the external costs
   b. the government
   c. the purchaser of the products
   d. nobody—when costs are internalized they no longer exist

(8.9) 14. Which one of the following policies to control pollution is the most common
in the United States?
   a. eco-taxes
   b. emission permits
   c. public utilities commissions
   d. command-and-control regulation

(8.9) 15. In many European countries charges are imposed on firms based on the
amount of environmental damage caused by the firm. Theses charges are often
referred to as
   a. eco-taxes.
   b. pollution prices.
   c. production charges.
   d. pollution-prevention fees.

True/False Questions *(Circle T or F.)*

(8.1) 16. The most important antimerger antitrust act is the Celler-Kefauver Act. T or
F

(8.3) 17. Elasticity of demand is the most important cause of natural monopolies. T
or F

(8.5) 18. Deregulation has been especially beneficial to labor unions. T or F

(8.6) 19. Without government intervention, the market would produce less than the
optimal amount of merit goods. T or F

(8.9) 20. Imposing an emission charge, or eco-tax, internalizes the external costs associated with pollution. T or F

Chapter 9

Government and Households

I. Chapter Outline

The U.S. government is involved not only in the business sector of our economy but in our daily lives as well. The amount of income that a household earns in the resource market depends on a number of things including human capital and ability to work. Because there are differences among households with respect to these characteristics, income is not distributed equally. The government intervenes and redistributes income through taxes and transfers in order to help households that might otherwise be impoverished. The government also protects consumers and workers.

Introductory Article: Cradle to Grave

Even though the United States is one of the most market-oriented economies in the world, the government is involved in many facets of the economy. These government activities are financed through taxpayers' dollars, and income tax rates in the United States are as high as 36%. However, in some of the welfare states of Western Europe, tax rates exceed 50%, and citizens are provided generous benefits from the cradle (birth) to the grave (death). There is a basic philosophical difference in these societies. In the United States, the prevailing belief is that people should be provided equal access to opportunities for advancement with the necessary result that some will be quite successful while others will not. In Western Europe, the prevailing belief is that everyone should be provided equal outcomes so that none are highly successful while others are unsuccessful.

Economic Analysis

This chapter examines the distribution of income in the United States and the role the government plays in redistributing it by examining the following questions:

1. **What Does the Government Do to Reduce Poverty?**

   Important Concepts: Poverty line, Personal income distribution, Dual labor market

   Case Application: Created Equal, But . . .

2. **What is the Answer to Poverty?**

   Important Concepts: Affirmative action program, Transfer payments, Temporary Assistance for Needy Families (TANF), Workfare, Earned income tax credit, Food stamps, Medicaid

   Case Application: The Rich Get Richer and the Poor Get Ketchup

3. **What Does the Government Do to Help Older Americans?**

   Important Concepts: Social Security, Social insurance, Social Security Trust Funds, Medicare, Payroll tax, Social Security reform, Defined benefits retirement plan, Defined contributions retirement plan

   Case Application: Taking Cookies From Strangers

4. **What Is the Role of Government in Protecting Consumers and Workers?**

   Important Concepts: Consumer protection, Worker protection

   Case Application: Depending on the Next Generation

Perspective: The New Deal

II. Summary of Economic Analysis

1. The official U.S. **poverty line** is determined by income level and varies with the size of the family and whether it is a farm or nonfarm household.

2. The **personal distribution of income** shows the relative size of household incomes.

3. One of the most important factors contributing to inequality in earnings is technology. A **dual labor market** has emerged that is increasingly divided between high-skilled and low-skilled workers and jobs.

4. Differences in household incomes can also be attributed to differences in the types of assets owned, differences in opportunities due to differences in gender, race, and ethnic group, and differences in abilities to work.

5. In the United States, the government tries to help families escape poverty by providing equal education and employment opportunities through **affirmative action programs.** The government also provides tax-financed **transfer payments** to the poor.

6. Transfer payments are expenditures for which no goods or services are exchanged. These include public assistance programs such as **Temporary Assistance for Needy Families (TANF)** and **Supplementary Security Income (SSI).** The government also grants poor families an **earned income tax credit** and provides specific types of goods to supplement cash income through such programs as **food stamps** and **Medicaid.**

7. Unlike public assistance, **Social Security** is a **social insurance** program designed to keep older Americans from falling into poverty.

8. The Social Security program is made up of four separate **trust funds.** One fund pays retirement benefits to those who are past retirement age or their survivors, and a second fund provides disability payments to those who are physically or psychologically unable to work. The other two funds make up the **Medicare** program and provide hospital and supplementary medical care for older people.

9. The Social Security program is a transfer program that is financed through a **payroll tax** levied on current workers' wages and salaries.

10. Because of demographic changes in the population as the "baby boom" generation retires and people live longer, the Social Security and Medicare programs are facing future financial difficulties. Surpluses earned today are being used to balance the federal budget.

11. Proposals to reform the Social Security program include continuing the program as a **defined benefits retirement plan,** extending the retirement age and increasing the payroll tax rate, and changing the program to a **defined contributions retirement plan,** where individuals are required to contribute to personal security accounts that are similar to **individual retirement accounts (IRAs).**

12. Because consumer products have become increasingly complex and difficult for consumers to evaluate, the government promotes **consumer protection** by testing, regulating, and controlling the products that businesses sell.

13. Because of the dangers involved in some types of work, the government promotes **worker protection** by setting and enforcing standards for worker safety.

III. Review of the Learning Objectives *(Answers begin on p. 271.)*

What Does the Government Do to Reduce Poverty?

> **PERSONAL DISTRIBUTION OF INCOME**
>
> The personal distribution of income shows the relative size of household incomes and is unequal in the United States.
>
> > **The poverty line** is the official designation of who is considered poor in the United States and varies depending on the number of people in a household and whether or not they live on a farm.
>
> > Differences in households' income levels can be attributed to differences in:
> > - human capital
> > - assets owned
> > - opportunities or motivations based on differences in gender, race, or ethnic group
> > - abilities to work and earn income

9.1 Explain how poverty is defined.

A. The poverty line (the official definition of poverty) is defined in terms of _____. It varies depending on _____ and _____.

B. The poverty line is calculated based on a family's food budget. The government estimates how much it would cost to feed a family of a certain size for a year and multiplies this food budget by 3 to determine the poverty line because it is estimated that low-income families spend about 1/3 of their incomes on food.

   1. Suppose that it costs $5,000 a year to feed a nonfarm family of four people. If food costs constitute 1/3 of a household's budget, what is the "poverty line"?

   _____

   2. What would the poverty line be if food costs constituted 1/5 of a household's budget?

   _____

   3. Would the number of people under the poverty line be greater if the share was 1/3 or 1/5?

   _____

9.2 Understand how income is distributed in the United States and why it is unequal.

A.

   1. In 1996, the lowest quintile in the personal distribution of income (representing 20% of the population) earned what percentage of total income? _____

   2. In 1996, the highest quintile in the personal distribution of income (representing 20% of the population) earned what percentage of total income? _____

B. Since 1975, the distribution of income in the United States has become _____ (more or less) equal.

C. Four things that contribute to an unequal distribution of income are differences in

   1. _____

2. _____

3. _____

4. _____

D. Use the numbers of your above answers to indicate which one is reflected in each of the following situations:

1. ____ Taylor is eight years old and lives in poverty.

2. ____ Ms. Jones earns less than Mr. Smith although their jobs and productivity are the same.

3. ____ Ms. Schwartz is a skilled computer programmer.

4. ____ Shaquille O'Neal earns millions of dollars a year playing basketball for the Los Angeles Lakers.

5. ____ Mr. Johnson hurt his back and is no longer able to hold a job.

6. ____ Katrina earned $19,000 in capital gains last year.

9.3 Explain how rapid advances in technology can lead to a dual labor market.

A. There are an increasing number of job openings in the _____ industry that require highly skilled workers.

B. The emerging dual labor market is increasingly divided between _____ and _____ workers.

C. Describe two ways a worker can increase his or her human capital.

1. _____

2. _____

9.4 Understand how income is distributed among people of different genders and different ethnic groups.

A. Based on the descriptions below, rank the individuals in order from 1 to 6 of median income earned during 1997, where 1 means this individual earned the most, on average, and 6 means this individual earned the least, on average.

1. ____ Female Hispanic

2. ____ Male black

3. ____ Female white

4. ____ Female black

5. ____ Male Hispanic

6. ____ Male white

B. What has the government done to remove obstacles to economic opportunities caused by racial, religious, gender, age, or disability discrimination?

_____ _____

_____

Case Application: The New Poor

This country is witnessing the emergence of a new class of poor people. These are families in which the head of the household previously held a well-paying job—as a manufacturing, construction, or service industry worker—and lost the job because of recession, downsizing, or obsolescence.

When their unemployment compensation expires and their savings are depleted, many of these people can no longer meet their mortgage or rent payments and have to move out of their homes. Many take to the road, traveling from state to state in search of work. Some families resort to living in tents in national, state, or county parks because it is all they can afford. In many cases, even when they find work, it is only temporary, and they are soon laid off and back on the road again. They are ineligible for welfare, unemployment insurance, and food stamps because they have no permanent address. Also, they are ineligible to vote.

Those who remain in the cities looking for jobs sometimes show up in the soup kitchens of charitable organizations. Previously, those partaking of the free meals had been, for the most part, society's outcasts, the down-and-out denizens of the cities' skid rows. But recently the free food lines have come to include families who previously had been self-sufficient.

Even when economic conditions are stable, there is a constant flow of people in and out of poverty. Studies by James Morgan at the University of Michigan show that only a small minority of those living in poverty remain poor permanently. The majority move in and out of poverty status depending upon changing personal circumstances. According to Professor Morgan, those who do continue to live in poverty are individuals who are uneducated, disabled, or very old. These people constituted the hard core of the "old poor." Now they have been joined by the "new poor."

Economic Reasoning *(Write your responses on a separate sheet. Answers begin on p. 271.)*

1. What are the differences in the causes of poverty between the "old poor" and the "new poor"?
2. Which group is likely to move out of poverty first when economic conditions improve, the "old poor" or the "new poor"? Why?
3. Should private welfare agencies divert part of their resources away from aiding the "old poor" in order to provide assistance to the "new poor"? Why or why not?

What Is the Answer to Poverty?

INCREASED OPPORTUNITY

One way to achieve more equitable income distribution is to remove obstacles to economic opportunity caused by racial, sexual, or age discrimination. Affirmative action programs are aimed at increasing educational, training, and employment opportunities for minorities and women.

Workfare

Originally a program that required nonexempt welfare recipients to work at public service jobs for a given number of hours a month; now it may also include job training and wage subsidies.

TRANSFER PAYMENTS

- Money transfers—public assistance
- Temporary Assistance for Needy Families— an entitlement program for families below the poverty line
- Supplementary Security Income— an entitlement program for those who cannot work because they are aged, blind, or disabled
- Food stamps—food subsidies for low-income households
- Medicaid—federally financed health care for low-income families
- Housing—housing subsidies and public housing

Earned Income Tax Credit (EITC)

A type of negative income tax for the working poor. Provides increasing tax credits the lower earnings are, with credits for the lowest income earners that exceed their tax liabilities.

9.5 Describe different public assistance programs used to help the needy.

A. Match each of the following public assistance programs with its description below.

    1. ____ Temporary Assistance for Needy Families

    2. ____ Workfare

    3. ____ Supplemental Security Income

    4. ____ Earned Income Tax Credit

    5. ____ Food stamps

    6. ____ Medicaid

a. certificates that can be used in place of money to purchase food items

b. government benefits for those who cannot work because they are aged, blind, or disabled in some other way

c. federal tax credit for poor families with earnings, which offsets their liabilities

d. federally subsidized public assistance program that provides income to needy families for a limited period of eligibility

e. federally subsidized, state-administered program to pay for medical and hospital costs of low-income families

f. program that requires nonexempt welfare recipients to work at public service jobs for a given number of hours a month and may include job training and wage subsidies

B. From the list of public assistance programs given in exercise A, use the numbers to indicate which ones best apply for each individual described below. (Note: There may be more than one answer for each.)

    1. ____ Charlotte is a single mother with two young children, and she cannot afford child care while she works.

    2. ____ Kenneth is a single male who is out of work because the company he worked for went out of business. He needs to learn new skills in order to find a new job.

    3. ____ Jack has a wife and a young son. He also has a low-wage, part-time job without benefits such as health insurance, and he thinks he may have pneumonia.

    4. ____ Teresa is 25 and was born with mental and physical disabilities that prevent her from holding a job.

C.

1. What types of programs provide the best long-run solutions to reducing poverty?

_____

2. What types of programs provide the best short-run solutions to reducing poverty?

_____

Case Application: Increased Opportunities for People with Disabilities

Since 1973 federal law has forbidden employers who are receiving funds or contracts from the federal government to deny jobs to people with disabilities. Most states now have laws prohibiting discrimination against those with disabilities by companies not covered under the federal law. These laws have opened job opportunities to people with disabilities—one of the minorities most discriminated against in the past. As a result, overt discrimination by employers has been substantially reduced, and disabled people who had been excluded from the labor force and forced to live in poverty are now leading productive lives.

However, discrimination still persists, especially toward people with "hidden" disabilities. This includes those with epilepsy, cancer, AIDS, and other hidden health problems. Even though their problems may be under control or in remission, when their health histories are revealed to employers or prospective employers they are not given the same consideration for jobs as other applicants. Employers view them as potential problems either on the job or in costs to the firm's medical coverage program.

Employers who do hire people with disabilities often find that such workers are not only productive but also stick with the job longer than other workers. Affirmative action programs to hire people with disabilities have usually proved rewarding to the firm as well as to the disabled workers themselves. Society also benefits from a reduction in the ranks of the poor and the consequent decrease in transfer payments and other costs.

Economic Reasoning *(Write your responses on a separate sheet. Answers begin on p. 271.)*

1. How has the number of people with disabilities who are poor been reduced since 1973?
2. Why are affirmative action programs to employ people with disabilities needed?
3. Should the government subsidize firms to hire people with disabilities? Why or why not?

What Does the Government Do to Help Older Americans?

SOCIAL SECURITY

The Old Age, Survivors, Disability and Health Insurance (OASDHI) program was established in 1935 to provide retirement and health benefits to the elderly, and public assistance to the aged, blind, and disabled.

- Social insurance for the elderly, not public assistance
- Medicare—A health and medical care program for older Americans funded through the Social Security Trust Funds.
- Payroll tax—Social Security is funded by taxes levied on wages and salaries of current workers. You "pay as you go" through the system.

Social Security Reform

Because of demographic changes in the population as the "baby boomer" generation retires and people live longer, the Social Security and Medicare programs are facing future financial difficulties. Proposed reforms fall into broad categories.

- Defined benefits retirement plan—a pension plan that guarantees participants a specified level of income when they retire, regardless of how much they contributed to the plan
- Defined contributions retirement plan— a requirement plan that requires participants to contribute a specific amount of income, with retirement benefits to be determined by the amount contributed plus earnings on the contributions

9.6 Explain the basic difference between public assistance and social insurance and the difference between public assistance and Social Security.

A. Programs designed to help people who are *in poverty* are _____ while programs designed to keep people *from falling into poverty* are _____.

B. Describe two ways in which Social Security differs from public assistance.

1. _____

2. _____

9.7 Understand the difference between Medicaid and Medicare.

A. Medical care for low-income people is _____, and medical care for older Americans is _____.

B.

1. Theodore is a 70-year-old American citizen. In 1978, he lost his job and did not work for a couple of years. During that time, his medical care was provided by the government. What government program most likely provided his health and medical care? _____

2. Today, Theodore is retired, and he is again receiving medical care through a government program. What government program is most likely providing his health and medical care today? _____

3. Why are the answers to questions 1 and 2 different?

_____

_____

9.8 Explain why the Social Security program is facing financial difficulties.

A. Explain how society's changing demographics will cause financial difficulties for the Social Security program unless the program is reformed.

_____

_____

B. How have advancements in technology and improvements in health care contributed to possible financial difficulties for the Social Security program?

_____

_____

C. How can the Social Security program be facing financial difficulties if the program is generating a surplus of funds today?

_____

_____

9.9 Explain how Social Security differs from private pension plans.

A.

1. Jasmine has a job where she is allowed to allocate a portion of her paycheck each month into a private pension plan. She can choose among a variety of funds in which her money will be invested. For each dollar that she saves, her company contributes $.50 to her account. What happens to this money?

_____

_____

2. Jasmine also contributes a percentage of her earnings each month to the Social Security program through a payroll tax. What happens to this money?

_____

_____

3. When Jasmine retires, she will receive two checks each month—one from the private pension plan and one from the Social Security program. Where does the money come from for each of these checks?

_____

B. What is the basic difference between the Social Security program and a private pension plan?

_____

_____

9.10 Understand how Social Security benefits are financed.

A. The Social Security program is financed through a _____ tax that is levied on the wages and salaries of _____.

B. Are contributions to the Social Security program voluntary? Explain.

_____

C. Roberto recently got his first job and is earning minimum wage. When he got his first paycheck, he was surprised to see that he "contributed" a significant portion of it to the Social Security program. Roberto's grandfather currently receives a Social Security check every month. How is the money taken by the government from Roberto's paycheck related to the money Roberto's grandfather receives from the government?

_____

_____

9.11 Understand the significance of the proposed changes to the Social Security system.

A. List two reforms to today's Social Security program that would not require significant changes in the structure of the program but would help it last longer.

1. _____

2. _____

B. A retirement plan that guarantees participants a specified level of income when they retire, regardless of how much they contributed to the plan, is called a _____. A retirement plan that requires participants to contribute a specific amount of income, with retirement benefits to be determined by the amount contributed plus earnings on the contributions is called a _____.

C. One proposal for reforming the Social Security program is to require individuals to invest in "personal security accounts." How is a personal security account similar to an individual retirement account?

_____

_____

D. What do you think should be done to reform the Social Security program? Explain.

_____

_____

Case Application: A Three-Legged Stool?

When the government passed the Social Security Act on August 14, 1935, to create the Social Security program, the plan was to provide health and retirement benefits to older Americans and to provide adequately for the aged, blind, and disabled. The program was not intended to provide a primary source of retirement income. Instead, Social Security was to be "one leg" of a "three-legged stool" that would support older Americans in retirement. It was intended to supplement private pensions and savings.

However, as shown in the table below, most older Americans today report that Social Security is their major source of income. In a 1998 Profile of Older Americans, the Administration on Aging reported that 91.9% of older Americans stated that Social

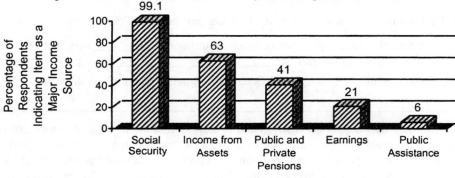

Major Sources of Income as Reported by Older Americans

Security was a major source of income, while fewer than two-thirds identified income from assets as a major source, and fewer than one-half identified income from public and private pensions as a major source.

It is evident that older Americans have come to depend on Social Security benefits as a source of retirement income. However, even taking into account Social Security benefits, the Administration on Aging reports that 17% of older Americans were below or near (within 125% of) the poverty line in 1997. Some estimates suggest that without Social Security, 60% of our elderly would be living in poverty.

Economic Reasoning *(Write your responses on a separate sheet. Answers begin on p. 272.)*

1. What are the "three legs" that are supposed to support retired Americans in today's society?
2. How have attitudes and behavior about retirement funds changed since the inception of the Social Security program?
3. Do we need a government-run program for retirement benefits?

What Is the Role of Government in Protecting Consumers and Workers?

CONSUMER PROTECTION	WORKER PROTECTION
Government agencies involved in the protection of the consumer include the following: • Department of Transportation (DOT) • Food and Drug Administration (FDA) • Consumer Product Safety Commission (CPSC) • Federal Trade Commission (FTC)	The principal legislation for government protection of workers is the Occupational Safety and Health Act. Its provisions are enforced by the Occupational Safety and Health Administration (OSHA).

9.12 Understand how the government protects workers and consumers.

A. Consider the following government agencies:

DOT (Department of Transportation)
FDA (Food and Drug Administration)
CPSC (Consumer Product Safety Commission)
FTC (Federal Trade Commission)
OSHA (Occupational Safety and Health Administration)
SEC (Securities and Exchange Commission)

Indicate which one protects consumers or workers in each of the following situations:

1. _____ You were swindled out of your life savings after investing in a bogus stock.

2. _____ Your automobile blew up when a neighbor's child bounced a baseball off the gas tank.

3. _____ Your G.I. Joe doll came with a live grenade that blew off your big toe.

4. _____ The product that you handled at work causes cancer.

5. _____ A new cold remedy had side effects that caused your hair to fall out.

6. _____ A deceptive advertisement caused you to pay $100 for a worthless product.

B. Why do we need the government to protect us in so many ways? Why can't we figure out for ourselves which products are safe and which products are not safe?

_____

_____

C. Which industry is the most dangerous in the United States in terms of the number of injuries incurred on the job?

_____

Case Application: **Are Herbal Remedies Safe?**

Millions of Americans use herbal remedies every year for ailments such as headaches and digestive problems as well as to have more energy or "feel better." One herb that has been receiving much attention lately and is used by increasing numbers of consumers is St. John's wort.

The news media, several new books, and testimonials on the Internet have touted the effectiveness of the herb in curing mild depression. As for side effects, users have reported occasional constipation, dizziness, and sleeplessness. However, doctors and pharmacists argue that the herb's health benefits have not been proven, and there have been no systematic, long-term studies of the effects of taking St. John's wort.

In response to the demand for information about the effectiveness of the herb, the federal government, through the National Institutes of Health, has launched a three-year study. However, millions of Americans are not waiting for the results. In fact, consumers' eagerness to take the herbal supplement has caused a shortage in this market.

Some doctors argue that, even if the NIH study proves that the herb can relieve mild depression, consumers should still be cautious when taking herbal supplements. There is currently no regulatory oversight for dietary supplements, and side effects are not listed on the labels. Therefore, consumers ingest them at their own risk.

Economic Reasoning *(Write your responses on a separate sheet. Answers begin on p. 272.)*

1. What agency would be involved if the safety and effectiveness of dietary supplements were regulated?

2. Why would consumers purchase herbal supplements such as St. John's wort without approval from a government agency?

3. Would it be a good use of society's scarce resources for the government to study the safety and effectiveness of dietary supplements? Why or why not?

IV. Practice Test (Answers begin on p. 273.)

Multiple-Choice Questions *(Circle the correct answer.)*

(9.1) 1. The poverty line is defined in terms of
   a. race.
   b. income.
   c. occupation.
   d. productivity.

(9.1) 2. In 1996, the U.S. poverty line for a nonfarm family was an income of approximately
   a. $5,000.
   b. $12,000.
   c. $16,000.
   d. $25,000.

(9.2) 3. Given the two income distributions shown below for a hypothetical country in the years 1990 and 1995, which one of the following statements is *true*?

| | 1990 | | 1995 | |
Income Group	Average Income ($)	Share of Total Income(%)	Average Income ($)	Share of Total Income (%)
Lowest quintile	$7,708	4.1	$8,547	3.3
Second quintile	20,496	10.7	20,626	10.3
Third quintile	33,006	17.4	33,948	16.8
Fourth quintile	46,527	24.5	49,985	24.9
Highest quintile	82,378	43.3	87,797	44.7

   a. The distribution of income was less equal in 1990 than in 1995.
   b. The distribution of income was more equal in 1990 than in 1995.
   c. The rich (top quintile) did not get richer in 1995 as compared to 1990.
   d. The middle class (third quintile) increased its share of income in 1995 as compared to 1990.

(9.3) 4. According to the *1997 Economic Report of the President,* which one of the following is the most important factor contributing to inequality in earnings?
   a. gender
   b. technology
   c. productivity
   d. asset ownership

(9.4) 5. Which one of the following groups earned the highest median income in 1997?
   a. black males
   b. black females
   c. white females
   d. Hispanic males

(9.5) 6. Which one of the following public assistance programs requires working at a public service job?
   a. Workfare
   b. Food stamps
   c. Supplemental Security Income
   d. Temporary Assistance for Needy Families

(9.5) 7. Which one of the following public assistance programs is specifically designed to help disabled people?
   a. Workfare
   b. Food stamps
   c. Supplemental Security Income
   d. Temporary Assistance for Needy Families

(9.6) 8. Which one of the following is a form of social insurance?
   a. Workfare
   b. Food stamps
   c. Social Security
   d. Temporary Assistance for Needy Families

(9.7) 9. A retired grandmother receives government-provided medical care through which one of the following programs?
   a. Medicaid
   b. Medicare
   c. Supplemental Security Income
   d. Temporary Assistance for Needy Families

(9.8) 10. Which one of the following is a cause of financial difficulties facing the Social Security program in the future?
   a. The program is generating surpluses today.
   b. Poverty among older Americans is decreasing.
   c. Baby boomers will be retiring in the coming years.
   d. The percentage of elderly in our population is declining.

(9.10) 11. Which one of the following is financed through the FICA payroll tax paid by current workers?
   a. Workfare
   b. Food stamps
   c. Social Security
   d. Temporary Assistance for Needy Families

(9.11) 12. Social Security reform is necessary because
   a. the program is currently losing money.
   b. without it, the program will become bankrupt.
   c. Congress has mismanaged the funds in the program.
   d. the money in the program has been accumulating in trust funds for a number of years.

(9.11) 13. Which one of the following reforms involves privatizing the Social Security program?
   a. extending the retirement age
   b. increasing the payroll tax percentage
   c. increasing taxes on Social Security benefits checks
   d. establishing personal security accounts for individual workers

(9.12) 14. Which one of the following government agencies protects workers on the job?
   a. FTC
   b. FDA
   c. CPSC
   d. OSHA

(9.12) 15. Which one of the following government agencies issued a recall of asbestos-insulated hair dryers in order to protect consumers?
   a. FTC
   b. FDA
   c. CPSC
   d. OSHA

True/False Questions (Circle T or F.)

(9.2) 16. The distribution of income in the United States has become more unequal during the past 20 years. T or F

(9.4) 17. Children are the poorest segment of American society today. T or F

(9.6) 18. Social Security is a form of public assistance. T or F

(9.7) 19. Medicaid is a program designed to provide medical care to the elderly. T or F

(9.12) 20. Economists agree that government regulation to protect consumers is cost-effective. T or F

Microeconomics Crossword Puzzle (Chapters 5–9)

Across

5. Earnings from asset ownership
6. Consumer____, influenced by advertising, determines what is produced.
7. The smallest share of income receipts in the United States
12. Purchasing goods because they are expensively chic is called the _____ effect.
14. The use of computer-controlled equipment to enhance production
15. Government agency that regulates conditions in workplaces
16. Government agency that regulates food, drug, and cosmetics industries
18. A movement to turn those natural monopolies that are not obviously "natural" over to the private sector
20. A(n)_____ is opposed to employee-involvement programs.

Down

1. OPEC is an example.
2. In coming years, the shortage of this in Japan will likely cause their industries to become more capital intensive.
3. These production costs do not change with the change in the quantity of goods or services.
4. They enable two or more people to pool their capital and/or talents to make a business successful.
8. These types of goods enrich our entire culture, not just individuals.
9. Enables consumers to obtain a greater utility from their income
10. If demand for an item is this, the quantity demanded will decrease a great deal with a small increase in its price.
11. To protect the consumer, this government organization requires proper seat belts and secure gas tanks on automobiles.
13. Law that states that employers cannot "interfere with, restrain, or coerce employees"
17. Just-in-____ manufacturing provides for raw materials to be delivered by suppliers when needed.

Chapter 10
Money

I. Chapter Outline

Although all of us are interested in money, most of us do not understand just exactly what money is, what it does, or where it comes from. Money is a very curious commodity. Coins, bills, and checks have little value in and of themselves. What can you do with a rectangular piece of paper or a small metal disk? The only value money has is that people are willing to accept it in exchange for the things that they really want—goods and services.

Introductory Article: That Curious Commodity

As long as you can transport it, people will accept it, and other people cannot easily reproduce (forge) it, anything can function as "money." Although everything from cows to tobacco has been used as money, most countries today use paper money. The use of paper money was introduced in the 1700s. Prior to 1913, private banks in the United States were allowed to issue their own paper money. With the formation of the Federal Reserve System in that year, the United States for the first time had a standardized type of paper money. Today, we are moving toward increased use of electronic payments instead of cash or checks.

Economic Analysis

This chapter explores what money is and where it comes from by examining the following questions:

1. **What Is Money?**

   Important Concepts: Currency, Demand deposits, Near money, Money supply, M1, M2, M3, L

   Case Application: Dealing the Cards

2. **What Does Money Do?**

   Important Concepts: Medium of exchange, Unit of measurement, Store of value

   Case Application: POW Money

3. **How Is Money Created?**

   Important Concepts: Promissory notes, Treasury bills and bonds

   Case Application: How to Create Money

4. **How Is the Supply of Money Controlled?**

   Important Concepts: The Federal Reserve System, Required reserves, Excess reserves, Discounting, Money multiplier, Open market operations

   Case Application: Cheap Money

Perspective: The Big Bank Controversy

II. Summary of Economic Analysis

1. In the United States, money consists primarily of **currency** in circulation (about 37%), **demand deposits** in commercial banks, and other checkable deposits.

2. Currency is produced by the federal government and is distributed through the economy by the banking system to satisfy the needs of businesses and households.

3. Demand deposits are checking accounts in banks and other financial institutions. Changes in the money supply result primarily from changes in the amount of demand deposits.

4. The usual measure of the money supply is **M1**, the total of coins and currency in circulation, demand deposits, and traveler's checks.

5. **Near money** consists of financial assets that are less **liquid** than money. These include **savings deposits, certificates of deposit**, and **shares in money market funds.**

6. In addition to M1, other measures of the money supply, such as **M2, M3,** and **L,** can be defined by adding different kinds of near monies to M1.

7. Money serves three basic functions: it serves as a **medium of exchange**, a **unit of measurement**, and a **store of value**.

8. Money is created and the money supply increases when individuals, businesses, and governments borrow money. The money supply decreases (or fails to increase) when loans are repaid and/or no new loans are being made.

9. The money supply in the United States is controlled by a central bank, called the **Federal Reserve System**, or simply the **Fed.** The Fed controls the money supply by controlling the excess reserves available to banks. As excess reserves increase, the money supply increases; as they decrease, the money supply decreases.

10. The tools that the Fed uses to control the money supply include changing the level of required reserves, changing the **discount rate**, and **open market operations.**

11. Banks must hold a required percentage of their deposits as **required reserves.** Any deposits in excess of the required reserves are **excess reserves**. Excess reserves represent the amount of funds that banks have to lend.

12. When the ratio of required reserves to total deposits increases, banks will have less excess reserves to loan and the money supply will be unable to increase. When the ratio decreases, banks will have more money to loan and the money supply will increase.

13. The discount rate is the interest rate that regular banks are charged when they borrow money from the Fed. Lower rates result in more money being borrowed by banks and re-lent to businesses and individuals. This increases the money supply.

14. Open market operations refer to the Fed's buying and selling existing government bonds from banks and individuals. When the Fed buys bonds it takes bonds out of the economy and replaces them with new reserves that can be loaned. When the Fed sells bonds, it takes potentially loanable funds out of the economy and replaces them with nonloanable bonds.

III. Review of the Learning Objectives *(Answers begin on p. 273.)*

What Is Money?

MONEY

Currency	**Demand Deposits**
Currency is that part of the money supply that consists of coins and bills. Currency constitutes almost 40% of the money supply. The amount of currency in circulation depends on the demands by individuals and businesses for holding their financial assets in the form of currency.	Demand deposits are liabilities of depository institutions that are payable on demand, such as checking accounts. Deposits payable on demand constitute more than 60% of the money supply.

M1

The most commonly used measurement of the money supply includes currency, traveler's checks, demand deposits, and other checkable deposits such as negotiable order of withdrawal (NOW) accounts.

NEAR MONEY

Near money is a type of financial asset that can, more or less easily, be turned into money. This includes savings deposits, certificates of deposits (CDs), and shares in money market mutual funds.

10.1 Explain the history of money.

A. Other than coins or currency, what are three things that have served as money in different societies?

1. _____

2. _____

3. _____

B. Paper money was first introduced in the _____ century by _____ [what profession]?

C. During the 1800s in the United States, what institutions were allowed to issue paper money?

_____

D. In 1913, what U.S. institution was granted the sole right to issue paper money?

_____

10.2 Define the M1 money supply and describe its components.

A. List the components of the M1 money supply.

1. _____

2. _____

3. _____

4. _____

B. The largest component of the M1 money supply is

_____

C. Why do U.S. dollar bills have value?

_____

10.3 Explain how near money differs from money.

A. Assets that can be converted to money more easily than other assets are more

_____

B. Rank the following from most liquid (1) to least liquid (5).

1. __5__ A house
2. __2__ A savings account
3. _____ An automobile
4. __1__ A checking account
5. __3__ 100 shares of AT&T

C. What are three financial assets included in "L" but not in M1?

1. _____
2. _____
3. _____

D. Indicate which measure(s) of the money supply (M1, M2, M3, L) include(s) each of the following.

1. ____ ____ ____ ____ Traveler's checks
2. ____ ____ ____ ____ Your passbook savings account
3. ____ ____ ____ ____ A checking account
4. ____ ____ ____ ____ Short-term government bonds
5. ____ ____ ____ ____ Large certificates of deposit (CDs)
6. ____ ____ ____ ____ Coins and currency
7. ____ ____ ____ ____ Money market funds

Case Application: What Isn't Money?

It is getting more difficult all the time to tell what money is—although this may not seem to be a problem to you. If you have $500, you can keep it in currency under your mattress, deposit it in a NOW account in a savings and loan association, or put it in a money market fund. It's all money to you. But it's not all money to the nation's monetary authorities. Currency and checkable accounts in depository institutions are considered money, but not money market funds.

The first money market fund was started in 1972. By 1992 the value of money market funds had grown to $548 billion. Most of the money was taken out of banks, especially savings and loan associations. Checks can be written on the money market funds, although there is usually a minimum amount per check. One drawback to the money market funds is that, unlike deposits in banks and S & Ls, the customer's money is not insured by the federal government. However, the assets of money market funds are invested in government and other blue-chip securities with short maturity periods of one month or up to one year. The risk can be minimized by investing in a money market fund holding only federal government securities.

Because people treat their money market fund accounts as disposable money, it can be arbitrary and misleading not to include those funds as part of the money supply.

The money supply situation became even more cloudy when the Depository Institutions Act of 1982 permitted banks to establish money market funds of their own. Under one type of plan, a specified amount of a customer's deposits is kept in a checking account which pays a relatively low interest rate. Amounts deposited over and above that minimum are automatically "swept" into a money market account paying the market interest rate. This type of account has blurred significantly the line between what is part of the money supply and what is near money.

It is not only increasingly difficult to tell what money is, it is even hard to tell what a bank is. Other financial institutions such as brokerage firms and insurance companies are taking on banking functions. For their part, the banks are moving into new areas of business. Financial institutions once limited to specified activities are now expanding into "supermarkets" of financial services. Deregulation of the industry is creating new opportunities and types of competition, but this change is accompanied by flux and uncertainty in the management of the nation's money supply.

Economic Reasoning *(Write your responses on a separate sheet. Answers begin on p. 273.)*

1. The expansion of money market funds represented an increase in what type of money?
2. Why are money market funds more like money than are certificates of deposit?
3. Is the deregulation of financial institutions a good idea? Why or why not?

What Does Money Do?

MEDIUM OF EXCHANGE	UNIT OF MEASUREMENT	STORE OF VALUE
Money plays the role of an intermediary in the exchange of goods and services, in place of direct barter, because it simplifies making transactions.	The money unit serves as a common denominator in which the value of other things can be measured.	Money serves as a liquid form in which wealth can be held.

MEDIUM OF EXCHANGE — Attributes of a good medium of exchange:
- Universally recognized
- Adequate but limited supply
- Not easily reproduced
- Easily portable
- Durable

UNIT OF MEASUREMENT — Attribute of a good unit of measurement:
- Should itself be stable in value

STORE OF VALUE — Attribute of a good store of value:
- Should be liquid—readily convertible without loss of value

10.4 List the three functions of money.

A. List the three functions of money.

1. _____
2. _____
3. _____

B. Using the numbering in the above list, indicate which function is being described in each of the following situations:

1. ____ You hide your money under your mattress.

2. ____ You estimate how much you should charge to do a job based on what you can buy with your earnings.

3. ____ You pay $1.95 for a burger.

4. ____ You pay tuition.

5. ____ World oil prices are quoted in dollars.

6. ____ Prices influence how much a producer will produce.

10.5 Explain the characteristics that money must have in order to be functional.

A. List the five characteristics that money must have in order to be a good medium of exchange.

1. _____
2. _____
3. _____

4. _____

5. _____

B. Using the numbering from the above list, indicate which characteristic would be missing if each of the following were to be used as money (there may be more than one):

1. _____ Flawless diamonds

2. _____ Dead fish

3. _____ Cows

4. _____ Pebbles

5. _____ Notebook paper

6. _____ Your IOUs

C. Why are credit cards not considered "money"? What necessary characteristic(s) do they lack?

_____

D. What attribute makes a good unit of measurement?

_____

Case Application: Primitive Money

Debate over the nature of primitive money has recently surfaced in anthropological circles. Are the foodstuffs, cattle, brass rods, bits of porcelain, and cowrie shells used in various primitive cultures really money? The Tiv in Nigeria, for example, have three separate classes of transactions. Foodstuffs are used to exchange within one class; cattle and brass rods are used in the second. Before slaves were freed, their price was quoted in cows and brass rods. The third class is limited to marriage arrangements and involves the "payment" of cattle. Services and labor, on the other hand, are acts of generosity, and to offer payments for them would be insulting.

Some anthropologists argue that the shells, cattle, and brass rods have a particular social value and a limited purpose. These goods do not serve as a medium of exchange except in special instances; often, as in the case of bride-price, only special people may use the cattle or shells. These items act more as the concrete sign of a contract than as a medium of exchange. A person's concept of money is closely related to the society in which he or she lives. It can be misleading to assume that what we call money always has the same functions in different cultures.

One anthropological view maintains that the shell money of the Russell Island inhabitants was used in basically the same way as, say, U.S. money. Perhaps the most telling point against this stand is that there was little or no conversion of denominations of one class of shells into another class. Some classes of shells were obviously special-purpose money.

Economic Reasoning (*Write your responses on a separate sheet. Answers begin on p. 273.*)

1. When the price of slaves was quoted in cows and brass rods in Nigeria, which function of money were the cows and rods performing?
2. Why should the lack of conversion of denominations of one class of shells into another class among the Russell Islanders indicate that the shells did not serve the same function as money does in the United States?
3. Are there ways in which money in our society performs social functions as well as economic functions? For example?

How Is Money Created?

CURRENCY	PRIVATE BORROWING	GOVERNMENT BORROWING
The government prints paper money and mints coins in the amounts required by the public. The currency is distributed to businesses and households through the banking system.	Borrowing from a bank results in increasing the money supply by increasing the amount of demand deposits. Repayment of a loan decreases the money supply.	When a local, a state, or the federal government sells bonds or Treasury bills acquired by banks, new demand deposits are created that increase the money supply just as in the case of private borrowing.

10.6 Explain how money is created.

A. Which of the following would result in an increase (I) in the demand for currency, and which would result in a decrease (D) in the demand for currency?

1. _____ An increase in the use of automated teller machines (ATMs) in shopping malls

2. _____ A very large increase in the interest rate paid on certificates of deposit

3. _____ A decrease in incomes

4. _____ The approach of the holidays

5. _____ Individuals trying to avoid paying income taxes

6. _____ A decrease in illegal activity

B. When an individual, a business, or the government borrows money from a bank, the loan is usually in the form of which component of the money supply?

_____

C.

1. Have you ever received a student loan, a car loan, or any other kind of loan from a bank? _____

2. If so, how much of the loan did you actually see in "cold, hard cash"?

_____

D. When the money supply is increased (when money is created), it is usually done by increasing which component of the money supply?

_____

E.

1. When someone gets a bank loan, does the amount of money that the borrower has change? How?

_____

2. When someone gets a bank loan, does anybody else *outside the banking system* have less money?

_____

3. What happens to the amount of money in an economy if someone gets a bank loan?

_____

Case Application: How the Government Creates Money

If the government needs money, it doesn't just crank up the printing presses and print currency. Instead, it prints bonds or Treasury bills and sells these government securities to the public, financial institutions, or other businesses. The money received from the sales of securities is deposited in the U.S. Treasury's bank accounts.

The Treasury writes checks drawing on the money from sales of securities to pay for government programs, public projects, or employees' salaries. The recipients of these checks, of course, deposit them in their own banks. The banks send them to the Federal Reserve banks in their districts. The checks are cleared by the Fed, reducing the Treasury's deposit balance and increasing the commercial bank's reserve account by a like amount. Thus, the money becomes new reserves for the banking system, and these new reserves can result in a multiple expansion of the money supply.

The sale of government securities is most expansionary when they are acquired by the Fed or by other banks. When this happens, the funds used to purchase the securities are new money created by the credit expansion of the banking system. On the other hand, when the securities are sold to the public or to businesses other than banks, they may be paid for from existing demand deposits and thus would not represent an increase in the money supply.

Economic Reasoning *(Write your responses on a separate sheet. Answers begin on p. 273.)*

1. If the U.S. treasury prints a $10,000 bond and you borrow $10,000 from your bank to purchase the bond, by how much is the money supply increased? Who is directly responsible for the expansion of the money supply, you or the government?
2. If the government paid its bills by printing currency rather than by selling government securities, would this increase the money supply more, less, or the same amount? Why?
3. The only government securities issued in the smaller denominations that everyone can afford are savings bonds, which pay lower interest rates than other types of government securities. Is this fair? Why or why not?

How Is the Supply of Money Controlled?

THE FEDERAL RESERVE SYSTEM (FED)

The Fed is the central bank of the United States, a government institution that serves as a "banker's bank," provides for the monetary needs of the federal government, and controls the money supply. Control of the money supply is the Fed's most important function, which it accomplishes by the following means:

Reserve Requirements	Discounting	Open Market Operations
The Federal Reserve specifies the amount of reserves that banks must have on deposit with the Fed as a percentage of their deposit liabilities. The magnitude of the required reserve ratio determines the money multiplier. Thus by changing the banks' reserve requirement ratio, the Fed can permit a larger or smaller money supply.	The Fed can reduce the amount of bank lending by raising the discount rate that it charges the banks on funds they borrow from the Fed to supplement their reserves. Alternatively the Fed can encourage bank lending and increase the money supply by reducing the discount rate that it charges the banks.	The Fed can draw funds out of bank reserves by selling government securities on the open market, thus reducing the amount of money the banks can create. Alternatively it can encourage bank lending by buying bonds and Treasury bills on the open market, thus adding to bank reserves.

10.7 Describe the Federal Reserve System and explain what it does.

A. The central bank of the United States is called the

_____

B.

    1. How many branches of the Federal Reserve are there in the United States?

    _____

    2. Which branch of the Federal Reserve serves the area where you live?

    _____

C. What are the three functions of the Fed?

    1. _____

    2. _____

    3. _____

D. Some economists believe that the Fed has more economic power than any other institution in the United States. Which of the above functions do you think gives the Fed so much power?

_____

E.

    1. How many members are there on the Board of Governors of the Federal Reserve? _____
    2. For how many years does each member of the board serve? _____
    3. Compare the terms of office for members of the Board of Governors with those for members of the House of Representatives and the Senate and that of the president of the United States. What advantage is there in these relative terms of office?

_____

_____

10.8 Explain the difference between required reserves and excess reserves.

A.

    1. The minimum reserve of money that banks are required to have in their vault or on deposit with the Federal Reserve bank in their district is called

_____.

    2. The amount of money that a bank holds in its vault or on deposit with the Federal Reserve bank in its district in excess of the minimum amount required is called _____.

B.

    1. Suppose the reserve requirement is 10%. If Bank ABC has assets of $300,000, how much is this bank required to hold in reserves? _____
    2. Suppose the reserve requirement is 5%. How much is Bank ABC required to hold in reserve? _____
    3. Suppose the reserve requirement is 10%, and Bank ABC has $50,000 either in its vault or on deposit with the Federal Reserve bank in its district. What is the amount of Bank ABC's excess reserves? _____

C. Why would a bank hold excess reserves?

_____

10.9 Explain how changing the required reserve ratio, changing the discount rate, and open market operations can all lead to a change in the money supply.

A. What are the three tools that the Fed can use to change the money supply?

    1. _____

2. _____

3. _____

B. Other than deposits by customers, what are two places from which banks can get money in order to increase reserves?

   1. _____

   2. _____

C. Indicate whether each of the following will result in an increase (I) or a decrease (D) in the money supply:

   1. ____ The Fed buys bonds from banks.

   2. ____ The Fed sells bonds to banks.

   3. ____ The discount rate is increased.

   4. ____ I buy bonds from the Fed and pay for them with a check.

   5. ____ The required reserve ratio is decreased.

D. Use this bank "balance sheet" to answer the questions that follow.

Bank Assets		Bank Liabilities	
Total Reserves	$100,000	Demand Deposits	$100,000
Loans	0		
Government Bonds	0		
Total	$100,000		$100,000

   1. If the required reserve ratio is 10%, how much must the bank put into required reserves?

   _____

   2. How much will be left in excess reserves?

   _____

   3. How much can the bank lend?

   _____

   4. The money multiplier will be equal to

   _____

   5. The money supply can increase by how much?

   _____

   6. If the bank buys $20,000 in government bonds, how much will it have available to loan to individuals and businesses?

   _____

   7. After the bank buys the government bonds, how much can the money supply increase?

   _____

E. Use the balance sheet from exercise D to answer the following questions, but now assume that the reserve ratio is equal to 20%.

   1. How much must the bank put into required reserves?

   _____

   2. How much will be left in excess reserves?

   _____

3. What is the money multiplier?

_____

4. The money supply can be increased by how much?

_____

5. If the bank buys $40,000 in government bonds, how much will it have available to loan to individuals and businesses?

_____

6. After the bank buys the government bonds, how much can the money supply increase?

_____

F. The interest rate (the price of money) is *inversely* related to the price of government bonds; that is, when bond prices increase the interest rate decreases, and, conversely, when bond prices decrease the interest rate increases.

1. If the Fed increases the amount of bonds it buys, what happens to the demand for bonds?

_____

2. What happens to the money supply?

_____

3. What happens to the price of bonds?

_____

4. What happens to the interest rate?

_____

G.

1. If the Fed increases the amount of bonds that it sells to banks, what happens to the supply of bonds?

_____

2. What happens to the money supply?

_____

3. What happens to the price of bonds?

_____

4. What happens to the interest rate?

_____

H. Indicate which of the following items are directly (D) related to each other and which are inversely (I) related to each other.

1. _____ The money supply and interest rates
2. _____ The price level (inflation) and the real interest rate
3. _____ The amount of government bonds purchased by the Fed and the money supply
4. _____ The money supply and the price level
5. _____ The discount rate and the money supply
6. _____ The required reserve ratio and the money supply

I. The supply of money is usually considered to be *interest inelastic*. This means that the quantity supplied does not change as the price of money (the interest rate) changes.

1. On the graph below, draw the supply curve for money (S₁) and a "typical" downward-sloping demand curve for money (D₁). Label the equilibrium interest rate R₁.

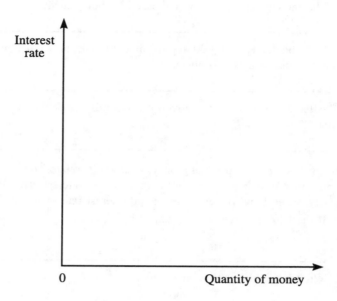

2. Show what happens to the interest rate if the demand for money increases (D₂) while the supply of money does not change. Label the new interest rate R₂.

3. On the same graph, show what happens if the supply of money increases (S₂). Label the new interest rate R₃.

4. What might be one drawback of increasing the money supply in order to keep interest rates low?

Case Application: **Who's in Charge around Here?**

Who is in charge of the nation's banks? The Federal Reserve? The Comptroller of the Currency? The Federal Deposit Insurance Corporation (FDIC)? At present, authority over the 4,000-plus national banks is divided among all three.

This confusion of authority has led to proposals to delineate the spheres of control among the different agencies. A White House task force was designated to draft a plan to overhaul bank regulation. In essence, the plan would have stripped the Fed and the FDIC of their bank-regulatory functions and set up a new federal banking agency under the Comptroller of the Currency. The FDIC would have confined its activities to insuring bank deposits, and the Fed's role would have been to serve as a central bank for its members and control the money supply.

The plan was torpedoed by then–Federal Reserve Board chairman Paul Volcker. He contended that, without its regulatory powers, "It would indeed be dangerous to look to the Federal Reserve to pick up the pieces in a financial crisis."

Economic Reasoning *(Write your responses on a separate sheet. Answers begin on p. 274.)*

1. The task force recommendation would reduce the authority of the Fed. What legislation expanded its authority in 1980?

2. What regulatory powers does the Fed need in order to implement monetary policy?

3. Should jurisdiction over the different areas of banking system control be assigned to specific agencies, or should the present system of divided authority be retained? Why?

IV. Practice Test (Answers begin on p. 274.)

Multiple-Choice Questions (*Circle the correct answer.*)

(10.1) 1. Paper money was first introduced by which one of the following types of workers?
    a. bankers
    b. spice and silk traders
    c. goldsmiths
    d. soldiers in the Crusades

(10.1) 2. Which one of the following describes the way making payments for goods and services is changing?
    a. increased use of paper money
    b. increased use of electronic payments
    c. more government regulation of banking
    d. increased investment in precious metals and coins

(10.2) 3. Which one of the following is *not* a part of M1?
    a. currency
    b. traveler's checks
    c. checking accounts
    d. savings accounts

(10.2) 4. Which one of the following is the "technical" term used to describe checking accounts?
    a. certificate accounts
    b. demand deposits
    c. time deposits
    d. negotiated orders of withdrawal (NOW accounts)

(10.3) 5. Near money is _____ than money.
    a. more valuable
    b. scarcer
    c. less liquid
    d. less risky

(10.3) 6. Which one of the following measures of the money supply includes the greatest number of different financial assets?
    a. M1
    b. M2
    c. M3
    d. L

(10.4) 7. To be functional, money must
    a. not be too liquid.
    b. be easily reproduced.
    c. be difficult to transport.
    d. be universally recognized.

(10.5) 8. Which one of the following would *not* function well as money?
    a. amber beads
    b. cigarettes
    c. flowers
    d. metal disks

(10.6) 9. Which one of the following determines the amount of currency that the Fed provides to the economy?
    a. the level of the interest rate
    b. the level of cash transactions
    c. the need to increase or decrease the money supply
    d. the level of bonds in the economy

(10.6) 10. The supply of money in an economy is usually controlled by controlling the
  a. amount of money that is borrowed.
  b. amount of money deposited in savings accounts.
  c. amount of currency printed.
  d. demand for money.

(10.7) 11. Which one of the following is responsible for controlling the supply of money in the United States?
  a. Congress
  b. the president
  c. the Federal Reserve Bank
  d. the Department of the Treasury

(10.8) 12. If a bank has $10,000,000 in assets and $1,000,000 in reserves, and the required reserve ratio is 10%, what is the value of this bank's excess reserves?
  a. $0
  b. $100,000
  c. $900,000
  d. $1,000,000

(10.9) 13. Which of the following would lead to an *increase* in the money supply?
  a. The Fed sells government bonds.
  b. The discount rate is lowered.
  c. The required reserve ratio is increased.
  d. all of the above

(10.9) 14. The money supply is *most commonly* changed by changing the
  a. rate at which bills are printed.
  b. discount rate.
  c. required reserve ratio.
  d. amount of government bonds bought and sold by the Fed.

(10.9) 15. Which one of the following is a *true* statement?
  a. When the Fed buys bonds, the money supply decreases and interest rates increase.
  b. When the Fed buys bonds, the money supply decreases and interest rates decrease.
  c. When the Fed buys bonds, the money supply increases and interest rates decrease.
  d. When the Fed buys bonds, the money supply increases and interest rates increase.

True/False Questions *(Circle T or F.)*

(10.1) 16. In the United States, the amount of currency in circulation is limited to the value of the banking system's gold reserves. T or F

(10.2) 17. The largest measure of the money supply (L) is also the most commonly used measure of the money supply. T or F

(10.6) 18. The main determinant of changes in the money supply is the amount of money deposited in savings accounts. T or F

(10.7) 19. The most important function of the Federal Reserve System is to control the creation of money by depository institutions. T or F

(10.8) 20. Increasing the required reserve ratio results in a decrease in the money supply. T or F

Chapter 11

Economic Instability

I. Chapter Outline

An economy is generally evaluated by how well it deals with the problems of unemployment and inflation. Prior to the 1970s economists believed that the U.S. economy could suffer from one or the other, but not both at the same time. Since then we have found that this, unfortunately, is not always true. However, we have also discovered in the 1990s that we can have low unemployment and low inflation at the same time.

Introductory Article: Movin' on Up!

During the 1990s, the United States has experienced unprecedented levels of both low unemployment and low inflation. Although this has puzzled economists who believe that there is a trade-off between unemployment and inflation, many Americans have enjoyed this period of prosperity. However, the labor market has become so tight that some companies have cut costs by laying off workers, reducing wages, or restricting hours worked. In order to obtain the high-wage jobs that are available, members of today's labor force must acquire skills in areas such as information technology and engineering. Otherwise, their incomes may be so low that they will not be able to maintain a satisfactory standard of living.

Economic Analysis

This chapter explores the phenomena of unemployment and inflation by examining the following questions:

1. **What Causes Unemployment?**

   Important Concepts: Frictional unemployment, Structural unemployment, Cyclical unemployment, Aggregate demand, Natural rate of unemployment, Hidden unemployment

   Comparative Case Application: El Desempleo

2. **What Causes Inflation?**

   Important Concepts: Consumer price index, Demand-pull inflation, Cost-push inflation, Monetary inflation

   Important Model: The quantity equation

   Case Application: The High Cost of Loving

3. **Is There a Trade-off between Unemployment and Inflation?**

   Important Concepts: The Phillips curve, Stagflation

   Important Model: Aggregate demand and supply

   Case Application: Going Down?

4. **What Are the Consequences of Unemployment and Inflation?**

   Important Concepts: Income effects of unemployment, Real output effects of unemployment, Social effects of unemployment, Income effects of inflation, Real output effects of inflation

   Comparative Case Application: Inflation—How High Is Up?

Perspective: Black Thursday and the Great Crash

II. Summary of Economic Analysis

1. The three reasons that people may be involuntarily out of work are **frictional unemployment**, **structural unemployment**, or **cyclical unemployment**.

2. Frictional unemployment results from job changes. It is not unexpected in a healthy economy, and it usually will be of short duration.

3. Structural unemployment results when skills become obsolete or there are geographic shifts in job locations.

4. Cyclical unemployment results from the inadequate **aggregate demand** for an economy's goods and services. It occurs when the economy is in a recession or a depression.

5. The **natural rate of unemployment** is the lowest level of unemployment that can be maintained without setting off increases in inflation.

6. The reported number of unemployed persons includes only those who are unemployed and actively looking for work. This does *not* include **hidden unemployment**: those who are not counted because they are discouraged and have stopped looking, those who work part-time when they desire full-time work, and those who are working in jobs for which they are very overqualified (the **underemployed**).

7. **Inflation** is a continual rise in the general level of prices in an economy.

8. The level of inflation is measured by price indices such as the **consumer price index**. These indices are computed by comparing the prices of goods in the same **market basket** at different points in time.

9. **Demand-pull** inflation is caused by the level of aggregate demand in product markets exceeding the productive capacity of the economy.

10. **Cost-push** inflation is caused by a rise in the prices of productive inputs (land, labor, and capital) in factor markets.

11. **Monetary inflation** occurs when the money supply increases faster than an economy's output of goods and services. The direct relationship between the money supply and the price level is shown by the **quantity equation**.

12. The **Phillips curve** shows the *inverse* relationship between the level of unemployment and the level of inflation.

13. The trade-off between unemployment and inflation shown by the Phillips curve is not constant over time. **Stagflation** occurs when the Phillips curve shifts so that *both* unemployment and inflation increase at the same time.

14. The consequences of unemployment include reduced household incomes, lower real output in the economy, and increased social and health problems.

15. Inflation reduces the **real income** of those whose incomes do not rise as fast as the price level, those holding their assets in the form of money, and lenders. Those in the opposite positions will gain. The effects of inflation on real output are unclear, but the longer the inflation lasts, the greater the negative effects on output.

III. Review of the Learning Objectives *(Answers begin on p. 274.)*

What Causes Unemployment?

FRICTIONAL UNEMPLOYMENT	STRUCTURAL UNEMPLOYMENT	CYCLICAL UNEMPLOYMENT
In a market economy there will always be people in between jobs. Those who are out of work for a short period of time while changing jobs constitute frictional unemployment in the economy. From the end of World War II to the 1970s, 3%–4% frictional unemployment was considered normal.	When changes in market supply or demand conditions affect major industries or regions, it can result in what is called structural unemployment. **Causes of structural unemployment:** • Decline in demand for a product • Increased foreign competition • Automation of production • Increased raw material costs • Lack of labor mobility between occupations or between regions	When aggregate demand in the economy is not sufficient to provide jobs for all those who are seeking work, cyclical unemployment results. When the economy is operating at production capacity there is full employment aggregate demand.

Hidden Unemployment

In addition to those officially counted as unemployed, there are others who have become discouraged about the possibility of finding a job and have given up looking. Consequently, they are not counted as unemployed, constituting hidden unemployment. There are other workers who are involuntarily working only part-time. They are not counted among the unemployed either, even though they cannot find full-time jobs and are underemployed.

11.1 Describe the three major causes of unemployment. *(Write in answers below.)*

A. Indicate whether each of the following represents frictional (F), structural (S), or cyclical (C) unemployment.

1. ____ Unemployed blacksmiths

2. ____ Assembly-line workers laid off during a recession

3. ____ A new graduate looking for her first job

4. ____ A Pittsburgh steelworker who loses his job when the steel mill moves to Alabama

5. ____ An unemployed oil worker in Houston during the 1986 oil glut

6. ____ A textile worker who loses her job when aggregate demand in the economy declines

7. ____ A textile worker who loses her job when the textile mill shuts down because of foreign competition

B.

1. Which type of unemployment is expected in a healthy economy?

_____

2. Which type of unemployment is expected to last the shortest amount of time?

_____

3. Which type of unemployment is considered the most serious problem for the economy as a whole?

_____

4. What type of unemployment exists when the economy is at full employment?

_____

C. Indicate which type of unemployment, frictional (F), structural (S), or cyclical (C), could be reduced by each of the following:

1. _____ Publishing lists of all available jobs in an area

2. _____ Increasing the demand for goods and services in an entire economy

3. _____ Retraining programs

4. _____ Policies that increase the mobility of workers between different regions of the country

5. _____ Job placement services at high schools and colleges

11.2 Explain why some unemployment is hidden.

A. To be classified as unemployed, a person must be unemployed and

_____

B. Indicate whether each of the following would be officially counted (C) or not counted (N) as being unemployed (those not counted represent _hidden_ unemployment).

1. _____ A person works at a part-time job at night while looking for a full-time job during the day.

2. _____ A person with a Ph.D. in economics works as a cab driver.

3. _____ A person loses her job as a mechanic and is looking for a new job.

4. _____ A person who has been unemployed for 6 months stops looking for work.

5. _____ A new mother decides to leave her job in order to stay at home with her child.

6. _____ A person is in prison because he lost his job as a bank robber when he got caught.

7. _____ A person who works on an assembly line has her hours reduced from 40 to 25 hours per week because of a decline in aggregate demand.

C. The official unemployment rate is calculated by dividing the number of unemployed persons actively looking for work by the total labor force.

1. If the amount of hidden unemployment increases, what happens to the official unemployment rate?

_____

2. Every June the number of students looking for work causes the size of the labor force to increase. What effect will this have on the unemployment rate if none of the students finds a job?

_____

3. Does the existence of hidden unemployment mean that the official unemployment rate understates or overstates the actual unemployment rate in the economy?

_____

4. Does the existence of people "working" full-time in illegal activities mean that the official unemployment rate understates or overstates the actual unemployment rate in the economy?

_____

11.3 Define the natural rate of unemployment and explain what happens when it differs from the actual rate of unemployment.

A. The natural rate of unemployment is the lowest level of unemployment that can exist with _____ and _____ prices.

B. What will happen to the inflation level if the actual rate of unemployment falls below the natural rate?

_____

C. Indicate what happens in each of the following scenarios:

  1. When prices increase faster than wages, the real wage will (decrease, increase, stay the same).

  2. This will cause employers to hire (more, fewer, the same number of) workers.

  3. When workers understand what has happened to their real wage, they will demand (higher, lower) wages in order to keep up with inflation.

  4. When workers get their (higher, lower) wages, employers will adjust by hiring (more, fewer, the same number of) workers.

  5. It follows from the above, that when workers adjust their wage expectations to account for inflation, unemployment will (increase, decrease).

Case Application: Where the Jobs Went

The unemployment level remained stubbornly high from 1980 through the early 1990s, despite the second longest economic expansion since World War II, with employment reaching the full employment level in only 3 of those years. With 8.7 million people out of work in 1993, nearly 7% of the labor force, what happened to all of the jobs? Who was out of work and why? Would the jobs return or were they lost forever?

Much of the job loss was due to the decline of older manufacturing industries such as steel, rubber, textiles, and automobiles. Those heavy industries, once the foundation of the nation's prosperity, are being replaced by high technology industries. The auto industry, for example, has had to automate in order to be competitive with Japanese and other foreign producers. Many of the jobs are thus gone forever. It is estimated that at least 100,000 jobs have been permanently eliminated in the automobile industry, and a million jobs in manufacturing overall.

Also, the high unemployment levels have been associated with an exceptionally large increase in the size of the labor force. The members of the "baby boom" generation swelled the ranks of labor, and an increasing percentage of women entered the job market, so that the capacity of the economy to create new jobs was strained beyond the limit. In order to absorb the new entrants into the workforce, the growth of output would need to have been much higher than it was at the time. Since then, the economy has adjusted, and unemployment rates have declined.

Economic Reasoning *(Write your responses on a separate sheet. Answers begin on p. 274.)*

  1. The 100,000-plus jobs that were permanently lost in the automobile industry represented what type of unemployment?
  2. About one in every four women workers who were displaced from jobs that they had held for 3 years or more gave up looking for a new job. Were they counted as unemployed? What type of unemployment did they represent?
  3. What would you recommend to a 40-year-old steelworker, with a wife and four children to support, who lost his job when the steel mill shut down in Donora, Pennsylvania?

What Causes Inflation?

Measuring Inflation
The most commonly used measure of average prices in the economy as a whole is the consumer price index (CPI).

DEMAND-PULL INFLATION

When the demand for goods and services exceeds the production capacity of the economy, the excess demand spills over into demand-pull inflation. Inflation is compounded when prices are rising due to shortages as goods and resources are bought and held off the market by those who are speculating on a rise in the price.

COST-PUSH INFLATION

Inflation can arise from changes in the costs of production of goods and services. An increase in prices of raw materials, labor, or capital results in cost-push inflation. Cost-push inflation may reinforce demand-pull inflation through labor contracts containing cost-of-living adjustment (COLA) clauses.

MONETARY INFLATION

The monetarists maintain that inflation is caused by excessive growth of the money supply.

Quantity Equation

According to the quantity equation, the money supply times the velocity at which it changes hands equals the number of transactions times the average level of prices.

$$M \times V = T \times P$$

11.4 Understand what inflation is and how it is measured by the CPI.

A. Define inflation.

_____

_____

1. The most common measure of inflation is the

_____

2. This index is computed by comparing the price of the same _____ of goods in two different time periods.

B. The following represent the cost of the same market basket of goods purchased in successive years. If 1985 is the *base year*, use the data to construct a price index. (Use the following formula to compute the index.)

Price Index = $\dfrac{\text{(Cost in year of interest)}}{\text{(Cost in base year)}} \times 100$

Year	Cost of Market Basket	Price Index
1985	$200.00	_____
1986	$220.00	_____
1987	$230.00	_____
1988	$250.00	_____
1989	$260.00	_____

C. The inflation rate between two years is calculated as the percentage change in the price index for those years. What are the inflation rates for the indices you computed in the previous question? (Use the following formula.)

% Change = $\dfrac{\text{(Index in one year)} - \text{(Index in previous year)}}{\text{Index in previous year}}$

1985 to 1986 inflation rate equals _____.

1986 to 1987 inflation rate equals _____.

1987 to 1988 inflation rate equals _____.

1988 to 1989 inflation rate equals _____.

11.5 Describe the three causes of inflation.

A. In terms of the circular flow model of the economy presented in chapter 3, demand-pull inflation arises in the _____ market, and cost-push inflation arises in the _____ market.

B. Identify the probable causes of inflation in each of the following instances:

1. The Fed buys increasing amounts of bonds.

_____

2. Even though real income and output do not change, everybody goes out and charges their credit cards up to their limits.

_____

3. The price of oil increases as a result of political unrest in the Middle East.

_____

4. People see that prices are increasing and they stock up on goods.

_____

5. A large proportion of the economy receives cost-of-living adjustments.

_____

11.6 Use the quantity equation to explain the relationship between the money supply and the price level.

A. Define each of the four components of the quantity equation:

1. M _____

2. V _____

3. P _____

4. T _____

B.

1. What does M × V represent?

_____

2. What does P × T represent?

_____

C. Use the quantity equation to answer each of the following:

1. What happens to the price level if output and velocity do not change when the money supply decreases?

_____

2. What happens to the value of total purchases if increases in the money supply are offset by equal decreases in the velocity of money?

_____

3. If prices and the supply of money cannot change, what must happen if the number of transactions in an economy are increasing?

_____

D. Suppose that the velocity of money is fixed, but that prices and/or transactions can change. Then suppose the Fed buys bonds in order to increase the money supply.

1. What will happen to prices and transactions if the economy is in a recession? (**Increase, Decrease,** or **Stay** the same?) P: _____ T: _____

2. What will happen to prices and transactions if the economy is at full employment? P: _____ T: _____

3. What will happen to prices and transactions if the economy is somewhere between recession and full employment? P: _____ T: _____

4. Based on your answers in parts 1, 2, and 3 of this exercise, when do you think monetary policy would be best used to combat unemployment?

Case Application: **Talk about Inflation . . .**

The United States experienced unprecedented levels of inflation— unprecedented since price controls were lifted at the end of World War II—in the late 1970s and the beginning of the 1980s. Prices rose at a rate of 13.3% in 1979 and 12.4% in 1980. This rate of inflation was very disturbing to the public and to policy makers in Washington, but compared to inflation rates in some other countries, the U.S. inflation rate was quite tame.

Latin American, African, and Eastern European countries have had the highest inflation rates in recent years. Russia had an annual rate of 245% in January 1992, and Poland reached a peak rate of 640% in 1989. However, even the advanced economy of Israel reached an inflation rate of 370% in 1983–84. A tankful of gasoline in Israel cost an amount of shekels that would have paid for the car 5 years earlier.

Such extreme inflation rates are the consequence of large government budget deficits and increases in the money supply. When the government is spending more than it collects in tax revenues, the extra money spent by the government is chasing the same resources as the money in the taxpayers' pockets. Hence, the prices of resources and finished products are bid up. When the government finances its deficit spending by putting more money into circulation, it compounds the inflation.

Economic Reasoning *(Write your responses on a separate sheet. Answers begin on p. 275.)*

1. If dinner in a Tel-Aviv restaurant cost 10 shekels at the end of 1983, what would a restaurant patron have to pay for the same meal at the end of 1984?
2. What types of inflation are described in this application?
3. Why do you think inflation was so much greater in some other countries than in the United States?

Is There a Trade-off between Unemployment and Inflation?

PHILLIPS CURVE

The relationship between the rate of inflation and the unemployment rate is shown by the Phillips curve. In the 1960s the trade-off between inflation and unemployment was at levels that now seem moderate.

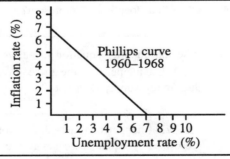

Stagflation

In the 1970s the Phillips curve shifted upwards to the right, with the trade-off between inflation and unemployment at much higher levels. This has been termed stagflation—a combination of stagnation and inflation.

Causes of the 1970s stagflation:

- Spending on the Vietnam War plus spending on domestic social programs
- Inflationary expectations
- Rise in energy costs touched off by OPEC
- Monopolistic pricing

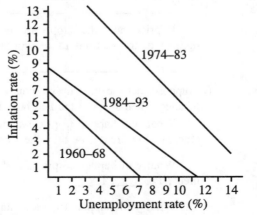

11.7 Use the Phillips curve to explain the relationship between unemployment and inflation.

A. Indicate whether the following are directly (D) or inversely (I) related to one another.

    1. ____ Output and employment

    2. ____ Output and unemployment

    3. ____ Output and inflation (the price level)

    4. ____ Inflation and employment

    5. ____ Inflation and unemployment

B. Which of the above relationships (1 through 5) describes the Phillips curve? _____

C. Use the data provided below to construct a Phillips curve for the economy.

Year	Unemployment	Inflation
1986	10%	1%
1987	8%	3%
1988	6%	6%
1989	4%	9%
1990	2%	12%

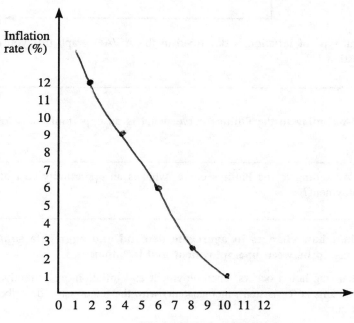

D. Use the space provided below to construct an aggregate supply and aggregate demand graph that reflects the economy described in exercise C for 1986 and 1990. (You should have one AS curve and two AD curves. Be sure to label both axes and both AD curves.)

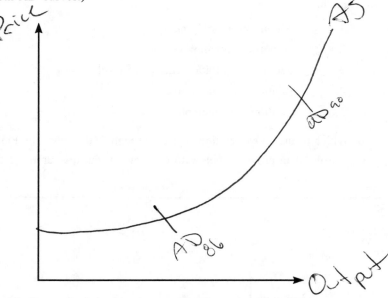

E. What type of inflation is described in the AS/AD graph that you constructed in question D?

_____

F.

1. According to the Phillips curve, what is an opportunity cost of reducing inflation?

_____

2. According to the Phillips curve, what is an opportunity cost of reducing unemployment?

_____

11.8 Explain how changes in aggregate demand and aggregate supply affect the relationship between unemployment and inflation.

A. When stagflation occurs, unemployment and inflation are (directly, inversely) related. This is (consistent, inconsistent) with the relationship described by the Phillips curve.

B. What are three possible causes of stagflation?

1. _____

2. _____

3. _____

C. Use the axes provided below to construct an AS/AD graph with the initial inter-section in the stable price (horizontal) range of the AS curve. Then draw a new AD curve (AD₂) that indicates an increase in both output and prices.

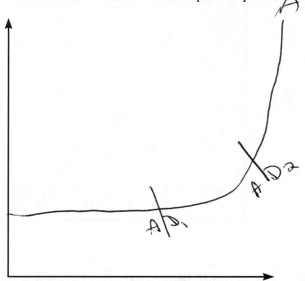

D. Use the axes provided below to construct an AS/AD graph with the initial inter-section in the stable price (horizontal) range of the AS curve. Then draw a new AS curve (AS₂) that indicates an increase in prices and a *decrease* in output.

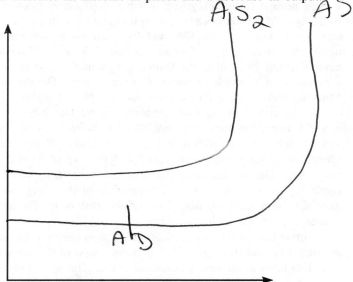

E. Which of the two preceding graphs (question C or D) depicts the presence of stagflation? Explain_____

_____

F. Use the aggregate supply and aggregate demand curves drawn below to answer the following questions about the price level and the level of transactions (Increase, Decrease, Stay the Same):

1. If aggregate demand shifts from AD₁ to AD₂, what happens to P and T?

P: _____S_____   T: _____I_____

2. If aggregate demand shifts from AD₂ to AD₃, what happens to P and T?

P: _____I_____   T: _____I_____

3. If aggregate demand shifts from AD₃ to AD₄, what happens to P and T?

P: _____I_____   T: _____S_____

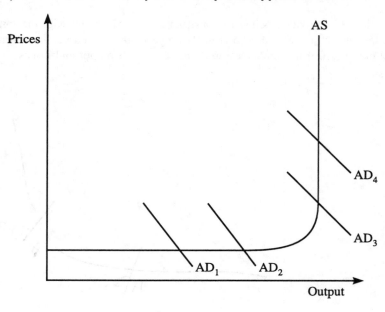

Case Application: **Phillips Curve International**

Traditionally, the countries of Western Europe have been more willing to trade off inflation for less unemployment than has the United States. A 4% unemployment rate, considered normal full employment in the United States prior to the 1970s, was excessive in the eyes of the Europeans. Unemployment rates that high could cause European governments to fall. Between 1960 and 1975, the unemployment rate in West Germany was never more than 1.6%, in Sweden not over 2%, and in France less than 3%. In Italy it never reached 4%, and in the United Kingdom it did so in only one year. There was an abhorrence of unemployment in Western Europe. On the other hand, those countries generally had higher inflation rates than the United States.

As described in the Case Application "El Desempleo," on pages 293–294 of the text, the European unemployment situation in recent years has been quite different. In 1994, when the unemployment rate in the United States was 6.5%, over 12% of the French labor force was unemployed and in Italy more than 11%. The unemployment rates in the United Kingdom, Germany, and other European countries were also significantly higher than in the United States. But at the same time, European inflation rates have also been relatively high. The upward shift in the Phillips curve in Western Europe was even greater than in this country.

Differences in the positions of the Phillips curve reflect such things as variations in industry structure, the age and skill composition of the labor force, institutional factors, including labor union practices and the tax structures, and government economic policies. The economies of the European countries were hit even harder by the rise in energy prices than the U.S. economy because they are more dependent on foreign energy supplies.

Economic Reasoning *(Write your responses on a separate sheet. Answers begin on p. 276.)*

1. Prior to 1975, were the European countries operating more to the lower right or to the upper left on their Phillips curves, compared to the United States?
2. How did the rise in energy costs in the 1970s contribute to the upward shift in the Phillips curve in Western Europe?
3. Where on the Phillips curve do you think it is better for a country to be located, the lower right or the upper left? Why?

What Are the Consequences of Unemployment and Inflation?

UNEMPLOYMENT

Income effects:

- Loss of income and benefits (health insurance) by unemployed
- Loss of income to others because of reduced purchasing power
- Reduced tax income and increased outlays for governments

Real output effects:

- Each 1% of unemployment results in a reduction of $100 billion in output
- Lower real investment means less growth and reduced future output

Social effects:

- Health problems (e.g., depression)
- Increased suicides
- Break up of families
- Increased child abuse
- Increased crime

INFLATION

Income effects:

- Reduced purchasing power of the dollar
- Reduced real income for fixed income receivers
- Reduced real wealth of savings
- Benefits those whose incomes rise faster than the inflation rate
- Benefits owners of real assets (for example, precious metals, real estate)
- Benefits debtors

Real output effects:

- Inflation initially stimulates output
- Near full employment, there arise bottlenecks in supplies
- Costs begin rising faster than prices
- Interest rates accelerate, discouraging new investment

11.9 Explain the consequences of unemployment and inflation.

A. List three undesirable consequences of unemployment.

1. _____
2. _____
3. _____

B. Use the list from question A to indicate which consequence is represented in each of the following:

1. ____ Suicides increase.
2. ____ The economy produces fewer cars.
3. ____ Living standards decrease.
4. ____ Government tax receipts decrease.
5. ____ Child abuse increases.

C. Indicate which of the following groups would benefit (B) and which would lose (L) as a result of unanticipated inflation.

1. ____ Borrowers
2. ____ People on fixed incomes
3. ____ People who put their money under their mattresses
4. ____ People who put their money in savings accounts at fixed interest rates
5. ____ Lenders
6. ____ Members of strong labor unions
7. ____ Collectors of rare coins
8. ____ Homeowners
9. ____ The U.S. government

D.

    1. Describe a situation in which a business would benefit from inflation.

    _____

    _____

    2. Describe a situation in which a business would be harmed by inflation.

    _____

    _____

Case Application: **Disinflation Losers**

Lowering the rate of inflation has been a major economic goal, and inflation has been accused of robbing everybody's pocketbook. But as inflation came down, it appeared there were some losers from "disinflation" as well.

The people visibly hurt by the end of the high inflation rates included those who had purchased houses when real estate prices were rising at 5%–20% a year. Some purchased those houses at mortgage interest rates of 15% or more with the expectation that the continued rise in the value of real estate would enable them to refinance their loans in the future. The sudden end to those rising housing prices, even price declines in many areas, resulted in many foreclosures because owners could not meet the high mortgage payments and could not refinance. In a sense all homeowners suffered from the end of the inflation in housing prices. The rise in real estate prices, which was higher than the inflation of prices in general, had greatly increased the value of their homes as a financial asset. It made homeowners wealthier, although they might not be able to take immediate advantage of it. The end of inflation terminated their "windfall" gains in the value of their houses.

Others who suffered from the end of inflation were those who invested in gold, precious gems, or other commodities. Disinflation meant an end to the rising prices of those inflation hedges. As a result, there was a decline in the demand for them, and their value fell. The price of gold fell by over 50% in a 2-year period. The price of diamonds took a nosedive. Those who tried to protect themselves from inflation by investing in those commodities were savaged by the disinflation.

Government finances also suffered from the end of inflation. Inflation had accelerated government tax receipts and reduced the real cost of government debt. The disinflation and recession put a severe squeeze on government budgets. As a result, many government services had to be sharply curtailed.

Economic Reasoning *(Write your responses on a separate sheet. Answers begin on p. 276.)*

    1. Whose wealth and income were negatively affected by an end to inflation?
    2. How would a decline in the price of gold and other commodities be likely to affect the output of those commodities? Why?
    3. Is disinflation as bad as inflation? Why or why not?

IV. Practice Test (Answers begin on p. 276.)

Multiple-Choice Questions *(Circle the correct answer.)*

(11.1) 1. Unemployment that results from a decrease in aggregate demand is called _____ unemployment.
        a. inflationary
        b. cyclical
        c. frictional
        d. structural

(11.1) 2. The type of unemployment that can be reduced by increasing training and retraining programs is called _____ unemployment.
   a. inflationary
   b. cyclical
   c. frictional
   d. structural

(11.1) 3. For the economy as a whole, which type of unemployment represents the greatest problem?
   a. cyclical unemployment
   b. frictional unemployment
   c. structural unemployment
   d. all of the above

(11.2) 4. Which one of the following is an example of "hidden" unemployment?
   a. A worker is laid off because of decreased demand for his product.
   b. A worker loses her job when she is replaced by a machine.
   c. A worker works at a part-time job while desiring a full-time job.
   d. A worker quits a job in order to find a better job.

(11.2) 5. Which one of the following individuals could be characterized as "underemployed"?
   a. Christine works in illegal activities.
   b. Samantha is overqualified for her job.
   c. Geraldo is temporarily laid off from his job.
   d. Nathan is a househusband who works in the home.

(11.3) 6. What is the natural rate of unemployment?
   a. the rate that exists when there is the greatest amount of employment without increased inflation
   b. the rate that exists when everyone who wants a job has one
   c. the rate that exists when there is no hidden unemployment
   d. the rate that exists when the unemployment and inflation rates are equal

(11.4) 7. Price indices are constructed by comparing the prices of
   a. different market baskets at the same point in time.
   b. different market baskets at different points in time.
   c. the same market basket at the same points in time.
   d. the same market basket at different points in time.

(11.4) 8. If prices double from the base year to the current year, the price index in the current year is equal to
   a. 0.20.
   b. 50.00.
   c. 100.00.
   d. 200.00.

(11.5) 9. When the economy is near full employment an increase in aggregate demand will result in inflation. What kind of inflation is this?
   a. disinflation
   b. cost-push inflation
   c. demand-pull inflation
   d. cost-of-living adjustment

(11.6) 10. Which one of the following is the quantity equation?
   a. $M \times V = P \times T$
   b. $P \times V = P \times T$
   c. $C \times P = I$
   d. $M \times T = P \times V$

(11.6) 11. If the level of transactions and the velocity of money are fixed (constant), an increase in the supply of money will result in which one of the following?
   a. an increase in output
   b. a decrease in employment
   c. an increase in prices
   d. a decrease in inflation

(11.7) 12. The Phillips curve shows the relationship between which one of the following?
   a. inflation and the price level
   b. inflation and unemployment
   c. employment and unemployment
   d. inflation and total output

(11.7) 13. Which one of the following is a *true* statement?
   a. The Phillips curve does not shift over time.
   b. The Phillips curve shifted to show greater levels of both inflation and unemployment in the 1970s.
   c. The Phillips curve shifts when the level of unemployment changes.
   d. The Phillips curve shifts when the inflation rate changes.

(11.8) 14. Stagflation may occur as the result of which of the following?
   a. a rightward shift of the aggregate demand curve
   b. a leftward shift of the aggregate demand curve
   c. an upward shift of the aggregate supply curve
   d. a downward shift of the aggregate supply curve

(11.9) 15. Unemployment affects everyone because
   a. it reduces the demand for goods and services.
   b. lost production is lost forever.
   c. the unemployed usually require tax-financed government assistance.
   d. all of the above

True/False Questions *(Circle T or F.)*

(11.1) 16. Frictional unemployment is normal in a healthy economy. T or F

(11.2) 17. In an economy with a significant amount of hidden unemployment, the "official" unemployment rate is artificially high. T or F

(11.3) 18. When the economy is at full employment, increases in aggregate demand will lead to increased prices but no increased output. T or F

(11.5) 19. Demand-pull inflation is the same as cost-push inflation. T or F

(11.9) 20. Because it is the biggest debtor in the world, the U.S. government will be a net loser if inflation occurs. T or F

Chapter 12

The Economy's Output

I. Chapter Outline

There are two different ways of measuring the total output of the economy. Although it is calculated differently, you will get the same total amount whether you add up the total amount of money spent or whether you add up the total amount of money earned. There are also two different explanations of what determines how much an economy produces: the demand-side and the supply-side points of view. Unlike the two different ways of measuring output, however, these two points of view come to distinctly different conclusions.

Introductory Article: Forecasting or Fortune-Telling?

Despite the intricate complexity of modern statistical economic forecasting models, they are often no more reliable than the oracles at Delphi in ancient Greece at predicting the future. Problems confronting forecasters include the unreliability of the data they put into their models and the unpredictable nature of the world and the events which shape it. Nonetheless, there is a strong demand by business and government for information that can be used to shape future plans. As an anonymous economist once pointed out, "Forecasting is difficult, especially about the future."

Economic Analysis

This chapter examines how the levels of total output and employment are determined in a market economy by addressing the following questions:

1. **How Much Does the Economy Produce?**

   Important Concepts: Consumption, Investment, Government spending, Net exports, National Income, Excise taxes, Current and constant dollar Gross Domestic Product (GDP)

   Case Application: The Roller-Coaster Ride

2. **What Determines Domestic Output from the Demand-Side Point of View?**

   Important Concepts: Disposable income, Budget deficits and surpluses, Aggregate demand, Equilibrium output

   Important Model: The Keynesian economic model

   Case Application: Squaring the Economic Circle

3. **What Determines Domestic Output from the Supply-Side Point of View?**

   Important Concepts: Supply-side economics, Say's Law, Incentives, Crowding out

   Case Application: Spending Like There Is No Tomorrow

Perspective: The Keynesian Revolution

   Biography—John Maynard Keynes

II. Summary of Economic Analysis

1. The **Gross Domestic Product (GDP)** of an economy is the value of all the goods and services it produces domestically within a year.

2. An economy's GDP can be computed either by adding together all the **expenditures** made on goods and services or by adding together all the **incomes** earned by producing these goods and services. Either method of measuring will result in the same value for GDP.

3. The expenditures method computes GDP by adding together the four types of expenditures that occur in a market economy: **personal consumption (C), private domestic investment (I), government spending (G)**, and **net exports (X − M)**. Therefore, GDP = C + I + G + (X − M).

4. The sum of all incomes earned as wages, rents, profits, and interest is equal to **National Income**. National Income plus **capital consumption allowances, indirect business taxes**, and other business transfers equals GDP.

5. In order to avoid **double-counting**, only the **value added** by each firm at each stage of the production is included when computing the size of the GDP.

6. **Current dollar GDP** is the value of GDP with no adjustment for inflation. **Constant dollar GDP** is the inflation-adjusted value of GDP.

7. The **demand-side** (Keynesian) view of the economy is that the size of the GDP depends on aggregate demand: the total amount of consumption, investment, government, and export demand.

8. Insufficient aggregate demand can result in **underconsumption** or **overproduction**. This in turn leads to a slowing of economic activity and an increase in unemployment. If aggregate demand remains low, the economy will not correct itself and high levels of unemployment might remain for extended periods (like the Great Depression).

9. Savings (S) and taxes (T) are **leakages** out of an economy's flow of income. Investment (I) and government spending (G) are **injections** into the flow of income.

10. When I + G > S + T, additions exceed leakages, aggregate demand increases, and income, output, and employment increase (if the economy was not already at full capacity).

11. When I + G < S + T, leakages exceed additions, aggregate demand decreases, and income, output, and employment decrease.

12. **Equilibrium output** in the **Keynesian model** of an economy occurs whenever the level of leakages out of the economic flow are just offset by the injections into it: I + G = S + T.

13. Keynesian economics is based on the premise that the supply of goods and services in an economy will increase in response to increased demand. In contrast, early **supply-side** economic views were based on **Say's Law of Markets**, which states that "supply creates its own demand." Say's Law implies that underconsumption cannot occur.

14. Modern supply-side economics emphasizes the importance of profit **incentives** in motivating an economy to increase its output. According to this view, big government and high tax rates discourage productive work and investment and consequently limit economic growth.

15. According to the supply-side point of view, a very real danger of increased government borrowing is that it **crowds out** private investment.

III. Review of the Learning Objectives *(Answers begin on p. 276.)*

How Much Does the Economy Produce?

GROSS DOMESTIC PRODUCT

The measure of the total amount of goods and services produced in the economy is the Gross Domestic Product (GDP). There are two methods of measuring GDP:

Expenditure Categories	**Income Categories**
C — personal consumption expenditures	National Income (NI)
I — gross private domestic investment	Wages and salaries
(buildings, equipment, inventories)	Proprietor's income
G — government spending	Corporate profits
(X – M) — net exports (exports minus imports)	Interest
	Rent
	+ Capital Consumption Allowances
GDP = C + I + G + (X – M)	+ Indirect Taxes
	= GDP

Value Added

To avoid double-counting in adding up the total amount of goods and services produced, only the value added at each stage of production is counted, excluding the cost of intermediate goods.

Current and Constant Dollar GDP

In order to measure real changes in GDP, eliminating the effect of inflation on the figures, the current dollar values are adjusted by a price index to give the values in the constant dollar value of an earlier base year.

12.1 Define the GDP and explain the two ways of measuring it and why they give the same result.

  A.

     1. The *expenditure* approach to calculating GDP adds up all the money that people

     _____

     2. The *income* approach to calculating GDP adds up all the money that people

     _____

  B. In terms of the circular flow diagram:

     1. the expenditure approach to calculating GDP adds up all the transactions in the _____ market.

     2. the income approach to calculating GDP adds up all the transactions in the _____ market.

  C. The following table shows the prices received by producers at each stage of the production of a loaf of bread. Calculate the *value added* at each stage of production and indicate how much the production of a loaf of bread adds to GDP.

Producer	Price Received	Value Added
Wheat farmer sells to miller	$0.30	_____
Miller sells to baker	0.45	_____
Baker sells to wholesaler	0.65	_____
Wholesaler sells to retailer	0.85	_____
Retailer sells to consumer	0.95	_____
	ADDITION TO GDP =	_____

  D. GDP is a measure of the total amount of goods and services *produced in an economy in the current year*. With this in mind, indicate whether the dollar value of each of the following should be included (I) or not included (N) in this year's GDP.

1. ____ Harry buys a meal at a restaurant.

2. ____ Harry buys 100 shares of AT&T from a stockbroker.

3. ____ Harry buys a 1984 Ford station wagon.

4. ____ Harry buys a new pair of jeans.

5. ____ Harry sells 1,000 bushels of wheat to the Chinese.

6. ____ Harry sells 1,000 bushels of wheat to an American baker.

7. ____ Harry mows his neighbor's lawn for $10.00.

8. ____ Harry pays his housekeeper $100 per week.

9. ____ Harry's wife cleans their house but is not paid for doing the job.

E. What are the four components of National Income?

1. _____

2. _____

3. _____

4. _____

F. To determine GDP using the income approach, what two things must be added to National Income?

1. _____

2. _____

12.2 List the four types of expenditures that make up the aggregate demand for goods and services.

A. Indicate whether each of the following expenditures is a part of consumption (C), government spending (G), investment (I), or exports (X):

1. ____ The Air Force buys a Stealth bomber.

2. ____ A pair of Levi's jeans is sold in Rome.

3. ____ Japanese tourists buy New York City souvenirs.

4. ____ A family buys a new house.

5. ____ A family buys a Thanksgiving turkey.

6. ____ A toy company increases its inventory.

7. ____ An electric company buys a new generator.

8. ____ A family pays its electric bill.

B. The same good could be classified as consumption, a government purchase, investment, or an export, depending on who the buyer is. Give an example of how each of the following goods could be classified as C, I, G, or X.

1. A pickup truck

C: _____

I: _____

G: _____

X: _____

2. A television
   C:_____
   I:_____
   G:_____
   X:_____

C. Which component of total expenditures:

1. is the largest? ____
2. is the most stable over time? ____
3. depends the most on interest rates? ____
4. increases when we buy more French wine? ____
5. includes inventories? ____
6. depends on disposable income? ____
7. is directly related to savings levels? ____
8. is inversely related to savings levels? ____

12.3 Define constant dollar GDP and explain how it is related to current dollar GDP.

A. When we add up everybody's incomes or add up the total amount of expenditures in the economy in order to calculate GDP, we do so in terms of dollars. However, the value of a dollar changes over time.

1. If an analyst wishes to compare changes in an economy's output over a number of years, she must first adjust the level of GDP to reflect changes in the _____ in each of the years.
2. This implies that the analysts should compare the values of _____ GDP rather than _____ GDP.

B. If P represents the average price level and Q represents the total amount of goods and services produced in an economy, then:

1. constant dollar GDP equals _____.
2. current dollar GDP equals _____.

~ C. To convert current dollar GDP to constant dollar GDP, one must divide current dollar GDP (P × Q) by the appropriate price index (P) and then multiply by 100 (because the price index starts from a base of 100—see chapter 11). If constant dollar GDP is defined as Q, then:

$$\frac{(P \times Q)}{P} \times 100 = Q, \text{ or} \qquad \frac{Current \ \$ \ GDP}{Price \ Index} \times 100 = Constant \ \$ \ GDP$$

Use the above formula to calculate the level of constant dollar GDP from the given levels of current dollar GDP and the price index.

Year	Current Dollar GDP	Price Index	Constant Dollar GDP
1994	$2,000,000	100	2000 000
1995	$2,310,000	105	_____
1996	$2,640,000	110	_____
1997	$3,055,000	130	_____
1998	$3,500,000	140	_____

D. In the previous question, the economy was in a recession in which year?

_____

E. If the price index increases each year, then which will be bigger, current or constant dollar GDP? Explain.

_____

_____

_____

12.4 Explain why GDP is not a good measure of economic or social well-being.

A. GDP is not a good measure of well-being because it excludes many "goods" that we value and includes expenditures for many "bads" that we would prefer not having to buy. Which of the following are "goods" (G) that would not be included in GDP, and which of the following are "bads" (B) that result in a larger GDP? (Be careful, some might not fit either category!)

1. _____ Julio buys a lock for his bicycle.

2. _____ Anna Maria goes to the dentist.

3. _____ Increased amounts of leisure time

4. _____ A beautiful autumn day

5. _____ Jerry buys an air filter because the smog makes his lungs hurt.

6. _____ The government builds a new jail.

B. Economists have attempted to formulate better measures of well-being than GDP. One such measure created by Nordhaus and Tobin is called the Measure of Economic Welfare (MEW). The adjustments they made to get from GDP to MEW are described below. For each, state whether you think the adjustment would result in additions to the traditional measure of GDP (+), or subtractions from the traditional measure of GDP (−) for a given year.

1. _____ Include a measure of the value of leisure time.

2. _____ Include a measure of environmental damage caused by pollution.

3. _____ Include a measure of government services provided to consumers.

4. _____ Exclude consumer expenditures, such as commuting to/from work, that do not seem to increase welfare.

5. _____ Include a measure of the value of nonmarketed household activities (for example, ironing clothes).

6. _____ Instead of adding the value of a durable good at the time of purchase, add the value of services obtained from the good over the life of the good.

Case Application: **Helen's Gift City, Inc.**

Late in 1993, a gift store located in a shopping mall in a well-to-do suburban area of northern New Jersey was on the verge of bankruptcy. Internal management and external coordination problems with corporation headquarters in California appeared to be behind the trouble.

Helen Bidwell had always dreamed of owning her own business. At the end of December 1993, she bought the store. She reorganized, incorporated, and named it "Helen's Gift City, Inc."

Mrs. Bidwell has a good business mind, and she seemed to know where the "market" was for the gift industry. She immediately acquired a selection of merchandise in all materials and colors, from all geographic and national origins. Boutique specialties, costume jewelry, decorative hardware, flatware, figurines, sculpture, purse accessories, and woodenware were only a few of the items she carried. Because her line of giftware was so comprehensive in its appeal, she turned the store into a lucrative enterprise. By the year's end, Helen, who had some elementary accounting, drew up the following income statement:

Helen's Gift City, Inc.
Account's Income Statement For the Year 1994

Sales		$200,000
Cost of gifts sold		
Merchandise	$90,000	
Wages and salaries	60,000	
Rent	15,000	
Depreciation	10,000	
Excise tax	14,000	
		−189,000
Gross Profit	11,000	
Allowance for corporation		
income tax	2,000	−2,000
Net profit		$ 9,000

Based on the income statement of Helen's Gift City, Inc., Mrs. Bidwell's husband, who happens to be an economist, drew up the following national income accounts for the same year.

National Income Accounting
(for Helen's Gift City, Inc. 1994)

Sales	$200,000	
Purchases from all		
intermediate firms		
(wholesale)	−90,000	
Value-added GDP		$110,000
Wages and salaries	60,000	
Rent	15,000	
Capital consumption allowance	10,000	
Business taxes	14,000	
Corporation income taxes	2,000	
Profit	9,000	
Income and other contributions		$110,000

Economic Reasoning *(Write your responses on a separate sheet. Answers begin on p. 277.)*

1. What was the contribution of Helen's Gift City to total output?
2. How much did the firm add to National Income? What accounts for the difference between its contribution to GDP and its contribution to NI?
3. Which provides the more useful information about Helen's Gift City, the business accounting statement or the national income accounting statement? Why?

What Determines Domestic Output from the Demand-Side Point of View?

KEYNESIAN ECONOMICS

One of the two principal interpretations of what determines total output is the demand-side analysis based on the writings of British economist John Maynard Keynes in the 1930s. The Keynesian model assumes four demand sectors, of which we consider at this point only the three domestic sectors.

Consumption	**Investment**	**Government**
Consumption demand (C) is the largest flow of purchasing power into the economy. The size of C is determined for the most part by the amount of people's disposable income that they choose to allocate to consumption.	Investment demand (I) consists of the spending by businesses for equipment, factories, office buildings, and inventories. The investment also includes new residences. The corresponding allocation of income is savings (S), which flows to money markets.	Government demand (G) is the purchases of goods and services by federal, state, and local governments. The corresponding outflow consists of the taxes (T) paid by households and businesses.
		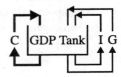

Equilibrium Output

Total output is at the domestic equilibrium level, with no tendency to increase or decrease, when the aggregate demand from the three domestic demand sectors is just equal to the amounts allocated from income to the three sectors. The economy thus will not be rising or falling when C + I + G = C + S + T. Since the allocation of income to consumption expenditures is identical to consumption demand (C = C), the condition for equilibrium GDP can be stated as:

$$I + G = S + T$$

12.5 Explain the Keynesian economic model and describe under what conditions it claims the output of the economy is at equilibrium.

A. According to the Keynesian economic model, the level of output in an economy depends upon the level of

_____

B.

1. Most people think that saving some of their money is a wise thing to do. According to the Keynesian economic model, what is a negative aspect of saving?

_____

_____

2. What is a positive aspect of saving?

_____

_____

C. Using the Keynesian point of view, indicate which of the following will result in GDP growth (G) and which will result in GDP decline (D).

1. __D__ An increase in taxes

2. __G__ An increase in business investment

3. __G__ An increase in consumer spending

4. __D__ An increase in leakages

5. __G__ An increase in government spending

6. __G__ An increase in net exports

7. __D__ An increase in net imports

D. Unlike most state and local governments, the federal government is not required to balance its budget.
   1. When the government spends more than it receives in taxes, the result is a
_Deficit_____

   2. This will have what impact on GDP?
_Increased spending_____

E.
   1. When the government spends less than it receives in taxes, the result is a
_Surplus_____

   2. This will have what impact on GDP?
_Decrease_____

F. According to the Keynesian economic model, the economy is in equilibrium when
_____

12.6 Describe what happens to GDP when leakages exceed injections of purchasing power and what happens when injections of purchasing power exceed leakages.

A. The four leakages from the GDP tank reenter the tank as additions to demand. Indicate each of the leakages and its corresponding addition.
   1. Leakage: _____C_____ Addition: _____I_____
   2. Leakage: _____S_____ Addition: _____T_____
   3. Leakage: _____T_____ Addition: _____G_____
   4. Leakage: _____I_____ Addition: _____E_____

B. Using the leakage/addition list constructed in the previous question, indicate what (if anything) will cause the leakage to be greater than the addition.
   1. _____

   2. _____

   3. _____

C. Indicate what happens to the level of output (GDP) in each of the following instances:
   1. Leakages exceed additions. _____lower_____
   2. Additions exceed leakages. _____higher_____
   3. Additions equal leakages. _____

D. Additions and leakages are very important parts of the Keynesian economic model.
   1. According to the Keynesian model, what will happen to output and employment if leakages are greater than additions?
_____

   2. What could the government do to increase additions?
_____

   3. What could the government do to decrease leakages?
_____

   4. If the government does act to increase additions and decrease leakages, what will happen to its budget?
_____

   5. If the economy is operating at full capacity, what might be a negative result of additions being greater than leakages?
_____

   6. What could the government do to decrease additions?
_____

   7. What could the government do to increase leakages?
_____

8. If the government does act to decrease additions and increase leakages, what will happen to its budget?

Case Application: Changes in Demand

Most demand that makes up GDP is consumption demand, 67% in 1993. But changes in GDP are not attributable to changes in consumption. Consumption spending does not fluctuate a great deal; it does so mainly as a result of changes in GDP and income. Consumption expenditures generally follow income changes rather than initiating them.

The variability in the different demand sectors is shown in the following table:

Growth in Major Components of Real Gross Domestic Product 1989—1993, Percentage Change

Component	Percentage Change				
	1989	1990	1991	1992	1993
Real gross domestic product	2.5	1.2	−0.7	2.6	2.9
Personal consumption expenditures	1.9	1.6	−0.4	2.5	3.3
Business fixed investment	1.7	1.3	−5.9	2.7	11.7
Residential fixed investment	−4.0	−8.9	−12.8	15.9	8.6
Government purchases of goods and services	1.9	3.2	1.4	−0.1	−0.6
Federal	−0.3	2.1	0.8	−3.6	−4.8
State and local	3.5	4.0	2.0	2.1	1.9
Net exports	−26.0	−25.7	65.1	−78.9	−132.4
Exports	11.8	8.3	6.3	6.4	3.1
Imports	3.6	3.7	−0.4	8.7	10.6

Source: U.S. Department of Commerce, Bureau of Economic Analysis.

The most stable components of aggregate demand are consumption and government spending. Investment and net foreign demand are much more variable.

Economic Reasoning *(Write your responses on a separate sheet. Answers begin on p. 277.)*

1. In 1993, which GDP component was the strongest? Which was the weakest?
2. What could account for the much more rapid growth in imports than in exports in 1993?
3. In the national income accounts, consumption spending appears to be more stable than income. Is your spending more stable than your income? Why or why not?

What Determines Domestic Output from the Supply-Side Point of View?

SUPPLY-SIDE ECONOMICS

The main alternative explanation of what determines the total output of the economy is supply-side economics, which was the foundation of "Reaganomics."

Say's Law

The roots of supply-side economics go back to the ideas of J. B. Say. According to Say's Law of Markets, "supply creates its own demand" so that production creates enough income to purchase what is produced and there will not be overproduction and unemployment.

Incentives

Modern supply-side economics emphasizes the importance of incentives in determining output. Increasing the returns to producers by reducing taxes and other costs provides an incentive for them to produce more, thereby creating jobs and income to purchase what is produced. Reducing taxes is also assumed to result in larger savings, which makes more funds available for investment.

Government Deficits

Supply-side economics emphasizes the negative effects of government deficits on the availability and cost of capital to investors in the private sector, with government borrowing crowding out private investment borrowing in the money market.

12.7 Explain Say's Law.

A. According to Say's Law, the level of aggregate demand in an economy will depend upon

_____

B.

   1. Prior to the Keynesian revolution, economists believed that if overproduction existed (if there were too many goods on the market), the problem would be corrected by

_____

   2. Keynes argued that this would *not* occur because

_____

C. If Say's Law had been correct, what would have happened to end the Great Depression of the 1930s?

_____

_____

D. In the following space draw demand (D_1) and supply (S_1) curves for the labor market. Draw a new demand curve (D_2) that represents a decrease in demand. Indicate the levels of employment and wages that J. B. Say believed would occur (Q_s and W_s), and the levels of employment and wages that J. M. Keynes believed would occur (Q_k and W_k).

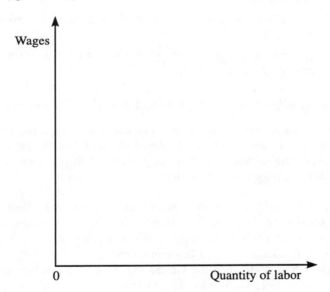

12.8 Explain how supply-side economics differs from demand-side economics.

A. Supply-side economists take a different view of the world than do Keynesian economists.

   1. According to supply-side economists, the key to increasing output is increasing the

_____

   2. Accordingly, supply-side economists believe that the best government policy for expanding output would be

_____

B. According to supply-side economists, lower tax rates will result in more output because they will increase

1. _____

2. _____

3. _____

C. Supply-siders and Keynesians have different opinions about government deficits.

   1. According to the Keynesian (demand-side) point of view, increased government deficits result in _____ aggregate demand and _____ levels of income and output.

   2. According to the supply-side point of view, increased government deficits result in higher _____ that _____ private investment and result in _____ levels of income and output.

D. Indicate which of the following statements would be favored by demand-side (Keynesian) economists (D) and which would be favored by supply-side economists (S).

1. ____ Government spending helps keep GDP high.

2. ____ Transfer payments to the poor harm the economy.

3. ____ High tax rates reduce output because they reduce incentives to produce.

4. ____ Government borrowing crowds out private investment.

5. ____ The most important benefit of lower taxes is increased disposable income and spending.

6. ____ The most important benefit of lower taxes is increased savings and investment.

7. ____ Private sector activity is more important than government activity in ensuring economic growth.

Case Application: Is War Good for the Economy?

The conventional viewpoint in the past was that war is good for the economy. The reasoning for such a view was found in the observation that the production of armaments and the supplying of troops with food, clothing, transportation, and other goods and services stimulated an increase in output and raised incomes.

The view of war as a cure for recession was bolstered by the experience at the beginning of World War II, as the United States supplied the Allies with armaments and civilian materials when hostilities began in Europe. Even before America entered the war, the increased production brought the country out of the Depression of the 1930s and caused a rapid expansion to full employment.

On the other hand, when the United States became involved in war in the Persian Gulf in January 1991 there was concern that the war would make the recession that began in the previous quarter even worse. What was the cause of this change in the conventional wisdom about the effects of war on the economy?

In part, the changed opinion about the effects of war was peculiar to that particular war. It was anticipated that the war would reduce the supply of petroleum on world markets, raising the prices of gasoline, fuel oil, and energy as a whole. If that happened, production costs would rise throughout the economy, and consumers would have less money with which to buy goods and services.

Other causes of the changed expectations about the effect of war on the economy were more general. One change in the economy since World War II has been the decline in the relative importance of manufacturing to total output. A boost to the output of military hardware would have a smaller effect on overall economic activity than it did when manufacturing was the principal production sector.

But even more important in the changed thinking was the anticipated effect of the costs of the war and how they would impact the investment sector of the economy. With government spending increased by billions of dollars to wage war, it was feared that the rising government deficit would siphon off funds from the financial markets, leaving a shortage of funds for investment.

As it turned out, the war was followed by continuing recession, which indicates that war, at least less-than-all-out war, does not have the stimulative effect on the economy that was presumed in the past.

Economic Reasoning *(Write your responses on a separate sheet. Answers begin on p. 277.)*

1. Was the earlier conventional view of the effect of war on the economy based on demand-side or supply-side economics?
2. Was the expected impact of war on the economy at the beginning of the Persian Gulf war based on demand-side or supply-side economics? What were those anticipated effects?
3. Should the U.S. government take into account the expected effects of war on the economy when it decides whether or not to go to war? Why or why not?

IV. Practice Test (Answers begin on p. 277.)

Multiple-Choice Questions *(Circle the correct answer.)*

(12.1) 1. GDP measures the total
    a. level of investment in an economy.
    b. output produced by an economy.
    c. disposable income in an economy.
    d. level of private sector output in an economy.

(12.1) 2. The largest component of GDP is
    a. personal consumption spending.
    b. business investment.
    c. government spending.
    d. net exports.

(12.1) 3. Why will the income and expenditure approaches to measuring GDP result in the same total?
    a. All leakages eventually reenter the economy as additions to aggregate demand.
    b. Total aggregate demand is always equal to the sum of its four components (C, I, G, and X).
    c. Aggregate demand is by definition always equal to aggregate supply.
    d. Every dollar spent in an economy becomes someone's income.

(12.2) 4. Which one of the following is *not* included as a part of investment spending when computing GDP?
    a. A family buys a new house.
    b. The government builds a new dam.
    c. A business increases its inventory stocks.
    d. An electric company builds a new generator.

(12.2) 5. Which one of the following is *not* one of the four expenditure categories used when calculating GDP?
    a. investment
    b. consumption
    c. savings
    d. net exports

(12.3) 6. Which one of the following will always be true during periods of inflation?
    a. The expenditure approach to measuring GDP will result in larger values than the income approach.
    b. Consumption spending will become the most volatile part of aggregate demand.
    c. Current dollar GDP will be greater than constant dollar GDP.
    d. Constant dollar GDP will decline.

(12.4) 7. Which one of the following would *not* be counted as part of GDP?
    a. production of a new home security system by ADS Security Co.
    b. Al's production of a new, finished basement in his mom's house
    c. Arista Records' production of the Crash Test Dummies' new CD
    d. government production of a new interstate highway in Nebraska

(12.5) 8. According to the Keynesian economic model, the equilibrium level of output occurs when
    a. $G + T = I + S$.
    b. $G + I = S + T$.
    c. $G + T = C + S$.
    d. $G + I = C + S$.

(12.5) 9. According to the Keynesian economic model, the most important factor in determining an economy's output is the level of
    a. taxes.
    b. aggregate demand.
    c. investment.
    d. government spending.

(12.5) 10. According to the Keynesian economic model, which one of the following will promote economic growth?
    a. Household savings increase.
    b. Investment exceeds savings.
    c. Taxes exceed savings.
    d. Government spending decreases.

(12.6) 11. According to the Keynesian model, if leakages exceed additions, output
    a. and prices will both rise.
    b. and prices will both decline.
    c. will decline, and prices will rise.
    d. will rise, and prices will decline.

(12.7) 12. What is Say's Law?
    a. the idea that all earned income will be spent
    b. the law that restricted government spending and led to the Great Depression
    c. an idea that served as the basis for the Keynesian revolution
    d. the belief that lower taxes lead to greater output

(12.7) 13. Prior to the Keynesian revolution in economic thought, economists believed that which of the following would protect an economy from prolonged recessions?
    a. flexible wages and prices
    b. the existence of government demand for goods and services
    c. the growth of GDP
    d. the existence of "crowding out"

(12.8) 14. Supply-side economists argue that which of the following is the key to economic growth?
    a. increased aggregate demand
    b. incentives to produce
    c. a strong government sector
    d. all of the above

(12.8) 15. An example of "crowding out" occurs when government
    a. tax revenues exceed government spending.
    b. taxes reduce the incentive to produce.
    c. borrowing results in less private investment.
    d. borrowing exceeds government tax revenues.

True/False Questions *(Circle T or F.)*

(12.1) 16. Both the expenditure approach and the income approach to measuring GDP should yield the same answer to the question of how much the economy produces. T or F

(12.2) 17. Personal consumption expenditures are the most unstable part of aggregate demand. T or F

(12.6) 18. According to the Keynesian economic model, GDP increases when "leakages" exceed "additions." T or F

(12.7) 19. Prior to the Keynesian revolution in economic thinking, economists believed that recessions could never last very long. T or F

(12.8) 20. Supply-side economists usually advocate a large government sector to ensure economic growth. T or F

Chapter 13

Public Finance

I. Chapter Outline

There are many goods and services that the market system cannot provide for the members of an economy. The market cannot provide national defense or public safety. The market cannot provide food, clothing, shelter, and medical care for those too poor to afford these basic necessities. When the members of a society collectively decide to provide goods and services, they do so through the institution we refer to as the "government" or the "public sector" of the economy. However, governments, whether local, state, or federal, are constrained by scarcity, just as individuals are. After determining where we, as a society, want our money spent, governments must collect money from us to pay for the programs by levying taxes.

Introductory Article: Rx Health Care Reform

Health care is taking an increasing share of both government and family budgets. Along with food and shelter, access to health care has come to be seen as a right of every American. But in recent years, increasing numbers of people have been without health insurance and, as a result, have overburdened costly emergency care facilities. This introductory article examines the reasons why health care reform has come to the forefront of public concern.

Economic Analysis

This chapter examines the issue of government (public) finance by addressing the following questions:

1. **On What Do Governments Spend Money?**

   Important Concepts: Transfer payments, Entitlements, Federal expenditures, State and local expenditures

   Case Application: Collective Choice

2. **Where Do Governments Get the Money to Spend?**

   Important Concepts: Income taxes, Payroll taxes, Excise taxes, Sales taxes, Property taxes, Fiscal federalism

   Case Application: The Numbers Game

3. **Who Pays for Government Spending?**

   Important Concepts: Horizontal equity, Vertical equity, Benefits principle, Tax efficiency, Tax incidence, Proportional taxes, Progressive taxes, Regressive taxes, Sin taxes, Marginal tax rate, Earned and nonearned income

   Case Application: Reflections in the Tax Mirror: Which Is Fairest of Them All?

Perspective: The Growth of Big Government

II. Summary of Economic Analysis

1. About one-third of the Gross Domestic Product in the United States passes through federal, state, or local governments. However, after adjusting this amount for funds that are simply **transfer payments** from some individuals to others, governments purchase about 18% of all the goods and services produced.

2. The largest federal direct expenditure is national defense, making up 16.4% of the budget. It is such direct spending that constitutes the G sector in determining GDP. Transfer payments, such as **interest on the federal debt**, are not included in GDP.

3. Most transfer payments are **entitlements**, meaning that the recipients are legally entitled to their benefits. Entitlement programs include **Social Security**, federal employee retirement benefits, **Medicaid**, **Medicare**, veterans' benefits and unemployment assistance.

4. The largest expenditure made by state and local governments is education spending.

5. Unlike the federal government, state and local governments must keep their current budgets in balance and can pay for new programs only by raising taxes.

6. The largest source of revenue for the federal government is the **individual income tax**. The second largest source is the **payroll tax** to finance Social Security.

7. State governments receive most of their revenue through the **sales tax** and local governments rely most heavily on the **property tax**.

8. Through the institutional arrangement known as **fiscal federalism**, state and local governments receive a significant share of their funds from the federal government in the form of grants.

9. In addition to providing funds to state and local governments, the federal government often **mandates** that they pay for specified programs. Often the funds provided are not sufficient to cover the costs of the programs, and this contributes to the financial squeeze felt at the state and local level.

10. A fair tax system requires **horizontal equity,** meaning that financially equal households pay the same amount of taxes. **Vertical equity** refers to the idea that those with greater financial means should pay more taxes.

11. The **benefits principle** of taxation refers to the idea that those who benefit from a government service should pay for it.

12. An **efficient tax** is one that does not result in a lower level of economic output or alter the economic behavior of citizens. A **sin tax** is a tax that is intentionally designed to be inefficient in order to provide people with an incentive not to use certain dangerous or unhealthy products.

13. The **incidence of a tax** refers to who ultimately pays the tax.

14. If a person's tax payments *as a percentage of income* increase as income increases, the tax is **progressive**. If taxes decrease as a percentage of income as income increases, the tax is **regressive**. If the proportion of income taken in taxes is constant across all income levels, the tax is **proportional**.

III. Review of the Learning Objectives *(Answers begin on p. 278.)*

On What Do Governments Spend Money?

Size of Government Spending
About 32% of all spending in the economy is channeled through governments. But governments account for only about 18% of purchases. The difference is transfer payments.

FEDERAL SPENDING	STATE AND LOCAL EXPENDITURES
National defense is the largest item in the federal budget (16.4%). Other direct expenditures account for 6.1%. The balance of federal expenditures are transfer payments for: • Social Security (22.5%) • Other income security (14.6%) • Medicare and other health programs (19.7%) • Interest on the national debt (15.2%)	Education absorbs the largest part of state and local budgets (28%). Other large expenditures include: • Public welfare (14%) • Health and hospitals (8%) • Police, fire, and corrections (7%) Interest costs on state and local government debt amount to only 4% of their budgets.

13.1 Discuss the relative size of the government in the U.S. economy.

    A. Although we think of ourselves as having a free-market economy, governments are involved in a great deal of the economic activity in the U.S. economy.

        1. Including transfer payments, governments account for what percentage of all economic activity in the United States? _____

        2. Excluding transfer payments, governments account for what percentage of all economic activity in the United States? _____

    B. Most of the growth in federal spending over the past two decades has occurred in which two types of spending?

        1. _____

        2. _____

    C. The level of total spending is greatest at the _____ level, but public employment is greatest at the _____ level of government.

    D. How have the numbers of government employees changed during the past two decades at:

        1. the federal level?_____

        2. the state and local level?_____

13.2 Distinguish between the total amount of money spent by the government sector and the amount spent on direct purchases.

    A. Money that the government spends on programs such as Social Security is not counted as direct purchases because_____.

B. The pie chart below shows the breakdown of government spending by category for 1997.

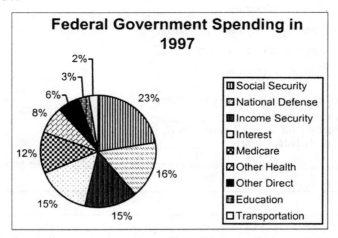

Federal Government Spending in 1997

- Social Security — 23%
- National Defense
- Income Security
- Interest
- Medicare
- Other Health
- Other Direct
- Education
- Transportation

2%, 3%, 6%, 8%, 12%, 15%, 15%, 16%

1. What percentage of government expenditures in 1997 were direct expenditures?

_____

2. What percentage of government expenditures in 1997 were transfer payments?_____

C. For each of the following, indicate whether it represents a direct government purchase (D) or a transfer payment (T).

1. ____ Alma receives a federal grant to help pay for her college tuition.

2. ____ Molly receives food stamps from the government every month.

3. ____ Tyrone works on a road crew repairing federal highways.

4. ____ The EPA purchased new copying machines for their offices.

5. ____ The Department of Defense has purchased new Army tanks.

6. ____ Jeremiah uses his Medicare prescription card to buy medicine.

13.3 List the largest expenditures made by the federal government.

A. The three largest *specific* federal government expenditures are:

1. _____

2. _____

3. _____

B.

1. Does the federal government have a bigger impact on the allocation of resources or on the allocation of incomes?

_____

2. How do you know?

_____

_____

C. Indicate which of the following expenditures Congress *can* reduce (C), and which *cannot* be reduced because they are entitlements or for some other reason (CN).

1. ____ Veterans' benefits

2. ____ Social Security payments

3. ____ Medicaid payments

4. _____ Defense expenditures

5. _____ Space exploration

6. _____ Interest payments

7. _____ Environmental programs

8. _____ Education programs

D. Which of the above programs (in exercise C) represent:
   1. Collective goods?_____
   2. Correcting for external economies?_____
   3. Income redistribution?_____

E. What are three federal expenditures that you personally benefit from?

   1. _____

   2. _____

   3. _____

13.4 List the largest expenditures made by state and local governments.

A. The largest state and local government expenditure is for

_____

B. State and local governments are allowed to borrow only in order to

_____

C. What two areas of spending have increased the most for state and local governments during the past decade?

   1. _____

   2. _____

D. Indicate which of the following are financed *primarily* by the federal government (F) and which by state and local governments (SL).

   1. _____ Education

   2. _____ Police and fire protection

   3. _____ Highways

   4. _____ Prisons

   5. _____ Defense

   6. _____ Income maintenance programs

   7. _____ Space exploration

   8. _____ Environmental cleanup

E. Indicate three expenditure programs that are creating financial pressure for your state or local government.

   1. _____

   2. _____

   3. _____

Case Application: Renovating America

Between 1948 and 1951 the United States spent nearly $12 billion helping to rebuild the Western European countries after the devastation inflicted by World War II. But the cost of that reconstruction pales in comparison to the cost of rebuilding our own country's public facilities after decades of neglect. The cost of repairing and upgrading our highways, bridges, and dams, bringing our water and sewerage systems to an adequate level, improving airports, and renovating our decrepit public transportation equipment will be in the hundreds of billions of dollars. In this time of strained government budgets, can we afford to do it?

Can we afford *not* to do it? The country's infrastructure of public facilities is deteriorating so rapidly due to lack of maintenance that failure to carry out a massive renovation program will result in increasing breakdowns, suspensions, and dangerous hazards in public services. The deterioration in the nation's infrastructure has caused a decline in private sector productivity and discouraged new private investment. Even Adam Smith noted in his 1776 book *The Wealth of Nations* (see Perspective, p. 115 of the text) that investment in infrastructure is a necessary function of government. Federal government spending on infrastructure, however, has fallen from roughly 5% of all U.S. budget outlays in the 1960s to less than 3%.

Lack of adequate infrastructure facilities is costly to individuals as well as businesses. The U.S. Department of Transportation estimates that Americans spend more than 2 billion hours a year tied up in highway traffic. It calculates an annual cost of $35 billion in lost interstate commerce due to traffic congestion.

Economic Reasoning *(Write your responses on a separate sheet. Answers begin on p. 278.)*

1. Federal spending on renewal of the nation's public facilities would increase the size of which of the pie slices in Figure 3 on page 355 of the textbook?
2. What state and local government spending in Figure 4 on page 360 of the textbook will be affected by the need to renovate the infrastructure?
3. What priority would you give to renewing America's infrastucture as compared to other types of government spending? Why?

Where Do Governments Get the Money to Spend?

FEDERAL REVENUES	STATE AND LOCAL REVENUES
• Personal income taxes (46.7%)— the largest federal revenue source • Payroll taxes (34.2%)— the second largest source • Corporate income taxes (11.5%) • Excise taxes (3.6%)	• User fees and miscellaneous (20%) • Sales taxes (17%) • Property taxes (14%) • Income taxes (12%) **Fiscal Federalism** The system by which the federal government collects revenues that it transfers to lower government levels to finance their activities

13.5 List the most important sources of revenue for the federal, state, and local governments respectively.

A. Indicate which of the following revenue sources are used *primarily* by federal (F), state (S), or local (L) governments.

1. _____ The personal income tax

2. _____ The sales tax

3. _____ Excise taxes

4. _____ Grants-in-aid

5. _____ The corporate income tax

6. _____ The property tax

7. _____ Payroll taxes

B. What is an advantage of the federal government's collecting taxes and giving grants to states and localities instead of state and local governments' raising their own tax revenues? (*Hint:* Think about the incidence of taxes and vertical equity.)

_____

_____

_____

C. Indicate which taxes it might be necessary to pay in each of the following situations (there may be more than one).

1. A person gets a paycheck.

_____

_____

2. A person spends some of his or her paycheck.

_____

_____

3. A person saves some of his or her money in a savings account or buys corporate stocks that pay dividends.

_____

_____

4. A person saves some of his or her money and buys a house.

_____

_____

D. The property tax in the United States is levied on both the value of land and the value of buildings on that land. Henry George was a late-nineteenth-century American writer who argued that the property tax should be imposed on land only. Keeping in mind that people respond to incentives, how would removing the tax on the value of buildings and taxing only land affect:

1. The supply of land?

_____

_____

2. The supply (size and number) of buildings?

_____

_____

Case Application: How to Pay for Schools

Ever since the beginning of the republic, America has paid for its schools out of property taxes. But that is changing.

One of the causes for change is taxpayer revolt over ever-mounting property taxes. The passage of Proposition 13 in California, rolling back property taxes and limiting future increases, reduced the amount of money available to school districts from local property taxes and shifted more of the financing burden to general state revenues. There were similar moves in other states.

Another factor prompting the shift of school financing is the increasing pressure for equability in funding between schools in rich and poor districts. The courts have found that vast inequities in funding between districts is not acceptable, and public policy is paying more attention to the social problems arising from the inequality.

In 1994, the people of Michigan took the biggest step yet to transform the funding of public schools. They voted to replace property taxes to finance the schools almost entirely by increasing the state sales tax from 4% to 6% and imposing higher taxes on cigarettes. Simultaneously, they mandated an increase in the minimum that a school must spend per pupil from $3,277 to $4,200.

Economic Reasoning *(Write your responses on a separate sheet. Answers begin on p. 278.)*

1. How will a change in the method of financing education affect the size of the pie slices in Figure 6 on page 362 of the text?
2. Shifting the funding of local school districts from property taxes to the state sales tax is an illustration of what principle of public finance? Why?
3. Would you want your state to follow Michigan's lead in shifting school funding from property to sales taxes? Why or why not? (You can find additional information bearing on this question in the last section of the chapter under the heading "Who Pays for Government Spending?")

Who Pays for Government Spending?

EQUITY	EFFICIENCY
Horizontal Equity People who are equally able to pay bear the same tax burden. **Vertical Equity** Those with higher incomes pay a larger percentage of their income in taxes. **Benefits Principle** Taxes are levied on the users of government services in proportion to the amount of use.	Taxes should be levied in such a way as to minimize their interference with the allocation of resources and their discouragement of production. **Sin Taxes** An exception to the above rule in the case of goods (tobacco, alcohol) that public policy wishes to discourage

INCIDENCE

Taxes are often shifted by those on whom they are levied to others. The incidence of the tax is on those who ultimately pay it. Income taxes cannot be shifted, but excise and property taxes are. Corporate profit taxes and payroll taxes are likely to be shifted to consumers in the form of higher prices and to workers in the form of lower wages.

Progressive Taxes	Regressive Taxes	Proportional Taxes
A higher percentage of tax is levied on larger incomes.	Lower-income earners pay a larger percentage of their income in taxes than higher earners.	The same percentage of income is paid in taxes at different income levels.

13.6 Explain the three criteria for equity in taxation.

A. While we all agree that taxes should be equitable, defining equity can be difficult.

1. The idea that people with equal incomes should pay equal taxes is referred to as

_____

2. The idea that taxes should be *directly* related to income is referred to as

_____

B. Many economists support a decrease in the capital gains tax so that capital gains are taxed at a lower rate than earned income. (Capital gains are the profits from the sale of assets.) Capital gains are primarily earned by people in the highest income categories. How would a reduction in the capital gains tax influence:

   1. Horizontal equity?

_____

_____

_____

   2. Vertical equity?

_____

_____

_____

C. Instead of basing taxes on some idea of equity, taxes can be based on the benefits principle of taxation.

   1. According to the benefits principle of taxation, who pays the tax that finances a specific government service?

_____

   2. Give one example of how the benefits principle is used in the United States.

_____

D. What are two types of government goods or services that cannot feasibly be financed according to the benefits principle of taxation? (*Hint:* One was discussed in chapter 8.)

   1. _____

   2. _____

E. Which of the following taxes are based on the benefits going to the taxpayer (B), and which are based on equity (ability to pay) grounds (E)?

   1. _____ The personal income tax

   2. _____ Highway gas taxes

   3. _____ The Social Security payroll tax

   4. _____ The general sales tax

   5. _____ Luxury taxes

   6. _____ Property taxes

   7. _____ Entertainment taxes on concert or movie tickets

13.7 Describe how "bad" taxes decrease economic efficiency.

A.

   1. What are "sin taxes"?

_____

   2. Explain how sin taxes could be justified because of "external" costs.

_____

_____

_____

_____

B. Indicate one way that each of the following tax policies may change behavior and cause a reallocation of resources.

1. Higher income taxes _____
2. A new tax on buildings_____
3. Higher taxes on dividends _____
4. Lower taxes on capital gains _____
5. Taxes on yellow pencils _____
6. Reduced tax deductions for charitable contributions_____

13.8 Understand what is meant by the incidence of a tax.

A. If the demand for a product is very *inelastic*, then people will continue to buy the product regardless of price increases. If the demand is *elastic*, people will switch to substitutes if the price of a product increases. Explain how the elasticity of demand can therefore influence the incidence of an excise tax.

_____

_____

_____

_____

B. Which of the following taxes is regressive, which is proportional, and which is progressive?

A		B		C	
Income	Tax	Income	Tax	Income	Tax
$10,000	$2,000	$20,000	$2,000	$10,000	$2,000
20,000	3,000	24,000	3,000	15,000	3,000
40,000	4,000	28,000	4,000	20,000	4,000

1. Tax A is_____.
2. Tax B is_____.
3. Tax C is_____.

C. If after-tax incomes are less equally distributed than before-tax incomes, then the overall tax system must be_____.

D. Which of the following taxes are regressive (R), which are progressive (P), and which are proportional (Pr)?

1. _____ The federal income tax

2. _____ Sales taxes

3. _____ Payroll taxes

4. _____ Excise taxes

5. _____ The U.S. tax system as a whole

6. _____ Gasoline taxes

7. _____ The lottery

Case Application: A Look at the Flat-Rate Tax

There are periodically proposals in Congress for a change in the income structure to a flat-rate tax. This change is a particular favorite of supply-siders, who believe that the existing tax structure discourages work and investment.

Another advantage claimed for the flat-rate tax is that it would greatly simplify the tax system, making it easier and cheaper for people to calculate their taxes and for the government to administer the system. Since it would eliminate a multiplicity of income exemptions from taxes, it should remove the existing inducements to invest in tax shelters and to devise other ways of avoiding taxes. It is alleged that this would increase the efficient allocation of our financial resources, reduce the time and expenses allocated to tax accountants and lawyers, and otherwise provide incentives for productive efforts in place of tax avoidance efforts.

Tax reforms in 1986 did eliminate most tax shelters, but the resulting tax system was at least as complicated to calculate and administer as the old system. In actuality, it increased the business of tax preparation firms.

The main objection to the flat-rate income tax is that it would make the tax system more inequitable. Federal taxes other than the income tax, as well as state and local taxes, are largely regressive. They take a higher percentage of the incomes of low-income earners than of high-income earners. Only income taxes counterbalance the regressivity of the rest of the tax system with their progressive structure.

Economic Reasoning *(Write your responses on a separate sheet. Answers begin on p. 279.)*

1. What would be the effect of a flat-rate income tax on the vertical equity of our tax system?
2. How might a flat-rate tax increase the efficiency of the tax system?
3. Are you in favor of a pure flat-rate tax, the modified flat-rate tax bill passed in 1986 (and amended in 1993), or the previous, progressive income tax system? Why?

IV. Practice Test (Answers begin on p. 279.)

Multiple-Choice Questions *(Circle the correct answer.)*

(13.0) 1. Which of the following is one of the reasons for the rapid increase in health care costs during the past 20 years?
   a. reduced government subsidies for health care insurance
   b. a lack of price competition and incentives to use every available high-tech medical procedure
   c. increasing numbers of businesses competing for employees by offering bigger and better health insurance programs
   d. the shift of health care responsibility from federal to the state and local levels of government

(13.1) 2. Government expenditures for entitlement programs are expected to increase in the coming years because
   a. more of the programs have been shifted to state and local governments.
   b. Congress has voted to expand benefits in the future.
   c. payroll tax receipts will increase and these funds are required by law to be used for entitlement programs.
   d. the U.S. population is aging and more people will become eligible for these benefits.

(13.2) 3. In the United States, about one-third of all money flow in the economy or about $2.5 trillion is channeled through the governments. However, a large part of this is in the form of transfer payments. About what percentage of federal spending is in the form of direct purchases?
   a. 12%
   b. 20%
   c. 28%
   d. 56%

(13.3) 4. Which one of the following is a *true* statement?

    a. State and local government employment has increased faster than federal government employment during the past 20 years.

    b. Federal government employment has grown faster than overall employment during the past 20 years.

    c. Both federal and state/local employment have grown at the same rate as overall employment during the past 20 years.

    d. Government employment at all levels has decreased during the past 20 years.

(13.3) 5. The three largest expenses of the federal government are

    a. defense, space exploration, and education.

    b. defense, education, and Social Security.

    c. defense, Social Security, and income security.

    d. defense, foreign aid, Social Security.

(13.3) 6. Which of the following is *not* an entitlement program?

    a. veterans' benefits

    b. Social Security

    c. grants-in-aid

    d. Medicaid

(13.4) 7. The largest state and local government expenditure is spending for

    a. income transfers and income maintenance.

    b. public safety (including police, prisons, and courts).

    c. transportation (including roads and mass transit).

    d. education.

(13.4) 8. State and local government budget deficits

    a. are collectively almost as large as the federal budget deficit.

    b. are small or nonexistent because state and local governments are more responsible than the federal government.

    c. do not usually exist because most state constitutions forbid state and local deficit spending.

    d. have increased at about the same rate as the federal budget deficit.

(13.5) 9. The largest source of federal tax revenue is the

    a. sales tax.

    b. individual income tax.

    c. corporate income tax.

    d. Social Security payroll tax.

(13.5) 10. The largest source of local tax revenue is the

    a. property tax.

    b. income tax.

    c. sales tax.

    d. excise tax.

(13.6) 11. Which one of the following helps achieve "vertical equity"?

    a. the use of state lotteries instead of taxes

    b. reducing the federal deficit by increasing everybody's taxes equally

    c. the use of more sales taxes and fewer property taxes

    d. the use of a progressive income tax

(13.6) 12. Which one of the following functions of government could *not* be financed by depending on the benefits principle of taxation?

    a. building roads

    b. providing fire protection

    c. providing a court (justice) system

    d. providing services for the poor

(13.7) 13. A tax is "efficient" if it
    a. is easy to collect.
    b. cannot be shifted from the taxpayer to someone else.
    c. is fair.
    d. does not change people's economic behavior.

(13.8) 14. The "incidence" of a tax refers to which one of the following?
    a. who ultimately pays the tax
    b. the fairness (equity) of a tax
    c. the effect of the tax on economic behavior and the allocation of resources
    d. the size of the tax relative to the taxpayer's income

(13.8) 15. Which one of the following is a tax that cannot be passed on to others?
    a. the property tax
    b. the sales tax
    c. the corporate income tax
    d. the individual income tax

True/False Questions *(Circle T or F.)*

(13.1) 16. The federal government employs about three times as many people as do state and local governments. T or F

(13.4) 17. State and local governments are usually forbidden from borrowing for any purpose. T or F

(13.5) 18. Property taxes are the primary source of local government revenues. T or F

(13.3) 19. Expenditures for entitlement programs will decrease as the population ages. T or F

(13.8) 20. The incidence of the Social Security payroll tax falls on both workers and employers. T or F

Chapter 14

Policies for Economic Stability and Growth

I. Chapter Outline

Economic growth, full employment, and stable prices are generally accepted by most economists as desirable economic goals. There is substantial disagreement, however, on the best ways to achieve these goals. Some economists believe that government intervention causes more problems than it cures and advocate a minimum of such intervention. Among those that believe that government intervention is necessary to achieve the above goals, there is disagreement as to whether the best policies are those that are based on changing government spending and taxation levels (fiscal policy) or those that are based on changing the money supply (monetary policy). Finally, there are significant disagreements between those that advocate policies that influence demand (Keynesian economics) and those that advocate policies that influence the supply side of the economy (supply-side economics).

Introductory Article: The Debt Bogeyman

The American people are rightly concerned about the immense growth in the national debt during 1981–1995, but perhaps for the wrong reasons. The debt is not bankrupting the country or shifting the payment burden to future generations. The burdens it imposes are higher interest rates and the consequent discouragement of investment, a constraint on anticyclical policy, and the threat of inflation. Americans should also view with skepticism the government's recent claims of a rapidly declining budget deficit. These figures are taken from the "unified budget" where the real budget deficit is made to look smaller due to surpluses in the Social Security trust funds. These surpluses will be depleted when the baby boom generation retires and begins to collect Social Security.

Economic Analysis

This chapter examines the ways that the federal government can influence the nation's economy by addressing the following questions:

1. **What Can the Government Do about Unemployment and Inflation?**

   Important Concepts: Stabilization, Fiscal policy, Cyclically balanced budgets, Functional finance, The golden rule

   Case Application: Who's at the Wheel?

2. **How Can Fiscal Policy Help Stabilize the Economy?**

   Important Concepts: Monetary policy, Discretionary fiscal policy, The multiplier effect, Automatic stabilizers

   Important Models: Keynesian economic model, Supply-side economic model

   Comparative Case Application: The Sun Also Sets

3. **How Can Monetary Policy Help Stabilize the Economy?**

   Important Concepts: Open market operations, Discount rate, Reserve requirement, Control of interest rates, Control of money supply, Monetary rule, Timing of discretionary policy, Recognition lag, Decision lag, Impact lag

   Important Model: The quantity theory

   Comparative Case Application: Coming Together

4. **How Can Economic Growth Be Increased?**

Important Concepts: Investment/GDP ratio, Stock options, Capital/output ratio, Labor force participation rate, Human capital

Important Model: Investment/GDP ratio

Case Application: Investing in the Future

Perspective: Monetarism—Does Money Matter?

Biography—Milton Friedman

II. Summary of Economic Analysis

1. Economic **stabilization** refers to policies that promote growth, employment, and price stability in an economy.
2. The two principal policy tools used to stabilize the economy are **fiscal policy** and **monetary policy**.
3. Fiscal policy is the use of federal government spending, taxing, and **debt management** to influence economic growth and price stability.
4. The way that the government manages its budget can have significant impacts on the economy. Four different budget philosophies are the **annually balanced budget**, the **cyclically balanced budget, functional finance,** and **the golden rule.**
5. **Discretionary fiscal policy** refers to intentional changes in tax or spending policies specifically designed to influence economic activity in a certain way.
6. **Keynesian economic theory** argues that discretionary fiscal policy should consist of government spending that makes up for inadequate or excessive aggregate demand. **Supply-side economic theory** argues that fiscal policy should be directed at stimulating savings and private investment.
7. The impact of any fiscal policy is magnified through the **multiplier effect** because increases in spending create income for individuals and/or businesses, and this income is in turn spent and becomes income for others.
8. **Automatic stabilizers** are built into the economy to help keep demand up during recessions and decrease demand during expansions. These automatically shield the economy from dramatic fluctuations in economic activity without requiring any action by the government.
9. **Monetary policy** consists of adjusting the money supply and interest rates in order to influence economic activity. Monetary policy is implemented by the Federal Reserve System.
10. Monetary policy tools include **open market operations,** changing the **discount rate,** and changing the **reserve requirement.** In order to curb inflation, the Fed may choose to reduce the money supply by selling government bonds, raising the discount rate, or raising the reserve requirement.
11. Monetary policy can be used either to control interest rates or to control the supply of money. The level of interest rates affects the economy by influencing investment. The impact of the supply of money on the economy can be evaluated by means of the **quantity equation**.
12. A problem with using monetary policy to control interest rates is that the timing of the Fed's actions becomes very important. A problem with using monetary policy to control the money supply is that the definition of the money supply and the velocity of money are constantly changing.
13. Increased **economic growth** is essential to increased standards of living.
14. To a large extent, economic growth depends on the quantity of capital in an economy. The rate of capital investment is measured by the **investment/GDP ratio**. The quality of this capital, as measured by the **capital/output ratio**, also influences the rate of growth.
15. The **labor force participation rate** measures the quantity of labor that is working with an economy's capital. **Human capital** investment improves the quality of that labor.

III. Review of the Learning Objectives *(Answers begin on p. 279.)*

What Can the Government Do about Unemployment and Inflation?

FISCAL POLICY

One arm of government stabilization policies is fiscal policy—the use of federal spending, taxing, and debt management to influence general economic activity.

BUDGET PHILOSOPHIES

Annually Balanced Budget

Balancing the federal budget each year rules out any discretionary fiscal policy by the government to counteract economic instability in the private sector.

Cyclically Balanced Budget

Balancing the federal budget over the course of the business cycle, with surpluses in boom years covering deficits during recessions, would make active government fiscal policy possible.

Functional Finance

Pursuing fiscal stabilization policies without regard to budget balance

Golden Rule

Covering current services with revenues while paying for capital expenditures with deficit financing

---

MONETARY POLICY

Monetary stabilization policies are under the control of the Federal Reserve System. The Fed implements monetary policy through its powers to manage the money supply by changing the reserves of depository institutions—reducing them to tighten the money supply in order to combat inflation or expanding them to loosen the money supply in order to encourage business expansion in a recession.

14.1 Discuss the issues surrounding the budget deficit and the national debt. *(Write in answers below.)*

A. People often argue that the national debt represents a burden on future generations of Americans.

1. The national debt represents the total amount of money that the federal government owes to lenders. What kind of securities does the federal government sell in order to borrow money?

_____

2. How does the federal government get the money to pay the people who own these securities?

_____

3. Who owns most (78%) of these securities?

_____

4. When the government pays back the people from whom it borrowed money, who is paying whom?

_____

B. As you know, the Federal Reserve System controls the supply of money in the U.S. economy, and government borrowing has a big impact on the demand for money. There is a fixed amount of money available to borrowers at a given point in time.

1. If the interest rate is the "price" of money, what happens to the rate when government borrowing causes the demand for money to increase?

_____

2. Which borrower do you think is more sensitive to changes in interest rates, the government or private business?

_____

3. What do you suppose happens to the amount of borrowing for private investment when the government must borrow billions of dollars to finance its debt?

_____

4. From the above, what is the opportunity cost (what is given up) when the government borrows to finance its debt?

_____

C. One often hears that the national debt is "large."
   1. What would be a lot of debt for you to owe to people?

_____

   2. Would the amount of debt that you indicated above be different if your last name was Rockefeller? Why?

_____

   3. It follows from the above that a given amount of debt is "large" only if it is large relative to one's _____.
   4. The national debt is therefore "large" only if it is large and growing relative to the United States' income, which is measured by the _____.

D. What is the difference between the national debt and the budget deficit?

_____

_____

14.2 Understand and explain how fiscal policy works.

A. Recall that aggregate demand is equal to $C + I + G + (X - M)$.
   1. How could fiscal policy increase C?

_____

   2. How could fiscal policy increase I?

_____

B. Suppose the U.S. economy is at the peak of a business cycle and fiscal policy is to be used to slow the economy down. How can an unexpected war in the Middle East frustrate the intent of fiscal policy?

_____

_____

C. What is the difference between Keynesian fiscal policy recommendations and supply-side fiscal policy recommendations to combat a recession?

_____

_____

14.3 Understand and explain how monetary policy works.

A. Fiscal policy is controlled by _____ while monetary policy is controlled by _____.

B. Match the stabilization policies 1–4 below with the uncontrollable event a, b, c, or d that could cause the policy to be *ineffective*.

1. Supply-side tax cuts are made in order to stimulate investment. _____

2. Demand-side (Keynesian) tax cuts are made in order to stimulate aggregate demand. _____

3. The Fed lowers the discount rate in order to increase economic activity. _____

4. The Fed increases the discount rate in order to decrease economic activity. _____

   a. Businesses decide not to borrow because their expectations about the future are gloomy.
   b. The velocity of money increases.
   c. People save their extra disposable income.
   d. People spend their extra disposable income.

C. How can "rational expectations" counteract a Fed policy of increasing the money supply to lower interest rates and stimulate investment?

1. Most people (like you!) now understand that if the money supply is increased, then the price level will __go up__ .

2. When that happens to the price level, lenders protect themselves by __increasing__ the interest rates they charge.

3. How effective will monetary policy be if people "rationally" predict the effects of the policy? _____

D. What are the effects of the following policies on GDP (up or down)? Indicate whether the policy is a fiscal policy (F) or a monetary policy (M).

	F/M	Up/Down	
1.	F	↓	Taxes increase.
2.	m	↑	The discount rate falls.
3.	m	↑	The Fed buys bonds.
4.	F	↑	Government spending increases (Keynesian theory).
5.	F	↓	Government spending increases (Supply-side theory).

14.4 Differentiate among annually balanced budgets, cyclically balanced budgets, and functional finance.

A. Independent of fiscal policies, the federal budget usually runs deficits during recessions and surpluses during expansions.

1. What causes the government budget to be in deficit during recessions?

_____

_____

2. Suppose the economy is in recession. How could requiring an annually balanced budget make the recession worse?

_____

_____

3. What causes the government budget to be in surplus during economic expansions?

_____

_____

4. Suppose the economy is at the peak of a business cycle. What problem could be caused by requiring an annually balanced budget?

_____

_____

_____

B. If the budget is to be cyclically balanced, then it will run a _____ during _____ and a _____ during _____.

C. Even though there have been a number of expansions during the past 30 years, the federal government has not had a surplus since 1969. Even if Congress believes in cyclically balanced budgets, why is it politically so much easier to have a deficit than it is to have a surplus? (*Hint:* How do you think voters feel about taxes? How do you think voters feel about federal spending projects in their regions?)

_____

_____

_____

D. Indicate whether each of the following is most descriptive of an annually balanced budget (A), a cyclically balanced budget (C), or functional finance (F).

1. _C_ The government should run a deficit during recessions.

2. _F_ Permanent budget deficits are acceptable.

3. _A_ Government spending would need to be cut during recessions.

4. ____ This would cause higher highs and lower lows in the business cycle.

5. _C_ Current deficits should be balanced by future surpluses.

Case Application: The Balanced Budget Amendment

A proposed amendment to the U.S. Constitution would require an annually balanced budget. Proponents of such an amendment maintain that Congress has been unwilling to curb the large federal deficits that have fueled inflation, increased the national debt, and caused higher interest rates. They claim that a constitutional amendment is necessary to prevent the government from running deficits except in times of emergency.

The text of one proposed balanced budget amendment is shown below.

SECTION 1. Prior to each fiscal year, the Congress shall adopt a statement of receipts and outlays for that year in which total outlays are no greater than total receipts. The Congress may amend such statement provided revised outlays are no greater than revised receipts. Whenever three-fifths of the whole number of both houses shall deem it necessary, Congress in such statement may provide for a specific excess of outlays over receipts by a vote directed solely to that subject. The Congress and the president shall, pursuant to legislation or through exercise of their powers under the first and second articles, ensure that actual outlays do not exceed the outlays set forth in such statement.

SECTION 2. Total receipts for any fiscal year set forth in the statement adopted pursuant to this article shall not increase by a rate greater than the rate of increase in national income in the year or years ending not less than six months nor more than 12 months before such fiscal year, unless a majority of the whole number of both Houses of Congress shall have passed a bill directed solely to approving specific additional receipts and such bill has become law.

SECTION 3. The Congress may waive the provisions of this article for any fiscal year in which a declaration of war is in effect.

SECTION 4. Total receipts shall include all receipts of the United States except those derived from borrowing and total outlays shall include all outlays of the United States except those for repayment of debt principal.

SECTION 5. The Congress shall enforce and implement this article by appropriate legislation.

SECTION 6. This article shall take effect for the second fiscal year beginning after its ratification.

Economic Reasoning *(Write your responses on a separate sheet. Answers begin on p. 279.)*

1. Could Congress circumvent the requirement for a balanced budget in this amendment? How?
2. What would be the consequences for implementing fiscal policy if the balanced budget amendment were to pass?
3. Are you in favor of or opposed to the balanced budget amendment? Why?

How Can Fiscal Policy Help Stabilize the Economy?

DISCRETIONARY FISCAL POLICY

Keynesian Approach

Keynesians focus on the use of fiscal policy to compensate for inadequate or excessive demand in the private sector by increasing government spending and decreasing taxes in a recession or by reducing government spending and increasing taxes in a period of inflation.

Multiplier

The impact on the economy of a change in taxes or government spending is increased by the multiplier effect:

$$\text{Multiplier} = \frac{1}{\text{Savings rate} + \text{Tax rate}}$$

Supply-Side Approach

Supply-side fiscal policy would reduce both taxes and government spending in a recession. The decreases in taxes would be directed toward savers rather than consumers.

Automatic Stabilizers

Besides discretionary fiscal policy, there are various automatic stabilizers in government spending and taxing, such as transfer payments and progressive tax rates, that counteract recession and inflation.

14.5 Explain how discretionary fiscal policy works from the Keynesian and supply-side viewpoints.

A. Indicate which of the following are Keynesian (K) and which are supply-side (S) views of the way that different policies affect the economy.

1. _S_ Tax cuts to upper-income groups will increase saving and investment.
2. _K_ Tax cuts to lower-income groups will stimulate aggregate demand.
3. _S_ Budget deficits "crowd out" private investment.
4. _K_ Budget deficits stimulate the economy.
5. _S_ If the government used fewer resources, more resources would be free to increase private spending.
6. _S_ Government policies should be directed toward increasing the economy's productive capacity.
7. _K_ Government spending is sometimes necessary in order to get the economy out of a recession.

B. Which of the two types of policy prescriptions, Keynesian or supply-side, takes a longer-run view of economic policy? How do you know?

Supply-side

C. Keynesians and supply-side economists look at the effect of policy on the "GDP tank" in different ways.

    1. _____ economic policy is directed at increasing economic activity by filling up the GDP tank.

    2. _____ economic policy is directed at increasing the size of the GDP tank.

14.6 Describe the multiplier and the multiplier effect.

A. For each of the following savings and tax rates, indicate the size of the *multiplier* and how much income will increase from an initial expenditure of $100 (include the original $100 in your calculations of how much income will increase).

	Savings Rate	Tax Rate	The Multiplier Equals	Total Income Will Increase
1.	0.10	0.00	_____	$_____
2.	0.10	0.10	_____	$_____
3.	0.20	0.10	_____	$_____
4.	0.40	0.10	_____	$_____
5.	0.50	0.50	_____	$_____

B. What would the multiplier be equal to if savings rates and tax rates together approached zero?

_____

C. An old proverb says that a fool and his money are soon parted. A Keynesian might revise the proverb to say that a fool and his money stimulate the economy.

    1. According to Keynesians, is there an inverse, direct, or constant relationship between the savings rate and the level of economic activity?

_____

    2. The "consumption rate" is equal to (1 − the savings rate): as the savings rate increases the consumption rate decreases, and vice versa. With this in mind, can you think of a good economic justification for encouraging people to spend rather than save?

_____

_____

    3. The savings rate and tax rate in the United States both decreased during the 1980s. From a Keynesian point of view, what impact would this have on income in the United States?

_____

D. Suppose the government determined that incomes needed to be increased by $1 billion in order to bring the economy out of a recession. How much would the government need to spend in direct spending (G) in each of the following situations?

    1. The multiplier equals 5._____

    2. Tax plus savings rates equal 0.25._____

    3. Tax plus savings rates equal 0.10._____

14.7 Define and give examples of automatic stabilizers.

A. Automatic stabilizers cannot reverse a trend in economic activity, but they can

_____

B. Automatic stabilizers are designed to automatically increase or decrease the level of economic activity in an economy.

    1. During downturns in the economy, automatic stabilizers

_____

Don't need to use the multiplier / Just know what it is a does

2. During upturns in the economy, automatic stabilizers

_____

C. Which of the components of aggregate demand is most influenced by automatic stabilizers?

_____

D. Indicate (with a check) which of the following are automatic stabilizers.

    1. ____ Unemployment compensation

    2. ____ Progressive income taxes

    3. ____ Defense spending

    4. ____ Aid to Families with Dependent Children

    5. ____ Property taxes

Case Application: What Happens to Tax-Cut Dollars?

A principal point of contention between Keynesian and supply-side proponents concerns the proper function of tax reductions. According to the Keynesians, tax-cut money should be used by consumers to purchase goods and services—thereby stimulating output, employment, and incomes. Supply-siders, on the other hand, believe that tax-cut dollars should go into savings, which would be available for real investment—thereby reducing costs, increasing output, creating jobs, and increasing incomes.

Tax legislation in the 1980s was oriented toward tax reductions for business and high-income taxpayers who have a larger propensity to save. Fully 35% of the total tax-cut dollars went to the 5.6% of income earners making over $50,000 a year. Increases in Social Security taxes and tax bracket creep resulting from inflation ate up all of the tax-cut dollars of those earning less than $50,000 a year.

The supply-side strategy requires an increase in the savings rate. However, research has shown the savings rate to be quite constant over time. Furthermore, although the average savings rate is greater for high-income earners than for low-income earners, the marginal propensity to save is about the same for both groups. Those earning over $50,000 a year are no more likely to save their tax-cut dollars than those earning under $50,000.

Another assumption of the supply-side tax cuts was that increasing the after-tax rate of return on savings would cause an increase in the savings rate. Studies do not support this assumption. Some people are induced to save more when the after-tax rate of return is increased. However, people whose objective is a specific level of future income from their assets can achieve that objective with a lower savings rate when the after-tax rate of return on savings is increased. These two groups cancel each other out, leaving the overall rate of savings unaffected by changes in the after-tax rate of return.

Economic Reasoning *(Write your responses on a separate sheet. Answers begin on p. 280.)*

1. What discretionary fiscal policy measure is discussed in this application?
2. Does the multiplier effect work on tax-cut dollars as well as on government expenditure dollars? How?
3. Was the tax legislation passed in the 1980s wise and effective fiscal policy? Why or why not?

How Can Monetary Policy Help Stabilize the Economy?

MONETARY POLICY TOOLS

Open Market Operations

The Fed offers to buy or sell government securities on the open market. Buying increases bank reserves and encourages expansion of money supply, while selling decreases reserves and reduces money supply.

Discount Rate Changes

The Fed reduces discount rate on loans to banks in order to encourage an increase in reserves and expand money supply and raises discount rate to discourage bank borrowing of reserves and to reduce money supply.

Required Reserve Ratio Changes

The Fed reduces the percentage of the banks' liabilities that they must have on deposit in their reserves in the Federal Reserve Bank to permit an increase in the money supply and increases the percentage required in order to reduce the money supply.

MONETARY POLICY TARGETS

Control of Interest Rates

The traditional target of Fed monetary policy was the control of interest rates. Bringing about a decline in interest rates stimulated economic activity, while raising interest rates was deflationary.

Control of Money Supply

The alternative target of monetary policy is control of the money supply. The Fed sets a target for growth of the money supply sufficient to finance expansion of the economy, but restrictive enough to prevent inflation.

Weakness of Both Monetary and Fiscal Policy Timing of Discretionary Policy

To be effective, expansionary policy should impact the economy as it is entering a recession, and contractionary policies when inflation is about to set in. However, there are lags in implementing such policies.

Recognition lag— time it takes policymakers to recognize the problem

Decision lag—time it takes government or Fed to determine course of action

Impact lag—time it takes policy to have an impact on economy

14.8 Explain how the Fed implements monetary policy.

A. Indicate what effect (increase or decrease) each of the following will have on the supply of money (MS), interest rates (R), investment (I), and aggregate demand (AD).

1. The Fed lowers the discount rate.
   MS __↑__   R __↓__   I __↑__   AD __↑__

2. The Fed buys bonds in the open market.
   MS __↑__   R __↓__   I __↑__   AD __↑__

3. The Fed increases reserve requirements.
   MS __↓__   R __↑__   I __↓__   AD __↓__

B. The Fed can use its policies to attempt to control interest rates or to attempt to control the size of the money supply.

1. Prior to 1979, the aim of the monetary policy carried out by the Fed was to control _____.

2. Since 1979, the Fed's monetary policy has concentrated on controlling the

_____.

3. A problem with this system is that it is difficult to know what makes up the money supply, much less control it. Financial deregulation has resulted in new types of bank accounts that function both as _____ deposits (money) and _____ accounts (near money).

C. Sometimes the actions of the Fed and the government counteract each other. The demand for money is directly related to the level of economic activity. The demand curve for money shifts to the right when the aggregate demand for goods and services increases, and vice versa.

   1. Using the graph below, show what happens if the Fed *decreases* the supply of money in order to reduce inflation while the government uses fiscal policy to *increase* economic activity. (*Hint:* A decrease in the supply of money is shown by a leftward shift of the supply curve.)

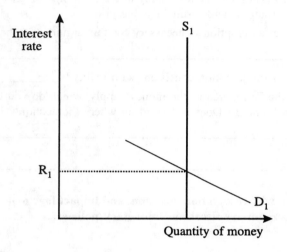

   2. What impact would the Fed's policy have on government plans to increase economic activity?
      a. Interest rates would_____.
      b. Investment would_____.
      c. Aggregate demand would_____.

   3. Would the Fed's actions help or hinder the government's fiscal policy efforts?

_____

D. Sometimes the actions of the Fed and the government reinforce one another.

   1. Using the graph below, show what happens if the Fed *increases* the supply of money while the government is conducting expansionary fiscal policy.

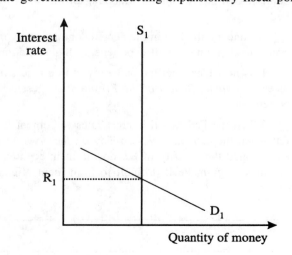

2. What happens to interest rates when the Fed increases the money supply while the government is using expansionary fiscal policy?

_____

3. What would be a *negative* consequence of keeping interest rates low in this situation?

_____

4. What would be the effect on interest rates if the Fed *does not* increase the money supply while expansionary fiscal policy is being used?

_____

E. According to monetarists, the quantity theory of money ($M \times V = P \times T$) shows that increasing the money supply at the same rate of growth as increases in transactions (output) will result in stable prices.

1. What assumption is necessary for this argument to be correct?

_____

2. Is this assumption consistent with reality? _____

3. If the Fed increases the money supply, which do you think will increase, P, T, or both P and T? Does it depend on where the economy is in the business cycle?

_____

_____

14.9 Explain why recognition, decision, and impact lags make it difficult to properly time discretionary fiscal and monetary policies.

A.

1. A recognition lag is the time that it takes _____ to recognize that the economy is entering a recession or that inflation is increasing.

2. A decision lag is the time that it takes _____ to determine a course of discretionary action.

3. An impact lag is the time that it takes _____ to have an impact on the country's economic activity.

B. In the space provided, identify each problem below as a Recognition lag (R), a Decision lag (D), or an Impact lag (I).

1. _____ The economic indicators suggest a recession on the horizon. This will be discussed at next month's meeting of the Open Market Committee of the Fed.

2. _____ In January, the Fed implemented contractionary monetary policies. However, the economy is still experiencing high inflation.

3. _____ It is now clear that the economy is in a recession even though the most recent *Economic Report of the President* suggested that the downturn would be temporary.

4. _____ When the Fed raised interest rates to combat inflation, the results were felt when the economy was already on the downturn. Therefore, the action exacerbated the severity of the downturn in economy activity.

C. Why do these lags make it difficult to implement effective fiscal and monetary policies?

_____

_____

Case Application: **The Interest Rate Yo-Yo**

In 1981 more than 2,000 construction firms went out of business. They went broke because housing construction fell to the lowest level in years, with hundreds of thousands of construction workers out of a job. The National Association of Realtors lost 70,000 members between 1978 and 1981. Other industries also had high mortality rates. In 2½ years some 2,600 automobile dealerships closed their doors. There was a 41% jump in business failures in 1981 as small businesses and farmers suffered foreclosures.

This havoc in the business world was not caused by a major depression but rather by sky-high interest rates—rates as high as 23% for construction loans alone. Potential housing buyers were unable or unwilling to take out mortgage loans at interest rates of 16% or 17%. Consequently, many construction firms were forced into bankruptcy by the banks that underwrote their construction loans.

New car dealers were in the same sort of bind, often paying $142 a month in interest costs on every $10,000 automobile they had in inventory. With new car sales moving so slowly, the interest costs simply became more than many dealers could handle.

It was previously unheard of for established businesses with excellent credit ratings to pay a prime rate over 20%, as they did for a short time in 1981. Home builders, farmers, and other small businesses frequently had to pay a premium of 2 or 3 percentage points above the prime interest rate. The super-high interest rates were a part of the government strategy for bringing down the inflation rate. It was a strategy that exacted a high price from thousands of small business owners.

With escalating government debt in the early 1990s, the question that is being asked is whether we will repeat the sky-high interest rate experience of a decade earlier.

Economic Reasoning *(Write your responses on a separate sheet. Answers begin on p. 280.)*

1. One reason interest rates were so high in 1981 was because of Federal Reserve open market operations. How would open market operations result in raising the interest rates paid by businesses?
2. As a result of the 1979 change in Federal Reserve Board strategy from controlling interest rates to controlling the money supply, interest rates have fluctuated widely. What are the consequences of wide fluctuations in interest rates?
3. Do you think the objective of controlling the money supply justifies the wide swings in interest rates? Why or why not?

How Can Economic Growth Be Increased?

IMPORTANCE OF ECONOMIC GROWTH
Our standard of living is largely determined by the rate of growth, and a higher growth rate makes it easier to solve many economic problems.

Increasing Capital Investment	Increasing Capital Efficiency	Increasing the Labor Force Participation Rate	Increasing Investment in Human Capital
Economic growth can be increased by raising the proportion of the nation's output that we put into the formation of capital.	Increasing the quality of capital investment by using more technologically advanced equipment and production methods is a major source of economic growth.	Economic growth is increased when a larger percentage of the population is active in the nation's labor force. Increased participation by women in the labor force in the last 2 decades has contributed in a quite significant way to U.S. economic growth.	The quality of the labor force is a determinant of the rate of economic growth. Investment in education and also in more occupational and on-the-job training increases the growth rate.
Investment/GDP Ratio The fraction of each year's GDP that is allocated to creating investment goods	**Capital/Output Ratio** The ratio of the cost of new investment goods to the value of annual output produced by those goods		

14.10 Explain the investment/GDP ratio and the capital/output ratio and explain why they are important.

   A.

      1. What is the primary opportunity cost of increasing the investment/GDP ratio?

          _____

      2. What is the primary benefit of increasing the investment/GDP ratio?

          _____

   B. Increased productivity is indicated by a(n) _____ in the capital/output ratio.

   C. Are the investment/GDP and capital/output ratios measures of the quality or quantity of capital in an economy?

      1. Investment/GDP ratio_____

      2. Capital/output ratio_____

   D. Indicate which of the following will result in an improved investment/GDP ratio (I) and which will result in an improved capital/output ratio (C).

      1. _C_ Improved technology

      2. _I_ Lower interest rates

      3. _C_ Better human capital

      4. _C_ The use of process innovations

      5. ____ A longer-term profit perspective

      6. ____ A smaller federal budget deficit

      7. ____ Computer-assisted manufacturing techniques

      8. ____ Just-in-time manufacturing techniques

   E. List three types of *public* investment that can lead to improved economic growth.

      1. _____

2. _____

3. _____

14.11 Describe the effects on economic growth of the labor force participation rate and investment in human capital.

A. Do the labor force participation rate and human capital investment reflect increased labor quantity or quality?

   1. Labor force participation rate_____

   2. Human capital investment_____

B. What are three reasons for the increased labor force participation rate in the United States?

   1. _____

   2. _____

   3. _____

C. What are two ways that people can invest in their human capital?

   1. _____

   2. _____

D. Similar to investing in physical capital, a person investing in human capital must compare the costs of the investment to the expected benefits.

   1. What is a person's biggest cost of investing in human capital?

   _____

   2. Why would you expect an *inverse* relationship between a person's age and that person's investment in human capital?

   _____

E. Rank the following in the order of time that it takes for each to occur (1 is the quickest, 4 the slowest).

   1. ____ Increases in the labor force participation rate

   2. ____ Increases in the investment/GDP ratio

   3. ____ Increases in productivity stemming from human capital investment

   4. ____ Increases in the capital/output ratio

Case Application: How to Grow

A growing economy is one that spends today to increase tomorrow's production. Money and effort are poured into education and research, as well as into new and better machines. However, disagreements arise over the relative effectiveness of money and time invested in different areas. The table below shows the relationship between changes in spending for research and development (R & D) and changes in the Gross Domestic Product for the years 1961–1992.

Average Annual Percentage Changes in Research and Development Outlays and Gross Domestic Product
Constant Dollars, 1961–1992

| | *Percent Change* | | | | | |
	1961–65	1966–70	1971–75	1976–80	1981–85	1986–92
R & D Outlay	6.5	1.2	−0.2	4.1	4.4	1.1
GDP	5.1	3.1	2.4	3.2	2.6	2.2

The figures on average annual changes in research and development outlays and Gross Domestic Product show a rough correlation between the two. Lower rates of increase in research and development spending are associated with lower rates of increase in Gross Domestic Product. The one exception is in the early 1980s.

This relationship does not necessarily show that changes in research and development spending cause changes in Gross Domestic Product, however. The benefits of research and development outlays may not show up in the growth of GDP for a period of time, perhaps years after the research and development takes place. The relationship may very well be the other way around: changes in the rate of growth of GDP may cause changes in the rate of growth of research and development outlays.

Another contributor to growth in GDP is education. The chart below shows the median years of education completed by those aged 25 to 29 years old.

Between 1940 and 1980 there was a 2.6-year increase in the median number of school years completed by those in the age group just having passed through the school-age period. That increase came to a halt in the decade of the 1980s. There was no increase whatsoever in the median number of school years completed by those in the post–school-age group. Considering the increasingly technical nature of production and the necessity for a more skilled and trained work force, the economic growth rate is thus impeded.

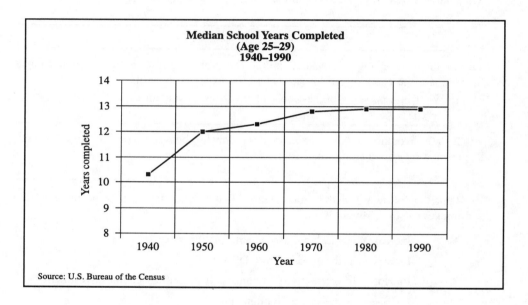

**Median School Years Completed
(Age 25–29)
1940–1990**

Source: U.S. Bureau of the Census

Economic Reasoning (*Write your responses on a separate sheet. Answers begin on p. 281.*)

1. What are the factors discussed in this application that affect economic growth?
2. Why should the rate of growth of R & D increase when GDP is growing faster and decrease when GDP growth slows?
3. Judging from the relationships shown in the data in this application, what measures do you think should be taken to increase the rate of growth in GDP?

IV. Practice Test (Answers begin on p. 281.)

Multiple-Choice Questions (*Circle the correct answer.*)

(14.1) 1. A very real problem with large budget deficits is that they result in _____ interest rates and _____ private capital formation.
    a. lower; lower
    b. lower; higher
    c. higher; lower
    d. higher; higher

(14.1) 2. It is often argued that the national debt imposes a burden on future generations. This would only be a valid argument if
   a. the Fed lowered interest rates at the same time.
   b. private investment was increasing.
   c. foreigners owned a large share of the debt.
   d. the government did not want to use fiscal policy.

(14.2) 3. Fiscal policy includes all of the following *except*
   a. controlling interest rates.
   b. controlling the size of government spending.
   c. automatic stabilizers.
   d. tax changes.

(14.3) 4. Monetary policy is controlled by
   a. Congress.
   b. the Federal Reserve System.
   c. the Department of the Treasury.
   d. the Office of Management and Budget.

(14.4) 5. Which one of the following problems might result from an annually balanced budget?
   a. an increased money supply and inflation
   b. decreased aggregate demand that could make an existing recession worse
   c. Congress's using fiscal policy to obtain political, rather than economic, objectives
   d. higher interest rates and less investment

(14.4) 6. The goal of functional finance is to
   a. keep the federal budget in balance.
   b. keep the economy growing.
   c. prevent inflation.
   d. all of the above

(14.5) 7. According to Keynesian economic policy, the objective of tax cuts is to
   a. increase government spending.
   b. stimulate saving and investment.
   c. increase the money supply.
   d. increase consumer spending.

(14.5) 8. According to supply-side economic policy, the objective of tax cuts is to
   a. increase government spending.
   b. stimulate saving and investment.
   c. increase the money supply.
   d. increase consumer spending.

(14.6) 9. The size of the multiplier depends on
   a. the velocity of money.
   b. tax and savings rates.
   c. the level of government spending.
   d. the size of the budget deficit.

(14.6) 10. The multiplier shows how much a change in _____ affects the level of _____.
   a. taxes; government spending
   b. spending; income
   c. saving; investment
   d. interest rates; investment

(14.7) 11. Which one of the following is considered to be an automatic stabilizer?
   a. investment in public infrastructure
   b. unemployment compensation
   c. health care
   d. defense spending

(14.8) 12. If the money supply increases at the same rate as output, prices will remain stable as long as
   a. the federal budget is balanced.
   b. taxes do not change.
   c. the capital/output ratio remains constant.
   d. the velocity of money is constant.

(14.9) 13. Five years ago, the government in the country of Nojobs increased government spending on goods and services in order to stimulate employment. However, the unemployment rate in Nojobs is still 64%. This unfortunate state of affairs is most likely attributable to which of the following types of lags in policy implementation?
   a. impact lag
   b. decision lag
   c. recognition lag
   d. standard-of-living lag

(14.10) 14. Increasing the investment/GDP ratio will result in
   a. an improved standard of living in the future.
   b. higher interest rates.
   c. increased consumption spending at the present time.
   d. improvements in the quality of capital.

(14.11) 15. The labor force participation rate in the United States
   a. is a measure of the quality of U.S. labor.
   b. decreased steadily in the 1970s because of high income taxes.
   c. is among the highest in the world.
   d. is directly related to investment in human capital.

True/False Questions *(Circle T or F.)*

(14.1) 16. The ratio of the national debt to GDP is higher now than it has ever been. T or F

(14.4) 17. Requiring an annually balanced budget would make it very difficult to implement fiscal policy. T or F

(14.5) 18. Supply-side economists and Keynesian economists both believe in the use of tax cuts as a policy to increase economic growth. T or F

(14.6) 19. The formula used to calculate the multiplier implies that income will increase the most when people have low savings rates. T or F

(14.8) 20. Fiscal policy involves adjusting taxes, government spending, and interest rates. T or F

Macroeconomics Crossword Puzzle (Chapters 10–14)

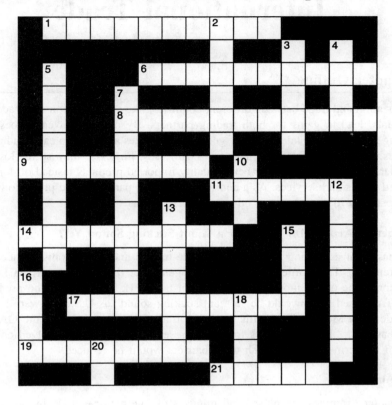

Across

1. Both the money supply and total income are affected by this process.
6. The lack of work that occurs from time lost changing jobs is _____ unemployment.
8. The largest revenue source for the federal government.
9. This type of inflation comes from supply-side economics.
11. British economist who developed the demand-side analysis of how the economy works.
14. A period of generally rising prices in the economy as a whole.
17. The paper money that the U.S. federal government printed in order to help finance the Civil War.
19. Social Security is this type of payment.
21. This type of tax is one of the largest sources of state and local government revenues.

Down

2. When measuring the economy, this should equal the value of output.
3. Education is a major expenditure for this level of government.
4. The CPI expresses the price of consumer goods as a percentage of the price prevailing in the _____ period.
5. _____increases the money supply.
6. The economic policies followed by the United States in the 1980s.
7. _____income determines the amount of consumer spending.
10. The central bank of the United States (slang).
12. If the amount of money in circulation in an economy is tied to the amount of gold held by the banking system, this is known as the gold_____.
13. The functional_____economic philosophy sees noninflationary full employment as the most important economic goal.
15. Unemployment occurs when there is a lack of _____.
16. One of the functions of money is that it is a common denominator for exchanges. It provides a _____ of measurement or account.
18. This clause, built into labor union contracts, automatically raises wages when the CPI reaches a specified point.

Chapter 15
International Trade

I. Chapter Outline

Specialization and trade between different countries, like specialization and trade between individuals, lead to gains for both trading partners. By doing what each does best and engaging in trade, the total amount of goods and services available to each trading partner increases. Some specific individuals and businesses, however, may suffer losses when consumers buy less expensive or better quality imported products instead of domestically produced goods and services. As a consequence, these parties would prefer to limit trade by imposing tariffs, quotas, and other trade restrictions.

Introductory Article: Do You Hear a Giant Sucking Sound Yet?

There has been a running battle between free-traders and protectionists since the birth of the republic. This battle was played out again over the North American Free Trade Agreement. One of the more vocal protectionists was H. Ross Perot, who predicted that if NAFTA passed there would be "a giant sucking sound" as U.S. jobs were drawn over the border into Mexico. The battle over free trade was intense during the GATT negotiations as well. It took 7 years for the representatives from the involved countries to agree on the terms through which trade barriers would be reduced.

Economic Analysis

This chapter examines the pluses and minuses of international trade by addressing the following questions:

1. **Why Do We Trade with Other Countries?**

   Important Concepts: Imports, Exports, Absolute advantage, Comparative advantage, Specialization, Increasing costs, Limited specialization

   Comparative Case Application: Europe Calling

2. **Who Benefits and Who Is Hurt by Foreign Trade?**

   Important Concepts: Consumer benefits, Import-competing industry, Producer and worker benefits, Free trade, Mobility of capital and labor, Trade adjustment assistance

   Case Application: Flying Carpets and Grounded Computers

3. **How Do We Restrict Foreign Trade?**

   Important Concepts: Tariffs, Bilateral trade negotiations, Multilateral trade negotiations, Most-favored nations, GATT, Quotas, Nontariff barriers, Export embargoes

   Case Application: Protection, Japanese-Style

4. **Should Foreign Trade Be Restricted?**

   Important Concepts: Protectionism, Infant industry argument, Terms of trade, Neomercantilists

   Case Application: Bastiat's Petition

Perspective: Smoot-Hawley Revisited

II. Summary of Economic Analysis

1. International trade can be based on either **absolute** or **comparative advantage**.
2. When a country has either type of advantage, it can gain by **specializing** in the production of one good and trading it for other goods.
3. Specialization is **limited** because of **increasing costs**.
4. **Consumers benefit** from foreign trade because competition from imports results in a greater selection and/or lower prices.
5. Many **producers benefit** from foreign trade because it gives them access to raw materials that can be found only in other countries, and it provides them with larger markets for their output.
6. When domestic output is exported, **workers benefit** from foreign trade because their exports provide jobs for domestic workers.
7. Producers and workers in **import-competing industries** can suffer if consumers purchase available imported goods instead of domestically produced goods.
8. If import-competing firms decline at the same time that exporting industries are growing, capital and labor should move from the former to the latter. Unfortunately, labor and capital are not always **mobile** between different types of production, and, as a consequence, they may suffer unemployment. **Trade adjustment assistance** is given by governments to firms and workers injured by foreign competition.
9. Taxing imported goods by placing a **tariff** on them raises their prices and improves the competitive position of domestic firms.
10. Domestic firms can also be protected from import competition by imposing **quotas** that limit the quantity of certain goods that can be imported.
11. **Nontariff barriers** to trade include licensing, testing, labeling, and other bothersome details that make it difficult for consumers to import foreign products.
12. **Export embargoes** prohibit the sale of certain goods to other countries in order either to protect domestic technology or to impose economic hardships on unfriendly countries.
13. In order to increase trade, countries often reduce tariffs and quotas through **bilateral trade negotiations** with another country. To reduce confusion and multiple tariff structures, **most-favored-nation clauses** extend such reductions to all nations that reciprocate.
14. Beginning in 1947, the United States and other countries began to negotiate trade agreements simultaneously through **multilateral trade negotiations**.
15. Among their arguments against free trade, **protectionists** claim that American workers need help in competing with cheap foreign labor, that imports reduce domestic aggregate demand and reduce GDP, and that **infant industries** need protection from import competition while they develop.
16. The amounts of a country's imports and exports can be influenced by the **terms of trade**—the relative prices of imports and exports.
17. The **mercantilists** were seventeenth-century economists who believed that a country's wealth came from its stocks of gold and that gold should not be exported. **Neomercantilists** are modern economists who believe that a country's comparative advantage lies in its technology and that a country should avoid exporting this technology.

III. Review of the Learning Objectives *(Answers begin on p. 281.)*

Why Do We Trade with Other Countries?

ABSOLUTE ADVANTAGE	COMPARATIVE ADVANTAGE
When a country has the resources that enable it to produce one good more cheaply than a second country, and the second country has the resources to produce another good more cheaply than the first country, each country will benefit from producing the good in which it has an absolute advantage and trading part of its production for the good in which it has the disadvantage.	When one country has an absolute advantage over a second country in the production of two goods but has a greater advantage in the production of one of the two goods than the other, it will benefit both countries for each to produce the good in which it has a comparative advantage and trade with the other country for the good in which it has a comparative disadvantage.

SPECIALIZATION

Nations tend to specialize their production in accordance with their available resources. Those countries with an abundance of capital relative to labor specialize in high-technology industries, while countries that lack large capital resources specialize in labor-intensive industries.

Increasing Costs

For most products, specialization is not complete. Because the amounts of resources that are suited to the production of a particular good are limited, as more of the good is produced there are increasing production costs that prevent the country from producing all of the good that it consumes. The difference is imported.

15.1 Explain the difference between absolute and comparative advantage. *(Write in answers below.)*

A. Suppose Mexico can produce 3 units of textiles and 6 units of oil with 1 unit of labor. Also suppose that Nigeria can produce 1 unit of textiles and 4 units of oil with 1 unit of labor.

1. Mexico has a(n) _____ advantage in the production of both goods.
2. One unit of textiles costs Mexico _____ units of oil.
3. One unit of textiles costs Nigeria _____ units of oil.
4. Which country is the lower-cost producer of textiles?

_____

5. One unit of oil costs Mexico _____ units of textiles.
6. One unit of oil costs Nigeria _____ units of textiles.
7. Which country is the lower-cost producer of oil?

_____

8. Which country has a comparative advantage in the production of oil?

_____

9. Which country has a comparative advantage in the production of textiles?

_____

10. Who should trade what for what?

_____

_____

15.2 Explain why specialization is sometimes complete, but normally is limited.

A. Under what conditions will complete specialization characterize the trade between two countries?

_____

_____

B. The effects of specialization can be analyzed with the production possibilities frontier.

1. What does a straight-line (uncurved) production possibility frontier imply about the cost of one good relative to the other as production increases?

_____

_____

2. In actuality, PPFs are curved because costs

_____

_____

3. This is due to the fact that resources are not

_____

4. When the PPF is curved, it indicates that when a country produces only one good, the last unit of that good produced is extremely

_____

5. Because of this, specialization will be

_____

15.3 Compare the types of goods exported by the United States to the types of goods imported.

A. Indicate whether each of the following is best characterized as a U.S. import (I) or export (E):

1. _____ Petroleum

2. _____ Autos and auto parts

3. _____ Food and animal products

4. _____ Textiles and clothing

5. _____ Chemicals

6. _____ Aircraft and parts

B. Where do people and businesses in other countries get the dollars necessary to buy goods and services from American producers?

_____

C. The United States tends to specialize in the export of goods that are _____-intensive while importing goods that are _____-intensive.

Case Application: U.S. Farmers Selling Overseas

The United States is a major source of food and other agricultural products for the rest of the world. We export a large percentage of the crops grown in this country—more than 40%. In 1992 we exported $42.1 billion of agricultural products, a new record.

The United States is by far the world's leading exporter of agricultural products. The following table shows the percentage of world exports accounted for by the United States for various major crops.

U.S. Share of World Agricultural Exports
Selected Crops, 1992

Commodity	U.S. Exports as a Percentage of World Exports
Wheat	36.0
Corn	69.7
Soybeans	66.3
Rice	13.9
Tobacco (unmanufactured)	14.4
Cotton	30.6

Source: U.S. Department of Agriculture, Foreign Agricultural Service

The United States produces 12.1% of the wheat grown in the world, but it supplies 36% of total world wheat exports. This is down somewhat from the nearly one-half (48.2%) that it supplied in 1981. It is still dominant in world soybean production and exports, but not to the extent that it once was as a result of increased planting of soybeans in Brazil.

Although the United States produces only 1.5% of the world rice output, it accounts for 13.9% of world rice exports. Some Asian countries, for whom rice is the main dietary staple, import rice that is grown in the United States more cheaply than they can grow it themselves.

In 1991, Asian countries received 42% of the agricultural exports of the United States. Almost half of that amount was purchased by Japan alone. Western Europe was the destination of 19% of our exports, down from 35% in 1970.

The largest consumer of U.S. farm products in Europe was the Netherlands, which purchased 43% more than second-place Germany, despite the great difference in their size and populations. Latin American countries took over 14% of our exports, half again as much as their share in 1970.

Economic Reasoning *(Write your responses on a separate sheet. Answers begin on p. 281.)*

1. Judging from the data on U.S. exports as a percentage of world exports, in what agricultural crop did the United States apparently have the largest efficiency advantage over the rest of the world?
2. Since the United States accounts for such a large percentage of world corn exports, it obviously has an advantage in corn production. Why, then, does it not completely specialize in corn production?
3. Because exporting so much of our agricultural output tends to raise domestic food prices, some people say that we should limit food exports in order to hold down the cost of living at home. What is your opinion of this proposal?

Who Benefits and Who Is Hurt by Foreign Trade?

BENEFITS	LOSSES
Consumer Benefits	**Import-Competing Firms' and Workers' Losses**
Consumers benefit from foreign trade by being able to consume some products that would not be available without trade. More importantly, consumers benefit by being able to purchase many products at lower costs than if there were no foreign trade, both because of the lower prices of imported goods and because competition from imports holds down the prices of domestic goods.	Competition from imports can be costly to the domestic firms and their workers in lost sales and lower prices. These costs are similar to the costs of competition from new domestic producers or from new substitute products.
	Mobility of Capital and Labor The costs of free trade to import-competing firms and workers can be minimized by mobility of capital and labor to alternative employments.
Producer and Worker Benefits	**Domestic Consumers of Export Industries**
Domestic industries that use imported inputs benefit. More importantly, export industries, their workers, and their suppliers benefit from the sales to markets abroad.	The export of part of the output of an industry tends to raise the price of the good to domestic consumers.

15.4 Describe the effects of foreign trade on economies.

A. The following tables show the production possibilities for oil and textiles produced in Mexico and Nigeria, assuming that these are the only two goods produced by both countries and that no trade takes place.

MEXICO

	A	B	C	D	E
Oil	0	2	4	6	8
Textiles	4	3	2	1	0

NIGERIA

	A	B	C	D	E
Oil	0	1	2	3	4
Textiles	16	12	8	4	0

1. What is the opportunity cost of a unit of oil in Mexico? (*Hint:* To determine the opportunity cost you must look at the changes from one combination to the next.)

2. What is the opportunity cost of a unit of textiles in Mexico?

3. What is the opportunity cost of a unit of oil in Nigeria?

4. What is the opportunity cost of a unit of textiles in Nigeria?

5. In the spaces provided below, draw the production possibility frontiers for each country.

MEXICO

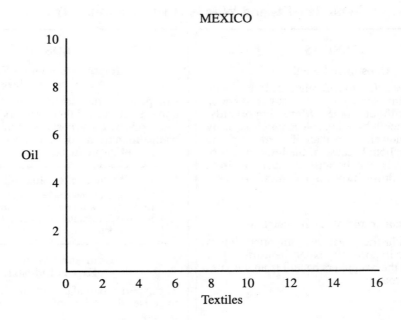

NIGERIA

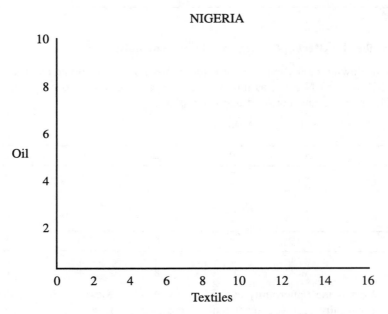

6. Suppose that Nigeria produces only textiles (16 units) and Mexico produces only oil (8 units) and that they trade oil for textiles at terms of trade equal to 2 units of textiles for 1 unit of oil. If Mexico gives up 3 units of oil in exchange for 6 units of textiles from Nigeria, then:

    a. Mexico will now have ___ units of oil and ___ units of textiles.

    b. Nigeria will now have ___ units of oil and ___ units of textiles.

    c. Compare these two combinations of oil and textiles to production possibility C on the above production possibility frontiers for both countries. (Plot the new points as point **X**.) How do they compare?

_____

_____

7. With trade, one production possibility for Mexico is to produce 8 units of oil and trade it all for 16 units of textiles. Plot this point (0 oil, 16 textiles) on the axes provided below and draw the new PPF for Mexico by connecting this to the

point where Mexico produces 8 oil and 0 textile units. Draw in the previous PPF that represented no trade.

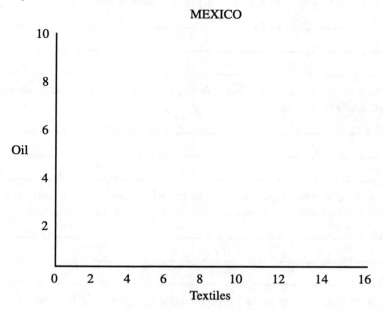

MEXICO

8. With trade, one production possibility for Nigeria is to produce 16 units of textiles and trade it all for 8 units of oil. Plot this point (0 textiles, 8 oil) on the axes provided below and draw the new PPF for Nigeria by connecting this to the point where Nigeria produces 16 textile and 0 oil units.

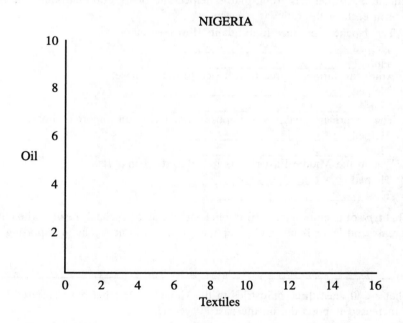

NIGERIA

9. What conclusions can you draw from your analysis in exercises 7 and 8?

_____

_____

15.5 Specify who benefits and who loses as a result of foreign trade.

A. What are three imported goods that you buy and/or use?

1. _____

2. _____

3. _____

B. For each of the three goods listed above, indicate the best possible *domestic* substitute available to you.

1. _____

2. _____

3. _____

C. For each of the three goods listed in exercise A, indicate a firm or worker in America who loses as a result of your buying an imported product.

1. _____

2. _____

3. _____

D. The discussion of foreign trade in the textbook implies that free trade is beneficial to economies in general. More specifically, the arguments assume that the purpose of trade is to benefit which group in every economy?

_____

E. Indicate one American group that is helped and one group that is hurt by foreign trade in each of the following instances:

1. The Japanese produce high-quality, low-cost autos.
   Helped_____
   Hurt_____
2. American farmers agree to sell rice to the Chinese.
   Helped_____
   Hurt_____
3. The American government imposes new tariffs on imported shoes.
   Helped_____
   Hurt_____
4. War in the Middle East results in reduced oil imports.
   Helped_____
   Hurt_____

F. What *type* of unemployment (frictional, structural, or cyclical) results when imports increase and labor is not mobile enough to move to new jobs in exporting industries?

_____

G. What are at least three industries in the United States that have suffered because of increased imports during the past 20 years?

1. _____

2. _____

3. _____

Case Application: NAFTA Winners and Losers

As consumers, we are all winners from the passage of NAFTA. But as producers, some individuals and companies benefit, some lose, and some are not affected one way or the other.

The following table shows major exports to and imports from Canada and Mexico in 1992, prior to NAFTA.

Leading Industries in Western Hemisphere Trade
1992

	Canada ($mil.)	Mexico ($mil.)
Exports		
Industrial Machinery	12,502	4,164
Electrical equipment	7,936	4,340
Vegetables and fruit	2,278	155
Imports		
Petroleum	6,636	4,564
Paper	6,111	119
Vegetables and fruit	273	1,382

The United States exports a great deal of industrial machinery and electrical equipment to Canada and Mexico.

On the import side, the United States depends on Canada and Mexico for petroleum supplies and on Canada for paper.

With respect to vegetables and fruit, it exports these items to Canada and imports them from Mexico.

Economic Reasoning *(Write your responses on a separate sheet. Answers begin on p. 283.)*

1. Judging from the table, which industries are hurt by U.S. Western Hemisphere trade?
2. Which industries benefit from U.S. Western Hemisphere trade? How?
3. Should U.S. farm workers favor increased Western Hemisphere trade, oppose it, or neither? Why?

How Do We Restrict Foreign Trade?

TARIFFS	**QUOTAS**
Taxes on imports are not imposed primarily for revenue but rather to shelter domestic firms from foreign competition. They may be based either on value or on quantity.	Restrictions imposed on the quantity of a good that may be imported may be set in terms of physical quantity or value and may be by country or in total.

Bilateral trade negotiations	**NONTARIFF BARRIERS**
reduce the trade restrictions between two countries. Most-favored-nation clauses in trade agreements extend trade concessions to other countries.	Protectionist measures in addition to tariffs and quotas include label of origin requirements, additional tests and inspections, and intentionally slow customs clearance.

Multilateral trade negotiations	**EXPORT EMBARGOES**
reduce the trade restrictions among many nations simultaneously. The General Agreement on Tariffs and Trade (GATT) provides for nondiscrimination between nations.	Exports may be restricted, rather than imports, to keep new technologies out of the hands of other countries for political reasons, or to hold down domestic prices.

15.6 Compare the different types of restrictions imposed on foreign trade.

A. A tariff on an imported good is similar to any increase in the cost of production.

In the following space, draw a demand and supply curve that shows the *domestic market* for a product before and after the imposition of a tariff. Then indicate the pre- and post-tariff equilibrium prices and quantities.

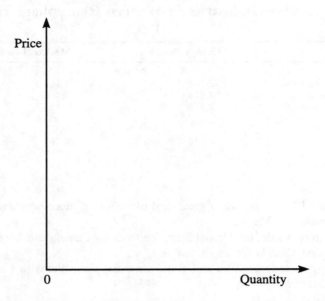

B. Quotas are effective at reducing trade only if the quota is less than the equilibrium quantity in the domestic market. On the axes that follow, draw a demand and supply curve that shows the *domestic market* for a good before a quota is imposed. Then show what happens to the supply curve if a quota lower than the equilibrium quantity is imposed. Indicate the quota limit by Q_q and the new domestic price by P_q. (*Hint:* The supply curve will become vertical at the quota level.)

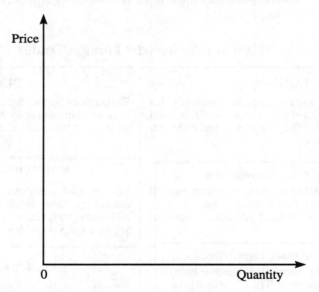

C. Suppose the demand for an imported product increases. In which case—quotas or tariffs—will the price increase be the greatest? Why?

_____

_____

_____

D. What are three reasons that the United States may place an export embargo on exports to a particular country?

1. _____

2. _____

3. _____

E. Be creative and make up three nontariff barriers that the United States could use to limit the import of Peruvian anchovies.

    1. _____

    2. _____

    3. _____

F. Government policies are often used to influence foreign trade.

    1. What bill did Congress pass in 1930 in order to raise tariffs?

    _____

    2. What was the objective of this bill?

    _____

    3. What was the effect of this bill?

    _____

15.7 Discuss the different vehicles for trade negotiations and explain the meaning of "most-favored-nation status."

A. GATT is an example of what type of trade negotiations?

    _____

B. Trade agreements can be worked out between only two countries or among many countries at the same time.

    1. What is a major problem that can arise from numerous bilateral trade agreements between one country and several others?

    _____

    2. What type of trade "clause" is designed to reduce or eliminate this problem?

    _____

    3. What do these clauses do?

    _____

Case Application: **Trade as an Instrument of Foreign Policy**

Foreign trade is sometimes used as an instrument of foreign policy. The United States has embargoed trade with Cuba for more than 20 years in order to weaken the Cuban economy and undermine the government of Fidel Castro. It imposed an embargo on Haiti to bring down the country's military regime and restore the democratically elected government. An embargo was imposed on Iraq by the United Nations as a result of its invasion of Kuwait and its refusal to accede to UN resolutions.

On the other side, favorable trade treatment is extended to friendly governments. The most-favored-nation clause originated as a means of giving tariff concessions to countries with which we have good relations. In years past, the United States had a policy of benefiting Caribbean countries by extending them sugar import quotas at favorable prices. Now, the United States provides payment guarantees through the Export-Import Bank on behalf of some countries, including Russia, to enable them to purchase U.S. exports.

But the use of trade restrictions to reward our friends and punish our enemies is contrary to the principles of free trade. Sanctions such as embargoes may injure the country imposing them as much as or more than they injure the target country. Unless sanctioned by the United Nations, embargoes are difficult to impose unilaterally. In general, trade discrimination is incompatible with multilateral trade agreements.

Economic Reasoning *(Write your responses on a separate sheet. Answers begin on p. 283.)*

1. Which types of trade restrictions have been used to implement foreign policy?
2. How do political embargoes affect comparative advantage?
3. Should the United States unilaterally use trade restrictions to implement foreign policy? Why or why not?

Should Foreign Trade Be Restricted?

TRADITIONAL PROTECTIONIST ARGUMENTS

Cheap Foreign Labor	Increase Aggregate Demand	Infant Industry
The argument for protecting American workers against competition from cheap foreign labor ignores the fact that workers' real income is primarily determined by their productivity, and productivity that is low means low wages but high real costs.	Restricting imports increases demand in the industries that compete with imports, but it reduces demand and reduces employment in export industries because of retaliation.	If there is a new industry that has the potential to be efficient and competitive, it may be justified to protect the industry from foreign competition while it matures. This is the only one of the traditional protectionist arguments that economists generally recognize as valid.

TERMS OF TRADE ARGUMENT

Imposing trade protection to lower the average price of imports relative to exports can obtain more imports per unit of exports, but is subject to retaliation.

NEOMERCANTILIST ARGUMENT

Like the mercantilists of Queen Elizabeth's time, today's neomercantilists want to restrict trade in order to maintain the advantages of technological superiority.

15.8 Critically evaluate the arguments in favor of trade restrictions.

A. The level of international trade has important consequences for the domestic economy.

   1. How do the levels of exports and imports affect aggregate demand in an economy?

     Exports_____

     Imports_____

   2. How do they affect domestic employment?

     Exports_____

     Imports_____

B. When Americans buy imported goods, they are buying goods made by foreign workers instead of goods made by domestic workers.

   1. U.S. workers earn higher wages than many foreign workers because they are more productive. This means that U.S. firms can hire U.S. workers and still be quite profitable. What is the main reason that U.S. workers are so productive?

2. Explain why U.S. workers, especially production workers, would accept the *neomercantilist* argument.

_____

_____

_____

C. The American steel and auto industries have consistently argued for protection from foreign competition. Can they use the *infant industry* argument to support their case? Explain.

_____

_____

_____

Case Application: Can Increased Poverty Be Blamed on Foreign Trade?

In the controversy over NAFTA, why did many liberals join with Ross Perot and other conservatives in opposing its passage? Are not liberals generally on the side of consumers? Since freer trade benefits consumers by lowering prices, why did those liberals oppose NAFTA?

One reason may lie in the belief that trade with low-wage countries, such as Mexico, lowers the wages of unskilled workers in this country. The real wages of many American workers have shrunk in the past 2 decades, as imports have doubled as a share of GDP. Between 1979 and 1989, the lowest decile of U.S. income earners experienced a 13% decline in their real wages.

Was the lowering of real wages caused by the increase in imports? Economic theory would support such a conclusion. According to theory, by putting unskilled American workers in competition with the large numbers of unskilled workers in the underdeveloped countries, the relative scarcity of such workers in this country is diminished, and, as a consequence, the price of their services lowered.

But recent studies have not supported this analysis. They show that in recent years the relative price of goods produced in low-skill industries has actually risen relative to the price of high-skilled industry goods.

Another expectation of the theory has not been supported by the evidence. If the theory held true, employers would be expected to economize on their use of expensive high-skilled workers by shifting to the use of more of the cheaper low-skilled workers as their relative wages fell. Just the opposite has happened. Industry by industry, the proportion of skilled labor has increased.

It appears that the increase in the wages of high-skilled workers relative to low-skilled workers is due to technological changes within the industries rather than to increased foreign trade.

Economic Reasoning (*Write your responses on a separate sheet. Answers begin on p. 284.*)

1. Which of the traditional protectionist arguments is involved in this case?
2. Why would a decrease in the wages of unskilled workers in the United States due to competition with workers abroad be expected to increase the number of such

workers employed relative to the number of skilled workers in a particular industry? Show with a labor market demand-supply diagram.

3. Should trade be restricted in order to reduce wage inequality between low-skill and high-skill workers? Why or why not?

IV. Practice Test (Answers begin on p. 284.)

Multiple-Choice Questions (*Circle the correct answer.*)

(15.1) 1. Which one of the following is a *true* statement?

a. Trade can be beneficial only if one trading partner has an absolute advantage.

b. Trade can be beneficial only if one trading partner has a comparative advantage.

c. Trade can be beneficial only if each trading partner has an absolute advantage in producing its export product.

d. Trade can be beneficial if either a comparative or an absolute advantage exists.

(15.1) 2. A country that has a comparative advantage in producing good X will

a. make economic profits by selling X.

b. be the low-cost producer of good X.

c. be the high-price seller of good X.

d. import good X.

(15.1) 3. The United States tends to have a comparative advantage in the production of

a. labor-intensive goods.

b. capital-intensive goods.

c. energy-intensive goods.

d. land-intensive goods.

(15.2) 4. Which one of the following tends to limit specialization in the production and export of a specific good?

a. decreasing capital/labor ratios as output expands

b. increasing costs due to resources that are not perfectly mobile between different industries

c. increasing labor force participation rates that lead to declining productivity

d. increasing tariffs and quotas as output and exports increase

(15.2) 5. Complete specialization can exist only when

a. there are no barriers to free trade.

b. both trading countries have an absolute advantage in producing the good that they export.

c. a particular good is produced only in one of the two countries that are engaging in trade.

d. both trading partners have most-favored-nation status.

(15.3) 6. The largest category of goods exported by American firms is

a. machinery.

b. autos.

c. food and animal products.

d. chemicals.

(15.3) 7. The largest category of goods imported by Americans is

a. machinery.

b. autos.

c. petroleum.

d. textiles and clothing.

(15.4) 8. Increased levels of U.S. imports will result in
   a. leakages from the U.S. GDP tank.
   b. increased unemployment in the United States.
   c. reduced aggregate demand in the United States.
   d. all of the above

(15.4) 9. How can increased foreign trade change a country's production possibility frontier?
   a. It can make the curve flatter.
   b. It can make the curve less flat (more bowed).
   c. It can cause the curve to move to the left.
   d. It can cause the curve to move to the right.

(15.5) 10. Which one of the following groups might suffer from increased exports of American wheat to France?
   a. American farmers
   b. French wheat consumers
   c. American wheat consumers
   d. French bakers

(15.5) 11. Which one of the following groups would gain from increased imports of Japanese cars?
   a. American auto manufacturers
   b. American auto workers
   c. American gasoline producers
   d. American car buyers

(15.6) 12. Why would the demand for American cars increase if a tariff is imposed on Japanese cars?
   a. The price of a complement would increase.
   b. The price of a complement would decrease.
   c. The price of a substitute would increase.
   d. The price of a substitute would decrease.

(15.6) 13. The effect of a quota on an imported good is to make the domestic
   a. demand curve for the good perfectly inelastic.
   b. demand curve for the good perfectly elastic.
   c. supply curve for the good perfectly inelastic.
   d. supply curve for the good perfectly elastic.

(15.7) 14. GATT is an example of
   a. most-favored-nation treatment.
   b. multilateral trade negotiations.
   c. a nontariff barrier to trade.
   d. a quota system.

(15.8) 15. Neomercantilists oppose
   a. the use of tariffs and quotas.
   b. trade adjustment assistance.
   c. the exporting of technology.
   d. complete specialization.

True/False Questions (*Circle T or F.*)

(15.2) 16. Complete specialization can exist only when an absolute advantage is present.
   T or F

(15.3) 17. Machinery is both the biggest U.S. import and a leading U.S. export. T or F

(15.5) 18. Workers in import-competing industries are harmed by foreign trade. T or F

(15.6) 19. U.S. firms have difficulty selling goods in Japan because of high Japanese tariffs on imported goods. T or F

(15.7) 20. GATT (the General Agreement on Tariffs and Trade) was initiated in 1986.
   T or F

Chapter 16

International Finance and the National Economy

I. Chapter Outline

Even if all trade barriers between countries were removed, other difficulties for trade would remain. For example, different countries use different currencies, and one currency must be exchanged for another in order to make purchases in a different country. Since a country pays for its imports through its exports, it is also necessary to determine a method of payment when imports exceed exports.

Introductory Article: Alice in the Wonderland of International Finance

Is a weak dollar good or bad for an economy? It depends on whom you ask, or, to put it another way, it depends on whose goose is getting plucked. Importers (such as consumers and raw material importers) dislike a weak dollar because it means that imported goods will be more expensive. On the other hand, exporters and workers in exporting industries like a weak dollar because it means that their exported goods will be less expensive to foreigners, and import-competing goods will become more expensive in this country.

Economic Analysis

This chapter examines how countries pay for their imports and how this affects the domestic economy by analyzing the following questions:

1. **How Do We Pay for Imports?**

   Important Concepts: Foreign exchange market, Correspondent banks, Exchange rates, The IMF, Depreciation, Appreciation, Devaluation, Revaluation, Exchange rate risk, Currency peg

   Comparative Case Application: Good as Gold

2. **What Happens When Exports and Imports Do Not Balance?**

   Important Concepts: Balance of payments, Current account, Balance of trade, Capital account, Basic deficit, Foreign currency reserves, Residual accounts

   Case Application: Going South

3. **What Is the Relationship between International Finance and the Domestic Economy?**

   Important Concepts: Economic equilibrium

   Case Application: Selling America

Perspective: Bring Back Gold?

II. Summary of Economic Analysis

1. Instead of using barter to conduct international transactions, businesses exchange their different currencies in **foreign exchange markets**. After buying a trading partner's currency, an entrepreneur can then use the currency to buy goods in that country.
2. Foreign exchange transactions for business purposes are usually done through **correspondent banks** in major financial centers.

3. When **exchange rates** are fixed, the price of one currency does not change with changes in its demand or supply in the foreign exchange markets. Shortages of a currency are met by reserves from each country's central bank or by borrowing from the **International Monetary Fund (IMF)**.

4. If shortages of one country's currency persist under a system of fixed rates, the country will **revalue**, or raise, the price of its currency. Persistent surpluses of a country's currency are met by a **devaluation**, or decrease in the price of its currency.

5. International financial markets today use a system of **freely fluctuating exchange rates** in which the price of one country's currency changes constantly depending on its demand and supply.

6. If people in the United States (or any other country) want to import increased amounts of goods from another country, the demand for that country's currency will increase and it will **appreciate**, or become more expensive. This, in turn, makes that country's goods more expensive and reduces the amount of goods that the United States imports.

7. If a country is importing more than it exports, it will be supplying the exchange markets with more of its currency while other countries have little demand for this currency. When the supply of a country's currency exceeds the demand for it, the currency will **depreciate**, or become less expensive. This, in turn, will make this country's goods less expensive and its exports will increase.

8. In order to insure foreign investors against **exchange rate risk,** the governments of smaller countries will sometimes **peg** the value of their currencies to the value of a larger country's currency.

9. The accounting record of a country's imports and exports is shown in its **balance of payments**. Exchanges of goods and services are reported in the **current account**.

10. The difference between the volume of goods and services exported and imported is called a country's **balance of trade**. If exports exceed imports, the balance is **favorable**; otherwise it is **unfavorable**.

11. In addition to the current account of goods and services, a country's balance of payments includes its **long-term** and **short-term capital accounts**. The long-term account compares the annual imports and exports of capital (investment), and the short-term account compares the international transfers of liquid funds such as bank deposits.

12. When total imports exceed total exports, the difference between the two is called a country's **basic deficit**.

13. One way in which a country can deal with a basic deficit is simply to pay for its imports with its currency. This amounts to the exporting country's giving the importing country credit. The currency that the exporting country holds serves as an IOU that can be redeemed for the importing country's goods in the future.

14. Another way that a country with a basic deficit can pay for its imports is by using gold or some other internationally accepted form of payment. Transfers such as these are called **residual accounts**.

15. Still another way for a country with a basic deficit to pay for its imports is to ask the IMF to loan it the currency it needs to pay the exporters to whom it is in debt.

16. If a basic deficit persists, a country's currency will be worth less and less to its trading partners, while their currency will be increasingly more valued. As a result, the currency of a country with a basic deficit will depreciate relative to its trading partners' currencies. Eventually, this will reduce the first country's imports, increase its exports, and eliminate its basic deficit.

17. A country's spending on imported goods results in money flowing out of its GDP tank, while the spending by others on its exports results in money flowing into its tank.

18. When imports exceed exports, there is a net flow out of a country's GDP tank, and aggregate demand, GDP, and employment will all fall.

19. When imports exceed exports, there will also be an excess supply of a nation's currency in the hands of foreign businesses. This currency will either stay in the bank for later use, or it will be used to buy assets in the country that has the basic deficit. In effect, a country with a basic deficit (such as the United States) trades its assets for imported goods and services.

20. **National economic equilibrium** occurs when leakages from the GDP tank—Savings (S) plus Taxes (T) plus Imports (M)—are equal to injections into the tank—Investment (I) plus Government Spending (G) plus Exports (X).

21. In the United States, S + T is less than I + G, so M must exceed X in order to bring the economy into equilibrium. A large part of the imports are in the form of liquid assets borrowed to finance our federal budget deficit.

III. Review of the Learning Objectives *(Answers begin on p. 284.)*

How Do We Pay for Imports?

FOREIGN EXCHANGE MARKET

The conversion of one currency into another takes place in the foreign exchange market, which is not a place but a set of banks and other institutions in the United States and other countries that deal in foreign currencies.

EXCHANGE RATES

SYSTEM	CHANGES IN RATES

Depreciation
The market exchange value of a currency falls due to a change in its market demand or in its supply.

Freely Fluctuating Exchange Rates
Exchange rates are allowed to float in response to demand and supply in the foreign exchange market.

Appreciation
The currency's value rises due to a change in its market demand or supply.

Fixed Exchange Rates
Governments stipulate the rate at which their currencies will exchange for other currencies and support that rate.

Devaluation
The government lowers the exchange value of its currency.

Pegged Exchange Rates
Governments of smaller countries fix the exchange rate between their currencies and the currency of a larger country.

Revaluation
The government raises the exchange value of its currency.

16.1 Explain how payments are made for imports. *(Write in answers below.)*

A. The price of an imported good is made up of two parts. First, an importer must purchase some of the other country's currency in the _____ market, and then it must purchase the good it wants to import.

B. Like other goods, currencies can be priced in terms of one another, for example, francs for dollars.
    1. If 1 dollar buys 5 francs, 1 franc buys _____ dollars.
    2. If 1 dollar buys 4 francs, 1 franc buys_____dollars.
    3. If 1 dollar buys 10 francs, 1 franc buys _____ dollars.

C. Assume that a U.S. importer of perfume can buy 5 French francs for 1 dollar.
    1. How many francs can the American importer buy for a dollar? _____

2. If a bottle of perfume costs 100 francs, how much does it cost in dollars?
_____

3. If the perfume increases in price to 120 francs, how much does it cost the American importer? _____
4. If the price of the perfume is still 100 francs but the American importer now gets only 4 francs for a dollar, how much does the perfume cost the importer in dollars? _____

D. Assume that a French importer of blue jeans must pay 5 francs for 1 dollar.
1. How many dollars can the French importer buy for 1 franc? _____
2. If a pair of blue jeans costs 15 dollars, how much does it cost in francs?
_____

3. If the price of the blue jeans increases to 18 dollars, how much do they cost in francs? _____
4. If the price of the jeans is 15 dollars, but the French importer needs only 4 francs to buy 1 dollar, then the price of the jeans in francs is _____.

E. Sometimes the dollar appreciates.
1. If francs become cheaper for Americans, dollars become_____
_____ to the French.
2. As a result, the price of French imports becomes _____ to Americans, and
3. the price of American imports becomes _____ to the French.

F. Sometimes the dollar depreciates.
1. If francs become more expensive for Americans, dollars become_____
_____to the French.
2. As a result, the price of French imports becomes _____ to Americans, and
3. the price of American imports becomes _____ to the French.

16.2 Distinguish among fixed, freely floating, and pegged exchange rates and explain how the rate of exchange is determined under each system.

A. When Americans demand pounds, they buy them with dollars, increasing the world's supply of dollars. When the British demand dollars, they buy them with pounds, increasing the world's supply of pounds. According to this:
1. The demand for pounds is the same as the _____, and
2. the demand for dollars is the same as the _____.

B. Assume that under a system of fixed exchange rates, 1 dollar is set to equal 1/2 pound (1 pound = $2). Now suppose that because of increased demand for British woolens, there is an increased demand for British pounds. The demand curve for pounds shifts from D_1 to D_2, while the supply curve for pounds remains unchanged. This will result in an increase in the supply of dollars from S_1 to S_2, while the demand for dollars remains unchanged. On the following graphs, draw the new demand and supply curves for dollars and pounds.

DOLLAR MARKET   POUND MARKET

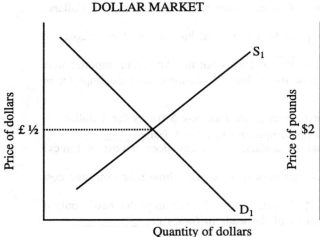
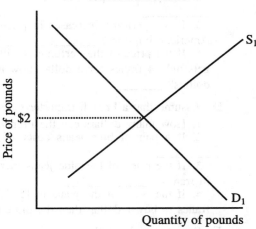

C. Fixed exchange rates can cause shortages or surpluses.

    1. In the above exercise, the graphs show that with a fixed exchange rate there would be a _____ of pounds. Show this on the graph.

    2. How could this be eliminated if exchange rates are fixed?

_____

_____

D. Shortages and/or surpluses exist in both currencies when exchange rates are fixed.

    1. In exercise B above, the graphs show that with a fixed exchange rate there would be a _____ of dollars. Show this on the graph.

    2. How could this be eliminated if exchange rates were fixed?

_____

_____

E. The demand and supply for dollars in terms of pounds and the demand and supply for pounds in terms of dollars are shown below. Initially, the foreign exchange markets are in equilibrium, with 1/2 pound = 1 dollar and 1 pound = 2 dollars. Now suppose that an increase in the demand for American jeans increases the demand for dollars and *exchange rates are allowed to fluctuate.* Show what happens in the markets for pounds and dollars and indicate possible new prices for each currency on the graph below. (*Hint:* When analyzing the pound market, remember the relationship between the demand for one currency and the supply of the other from exercise A.)

DOLLAR MARKET   POUND MARKET

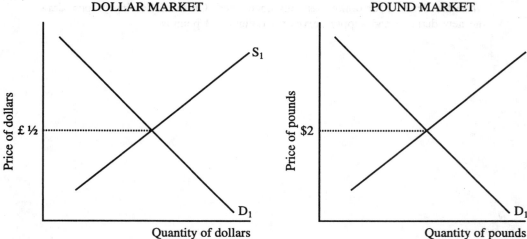

F. How is a fixed exchange rate system different from a pegged exchange rate system?

_____

_____

16.3 Differentiate among currency depreciation, appreciation, devaluation, and re-valuation.

A. If trade between Britain and the United States resulted in a surplus of dollars and a shortage of pounds under a system of *fixed* exchange rates, equilibrium in the foreign exchange markets would require that
   1. the pound be _____ and
   2. the dollar be _____ .

B. If trade between Britain and the United States resulted in a surplus of dollars and a shortage of pounds under a system of *fluctuating* exchange rates, equilibrium in the foreign exchange markets will occur when
   1. the pound _____ and
   2. the dollar _____ .

C. If exchange rates are fixed, countries sometimes find it beneficial to devalue or revalue their currency relative to others.
   1. If exchange rates are fixed, a country can make its goods cheaper to other countries by _____ its currency.
   2. This will lead to increased _____ and
   3. increased levels of _____ .
   4. What would be a negative aspect of this type of policy?

   _____

   _____

D. Is there any way for a country to influence the value of its currency under a system of freely fluctuating exchange rates? Explain.

   _____

   _____

   _____

E. Indicate whether each of the following will cause the U.S. dollar to appreciate (A) or depreciate (D).

   1. ____ Inflation increases in the United States, making U.S. goods more costly in other countries.

   2. ____ Interest rates are higher in the United States than in other countries.

   3. ____ There is an increase in the demand for U.S. exports.

   4. ____ The United States continually runs trade deficits with its trading partners.

   5. ____ The threat of war causes people in other countries to put their assets in the United States because it is safe.

16.4 Define exchange rate risk and understand how it can lead to smaller or larger returns on foreign investments.

A.
   1. Define exchange rate risk. _____

   _____

2. Name two countries that U.S. investors might avoid today because of exchange rate risk.

_____

_____

B. American citizen Chandler Bing decided to invest $100,000 in business ventures in Mexico because he thought that Mexico's participation in NAFTA practically guaranteed high returns on investments there. At the time Mr. Bing made his investment, the exchange rate was 3.5 pesos = $1, and the government had pegged the value of the peso to the dollar.

1. What was the value of Mr. Bing's initial investment in terms of pesos? _____ pesos

2. Assume that, to date, Mr. Bing has earned a 30% return on his investment. What is the value of his initial investment plus return in terms of pesos? _____ pesos

3. If Mr. Bing converted his initial investment plus return back into dollars, what would the dollar value be? $_____

Recently, unforeseen political instability and economic problems in Mexico caused the government to abandon currency pegging and allow the exchange rate to float freely. Assume that the new exchange rate is 6.5 pesos = $1.

4. What is the value of Mr. Bing's initial investment plus return in terms of pesos? _____ pesos

5. If Mr. Bing converted his initial investment plus return back into dollars, what would the dollar value be? $_____

6. Explain why your answers to exercises 3 and 5 are different.

_____

_____

C. During the first half of 1999, the value of the euro relative to the dollar fell. At the end of 1998, 1 euro was equal to $1.17 while in June of 1999, 1 euro was equal to $1.03. Suppose that during this time, Charles, an American citizen, invested his life savings in businesses in the European Union while Edward, also an American citizen, invested an equivalent amount in businesses in the United States. Based only on the change in the exchange rate (that is, all other things being equal), whose investment was harmed during the first six months of 1999? Explain why.

_____

_____

Case Application: **The End of the World Credit Binge**

The Mexican peso crisis in August 1982 signaled the end of a decade-long orgy of borrowing by developing countries that totaled some $360 billion. This credit consisted of private loans extended by U.S. and Western European banks to governments and private companies in Asian, African, Latin American, and Central European countries. A lot of the money, however, consisted of petrodollars, the earnings of the oil-exporting countries, which were recycled through Western banks to the borrowing nations.

Mexico was the biggest borrower, its foreign debt quadrupling between 1975 and 1982. Much of the borrowed money went to Pemex, the Mexican national oil company, for investment in new oil, gas, and petrochemical production facilities. As a result of its heavy international borrowing, Mexico was scheduled to make payment of $43 billion in interest and repayment on its foreign debts in 1982. This was nearly one-fifth of its national product and amounted to three times its estimated oil export earnings for the year. With world petroleum prices sagging due to the oil glut, Mexico did not have sufficient foreign exchange to satisfy its debt service obligations. As a result, in August the peso was devalued by nearly one-half to 70 pesos to the dollar. In September the private Mexican banks were nationalized and taken over by the government, and an interim loan was negotiated from the U.S. government to cover Mexico's foreign obligations until it could renegotiate its debt with the foreign banks. There was worldwide concern that a default by Mexico on the foreign loans could cause the banks that had extended it vast amounts of credit, based on its rapid growth rate and anticipated oil export earnings, to collapse.

A key to keeping Mexico from having to default on its foreign obligations was the participation by the International Monetary Fund in the financial rescue mission. Although the IMF would provide only $4.5 billion of the $15 billion to $20 billion needed, Mexico's agreement to the tough austerity measures imposed on it by the IMF was essential to obtain agreement from the private foreign banks to renegotiate their loans. These austerity measures included a reduction of Mexican deficit spending on government development projects and a lowering of the inflation rate.

Mexico was not the only country in trouble because of excessive foreign borrowing. Argentina, Bolivia, Brazil, Chile, Costa Rica, Peru, Poland, Romania, Venezuela, Yugoslavia, and a number of small African countries were also in danger of bankruptcy. If Mexico, Brazil, or some of the others had defaulted on their foreign obligations, the whole international financial structure could have collapsed as it did in the 1930s.

Economic Reasoning *(Write your responses on a separate sheet. Answers begin on p. 285.)*

1. Was Mexico employing a freely fluctuating exchange rate or a fixed exchange rate system? How can you tell?
2. How can petrodollars be recycled through Western banks to borrowing countries like Mexico?
3. The Mexican government resented the terms imposed by the IMF as a condition for extending it additional credit because Mexico felt that the demands infringed on its sovereignty. Do you think the IMF is justified in telling governments how to manage their internal affairs? Why or why not?

What Happens When Exports and Imports Do Not Balance?

BALANCE OF PAYMENTS

The annual accounting record of all transactions between a country's residents and residents of the rest of the world is the country's balance of payments.

MERCHANDISE AND SERVICES TRADE	CAPITAL FLOWS
Current Account	**Long-Term Capital Account**
The current account records imports and exports of goods and services.	The long-term capital account records the flow of public and private investment into and out of a country.
Balance of Trade The difference between merchandise exports and imports	**Short-Term Capital Account** The short-term capital account records the flow of liquid funds such as bank deposits between countries.

Basic Deficit

If the claims against a country from its merchandise and services trade, long-term capital, and other spontaneous transactions exceed the claims by the country on the rest of the world, the difference is the country's basic deficit.

Residual Accounts

The residual accounts balance short-term capital and gold movements to cover a basic deficit.

16.5 Define the balance of payments and distinguish among the different accounts in the balance of payments.

A. Indicate whether each of the following would be classified as an export (E) or an import (I) and whether it would be counted in the current (C), short-term capital (ST), or long-term capital account (LT).

Export or Import	Type of Account	
1. _____	_____	An American tourist visits Spain.
2. _____	_____	An American firm builds a factory in France.
3. _____	_____	An American in Maine earns interest on a money market fund in Germany.
4. _____	_____	A Japanese company buys a U.S. building.
5. _____	_____	A British citizen buys a pair of Levi's.
6. _____	_____	A Finnish citizen buys a 90-day U.S. government Treasury bill.
7. _____	_____	A Californian eats imported sushi.

B. Sometimes countries have a favorable balance of trade.

1. A favorable balance of trade occurs when _____ exceed _____ .

2. This is favorable to _____ because it results in increased sales.

3. It is not necessarily favorable to _____ because it reflects reduced choice.

4. A favorable balance of trade will eventually cause a country's currency to _____ .

C. Sometimes countries have an unfavorable balance of trade.

1. An unfavorable balance of trade occurs when _____ exceed _____ .

2. This is unfavorable to _____ because it results in decreased sales.

3. It is not necessarily unfavorable to _____ because it reflects increased choice.

4. An unfavorable balance of trade will eventually cause a country's currency to _____ .

D. Assuming freely fluctuating exchange rates, if country X has a favorable balance of trade, then:

1. the world's demand for X's currency will be

_____

2. the value of X's currency will

_____

3. the prices of imported goods in X will

_____

4. the volume of X's imports will

_____

5. the prices of X's exports to others will

_____

6. the volume of X's exports will

_____

7. as a result of #4 and #6, X's trade deficit will

_____

16.6 Understand how the basic deficit is determined and the role that foreign currency reserves play in balancing the balance of payments.

A. What are three ways that a country can offset a basic deficit?

1. _____

2. _____

3. _____

B. Are basic deficits more or less likely to persist if exchange rates are freely fluctuating? Explain.

_____

_____

_____

_____

C. The term "trade deficit" can be misleading. A country never really runs a total trade deficit because every transaction on one side of the balance of payments is offset by a payment on the other.

1. Existing trade deficits are brought into balance by

_____

2. These accounts are payments in the form of _____ or _____.

16.7 Explain how freely floating exchange rates cause currencies to appreciate to eliminate basic surpluses and depreciate to eliminate basic deficits.

A. Describe the course of events that occurs when a country has a basic deficit in its balance of payments and there is a system of freely floating exchange rates.

1. There is an excess of _____ (exports, imports).

2. There is a _____ (shortage, surplus) of its currency in the foreign exchange markets.

3. The exchange rate _____ (falls, rises) so that the currency _____ (appreciates, depreciates).

4. The basic deficit is eliminated by a subsequent increase in _____ (exports, imports) and decrease in _____ (exports, imports).

B. Describe the course of events that occurs when a country has a basic surplus in its balance of payments and there is a system of freely floating exchange rates.

1. There is an excess of _____ (exports, imports).

2. There is a _____ (shortage, surplus) of its currency in the foreign exchange markets.

3. The exchange rate _____ (falls, rises) so that the currency _____ (appreciates, depreciates).

4. The basic deficit is eliminated by a subsequent increase in _____ (exports, imports) and decrease in _____ (exports, imports).

C. Let's examine a freely floating exchange rate of American dollars for euros. The graph below illustrates the foreign exchange market where the demand curve represents the demand for dollars in the market, and the supply curve represents the supply of dollars in the market.

1. If (Q*,P*) represents equilibrium in the market, illustrate on the graph the current price of dollars assuming that the United States faces a basic deficit in its balance of payments and there is a system of freely floating exchange rates. Label this price $P_{deficit}$.

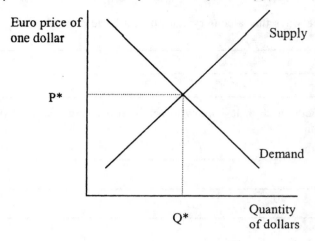

2. What will happen to the price (i.e., the exchange rate) in the market shown in the graph?

_____

3. What will happen to exports and imports as a result of the change in the exchange rate?

_____

Case Application: U.S. International Trade Position Takes a Nosedive

The last 15 years have seen dramatic changes in the United States' position in world trade. Judging by the behavior of its current account balance, the changes have been extraordinary.

Up until the 1970s the current account was close to being in balance. The values of U.S. exports and imports of goods and services were nearly equal, with a small but fairly consistent export surplus. (See chart below.) During the decade of the 1970s the behavior of the current account balance became much more erratic. The surpluses and deficits became much larger, but over the course of the decade they tended to cancel out.

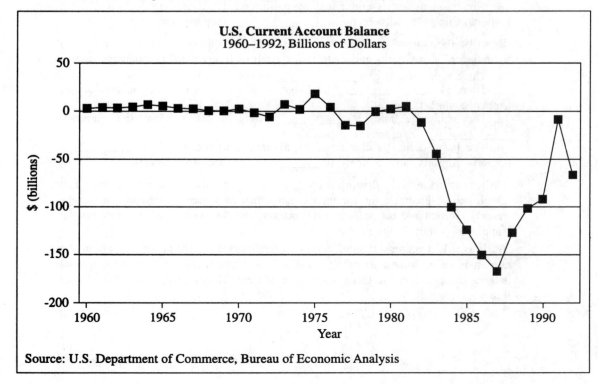

U.S. Current Account Balance
1960–1992, Billions of Dollars

Source: U.S. Department of Commerce, Bureau of Economic Analysis

Not so in the 1980s. Beginning in 1982 the current account balance took an unprecedented nosedive. It plunged to a low of a negative $167 billion balance in 1987. It recovered to a minus $8 billion during the recession of 1991, but then plunged again as other countries fell into recession and the U.S. economy began to recover.

Economic Reasoning *(Write your responses on a separate sheet. Answers begin on p. 286.)*

1. What types of balance-of-payments transactions are *not* included in the data shown in the chart?
2. What is the cause-and-effect relationship between recession and the current account balance? Explain how recession affects the balance of payments.
3. What do you think are the reasons for the drastic plunge of the U.S. current account balance in the 1980s?

What Is the Relationship between International Finance and the Domestic Economy?

FOREIGN SECTOR

The foreign sector of the economy consists of the country's external trade. Adding net foreign demand (X − M) to the domestic demand sectors (C + I + G) gives the aggregate demand for the nation's output of goods and services.

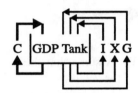

NATIONAL ECONOMIC EQUILIBRIUM

In the past decade the domestic sectors of the economy have been out of equilibrium because investment and government spending exceeded savings and taxes. The GDP has been in equilibrium as a result of the deficit in the foreign sector. The payments for the U.S. import surplus were invested by foreigners in the private sector and in government securities.

$$I > S$$
$$G > T$$
$$X < M$$
$$I + G + X = S + T + M$$

16.8 Understand the concept of national economic equilibrium in an open economy.

A. National economic equilibrium occurs when _____ + _____ + _____ = _____ + _____ + _____.

B. The GDP tank is subject to both leakages and injections.
1. _____, _____, and _____ are leakages out of the GDP tank.
2. Changes in each of these are _____ related to growth in GDP.

C.
1. _____, _____, and _____ are injections into the GDP tank.
2. Changes in each of these are _____ related to growth in GDP.

D. Label each of the flows (C [twice], G, I, M, S, T, X) in the GDP tank diagram on page 224.

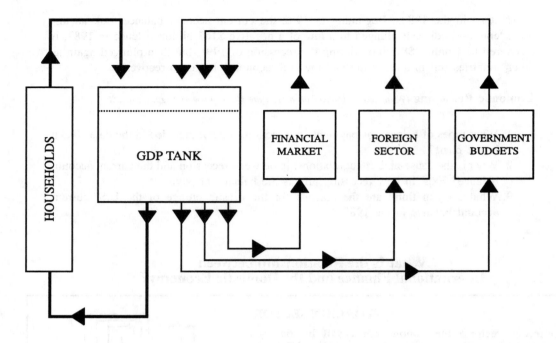

E. Assume that the above GDP tank diagram represents the U.S. economy during the 1980s.

1. In relation to the GDP tank, was more flowing into or out of the financial markets?

_____

2. Where did the "extra" funds in the financial sector go to or come from?

_____

3. Depict your answer to question 2, above, on the GDP tank diagram by drawing an arrow and labeling it **E.3**.

4. In relation to the GDP tank, was more flowing into or out of the government budgets?

_____

5. Where did the "extra" funds in the government budgets go to or come from?

_____

6. Depict your answer to question 5 on the GDP tank diagram above by drawing an arrow and labeling it **E.6**.

F. Sometimes a country's savings and tax revenues exceed its investment and government spending.

1. Suppose a country saves more than it invests and raises more in taxes than its government spends. Draw a GDP tank diagram in the space provided that shows this situation and indicate with a "+" those sectors that have inputs greater than outputs. Assume that there are no barriers to flows between financial markets, the foreign sector, and government budgets.

2. According to the diagram that you drew, which sector(s) must be net lenders and which sector(s) must be net borrowers?

Lender(s)_____

Borrower(s)_____

3. According to the diagram that you drew, what *must* be the relationship between this country's exports and imports?

_____

4. What is an example of a country that fits the description of the country described in this problem?

_____

16.9 Understand how an import surplus allows an economy to consume more than it produces.

A. America's trade deficit has received a great deal of negative publicity. However, there has been one positive aspect of the deficit. What is it? (*Hint:* Think of *short-term* consequences.)

_____

_____

_____

B. If the United States consistently imported more than it exported throughout the 1980s, then it must have supplied the rest of the world with lots of dollars that were not used to buy American exports. Where do you think these dollars have gone?

_____

_____

_____

_____

C. What (if anything) will be the price of consuming more than we produce in the United States, and who will pay this price?

_____

_____

_____

16.10 Describe the role of foreign investment in compensating for insufficient domestic savings and taxes.

A. Assume that the U.S. economy is in equilibrium with $S + T + M = I + G + X$. What would be the consequences if foreign investment in the United States suddenly declined?

1. What would have to happen in the government sector?

_____

_____

2. What would be the consequences for GDP?

_____

_____

3. What would have to happen in the financial markets?

_____

_____

4. What would be the consequences for GDP?

_____

_____

5. What would be the consequences of all of the above for consumer spending?

_____

_____

B. Investment can be categorized as either an import or an export.

1. Does foreign investment to build factories or buy real estate in the United States represent exports or imports?

_____

2. Do the profits generated from foreign investments in the United States represent exports or imports?

_____

Case Application: A Penny Saved Is a Rare Occurrence

Americans are big spenders. The proportion of our income that we save is the lowest of any major country.

This inclination to spend rather than save affects both the private and government sectors. As individuals, as businesses, and as a nation we have accumulated record levels of debt. In the private sector this has led to a massive number of bankruptcies. But the United States cannot take a Chapter 11 escape from its obligations. It must meet them in full.

Japan and the countries of Western Europe have savings rates two to three times higher than ours, as shown in the figure that follows. Canadians also save about twice as much of their income as Americans do.

High savings rates in a country provide loanable funds for investment. This facilitates productivity and faster economic growth. It also affects a country's international financial position.

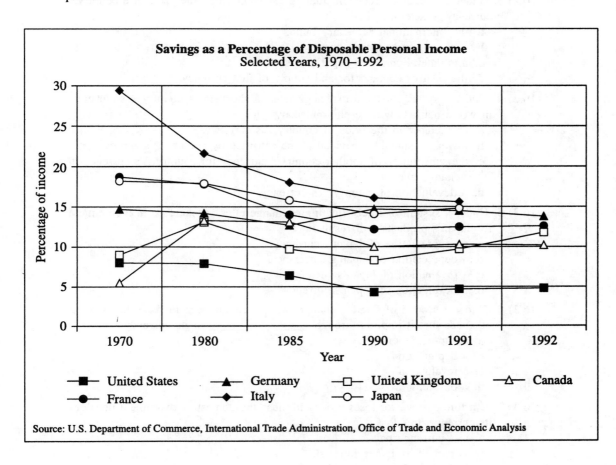

Savings as a Percentage of Disposable Personal Income
Selected Years, 1970–1992

Source: U.S. Department of Commerce, International Trade Administration, Office of Trade and Economic Analysis

Economic Reasoning *(Write your responses on a separate sheet. Answers begin on p. 287.)*

1. Referring to Figure 3 on page 458 in the text, if the U.S. savings (S) flow were greater, which of the other flows would be less?
2. What effect does the low national savings rate in the United States have on the country's international financial position?
3. Should any measures be taken to increase the national savings rate in the United States? If measures were to be taken, what should they be?

IV. Practice Test (Answers begin on p. 287.)

Multiple-Choice Questions *(Circle the correct answer.)*

(16.1) 1. Ultimately, a country pays for its imports with
    a. its own currency.
    b. its exports.
    c. its investments in other countries.
    d. credit.

(16.1) 2. Which one of the following is traded in foreign exchange markets?
   a. claims on foreign assets
   b. short-term capital assets
   c. physical quantities of goods and services
   d. currencies from different countries

(16.2) 3. Under a system of freely fluctuating exchange rates, the price of a country's currency is determined by
   a. the International Monetary Fund.
   b. each country's central bank.
   c. multilateral currency negotiations.
   d. the relative demand for and supply of that currency.

(16.2) 4. Under a system of fixed exchange rates, a shortage of country A's currency in world markets will be eliminated by
   a. an increase in the price of country A's currency.
   b. increased supplies provided at the set price by country A's central bank.
   c. the substitution of another country's currency for country A's currency in exchange markets.
   d. a devaluation of country A's currency.

(16.3) 5. Under a system of freely floating exchange rates, an increase in the demand for Japan's products will result in
   a. an appreciation of Japan's currency.
   b. a depreciation of Japan's currency.
   c. a revaluation of Japan's currency.
   d. a devaluation of Japan's currency.

(16.3) 6. Under a system of fixed exchange rates, a country can increase the amount of goods that it imports through _____ of its currency.
   a. an appreciation
   b. a depreciation
   c. a revaluation
   d. a devaluation

(16.4) 7. If a foreign investor loses money because the domestic government devalues its currency, this loss
   a. is a currency peg.
   b. is part of exchange rate risk.
   c. happens only during civil war.
   d. occurs when there is an import surplus.

(16.5) 8. Records of merchandise imports and exports are contained in a country's
   a. trade account.
   b. current account.
   c. capital account.
   d. residual account.

(16.5) 9. Who is helped when country A has a favorable balance of trade?
   a. consumers in country A
   b. a resident of country A who buys a lot from country A's exporting industries
   c. workers in export industries in country A
   d. import-competing firms in country A's trading partners
   e. everyone in country A

(16.6) 10. A country that has a basic deficit will have
   a. a positive residual account balance.
   b. a positive trade balance.
   c. an inflow of gold or similar assets.
   d. an appreciating currency.

(16.6) 11. Which of the following can be used to offset a basic deficit in the United States?
   a. an outflow of gold from the United States
   b. foreign countries holding more idle dollars
   c. outflows of short-term capital assets from the United States
   d. loans from the IMF
   e. all of the above

(16.7) 12. If a country has a basic deficit in its balance of payments and freely floating exchange rates,
   a. the exchange rate will increase.
   b. there is an excess of exports in the country.
   c. eventually higher imports and lower exports will eliminate the deficit.
   d. there is a surplus of the country's currency in the foreign exchange market.

(16.8) 13. National economic equilibrium requires that
   a. $I + X + T = S + M + G$.
   b. $X + M + T = S + G + I$.
   c. $S + M + T = G + X + I$.
   d. $S + G + X = T + M + I$.

(16.9) 14. The price of import surpluses in the 1980s will be
   a. an appreciation of the dollar.
   b. the necessity of producing more than we consume in the future.
   c. an increased residual account in the future.
   d. less trade in the future.

(16.10) 15. The biggest threat to the United States of foreign investment in the United States is the
   a. political power that it gives to foreign interests.
   b. increase in imports that such investment represents.
   c. increase in exports that such investment represents.
   d. possibility that this investment will be withdrawn.

True/False Questions *(Circle T or F.)*

(16.2) 16. Under a system of fixed exchange rates, a surplus of a nation's currency can be eliminated by devaluing the currency. T or F

(16.3) 17. An increase in inflation in France will result in the appreciation of the French franc. T or F

(16.5) 18. A country's balance of payments will always balance when *all* short- and long-term transactions are taken into account. T or F

(16.7) 19. Freely floating exchange rates cause currencies to appreciate to eliminate basic deficits. T or F

(16.9) 20. An import surplus is necessary for a country to consume more than it produces. T or F

Chapter 17

Economies in Transition

I. Chapter Outline

Since the collapse of communism in Central and Eastern Europe in 1989 and the collapse of the Soviet Union in 1991, these countries have been restructuring their economies into free-market systems. While Poland and most of the former Soviet countries relied on shock therapy, other CEE countries have adopted more moderate approaches. China has been slowly transitioning into a free-market economy since the death of Mao Zedong in the late 1970s. This chapter investigates in more detail the various processes of restructuring from a communist economy to a capitalist economy in these countries.

Introductory Article: State Socialism, Soviet-Style

The former Soviet Union, established in 1922, was the world's first communist nation. While there were some positive attributes, such as no official unemployment and affordable food, housing, and medical care for citizens, there were many problems with government control of the economy. During the 70 years following the country's origination, the problems associated with inappropriate incentive structures intensified until individual states began to secede from the Soviet Union, and it collapsed.

Economic Analysis

This chapter investigates the transformation from communism to capitalism by analyzing the following questions:

1. **How Is the Former Soviet Union's Economy Being Restructured?**

   Important Concepts: Communism, Socialism, Restructuring, Shock therapy, Getting prices right, Privatization, State-owned enterprises, Dinosaurs, Nomenklatura, Crony capitalism, Efficient capital markets, New role of government, Cold war, Rule of law

   Case Application: An Accident Waiting to Happen

2. **How Are the Economies of Central and Eastern Europe Being Restructured?**

   Important Concepts: CEE, Solidarity, Vouchers, Council for Mutual Economic Assistance (CMEA)

   Case Application: A Different Shade of Red

3. **How Is the Chinese Economy Being Restructured?**

   Important Concepts: Mao Zedong, Great Leap Forward, Communist ideology, Pragmatism, Town and village enterprises (TVEs), Special economic zones (SEZs), Purchasing power parity

   Case Application: The Odd Couple

Perspective: Marx on Capitalism

   Biography—Karl Marx

II. Summary of Economic Analysis

1. After **communism** collapsed, many of the newly independent countries of the former USSR began to restructure their economies through **shock therapy.** This has not proven successful during the 1990s.

2. In transforming from a communist economy to a capitalist economy, Russia must allow the market mechanism to **get the prices right** rather than relying on the government to set prices.

3. Since a market economy requires well-established and enforced private property rights, and these are lacking in Russia, the **privatization** of **state-owned enterprises** has proven to be difficult. The **nomenklatura** purchased many Russian firms and assets at less than one-fourth their true market value (on average), and through **crony capitalism,** they have pressured the government to continue to extend special treatment to them.

4. Financial markets in Russia, including banks, stock markets, and bond markets, continue to operate inefficiently because of corruption, poor management, and lack of regulation.

5. The new role that the Russian government must undertake includes establishing and enforcing laws and regulations governing the actions of firms, providing public goods and services to citizens, collecting taxes, and establishing stabilization policies.

6. Perhaps the biggest failure of the Russian government so far has been an inability to establish and enforce a **rule of law** whereby all people and businesses are treated fairly and equally.

7. The Poles opted for shock therapy just as the Russians did, but their transition to market capitalism has been more successful than the Russians'.

8. Privatization in Poland occurred through the use of **vouchers** that were distributed and could be used to buy shares in National Investment Funds, which in turn bought stock in different companies.

9. One difficulty for Poland and the other CEE countries is that the **Council for Mutual Economic Assistance (CMEA),** which controlled international trade among the CEE countries during the communist era, collapsed along with communism. Now these countries must become competitive in a global economy.

10. Shock therapy was unnecessary in Hungary because the economy already had a limited system of market capitalism in place when communism collapsed. Instead of using a voucher system, the Hungarians put their industries up for sale to anyone, including foreigners. Foreign investment in Hungary has also been encouraged through the use of incentives. Although Hungary faced some difficulties in restructuring the economy, the economy is steadily growing.

11. The other CEE countries had difficulties similar to those faced by Poland and Hungary when restructuring their economies. However, all have experienced improved economic performance following the transition period.

12. Mao Zedong proclaimed the establishment of the communist nation called the People's Republic of China in 1949. In 1957, he attempted to increase economic growth through the **Great Leap Forward.** This initiative failed, and communist ideology began to lose favor during the 1970s following another economic disaster.

13. A believer in **pragmatism,** Deng Xiaoping used small-scale experimentation with market capitalism to reform the Chinese economy beginning in the late 1970s. He began privatization initiatives including turning farms over to **TVEs,** requiring government agencies to become self-sufficient, and encouraging foreign investment in **SEZs.**

14. While China's economy is becoming more and more capitalistic, the Communist Party still retains control of the political system.

15. China's strategy for restructuring has been to move very slowly toward a free-enterprise economy. However, the economy is growing rapidly. If the current growth rates in China's GDP continue, the country will have the world's largest economy by 2020.

III. Review of the Learning Objectives *(Answers begin on p. 287.)*

How Is the Former Soviet Union's Economy Being Restructured?

> **COMMUNISM**
>
> Economic system in which government owns all nonhuman resources and answers the basic economic questions of what, how, and for whom to produce
>
> Collapsed with the dissolution of the USSR in 1991

> **RESTRUCTURING TOWARD CAPITALISM**
>
> **Shock Therapy**—Immediate imposition of free-market rules and institutions
>
> | **Getting Prices Right** | **Privatization** | **Efficient Capital Markets** | **New Role of Government** |
> |---|---|---|---|
> | Allowing prices to be set by market forces | Selling or turning over government enterprise to private-sector operators | Transferring financial resources from savers to borrowers | Providing legal systems, public goods/services, system of tax collection, and stabilization policies |

17.1 Explain why prices for most goods increased after the collapse of the former communist countries.

A. During communism, the government determined the prices of inputs and outputs in the economy. The graph below shows market supply and demand for loaves of bread. Suppose the government determines that the price should be $1.00 per loaf. This is an example of a price ceiling—a government-mandated price that is below the equilibrium price. It is intended to help consumers who cannot afford the higher equilibrium price. Let's look at the effects of price ceilings.

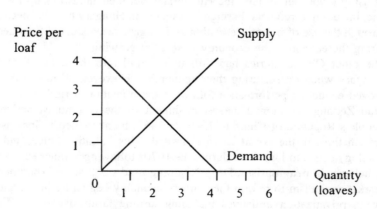

1. Indicate the ceiling price on the graph above. Label it $p_{ceiling}$.
2. What is the quantity demanded at the government-mandated price?
   _____
3. What is the quantity supplied at the government-mandated price?
   _____
4. Is there a shortage or a surplus at the ceiling price? _____

B. What would happen to the price in Exercise A if the government removed the price ceiling? Why? (This is what happened in Russia.)

_____

C. If the Russian government wanted to "get the right price," what price would this be in Exercise A? _____

17.2 Explain the reasons why privatization has proved to be so difficult to implement in Russia.

A. What problems resulted from the Russian government's inability to guarantee private property rights?

_____

_____

B. Who gained control of most of Russia's valuable resources during privatization?

_____

C. What is crony capitalism and how is it hurting the Russian economy today?

_____

_____

17.3 Explain why financial markets have been slow to develop in Russia.

A. Why do Russians possess the largest volume of U.S. currency outside of the United States?

_____

_____

B. Describe two reasons why the stock markets in Russia are inefficient.

1. _____
2. _____

17.4 Explain how the role of government in Russia is changing and the difficulties involved in making these changes.

A. Describe four new functions that the Russian government must fulfill in a market economy.

1. _____
2. _____
3. _____
4. _____

B. For each function listed above, describe a difficulty that the Russian government is facing in carrying out the activity.

1. _____
2. _____
3. _____
4. _____

17.5 Contrast crony capitalism as practiced in some countries with the rule of law, and understand why the latter is necessary for capitalism to work.

A. The principle that all people and businesses have equal protection under the law is known as _____ while an economic system based on the allocation of resources and goods according to favoritism is known as _____.

B. For each description below, indicate whether the information provided describes crony capitalism (C) or rule of law (R).

1. _____ Carl hires his nephew Al to build a new factory for his company.

2. _____ Tyra's firm provides plumbing for the new factory because they submitted the lowest bid for the contract.

3. _____ Mario's Manpower Co. collects applications and reviews qualifications to set up interviews for the new jobs that the factory will create.

4. _____ Wallace provides Al with the needed building permits as a favor to Carl.

5. _____ The government gives Carl a tax break on the new factory because he is building it in a rundown, inner-city area.

C. Why is it important to have a rule of law in order for capitalism to work?

_____

_____

Case Application: Funding Business Activities in Russia

Efficient financial markets are a necessary component of a successful market economy. In order to promote their development in Russia, a number of organizations have created programs that are specifically geared toward facilitating the lending of money.

In April 1994, the European Bank for Reconstruction and Development (EBRD) created the Russia Small Business Fund to help strengthen the capacity of the Russian banking system to make loans to small businesses. The program consists of a $300 million fund which is financed by the EBRD, the G-7 countries, and additional contributors. The money is made available to small businesses through 20–25 banks located throughout Russia. Loans of up to $125,000 with maximum maturities of 3 years are available through the Fund. Potential borrowers must meet cash-flow requirements, show sufficient demand for their products, and have sound management practices in place in order to obtain credit. They should also have their own funds to invest in the project. By August 1998, the Fund had provided 18,000 to 19,000 individual loans, and the repayment rate from the banks to the EBRD was about 97%. The repayment rate of the small businesses to the banks was also "remarkably high" according to Lou Naumovski, the senior banker on the EBRD's Russia team.

In May 1995, the Fund for Large Enterprises in Russia merged with the Russian-American Enterprise Fund to create the U.S. Russia Investment Fund (USRIF), which is a private investment firm that makes loans to, invests in, and provides technical assistance to Russian and Western enterprises operating within the country. The program is funded by the U.S. Congress through grants from the United States Agency for International Development (USAID) totaling $440 million. The Fund offers financing and management assistance to privatized Russian enterprises of all sizes, Russian-Western joint ventures, and Western firms interested in becoming involved in Russia. The Fund also has a Small Business Lending Program that works through a network of Russian banks and other lending institutions to make loans to small enterprises throughout the country. Potential recipients must be commercially viable and show potential for growth and profitability. They should also have a well-developed business plan and sound management principles in place. The Fund also provides training in underwriting and credit analysis to its bank partners.

USRIF has assisted many banks and business enterprises. Two businesses that have benefited from USRIF funds are Atlantic Cleaning Services in Moscow and G & D Bakery in Tula. Atlantic cleans Kazansky Railway Station in Moscow, and they sell their services to other railway stations. The company also operates a food store inside the station in a high traffic area. The company used the additional funds to expand operations to include cleaning electric trains, in order to increase sales. They also opened another food store and a cafeteria near the railway station. Diversification has helped the company mitigate risk. G & D used money borrowed from USRIF to purchase the building in which they operate so that they could keep their major costs constant. They also began using domestically produced equipment in order to reduce costs.

Economic Reasoning *(Write your responses on a separate sheet. Answers begin on p. 287.)*

1. Why are programs such as the Russia Small Business Fund and USRIF needed in Russia?
2. What are potential problems that investors might face if they invest in Russia?
3. Should other countries devote funds to programs such as the Russia Small Business Fund and USRIF?

How Are the Economies of Central and Eastern Europe Being Restructured?

POLAND	HUNGARY
Solidarity Shock therapy Privatization—use of vouchers Warsaw Stock Exchange	Market processes began while country was communist Privatization—encouraged foreign investment

OTHER CEE COUNTRIES

Czech Republic—used vouchers to proceed quickly toward privatization
Slovakia—less industrialized than the Czech Republic and proceeding more slowly toward a free-market economy
Romania/Bulgaria—agricultural economies moving very slowly away from communism
East Germany—unified with West Germany and received significant aid from them for development
Albania—still strictly communist today
Yugoslavia—long ago adopted own form of communism that allowed for some markets so they were more successful than traditional communist countries, but the country has broken apart during the 1990s due to civil war

17.6 Explain how the privatization policies followed in Poland and Hungary were different.

A. The following list describes characteristics of privatization policies used in Poland and Hungary. For each one, indicate whether it was used in Poland (P) or Hungary (H).

1. ____ Encouraged foreign investment

2. ____ Used vouchers to privatize industries

3. ____ Formed the noncommunist labor union Solidarity

4. ____ Used shock therapy

5. ____ Easily adopted use of equity markets

B. Describe two ways in which the privatization policies used in Poland and Hungary were different.

1. _____

2. _____

17.7 Understand why economic restructuring has been more successful in Central and Eastern Europe than it has been in the former USSR.

A. Describe four reasons why economic restructuring has been more successful in Poland than it has been in the former USSR.

1. _____

2. _____

3. _____

4. _____

B. How did Poland's method of handling so-called dinosaurs during privatization differ from the way dinosaurs were handled during privatization in Russia?

_____

_____

C. How did privatization in Hungary differ from privatization in Russia?

_____

_____

17.8 Understand what the Council for Mutual Economic Assistance was and why its demise presents a hardship for former communist countries.

A. What was the Council for Mutual Economic Assistance (CMEA)?

_____

_____

B. How did the Eastern European countries benefit from trade with the Soviet Union because of CMEA policies?

_____

_____

C. How did the demise of the CMEA affect exports from the Eastern European countries?

_____

Case Application: Marketing Drugs in Hungary

In a market economy, firms use marketing to increase demand for their products. Now that the CEE countries are restructuring toward capitalism, there is a huge increase in marketing and advertising. In Hungary, pharmaceutical companies spend billions of forints each year on radio and television advertisements, but they spend even more on advertising that is largely unseen. This money is spent to employ "medical representatives." These are doctors or pharmacists who pitch prescription drugs directly to doctors. The 1,800 medical representatives employed in Hungary must, by law, be doctors or pharmacists, and they easily earn twice as much as doctors make in their first year. Their job is to convince doctors to use their manufacturer's prescription drugs. So, while they provide professional information, their primary objective is to sell the drug.

The issue of money spent to employ medical representatives was raised by the director of the National Health Fund Administration (OEP) during recent discussions between the government and pharmaceutical companies about rising drug prices. The OEP decided that eliminating aggressive and expensive marketing practices could cut soaring drug prices and reduce the spread of expensive medications used in state health care. On the other hand, drug makers say that medical representatives are a necessity since they cannot advertise prescription treatments.

Some medical school graduates are choosing to become medical representatives right away without even practicing medicine because of the financial rewards. A medical representative begins with an annual salary of 140,000 to 160,000 forints while a first-year doctor earns about 60,000 forints. New "headhunter" companies have also sprung up to recruit doctors to become medical representatives.

While the government pushes to control drug costs by curtailing marketing, businesspeople complain that much higher marketing costs are built into drug prices in other countries. They believe that restraints will limit the industry's ability to compete as they progress toward consideration for membership in the European Union.

Economic Reasoning *(Write your responses on a separate sheet. Answers begin on p. 288.)*

1. Why is marketing unnecessary in a communist economy?
2. Why do beginning medical representatives earn much higher salaries than first-year doctors?
3. Are headhunter companies and jobs such as medical representatives a productive use of society's resources?

How Is the Chinese Economy Being Restructured ?

MAO ZEDONG'S LEADERSHIP
1949–1976

Work for the good of society.
Communist ideology—follow principles of communism whether or not they lead to economic successes.
Great Leap Forward—5-year plan to achieve accelerated economic growth by changing the motivation of the people (It failed miserably.)

↓

PRAGMATISM
Late 1970s–Present

Use economic policies that lead to success even if they are inconsistent with communist ideology.
Town and village enterprises (TVEs)
Self-sufficient government units
Special economic zones (SEZs)

↓

Fastest growing economy
Continued liberalization of economy
Political stability without political freedom (under communist control)

17.9 Know about Mao Zedong and his vision of China.

A. Mao Zedong's vision for China was to create a society in which the idea of _____ would be replaced with a desire to work for _____.

B. Suppose that Winnie, a high school graduate, earns $18,000/year while Pat, a college graduate, earns $26,000/year. That doesn't seem fair, does it? Suppose we split the money equally between the two. Let's pay each of them $22,000/year.

1. Is the new plan fair? Explain.

_____

_____

2. What kind of problems might result if we adopted the new plan?

_____

_____

3. How is the new plan similar to Mao Zedong's Great Leap Forward?

_____

_____

17.10 Explain how the Chinese experience with restructuring has been different than that in the former Soviet Union and the CEE countries.

A. From the list of countries provided below, match the countries with the restructuring policies they used and the characteristics of the countries. (More than one country may match each restructuring policy or characteristic, and each country may be used more than once.)

Countries:
   China (C)
   Hungary (H)
   Poland (P)
   Russia (R)

Restructuring Policies/Characteristics:

1. _____ Town and village enterprises

2. _____ Crony capitalism

3. _____ Pragmatism

4. _____ Vouchers

5. _____ Initial subsidization of dinosaurs

6. _____ Successful stock exchanges

7. _____ Encouragement of foreign investment in economy

8. _____ Continued existence of powerful communist political party

B. Why has the Chinese economy moved much more slowly toward capitalism than the CEE and former Soviet Union countries?

_____

_____

Case Application: E-commerce in China

China is the fastest-growing Internet market in Asia, and market research analysts predict that it will become one of the world's leading markets in the next 5 years. By the end of 1998, there were 2.1 million Internet users in China, and analysts predict this number will rise to more than 6.7 million by the end of 1999 and more than 33 million by 2003.

Many of the Chinese Internet users are single (64%) and male (86%), according to the *Statistical Report of the Development of China Internet.* As the pie chart below shows, most of them are also young.

Age of Internet Users in China

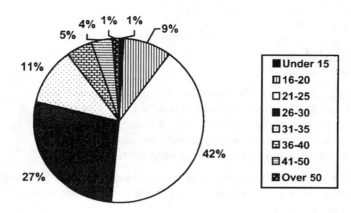

The growing Internet market in China presents several potential outlets for electronic commerce (e-commerce), or sales over the Internet. ChinaMallUSA.com, Inc. is an e-commerce company that facilitates trading between the United States and China. It recently announced the formation of a strategic alliance with *People's Daily Online Edition,* one of China's most popular web sites, in an effort to jointly promote development of e-commerce in China. *People's Daily Online* was created by *People's Daily,* the largest circulation newspaper in China, and since the site was launched in January 1997, it has received an average of 800,000 hits per day.

ChinaMallUSA.com foresees profitable opportunities for both companies resulting from this alliance. There will be opportunities to significantly expand the membership network of ChinaMallUSA.com in China and opportunities for *People's Daily Online* to increase revenues from advertising as more companies begin marketing online through the *People's Daily* website.

While the potential for e-commerce in China is great, investments at this stage necessarily involve risks and uncertainties. There are uncertainties about the development of technology, market acceptance of products and technology, existence of competitive market conditions, and the ability for companies to secure necessary sources of financing. Invest at your own risk.

Economic Reasoning *(Write your responses on a separate sheet. Answers begin on p. 288.)*

1. Use the demographic statistics about Internet users in China to describe which groups you think potential Internet advertisers might have the most success in reaching.
2. Why do analysts think there is so much potential for future development of e-commerce in China?
3. If you had money to invest, would you invest in an e-commerce business venture in China? Why or why not?

IV. Practice Test (Answers begin on p. 289.)

Multiple-Choice Questions *(Circle the correct answer.)*

(17.1) 1. When the Soviet Union collapsed, prices for most goods
    a. decreased because there was more competition.
    b. increased because consumers' incomes increased.
    c. increased because price controls were abandoned.
    d. decreased because the government mandated lower prices to help consumers.

(17.2) 2. When state-owned enterprises were privatized in Russia, which group ended up owning most of them?
   a. U.S. citizens
   b. nomenklatura
   c. Russian citizens
   d. labor union members

(17.2) 3. During privatization, the so-called dinosaurs in Russia were
   a. immediately shut down and abandoned.
   b. sold to the highest bidder (often a foreign buyer).
   c. broken up into smaller, more efficient companies.
   d. given government subsidies to keep them operating.

(17.3) 4. Which of the following types of financial markets in Russia adapted easily to privatization and were operating efficiently soon after privatization began?
   a. bond markets
   b. private banks
   c. stock markets
   d. all of the above
   e. none of the above

(17.4) 5. One of the most important roles that Russia's new government must fulfill is
   a. establishing and enforcing a rule of law.
   b. finding customers for Russian businesses.
   c. imposing high tariffs to collect revenue from importers.
   d. training lawyers and accountants so that the new systems will work.

(17.4) 6. Which one of the following problems became so severe in Russia that the IMF refused to make agreed-upon loan payments to the country unless the government dealt with the problem?
   a. tariffs that were too low
   b. insufficient system to collect taxes
   c. no subsidization of police and fire departments
   d. lack of spending on production of military goods

(17.5) 7. In order to extinguish crony capitalism in Russia, the government should
   a. establish and enforce a rule of law.
   b. subsidize police and fire departments.
   c. reduce spending on production of military goods.
   d. replace state-owned monopolies with private monopolies.

(17.6) 8. During privatization, which one of the following countries put state-owned industries up for sale to anyone, including foreigners?
   a. China
   b. Russia
   c. Poland
   d. Hungary

(17.6) 9. Which one of the following CEE countries opted for shock therapy to restructure its economy?
   a. Poland
   b. Albania
   c. Hungary
   d. Bulgaria

(17.7) 10. The transition to a capitalist economy has been most difficult for which one of the following countries?
   a. Russia
   b. Poland
   c. Hungary
   d. Czech Republic

(17.7) 11. Restructuring has been easier in the CEE countries than in the former Soviet Union countries because
    a. the former Soviet Union countries have higher populations than the CEE countries.
    b. the former Soviet Union countries developed stock markets and bond markets too quickly after privatization.
    c. the Soviet Union had devoted too many resources to protecting the environment instead of providing goods and services to its citizens.
    d. more citizens in the CEE countries had traveled to the West than USSR citizens, and they had seen how well capitalism worked compared to communism.

(17.8) 12. When the CMEA collapsed, CEE countries
    a. could not develop new markets for their goods.
    b. could purchase natural resources at lower prices.
    c. were restricted to trade with former USSR countries.
    d. improved the quality of export goods in order to compete globally.

(17.9) 13. Mao Zedong's plan to increase growth through the Great Leap Forward required that the Chinese people do what?
    a. work shorter days
    b. open more small businesses
    c. increase specialization, especially among intellectuals and laborers
    d. change their motivation for working from financial gain to the good of China

(17.10) 14. Which one of the following countries began a transition to capitalism first?
    a. China
    b. Russia
    c. Poland
    d. Hungary

(17.10) 15. In which one of the following countries does the Communist Party still have a strong hold on the political system?
    a. China
    b. Russia
    c. Poland
    d. Hungary

True/False Questions *(Circle T or F.)*

(17.1) 16. Market forces "get prices right" in a free market economy. T or F

(17.2) 17. Russia attempted to restructure its economy through shock therapy. T or F

(17.6) 18. So-called dinosaurs continued operating in Poland during restructuring because of crony capitalism. T or F

(17.6) 19. Hungary transformed to a capitalist economy without difficulties. T or F

(17.9) 20. China experienced a period of unprecedented economic growth under the leadership of Mao Zedong. T or F

Chapter 18

The Less Developed Countries

I. Chapter Outline

Four-fifths of the world's population live in nonindustrialized countries with low living standards and numerous obstacles to economic development. Overpopulation, malnutrition, illiteracy, depleted natural resources, inappropriate public policies, soaring debt, and lack of advanced banking systems and legal institutions all make it increasingly difficult for economies to pull themselves out of poverty. Adding even more to the problem, increased industrialization and economic growth will put increased pressures on the already threatened ecology of spaceship Earth.

Introductory Article: The Asian Flu

During the decades following World War II, the economies of East Asia became known as the Asian tigers and tiger cubs because they were the fastest-growing and most dynamic economies in the world. However, by the end of 1997, the tigers were sick with the Asian flu. GDPs fell and foreign investment evaporated as their economies based on socially guided market capitalism began to crumble.

Economic Analysis

This chapter addresses the problem of economic development in less developed countries by examining the following three questions:

1. **What Are the Characteristics of Less Developed Countries?**

   Important Concepts: Less developed countries (LDCs), Economic development, Per capita income, World Bank, Income distribution, Social indicators

   Case Application: The Dark Continent

2. **What Makes Countries Poor?**

   Important Concepts: Environmental determination, Cultural determination, Capricious universe view, Vicious circle of poverty, Economic surplus, Exploitation, Import substitution

   Case Application: The Sick Man of Asia

3. **What Are the Prospects for the Economic Development of the LDCs?**

   Important Concepts: Industrial development, Export promotion, Infrastructure, Overpopulation, Debt crisis, Environmental threats, Institutions, Transparency

   Case Application: Back to the Future

Perspective: The Malthusian Dilemma

Biography—Thomas Robert Malthus

II. Summary of Economic Analysis

1. Four-fifths of the world's population live in **less developed countries (LDCs),** where **per capita incomes** are low and **economic development** is lagging.

2. According to the **World Bank,** the average per capita income in the world in 1997 was $5,130. However, over 80% of the world's population have annual incomes of less than $2,000. Examining the per capita income as a measure of economic development in a country can be misleading because per capita figures do not take into account the distribution of income in a country.

3. The World Bank compiles **social indicators** of economic development such as rates of child malnutrition, life expectancy, child mortality, and adult illiteracy. Economic development could also be measured by the number of households who own modern conveniences such as televisions, personal computers, and telephone lines.

4. **Environmental determination** is a theory of economic development that empha- sizes the importance of natural resources and the physical environment of a country. **Cultural determination** is a theory of economic development that emphasizes the importance of the cultural attitudes and values of a country. People in some cultures adopt a **capricious universe view** believing that there is no connection between work effort and rewards.

5. LDCs must break the **vicious circle of poverty,** but there is no **economic surplus** that can be used to increase the quantity and quality of the countries' stocks of capital. LDCs also lack investment in human capital to improve worker literacy.

6. Both the LDCs that were colonized and some that were not suffered from **external exploitation** when the industrial countries forced them to be sources of raw ma- terials and markets for manufactured goods. Powerful families control much of the land and other means of production in LDCs, and they have used their positions to **internally exploit** their poor countrymen in order to enrich themselves.

7. Misguided economic policies such as exploitation of agriculture, **import substi- tution,** and excessive military expenditures frequently contribute to poverty in LDCs.

8. Economic development requires that the LDCs transform from agrarian economies to industrial economies through increased productivity in agricultural sectors, **ex- port promotion** policies, and reduced dependence on mining and other extractive industries. They must also build up their physical infrastructures.

9. Overpopulation contributes to a lack of economic development because increases in output need to be shared among an increasing number of people.

10. The increasing amount of money owed to foreign lenders has resulted in a debt crisis that limits growth because most foreign trade earnings must be used to pay interest instead of being used for new investment.

11. Rapid industrialization in LDCs is resulting in serious environmental threats as soot and fumes pollute the air, chemical wastes poison the water, and forests are burned for fuel.

12. In order to promote economic development, LDCs should adopt **transparency** in financial dealings and build strong banking and legal institutions. They should also strive for peace so that resources can be used to pursue economic development rather than fight wars.

III. Review of the Learning Objectives (*Answers begin on p. 289.*)

What Are the Characteristics of Less Developed Countries?

WORLD BANK

(The International Bank for Reconstruction and Development)

Agency of the United Nations whose major role is to help finance development of the world's LDCs; also publishes statistics describing economic development of countries of the world

---

Per Capita income—total national income (or GDP) divided by population; may be expressed in purchasing power parity dollars; common measure used to define LDCs

---

Income Distribution—may be used in conjunction with per capita income to gauge poverty in a country because distribution of income is often highly skewed in LDCs

---

Social Indicators—used to get a more complete picture of a nation's living standard

Various social indicators give a more complete picture of a nation's living standard:

- Growth in per capita GNP
- Life expectancy at birth
- Child mortality rate
- Adult illiteracy rate

Consumer Goods—In order to get a more complete picture of a nation's telecommunications infrastructure, the World Bank measures how many households have modern consumer electronic and telecommunications devices, such as:

- Televisions
- Personal computers
- Telephone main lines

18.1 Explain what economic development means.

A.

1. What does LDC mean? _____
2. What does economic development mean? _____

B. Use the data in the table below to find the 1997 per capita GDP for each country. (Round to the nearest dollar.)

Country	1997 GDP ($PPP)	1997 Population
Australia	$394 billion	18,613,087
India	$1.534 trillion	984,003,683
Mexico	$694.3 billion	98,552,776
Turkey	$388.3 billion	64,566,511
Uruguay	$29.1 billion	3,284,841
Yemen	$31.8 billion	16,387,963

1. Australia_____
2. India_____
3. Mexico_____
4. Turkey_____
5. Uruguay_____
6. Yemen_____

C. Based on per capita income, which three countries would you classify as most highly developed?

1. _____

2. _____

3. _____

18.2 Discuss the characteristics that set apart the developed and less developed countries of the world.

A. What are two economic indicators that can be used to compare living standards among countries?

1. _____

2. _____

B. What are four social indicators that can be used to compare living standards among countries?

1. _____

2. _____

3. _____

4. _____

C. The World Bank establishes minimum standards for amenities depending on the culture. What are three amenities that are "necessary" (to some) for life in the United States that probably are not necessary in an LDC?

1. _____

2. _____

3. _____

18.3 Identify those regions in the world where poverty is most prevalent.

A. In which two regions of the world is poverty the most prevalent?

1. _____

2. _____

B. List four countries in the region that you listed first in exercise A (either low-income or lower-middle-income countries).

1. _____

2. _____

3. _____

4. _____

C. List four countries in the region that you listed second in exercise A (either low-income or lower-middle-income countries).

1. _____

2. _____

3. _____

4. _____

18.4 Explain why per capita GDP alone is not always an accurate measure of world poverty.

A. What are two reasons why per capita GDP alone is not always an accurate measure of world poverty.

1. _____

2. _____

B. The concept of _____ allows economists to adjust for differences in buying power since the buying power of a dollar varies from country to country.

C. The table below describes per capita income that has not been adjusted for purchasing power parity (labeled **1997 Per Capita Income**) and per capita income that has been adjusted for purchasing power parity (labeled **1997 PPP Per Capita Income**) for five hypothetical countries.

Country	1997 Per Capita Income	1997 PPP Per Capita Income
A	$21,500	$20,860
B	$890	$1,675
C	$1,800	$3,445
D	$14,890	$12,306
E	$496	$2,484

1. Which country is poorest based on *unadjusted* per capita income? _____

2. Which country is poorest based on per capita income that has been adjusted for purchasing power parity?

_____

3. Explain why your answers for Exercises 1 and 2 are different. _____

_____

D. Country ABC has a per capita income of PPP $24,800, and 67% of the total income in the country is owned by the richest 20% of the population. Country XYZ has a per capita income of PPP $11,900, and 44% of the total income in the country is owned by the richest 20% of the population. Which country has more poverty? Explain.

_____

_____

E. List three methods that were used by the Asian tigers to make the distribution of income more equitable.

1. _____

2. _____

3. _____

Case Application: Capitalism versus Buddhism?

Currently, more than half of the world's poor people live in Asia. But since World War II, we have seen much economic development occur in the region. Despite the recent bout of Asian flu, it appears that much of Asia, especially East Asia, is on the way toward middle-class status within the next decade. While populations have been increasing in the region in recent years, the numbers of desperately poor people in the region have been falling.

As economic development continues and the population of Asia outstrips that of North America and Europe combined, there will be a large increase in the numbers of households with enough purchasing power to acquire at least some of the accoutrements of a middle-class lifestyle—color televisions, refrigerators, automobiles. Within the next decade as many as 40% of those households will have disposable incomes equal to the average of households in the countries now comprising the developed world.

However, the modernization of society that accompanies development may conflict with Asian traditions and philosophy. Asian social traditions emphasize continuity and stability, not change. Much Asian philosophy and religion, especially Buddhism, teaches renunciation of worldly desires, seeking instead to achieve oneness with spiritual values—nirvana. Can the requirements of capitalism coexist with the requirements of Buddhism?

Economic Reasoning (*Write your responses on a separate sheet. Answers begin on p. 289.*)

1. In 1996, how many households per 1,000 in South Asia had televisions? How many had personal computers? How many households per 1,000 in East Asia and the Pacific had televisions? How many had personal computers?
2. Why do increases in income from development activities do more to reduce poverty than increases in income from land ownership?
3. Do you think that it is necessary for Asian societies to sacrifice their philosophical values in order to escape poverty?

What Makes Countries Poor?

THEORIES OF ECONOMIC DEVELOPMENT

Environmental Determination—emphasizes the importance of natural resources and the physical environment of a country.
Cultural Determination—emphasizes the importance of the cultural attitudes and values of a country.

LACK OF PHYSICAL AND HUMAN CAPITAL

In order to break out of the vicious circle of poverty, a country needs an economic surplus over and above consumption needs to allocate to investment in real capital and human capital for intensive growth.

EXPLOITATION

The legacy of external exploitation in their colonial past may have retarded economic development for the LDCs. However, a greater obstacle to development may be the internal exploitation of one class by another, with ownership of land usually concentrated in the hands of a wealthy elite class that controls the government.

ECONOMIC POLICIES

Policies pursued by a number of LDCs have inhibited economic growth. These policies include the exploitation of agriculture by holding down agricultural prices to provide cheap food for residents of the cities and protectionist measures to favor import-substitution industries.

18.5 Explain the difference between environmental and cultural determination as causes of economic development.

A. The theory of economic development that emphasizes the importance of natural resources is _____. The theory of economic development that emphasizes the importance of attitudes and values of a country is _____.

B. For each description provided below, indicate whether the theory of environmental determination (ED) or the theory of cultural determination (CD) best applies.

1. ____ Brazil is the most highly developed country in South America because of its abundant rain forests.

2. ____ Vietnam is a less developed country because the peoples' values will not permit them to earn a profit.

3. ____ Economic growth in China is increasing because the young people are adopting Western behaviors.

4. ____ Russia will never be highly developed because Siberia is so desolate.

5. ____ Bermuda imports 80% of its food because there is a lack of suitable land for agriculture, but the country has one of the world's highest per capita GDPs because they have a tradition of working hard and providing good and faithful service.

C. Which theory do you think is more accurate in explaining economic development—environmental determination or cultural determination? Why?_____

_____

18.6 Describe the necessary preconditions for industrialization and economic development.

A. What is an economic surplus and why is it necessary for economic growth?

_____

_____

_____

_____

B. What are three factors leading to a lack of economic surplus in LDCs?

1. _____

2. _____

3. _____

C. In Chapter 14 of the textbook, four factors that lead to increased economic growth were presented. List these below and, for each one, discuss whether it is missing in LDCs.

1. _____

2. _____

3. _____

4. _____

D. Some parties benefit and some lose from the establishment of foreign trade barriers.

1. What two groups benefit from the presence of barriers to imports in an LDC?

_____

_____

2. How is the overall economy of an LDC harmed by the presence of barriers to imports?

_____

_____

_____

Case Application: Do You Like Company? How about 11 Billion?

The world population has more than doubled since 1950 to almost 6 billion people. In another 40 years, at current rates of increase, it will double again. More than 90% of the increase will come in the poor countries of the world. Will those countries be able to feed, house, clothe, educate, and otherwise provide for the increased numbers of people and at the same time generate the real savings necessary to increase their production efficiency?

In earlier centuries, population increase and prosperity went hand in hand. But in modern times, particularly in the second half of this century, income has been low where there is faster population growth. One reason why there is no longer a correspondence between prosperity and population growth is the introduction of improved public health services such as vaccines, antibiotics, and medical treatment into even the poorest areas, dramatically reducing death rates from epidemics and other health problems.

There is a population-education vicious circle at work in the LDCs. Poverty results in low levels of education, and education is associated with lower birthrates. In Ecuador, for example, women who have never gone to school give birth to an average of eight children, while those with at least 7 years of education have an average of fewer than three children. Low literacy levels in LDCs result in high birthrates that perpetuate the poverty that causes the low literacy.

Economic Reasoning *(Write your responses on a separate sheet. Answers begin on p. 290.)*

1. Does Table 2 in the text (p. 512) indicate that poverty is associated with illiteracy? What is the indication?
2. Are the population-education vicious circle and the vicious circle of poverty described in the text related? How are they different from each other?
3. Should the United States provide funding for international programs to reduce reproduction rates in the poor countries? Why or why not?

What Are the Prospects for the Economic Development of the LDCs?

INDUSTRIAL DEVELOPMENT	INFRASTRUCTURE
LDCs must make the structural transition from being agrarian economies to being industrial economies.	LDCs need to improve their physical infrastructures in order to support industrialization.
OVERPOPULATION	**DEBT CRISIS**
Economic growth must increase faster than the growth rate in population for living standards to improve. Many LDCs have exploding populations.	Many LDCs have defaulted on loans and have been forced by the IMF to implement unpopular austerity measures. Leaders walk a tightrope between defaulting on loans (and alienating creditors who may provide future assistance) and economically squeezing their people to the point of revolution.
ENVIRONMENTAL THREATS	**INSTITUTIONS**
Industrialization in LDCs is causing great harm to their local environments and contributing to worldwide problems such as ozone depletion and global warming. These costs are not internalized because of the shortage of funds to do so.	While the LDCs pursue economic development, they must be sure to put in place advanced banking systems and legal institutions to avoid problems experienced in East Asia during the late 1990s. Transparency in financial transactions is necessary.

18.7 Understand the differences between import-substitution and export-promotion and their consequences.

A.

1. Which kind of policy, import-substitution or export-promotion, can be described as "outward looking"? _____

2. Which kind of policy, import-substitution or export-promotion, can be described as "inward looking"? _____

B.

1. Which kind of policy, import-substitution or export-promotion, relies on trade barriers? _____

2. Which kind of policy, import-substitution or export-promotion, relies on free trade? _____

C. For each policy described below, indicate whether it is an import-substitution policy (IS) or an export-promotion policy (EP).

1. ____ Columbia places a high tariff on bananas so that local prices are cheaper than the prices of foreign bananas.

2. ____ In order to increase economic growth, Hong Kong adopted a policy of free trade during the 1980s.

3. ____ The Turkish firms petition the government to limit trade barriers, and they invest earnings in capital in order to increase opportunities for global expansion.

4. ____ Foreign sellers must obtain a license to import automobiles to the Ukraine. There are limited numbers of the licenses available.

5. ____ Russian citizens must purchase high-cost, low-quality, domestically-produced goods since trade barriers keep out many imports.

D. Which kind of policy, import-substitution or export-promotion, has been more successful in increasing economic growth for the countries that used it? Explain why.

_____

_____

18.8 Explain why external indebtedness is a problem for less developed countries.

A. Fill in the blanks below with the following: vicious circle of poverty, increased, decreased, interest, primary products, loans, economic surplus, economic reform.

1. Most of the world's underdeveloped debtor nations have economies that are based on the export of

_____

2. When inflation was high during the 1970s, the prices of these products

_____

3. This led foreign banks to think that these countries were good credit risks, and they increased their _____ to them.

4. When the prices of these products collapsed during the 1980s, the income earned by these countries _____

5. This led to a situation where these countries could not afford to make their _____ payments.

6. If these countries attempt to make these payments, there will be even less resources available to build a(n)

_____

7. As a result, these countries will be caught in a(n)

_____

8. In order to make their loan payments, the governments of many of these countries are forcing _____ on their people.

B. Inflation is not always so bad for everybody.

　1. Who gains from inflation—borrowers or lenders?

＿＿＿＿＿＿＿＿＿＿＿＿＿＿＿＿＿＿＿＿＿＿

　2. If inflation had increased in the 1980s, what would have happened to the price of primary products?

＿＿＿＿＿＿＿＿＿＿＿＿＿＿＿＿＿＿＿＿＿＿

　3. How would this have affected the ability of poor debtor nations to pay their debts?

＿＿＿＿＿＿＿＿＿＿＿＿＿＿＿＿＿＿＿＿＿＿

＿＿＿＿＿＿＿＿＿＿＿＿＿＿＿＿＿＿＿＿＿＿

C.

　1. What will be a real problem for debtor nations if they are unwilling or unable to pay their debts to the developed countries?

＿＿＿＿＿＿＿＿＿＿＿＿＿＿＿＿＿＿＿＿＿＿

＿＿＿＿＿＿＿＿＿＿＿＿＿＿＿＿＿＿＿＿＿＿

　2. What will be a real problem for debtor nations if they do pay their debts to the developed countries?

＿＿＿＿＿＿＿＿＿＿＿＿＿＿＿＿＿＿＿＿＿＿

＿＿＿＿＿＿＿＿＿＿＿＿＿＿＿＿＿＿＿＿＿＿

　3. What are two countries where economic conditions led to political revolution?

＿＿＿＿＿＿＿＿＿＿＿＿＿＿＿＿＿＿＿＿＿＿

＿＿＿＿＿＿＿＿＿＿＿＿＿＿＿＿＿＿＿＿＿＿

18.9 Describe the connection between overpopulation and economic development in the less developed countries.

A. Thomas Malthus was concerned that the world would suffer from food shortages because:
　1. populations grow at a(n) ＿＿＿＿＿＿＿＿＿＿＿＿＿＿＿＿＿
　2. while food supplies grow at a(n)＿＿＿＿＿＿＿＿＿＿＿＿＿＿＿

B. Suppose a population doubles each year while corn production increases by 1,000 ears per year. Use this information to fill in the following table:

Population	Ears of Corn	Ears per Person
100	1,000	＿＿＿＿
＿＿＿	＿＿＿	＿＿＿＿
＿＿＿	＿＿＿	＿＿＿＿
＿＿＿	＿＿＿	＿＿＿＿

C. What kind of mathematical relationship exists between a country's income and its population growth rate?

＿＿＿＿＿＿＿＿＿＿＿＿＿＿＿＿＿＿＿＿＿＿

D. In addition to pressures on the available food supply, population growth in developing countries also puts pressure on:
　1. ＿＿＿＿＿＿＿＿＿＿＿＿＿＿＿＿＿＿＿＿＿＿

　2. ＿＿＿＿＿＿＿＿＿＿＿＿＿＿＿＿＿＿＿＿＿＿

E. As sad as it may be, what two "natural" factors are currently limiting the population growth in the world's poorest countries?

1. _____

2. _____

Case Application: A Learning Experience

In a report entitled *Global Economic Prospects and the Developing Countries 1998/99: Beyond Financial Crisis,* the World Bank analyzed the East Asian financial crisis and made projections about its short- and long-term effects on developing countries. They concluded that the result of the crisis is a global slowdown that is predicted to hurt people in developing countries the most. However, the Bank is optimistic about future prospects for development in LDCs and views the recent crisis as an opportunity for learning.

Those hit hardest by the global economic slowdown will be countries that rely on exports of primary commodities, countries that depend on private capital flows to finance large current account deficits, and countries with major export markets where demand from other countries has slowed. These characteristics describe many LDCs.

According to the World Bank, protection of the poor should be central in the design of appropriate policy responses to the East Asian financial crisis. They believe that macroeconomic policies that promote economic growth should be combined with programs that offer "social safety nets" in order to mitigate the effects of the crisis.

While the developing countries will likely have the lowest growth rates since the 1980s debt crisis, the World Bank is optimistic that there will be improvements early in the 2000s. Although financial investment for development is shrinking today because of heightened risk aversion in global financial markets, policymakers in the LDCs are cautioned against interpreting the recent crises as reasons to retreat from globalization.

The primary problems discovered as a result of the East Asian financial crisis are weak domestic financial systems, shortcomings in macroeconomic policies, imperfections in international capital markets, and weaknesses in international financial systems to prevent and deal with crises, and these are problems that can be fixed. According to the World Bank, the lesson to be learned from the East Asian crisis is that developing countries must strengthen their regulatory systems and financial institutions and implement reforms that will allow them to benefit from globalization rather than withdraw from it.

Economic Reasoning *(Write your responses on a separate sheet. Answers begin on p. 290.)*

1. Why are countries that depend on private capital flows to finance large current account deficits hit particularly hard by the recent financial crises?
2. Why does the World Bank believe that social concerns are important to consider when formulating policies to assist the developing countries?
3. Do you expect the gap in living standards between developed countries and LDCs to diminish or get larger in the future?

IV. Practice Test (Answers begin on p. 290.)

Multiple-Choice Questions *(Circle the correct answer.)*

(18.1) 1. According to the World Bank, China is classified as being
    a. low-income.
    b. lower-middle-income.
    c. upper-middle-income.
    d. upper-income.

(18.2) 2. Which one of the following is generally a characteristic of developed countries rather than of LDCs?
    a. low incomes
    b. overpopulation
    c. low illiteracy rates
    d. low standards of living

(18.2) 3. Which one of the following is a specialized agency that helps finance development of LDCs?
    a. NATO
    b. World Bank
    c. World Trade Organization
    d. Organization for Economic Cooperation Among Countries

(18.3) 4. Poverty is most prevalent in which one of the following regions?
    a. Eastern Europe
    b. North Africa
    c. East Asia
    d. sub-Saharan Africa

(18.3) 5. Which one of the following is *not* classified by the World Bank as being a low-income country?
    a. China
    b. India
    c. Pakistan
    d. Malaysia

(18.4) 6. In order to compare the buying power of a dollar among countries, economists
    a. look at social indicators.
    b. convert all statistics to U.S. dollars.
    c. analyze the distribution of income.
    d. adjust for purchasing power parity.

(18.5) 7. The belief that only countries with abundant natural resources will become developed is based on the theory of
    a. internal exploitation.
    b. cultural determination.
    c. the Malthusian dilemma.
    d. environmental determination.

(18.5) 8. The capricious universe view that is prevalent in some countries can be attributed to
    a. overpopulation.
    b. crass materialism.
    c. import-substitution.
    d. cultural determination.

(18.6) 9. An economic surplus is necessary in order for a developing country to improve its
    a. labor force participation rate.
    b. population growth rates.
    c. investment/GDP ratio.
    d. import/export ratio.

(18.6) 10. The presence of a few large landowners taking advantage of the masses of people in a country is an example of
    a. appropriation.
    b. exploitation.
    c. reprobation.
    d. colonization.

(18.7) 11. Brazil's protection of its infant domestic car industry during the 1960s is an example of a(n)
    a. free-market policy.
    b. export-promotion policy.
    c. import-substitution policy.
    d. internal exploitation of its citizens.

(18.7) 12. In order to increase economic growth during the 1970s and 1980s, the Asian tigers
    a. encouraged population growth.
    b. adopted export-promotion policies.
    c. strengthened their financial institutions.
    d. implemented import-substitution policies.

(18.8) 13. A major cause of the debt crisis among LDCs is
    a. too much investment in infrastructure.
    b. the declining productivity of workers.
    c. declining prices for raw materials.
    d. the internal exploitation of workers.

(18.8) 14. LDCs that are attempting to make the payments on their outstanding loans are forced to do which one of the following?
    a. lower the standard of living for their citizens
    b. increase their imports of goods made in the lending country
    c. increase their per capita GDP
    d. borrow more at higher interest rates

(18.9) 15. Rapid population growth has negative impacts on
    a. nutrition levels.
    b. pollution levels.
    c. energy use.
    d. all of the above

True/False Questions *(Circle T or F.)*

(18.2) 16. If a country has a high per capita GDP, it must also have an equitable distribution of income. T or F

(18.3) 17. In 1997, sub-Saharan Africa had the lowest per capita GDP. T or F

(18.3) 18. The exploitation that results in poverty can come from both inside and outside a poor country. T or F

(18.8) 19. The debt crisis experienced by the tiger cubs has resulted in austerity measures that have caused social unrest. T or F

(18.6) 20. The world's underdeveloped countries may be poor in material goods, but they have much cleaner environments than the developed countries of the world. T or F

World Economics Crossword Puzzle (Chapters 15–18)

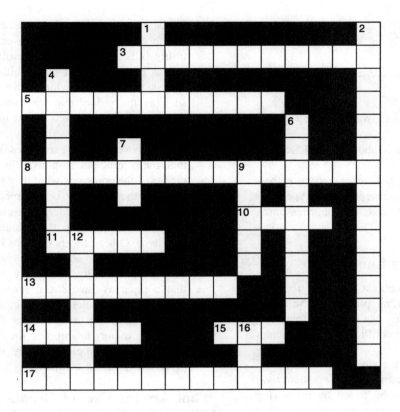

Across

3. The lowering of the foreign exchange rate of a currency by government regulation
5. Dissolved in 1991 into 15 separate republics
8. The doctrine that a country will retain a comparative advantage only as long as it retains a technological lead over other countries
10. The price of a currency in the foreign exchange market is the exchange_____.
11. A type of financial market that operates inefficiently in Russia
13. Agency of the United Nations that finances development
14. Established free trade area among Canada, Mexico, and the United States
15. Supplies foreign currency to a nation on a short-term loan basis
17. Designates nonindustrialized countries

Down

1. This is of more concern to many LDCs than the overpopulation problem.
2. One basic social indicator
4. The foreign exchange market does this to currency.
6. Trade negotiations between only two countries are_____trade negotiations.
7. A geographic area near the Chinese coast where foreign firms are allowed to operate and are given economic incentives
9. The _____of trade shows how many units of imports can be purchased with a given amount of exports.
12. Taxes on imports
16. Leader who established People's Republic of China as communist nation

Answers to Chapter Questions

Chapter 1

What Is Economics?

1.1. A. scarcity B. economic good C. wants D. You should check 1, 4, 5, and 7
1.2. 1.land 2.labor/entrepreneurship 3.labor 4.capital 5.capital 6.land 7.capital
1.3. A. predict B. testing hypotheses C. observation; gathering data; making a hypothesis; accepting the hypothesis
1.4. A. resources, people's wants B. choice C. economic reasoning

Case Application:

The Vanishing Land

1. Land is becoming more scarce as a result of urban development and wasteful farming practices. The actual amount of land has not changed, but it has become more scarce because the demand for conflicting uses is greater relative to the supply.
2. Likely hypotheses to explain the world loss of farmland are urbanization, strip mining, erosion, *or a combination of these.* The hypotheses can be tested by measuring changes in these conditions over time and correlating the changes with the amount of farmland available.
3. Since there are alternative possible answers, the answer to this question is open-ended. The answer given should be supported by accurate facts and valid reasoning. An answer that farmers should be required to use farming methods that reduce soil erosion might be supported by the fact that erosion is destroying much cropland and there is a need for food production to feed the expanding world population. An answer that farmers should not be forced to use such methods might be justified by the argument that farmers cannot afford to use more expensive conservation farming practices because they would be too costly. If they are forced out of farming by high costs, less food will be produced.

What Are the Tools of Economics?

1.5. A. 1.history 2.statistics 3.institutions B. 1.statistics 2.institutions 3.history 4.institutions 5.statistics C. describe, analyze, or interpret
1.6. A. concepts; models B. 1.C 2.C 3.M 4.C 5.M 6.M 7.M C. 1.diagrams 2.words 3.mathematical equations

Case Application:

Hot or Cold? Cost-Benefit Analysis

1. A cost-benefit analysis is a type of economic model.

2. Statistics are one factual tool used in this analysis, such as the data on costs of improvements and savings on utility bills. History is also involved, such as the historical experience that utility bills rise at 10% a year. The institutional behavior of the firm is also involved, such as the policy that the company should provide good working conditions for its employees even if that resulted in reduced profitability.
3. Open answer. Many executives in businesses believe that their principal responsibility is to maximize the profits of the company, what they refer to as "the bottom line." If the company is a corporation, they feel they owe it to the stockholders to earn as high a profit rate as possible, so long as they abide by legal and ethical standards. Other officers of firms believe company policies must take into account the welfare of their employees, the community, or society at large. They believe that companies have social responsibilities as well as profit responsibilities. In any event, executives should consider long-run profits rather than short-run profits. Spending money to improve the comfort and health of the company's employees may improve the long-run profitability of the company.

What Are the Uses of Graphs?

1.7.

A.

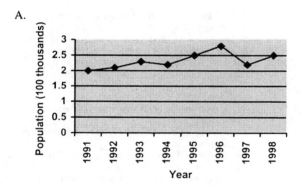

B.

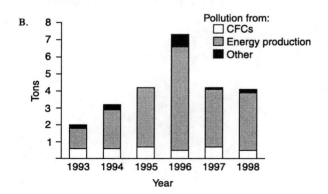

C.

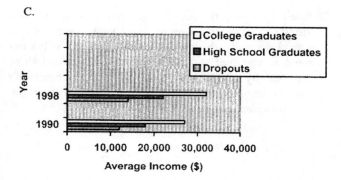

C.

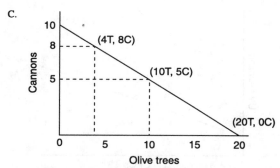

If MIC trades 2 cannons, it will have 4 trees and 8 cannons.
If MIC trades 5 cannons, it will have 10 trees and 5 cannons.
If MIC trades 10 cannons, it will have 20 trees and no cannons.

D.

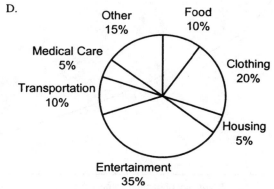

D.

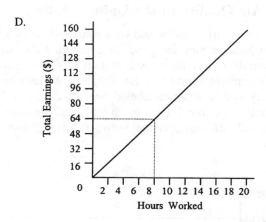

1.8. A. variables B. inverse C. direct D. charts; diagrams

1.9.

A.

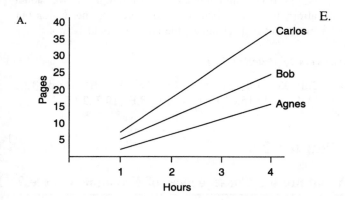

B.

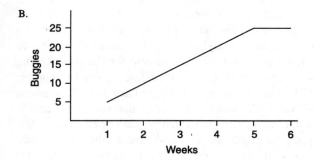

E.

1. An inverse relationship exists between CFC use and the ozone level.
2. An inverse relationship exists between the ozone level and the amount of ultraviolet radiation.

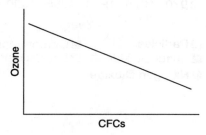

3. A direct relationship exists between CFC use and the amount of ultraviolet radiation.

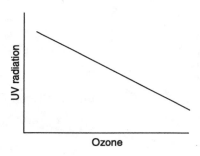

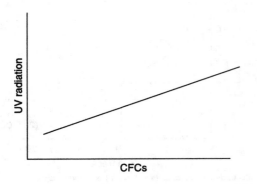

Case Application:

Air Quality in the United States

1. The best chart to use would be a column chart or a bar chart because they are good for comparing the values of variables over time. (A bar chart is shown below.) An alternative would be a line graph of the time series variety with a separate labeled line for each gas. The vertical axis shows the quantity of gas emissions in thousands of tons and the horizontal axis shows the years.

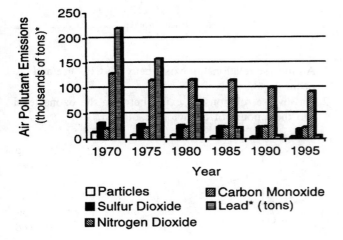

2. The relationship between the quantity of gaseous emissions and air quality is an inverse one. The vertical axis would normally show air quality (because it is the dependent variable) and the horizontal axis would show the quantity of gaseous emissions. The curve relating the two variables should slope downward to the right, indicating an inverse relationship.

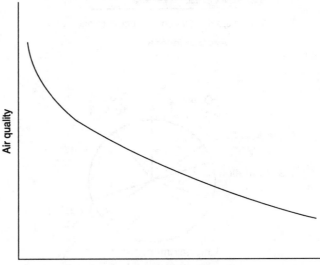

3. Open answer. If you put more value on a clean environment and think the cost is worth it, the answer would be yes. If you think that the cost is too high and we cannot afford it or that there are more pressing needs for our funds and real resources, the answer would be no.

Answers to Practice Test

1.c 2.d 3.c 4.b 5.a 6.d 7.d 8.a 9.a 10.c 11.d 12.c 13.d 14.d 15.c 16.T 17.F 18.F 19.T 20.T

Chapter 2

What are the Consequences of Economic Choices?

2.1. A. scarcity. B. (answers will vary) better health care; better roads; a safer environment C. (answers will vary) attending class instead of playing ball; watching television instead of studying; sleeping instead of getting up D. (answers will vary) 1.more help for the poor 2.using the land for a park 3.eating breakfast 4.going to a concert

2.2. A. Because of scarcity, everything has a cost. B. (answers will vary) Mr. Jones might think that the (high) cost is the educational programs that would not be funded; Ms. Applegate might see the (low) cost as the defense programs that will not be funded. C. (answers will vary) 1.baking brownies 2.going to a movie 3.planting a peach tree 4.the money you could earn on a job 5.fishing 6.buying something at the mall D. any other scrumptious desert *plus* the added calories!

2.3. A.

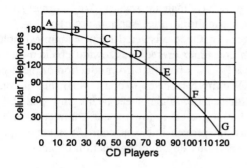

1. a. 10 cellular telephones b. 15 cellular telephones c. 20 cellular telephones d. 35 cellular telephones 2. increasing

B.

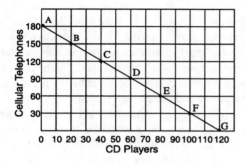

1. a. 30 cellular telephones b. 30 cellular telephones c. 30 cellular telephones d. 30 cellular telephones 2. constant

C. The country of Utopia (part A) has increasing costs, which implies the more realistic situation where resources are not perfect substitutes, while the country of Nirvana (part B) has constant costs, which implies that resources are perfect substitutes for one another.

Case Application:

Spotted Owls vs. Loggers

1. We need to determine the trade-offs between preserving the forests for the owls' habitat and cutting down the forests that provide jobs for loggers and income for their families.
2. The opportunity cost of saving the habitat of the spotted owl is a decrease in the production of other goods that could be produced with resources used to protect the owl. (These costs are experienced through losses of jobs for loggers, failure of businesses in the region, and so on.) The diagram showing the trade-offs between the owls and loggers could have the amount of owl preservation on one axis and the amount of other goods produced on the other axis. The curve showing the opportunity costs slopes downward to the right. The opportunity costs increase as more resources are used for one use (preserving owls) or the other (producing other goods) because some resources are better suited for one use or the other. For example, as the quantity of other goods produced decreases, some workers would have to

be retrained with new skills to be employed in preserving the owls. Therefore, the curve showing the opportunity costs is not a straight line but a line that curves towards the axes.
3. Open answer. The answer depends on how you value environmental goals such as species preservation compared to the value of other uses for our natural resources.

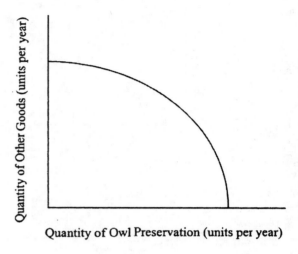

What Are the Basic Economic Questions

2.4. A. what and who 2.how 3.how 4.what (note: ultimately, each of these may affect "who")
B. what

Case Application:

Is Coal the Heir to the Energy Throne?

1. The choice between the use of underground tunneling or surface strip mining illustrates the "how" decision—how to produce the coal.
2. The reallocation of our resources has resulted from petroleum prices that are higher than before and the increased costs of nuclear power and our heightened awareness of its dangers. These considerations have increased the attractiveness of coal as a substitute, and more resources are being devoted to coal production.
3. Open answer. Some people believe that coal should be substituted for nuclear power in producing electricity, even if it results in an increase in air and water pollution, because nuclear power is dangerous due to the possibility of an accident and the problems of radioactive waste disposal. Others believe that we should not use more coal to produce electricity if it increases air and water pollution because that results in damaging the environment, people's health, and the quality of life.

What Are Society's Economic Goals?

2.5. A. 1.efficiency 2.price stability 3.full employment 4.growth

B. 1.growth 2.price stability 3.efficiency (or growth) 4. full employment (or growth)

2.6. A. 1.household incomes 2.increased output B. growth

C.

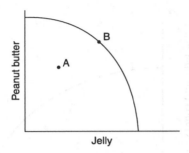

2.7.

A.

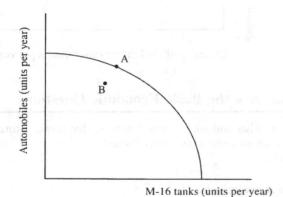

1. Point A must be located on the PPF (anywhere).
2. Point B must be located inside the PPF (anywhere).

B. 2 and 4

2.8. A. 1 and 2.

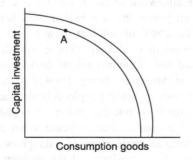

B. (answers will vary) 1.a new auditorium 2.a new water treatment plant 3.new highways 4.robots 5.a new computer system

2.9. A. 1.efficiency (or growth); safe environment 2.efficiency (or growth); job security 3.price stability; equity. 4.growth; equity B. (answers vary) 1.economic growth versus environmental protection with regard to logging of old-growth forests 2.full employment versus economic

equity with regard to raising of the minimum wage 3.efficiency versus financial security (for farmers) with regard to agricultural price support programs

2.10. A. shop B. Open answer. Recent examples include a shift in consumer preferences toward chicken and away from beef, which has affected production of these goods. Oprah Winfrey was taken to court when she said on television that she would not eat beef again, and the price of beef plummeted following her comments. Although she was not proven liable in court, it is clear that consumer decisions do affect production choices.

Case Application:

A Plastic World

1. The expansion of the plastics industry in recent years has definitely contributed to achieving the goal of economic growth. It most probably has also contributed to achieving the goal of full employment, despite the job losses in the older steel, wood, and fibers industries, because of the jobs created in the industry itself and the jobs created by industries using plastic.

2. An increasingly troublesome trade-off resulting from the growth of the plastics industry is the environmental pollution from the accumulating plastics garbage on land and in the oceans. Another trade-off is the loss of economic security by those workers who have been laid off in the more traditional materials industries because of the competition from plastics.

3. Open answer. On the environmental side, the answer is yes. If plastics garbage continues to accumulate in the environment, it will not only be aesthetically damaging and thus lower the quality of life, but it will be harmful to some animals, birds, and sea life. On the side of maximizing economic efficiency and minimizing costs, the answer is no. It is more costly to produce biodegradable plastics than standard plastics. It requires more resource inputs, and therefore we could not have as much consumption of other things as well as plastics.

Answers to Practice Test

1.a 2.c 3.d 4.b 5.d 6.b 7.a 8.c 9.a 10.a 11.c 12.c 13.d 14.b 15.c 16.T 17.F 18.F 19.T 20.T

Chapter 3

Why Are Economic Systems Needed?

3.1. A. comparative B. absolute C. comparative D. Answers will vary. Examples: The mother may be better at cooking and doing dishes, but she probably has a comparative advantage in cooking. The father probably has an absolute advantage in earning an income and washing the car, but probably a comparative advantage in washing the car.

3.2. A. specialize; efficiency; lower B. (open answers) 1. pluck chickens 2. make their own clothes 3. repair their own roofs C. boredom on the job D. 1. $70 2. $60 3. Bart—it saves Lisa $10 4. $80 5. $70 6. Lisa—it saves Bart $10 7. Lisa 8. Bart: cleaning; Lisa: tuning cars 9. Bart: cleaning; Lisa: tuning cars 10. $20

3.3. A. interdependent. B. specialization, interdependent. C. coordination problem. D. 1, 2, 5.

Case Application:

From Farm to City

1. People are more interdependent now than they were in 1790 because there is more specialization of production. In 1790 most families were rural and produced nearly everything they needed: food, clothing, shelter, tools, and so on. With industrialization and the movement to cities, families became dependent on others to supply their needs because they were now workers specialized in a particular type of production.

2. The growth of large metropolitan areas illustrates the principle of comparative advantage because they are efficient at providing services and many types of products. They have a comparative advantage in the types of production that benefit from population concentration, such as commerce, financial services, and communication. They are dependent on rural areas for those things, such as food, that are not as easily produced in densely populated areas.

3. Open answer. The answer to this question depends largely on people's value systems. If they think that simpler lifestyles, knowing one's neighbors, and self-sufficiency are the most important attributes, they might prefer a more rural society. If they believe higher living standards, the availability of more goods and services, and economic growth are the most important characteristics, they might prefer urbanization of society.

What Are the Principal Types of Economic Systems?

3.4. A. 1.C 2.T 3.M 4.C 5.T 6.M B. (open answers) 1. provides water 2. leases land to ranchers 3. inspects beef C. command (centrally directed) economy; mixed economy D. No

Case Application:

Digging a Subway in Calcutta

1. The use of manual labor rather than machinery is characteristic of traditional economies. The Calcutta subway has been dug in the fashion and with the implements that are traditional in India. The fact that it is a government project makes it characteristic of a mixed economy.

2. Private enterprise uses the production methods that are least expensive for the output obtained. If manual labor is cheaper than using machinery for the work to be done, which may be the case in India where labor is plentiful and capital scarce, private enterprise as well as the government may use traditional rather than modern methods of production.

3. Open answer. The answer to this question depends on how we evaluate the goals of efficiency versus full employment. If we make efficiency the overriding concern, the subway should be built by the method that minimizes total cost. On the other hand, if we consider providing jobs for unemployed workers to be as important as or more important than maximizing production efficiency, the subway should be built by manual labor, even if that raises the total cost of construction.

How Does a Market System Resolve the Three Basic Economic Questions?

3.5. A. profit B. more; less C. less; more D. land, labor, and capital; wages, rent, and interest E. finished goods; money payments

3.6. A. 1.F 2.P 3.P 4.P 5.F 6.P 7.F 8.P B. 1. a restaurant; a household kitchen 2. a law office; a student's room 3. a construction company; fixing a house's leaky pipes

3.7. A.

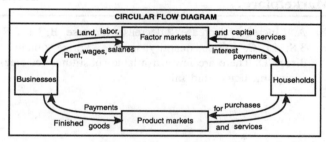

B. sell, to, factor. C. sell, to, product. D. In factor markets, consumers are the sellers and businesses are the buyers while in product markets, consumers are the buyers and businesses are the sellers. E. P, F, P, F, P, F

Case Application:

The Shale Age—Not Yet

1. Shale oil would be sold in a factor market because it requires additional processing to refine it into finished petroleum products. Only when it is sold directly to a consumer in the form of gasoline, heating oil, motor oil, or other final products will it be sold in a product market.

2. The oil companies would proceed with the development of shale oil when the profit incentives became adequate. Since these companies have petroleum reserves in wells that are cheaper to exploit at the present time than shale oil, they are not willing to risk large investments in the projects. Furthermore, bringing shale oil to market would reduce the value of their existing reserves in

wells. Further increases in oil prices or the development of shale oil by other companies or by the government would likely spur the oil companies to develop their leaseholdings.

3. Open answer. One position is that energy is a critical need for the country, both for civilian and national defense purposes. If it is worthwhile for the government to finance space exploration, it is certainly worthwhile to do at least as much to solve our energy problems. The opposite position is that the government should keep out of the energy business because it will spend tax money wastefully and energy will cost more than if the development is left to private enterprise.

Answers to Practice Test

1.c 2.b 3.a 4.b 5.c 6.d 7.c 8.c 9.b 10.c 11.d 12.b 13.d 14.b 15.b 16.F 17.F 18.F 19.T 20.T

Chapter 4

What Forces Determine Prices in the Marketplace?

4.1. A. 1.increase; decrease. 2.decrease; increase. B. 1.I. 2.S. 3.S. 4.I. C. 1.price; quantity; inverse. 2.price; quantity; direct. D. There are fewer available substitutes for electricity, medicine, and salt.

E.

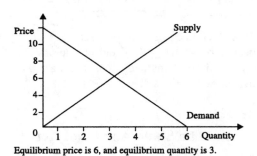

Equilibrium price is 6, and equilibrium quantity is 3.

Case Application: Are You An Oat Burner?

1. Both the demand and supply curves were affected—the demand curve by the reports of health benefits from eating oat bran and the supply curve by both the weather and the incentives offered to farmers by cereal companies.
2. The equilibrium price first rose to $4.25 a bushel and then fell to $1.15 a bushel the following year.
3. Open answer. It could be argued that the doubling of the price of oat bran cereal after the publishing of its health benefits was a bad thing because the cereal became much more costly and difficult for families, especially families on a limited budget, to afford. On the

other side, one that economists would generally take, the increased price served two necessary purposes in a market system: to ration a scarce commodity and to provide an incentive to produce more of the commodity.

What Determines Demand?

4.2. A. 1.tastes and preferences 2.price of complements 3.price of substitutes 4.population 5.income 6.tastes and preferences B. 1.I. 2.D. 3.I. 4.D. 5.I. 6.I.

Case Application: Upscale Munching

1. The determinants of demand responsible for the sales of gourmet snack products are the increase in the population size of that market, an increase in incomes, and changing tastes and preferences.
2. The cause of the change in the effective demand of the baby boom generation is their entry into the labor force and advancement to higher-paying jobs. The increase in their incomes has allowed them to indulge their tastes for higher-quality snack foods.
3. Open answer. Some people might consider the super-premium ice creams overpriced, since regular ice cream that is much less expensive can be very tasty. Others believe that the superpremium is worth the extra cost not only because it tastes better but because it is made with fewer artificial additives and more natural ingredients. The factors that need to be considered are the tastes and preferences of the consumers, their incomes, and the price and availability of the substitute.

What Determines Supply?

4.3. A. 1.W 2.W 3.WN 4.WN 5.W 6.W B. production costs. C. 1.The PPF will move outward. 2.economic growth 3.It will shift to the right. 4.Increases in supply are associated with economic growth.
4.4. A. productive capacity. B. capital C. 1.the dining room capacity 2.the number of chairs 3.classroom (number of desks) 4.factory size

Case Application: Black Walnut Worth Gold

1. The rustling of black walnut trees adds to the short-run supply of black walnut veneer. It shifts the short-run supply curve outward to the right.
2. The long-run supply curve for black walnut trees depends upon the length of growing time for the trees to reach maturity. With fertilizing and special care the long run can be reduced from 60–80 years to 30 years.
3. Open answer. Perhaps laws such as the one in Missouri should be enacted to discourage rustling of black walnut trees grown by individuals or in our national parks. On the other hand, such laws may be difficult to enforce, and they impose the burden of responsibility on log buyers, who claim that this is unfair.

Why Do Prices Change?

4.5. A. 1.income 2.price of substitutes 3.price of complements 4.tastes and preferences 5.size of the market population
B. 1. increase, increase 2. decrease, decrease 3. increase, increase 4. increase, increase 5. decrease, decrease

C.

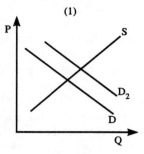

(1)

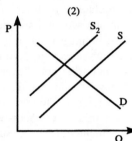

(2)

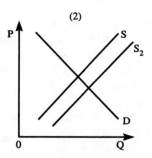

(2)

D. 1.price increases; quantity increases 2.price increases; quantity decreases

D. 1.increases; decreases 2.decreases; increases
4.7 A. 1.surplus; 20 2.shortage; 10 3.$6; 15

4.

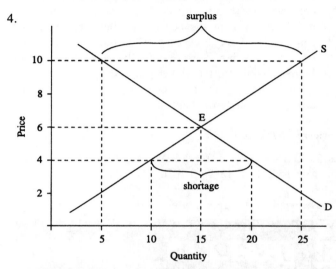

E.

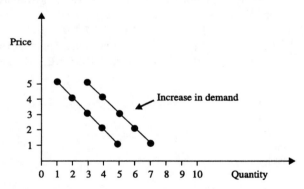

B. 1.surplus 2.fall 3.increase; decrease 4.surplus; disappear
C. 1.shortage 2.rise 3.decrease; increase 4.shortage; disappear D. equilibrium; surpluses; shortages
4.8. A. increase, demand B. decrease, quantity demanded C. 1. D 2. D 3. QD 4. D

4.6. A. 1.an increase; a decrease 2.a decrease; an increase 3.a decrease; an increase 4.a increase; a decrease B. lower prices and more goods and services

D.

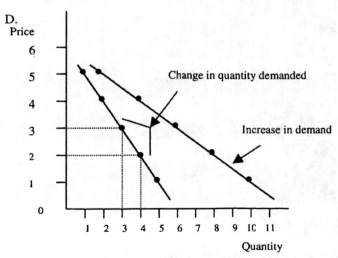

C.

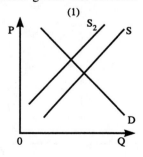

(1)

4.9 A. increase, quantity supplied B. decrease, supply C. 1. QS 2. S 3. S 4. S

Case Application: **Do Boycotts Work?**

1. If consumers respond to a boycott by reducing the amount of the product they would normally buy at any given price, the demand curve shifts backward to the left.

2. A boycott results in lower prices in the short run because the shift in demand causes sellers to move down their supply schedule to a lower price. However, in a competitive industry, such as the cattle industry, the lower prices may cause a reduction in investment in the industry that shifts the long-run supply curve backward to the left, resulting in higher prices in the long run.

3. Open answer. From the consumers' point of view, boycotts are fair when the price of something goes up much more rapidly than the consumers' incomes, and they cannot afford the higher prices. From the producers' point of view, boycotts are unfair because they may not be responsible for the higher prices that result from increased costs. To the producers, boycotts are a conspiracy that might force them out of business.

Answers to Practice Test

1.a 2.c 3.d 4.d 5.b 6.a 7.c 8.d 9.c 10.a 11.a 12.a 13.c 14.c 15.c 16.T 17.F 18.T 19.T 20. F

Crossword Puzzle for Chapters 1–4

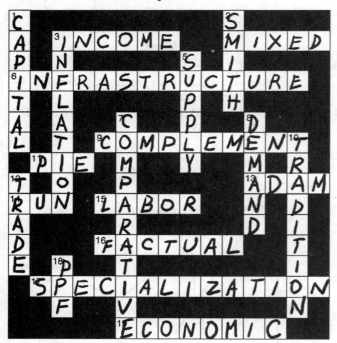

Chapter 5

What Determines Income?

5.1. A. functional distribution of income B. wages and salaries, rent, interest, profits C. 1.R 2.I 3.W 4.P 5.R 6.W

5.2. A. substitutes B. complements C. 1. complements 2. substitutes

5.3. A. fixed (or unchanging or limited) B. 1. price 2. quantity

Case Application:

Karl Marx's Prediction

1. As evidenced by the percentage of income generated as wages and salaries, labor's share increased until the 1980s when it began to level off. The percentage of national income generated as rental income (the payment for land) has decreased during the past century while the percentage made up of net interest (the payment for capital) fell, rose, and recently fell again in 1996. The percentage of income earned as profits has declined. There has been a steady decline in the percentage earned as proprietor's income while the percentage earned as corporate profits has fluctuated.

2. In a profit-sharing program, the average worker gets a share of the profits. Therefore, the capitalists or business owners cannot accumulate all of the income in the economy. It is shared among workers and business owners.

3. This would occur in countries that rely heavily on labor-intensive production processes. Agrarian (or agricultural) economies that do not have much capital equipment would have functional distributions of income that are more skewed toward labor as would economies that rely primarily on labor-intensive service industries. Examples include Rwanda, Sudan, and Bangladesh.

What Choices Do Consumers Make?

5.4. A. quantity demanded B. inelastic; elastic C. 1.availability of substitutes 2.the price of the good relative to your budget D. 1.I 2.E 3.E 4.E 5.I 6.I 7.I 8.I 9.E 10.E

5.5. A. There must be perfect substitutes. B. There are no substitutes. C. 1.PI 2.PE 3.PI 4.PE 5.RE 6.RE 7.RI 8.RE D.

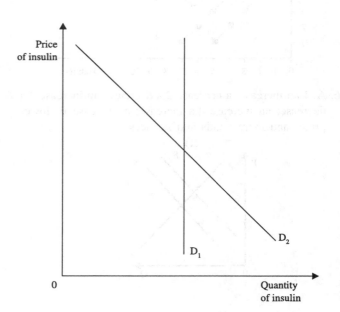

E.

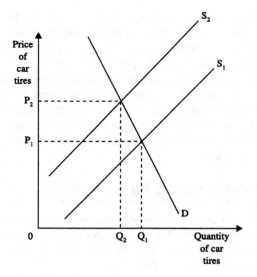

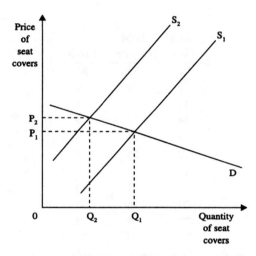

Price increases the most in the first case; quantity demanded decreases the most in the second case.

5.6. A. 1. 2.0 2. 1.0 3. 0.10 4. infinite 5. 0.00 B. Answers will vary for the example part of the question. 1.RE; broccoli 2.UE; frozen vegetables 3.RI; toothpaste 4.PE; wheat 5.PI; insulin

5.7. A. It produces what consumers want. B. Good question. Producers would need to guess, or perhaps tradition or a central administration would answer the "what to produce" question. C. Supply reacts to demand.

5.8. A. 1.pay taxes 2.spend 3.save B. APS = .15; APC = .85 C. 1.C 2.C 3.S 4.C 5.S 6.S D. They will be hurt because people will be spending and buying less. They will be helped because increased saving leads to more funds available to borrow for investment.

Case Application:

Going to the Movies

1. The Gardners consider going to the movies a luxury. This is indicated by their unwillingness to pay the higher ticket prices and by Martin's statement that if

the price of groceries continues to rise they will substitute groceries for movie attendance.

2. It appears that the Gardners' demand for theater movies is relatively elastic because they are substituting bicycle rides, picnics, and rental tapes or television for going to the movies.

3. Open answer. The answer depends upon the individual's preference for attending movies in comparison to other forms of leisure-time spending. If people rank movies very high on their preference scale relative to other types of activities, $7 may not be too much to pay for a ticket. If, on the other hand, there are substitute activities that cost less and provide almost as much satisfaction, $7 may be too high a price for a movie ticket. Another criterion is the amount of the individual's income. Those with high incomes may not consider $7 tickets too high, while those with lower incomes may consider it too high.

How Can Consumers Make Better Choices?

5.9. A. Answers will vary but should include such things as magazines that report on quality of consumer products (for example, *Consumer Reports*), newspapers, advertisements, government reports concerning product safety, reports/advertisements on the internet, word of mouth, and so on. B.1–B.4 Answers will vary, but just about any food, medicine, or natural fabric would apply. C.1–C.4 Answers will vary. D. Yes, it has most likely affected consumer behavior by making more information more readily available. Examples where consumers are using the Internet to gather information about potential purchases include automobiles and homes. Consumers are also making purchases through Web sites such as www.amazon.com and www.ebay.com.

5.10. A. less B. Yes, it would cause consumers to decrease demand for these brands of smoke alarms as preferences shifted away from the unreliable products. C. Answers will vary. D. 1. word of mouth 2. consumer publications or consumer shows on public TV and public radio E. more reliable because they do not have a vested interest in selling a product like an advertiser does.

Case Application:

Do You Have Time for Your Possessions?

1. The most common means by which consumers find out about the availability of new products is through advertising.

2. Purchasers could make better choices if they had information about the rate of failure and the frequency and cost of servicing the products that they buy.

3. Open answer. It would certainly help consumers to make better choices if they had that information. (For a few things, such information is already required—for example, refrigerator manufacturers are required to post on a refrigerator the average yearly energy cost of op-

erating it.) On the other hand, there is a cost involved in gathering, validating, and disseminating such information that would be passed on to consumers in a higher price for the product. Also, it would require government agencies to enforce the regulation—a cost to taxpayers.

Answers to Practice Test

1.b 2.d 3.d 4.a 5.d 6.b 7.a 8.d 9.a 10.a 11.b 12.c 13.d. 14.d 15.a 16.T 17.F 18.T 19.F 20.T

Chapter 6

What Are the Forms and Economic Functions of Business Firms?

6.1. A. 1.PR 2.C 3.PR 4.C 5.PA B. 1.C 2.PR 3.PA 4.PR 5.C 6.C C. 1.C 2.PA 3.PR 4.C 5.PA and PR D. The managers may be more interested in their *own* well-being than in the stockholders' income. For example, big company cars, fancy desks, and "business" trips to Bermuda do not help the stockholders.

6.2. A. organize production; allocate resources. B.1.(I) Consumers are environmentally conscious. (O) Production is geared toward the use of glass versus plastic. (A) Manufacturers of glass benefit relative to manufacturers of plastic. (C) The bottling machine is new capital. 2.(I) Concertgoers want better sound and lighting. (O) Bands and concert producers change the shows to utilize the new equipment. (A) The manufacturer of the new equipment makes money. (C) The sound and light equipment is new capital.

Case Application:

The Progressive Bike Shop

1. The Progressive Bike Shop was a limited partnership. Pat's parents invested in the business for a percentage return of the net earnings. This made them partners in the business.
2. The Progressive Bike Shop performed all four economic functions of a business. Pat and Jeff decided what goods and services would be offered in the economy by establishing a bicycle sales and service firm. Deciding to rent the storefront location in the inner city was an example of determining how goods and services would be provided. Deciding how the net receipts would be divided up affected the allocation of purchasing power by resolving the "for whom" question, which was also affected by providing their retail services to the campus community. Finally, the renovation of the store premises represented an increase in the economy's real capital investment.
3. Open answer. Locating the bike shop in a deteriorated neighborhood may have been a good idea from a business standpoint because of the low rent overhead, which

reduced the costs of operation, and because the neighborhood population contained an age group of potential customers. From a socioeconomic standpoint, it was a good idea because it helped to revitalize a rundown area. On the other hand, it might not have been a good business decision if the store's marketing area did not have sufficient purchasing power to provide adequate sales revenues for the firm to succeed. If the business failed, it would have been bad for the neighborhood as well as for the owners.

What Determines a Firm's Profits?

6.3. A. Fixed costs exist only in the short run because in the long run the firm has time to alter any and all productive capacity. B. 1.F 2.V 3.V 4.V 5.F 6.F 7.F C. depreciation; productive life; obsolete

6.4. A. profit B. total revenue; total cost; total revenue; total cost C.

Total Cost	Total Revenue	Profit
$2	$0	$2
7	9	2
11	16	5
14	21	7
16	24	8
17	25	8
18	24	6
20	21	1
23	16	-7
27	9	-22
32	0	-32

D. 1.0; 8 2. between 4 and 5 units of output
E. 1.Total revenue will increase because the effect of increased price dominates the effect of decreased quantity. 2.Total revenue will decrease because the effect of increased price is dominated by the effect of decreased quantity.

6.5. A. normal rate of return; economic profits B. the normal rate of return C. 1.$100,000 − $60,000 = $40,000 accounting profit. But her opportunity costs include $25,000 lost salary and $20,000 lost interest. Her net profit is a $5,000 loss! 2.She may stay in business for two reasons. First, she may expect business to improve—the first year is usually the toughest. Second, she may enjoy being her own boss enough to "subsidize" her business with her labor and capital.

Case Application:

The Fortunes of the Progressive Bike Shop

1. The $26,400 cost of the merchandise was a variable cost because it was directly related to the volume of sales.
2. Economic costs not included in the $43,200 total costs were the compensation to Pat and Jeff for the labor time

they put in the business and a normal return on the $6,000 of their capital investment in the business.

3. Open answer. Pat's parents put up over two-thirds of the capital invested in the business. They were entitled to a return on their investment. Such small businesses are risky investments and they stood a chance of losing their $14,000. Therefore, 20% of the net receipts might be a fair return. However, with the way the net receipts were calculated, they were greatly overstated. If Pat and Jeff had been paid a salary out of the receipts for the time they put into the business, the firm would not have shown a profit during its first year of operation. It might have been fairer if the return to Pat's parents' investment were calculated on the basis of net earnings after compensating Pat and Jeff for their time.

How Does Industry Market Structure Affect Price and Output Decisions?

6.6. A. Check 2, 3, 4, 5, and 6. B. Check 1, 2, 4, 6, and 7.

6.7. A. minimum; the lowest possible B. It would go out of business because consumers would buy from other purely competitive firms that sell the exact same product at a lower price. C. Consumers would purchase from a different purely competitive firm. This explains why the firms are price-takers that are always striving to improve product quality and offer output at the lowest possible price. Because of the competitive pressure, the firms also sell exactly the same products without any differentiation.

6.8. A. enter B. 1, 3, 6, 8 C. 2, 4, 5, 8 D. zero (the normal rate of return)

6.9. A. zero B. PM, DC, SM, SM, PM, PM, DC, PM, SM C. 1. PM, SM 2. DC, PM, SM 3. DC, SM 4. DC, PC 5. all 6. all 7. DC, PC 8. SM 9. SM

Case Application:

Wheat Farmers in Debt

1. The fact that he had to accept the going market price for his output. He had no choice in determining the price, but had to take it or leave it.

2. This application illustrates that under purely competitive conditions economic profits tend toward zero because profitable crop conditions result in more wheat being planted, and the increased supply reduces the price. The price decline results in profits disappearing.

3. Open answer. Farmers are engaged in a business that provides a necessity of life but that is subject to varied unpredictable conditions over which they have no control. The unstable effects of weather, insects, and crop diseases are magnified by the unpredictability of prices in the competitive markets for farm products. The uncertainties of farming combined with its importance to our economy have been justifications for government farm price-support programs. These programs have been attacked for misallocating resources by encouraging the production of unneeded crops, for contributing to inflation by

artificially raising food prices, for subsidizing mainly the large farmers, who are already wealthy and do not need government assistance, and for bureaucratic waste.

Answers to Practice Test

1.c 2.c 3.d 4.b 5.e 6.c 7.d 8.c 9.b 10.b 11.a 12.b 13.c 14.d 15.c 16.F 17.F 18.F 19.T 20.T

Chapter 7

What Determines Industry Performance?

7.1. A. (order of answers may vary) 1.productivity 2.quality 3.responsiveness to the market 4.responsiveness to social concerns B. 1.quality 2.responsiveness to social concerns 3.productivity 4.responsiveness to the market 5.quality 6.productivity 7.quality 8.quality 9.productivity, responsiveness to social concerns C. 1.responsiveness to the market 2.quality D. greater; smaller E. (answers will vary) 1.more burgers served per employee; a process innovation that streamlines worker's tasks 2.more cases litigated per hour; new capital—a computer system that makes it easier to keep track of cases 3.more electricity from a given amount of coal or oil; technological advance that converts more coal to energy and less to pollutants.

7.2. A. (answers will vary) 1.radiation leaks 2.too much fat 3.blurry print 4.too much "snow" 5.gears do not shift smoothly 6.roof leaks B. (answers will vary) 1."At Ford, quality is job one." 2.Maytag's lonely repairman 3.Any American car company that compares its cars to Japanese cars C. Winning the award will lead to more business and more profits.

7.3. A. (answers will vary) 1.discriminate in hiring practices 2.use packaging made of CFCs 3.dump their fry grease in a local stream B. 1.change their packaging to use less CFCs 2.use low-fat products 3.establish nonsmoking area C. 1.boycotts by consumers 2.fines levied by the government D. 1. environmental protection 2.equity

Case Application:

Academic Theory Put into Practice

1. Productivity is increased by the consolidation of the sales staff so that they are not competing with each other for the same accounts. Responsiveness to the market is evidenced by the firm's concentration on producing a long-lasting bulb that reduces worker fatigue and errors. (Incidentally, this bulb would improve production efficiency at the businesses that purchased it.) You could even say that the firm is satisfying social objectives by providing such a bulb.

2. An employee stock ownership plan should provide the company's workers with more incentive to produce a quality product efficiently. The larger the sales and the more efficiently the company operates, the greater will

be the company's profits and the higher the value of the employee's stock.

3. Open answer. As a teacher of business and law, Professor Lyons is doubtless up-to-date on management theory. On the other hand, it is often said that academics do not make good executives because managers frequently must make decisions without undue delay on the basis of incomplete knowledge.

How Can Industry Performance Be Improved?

7.4. A. direct B. decline C. (answers will vary) 1.use of uniform product codes (bar codes) 2.use of computers 3.use of robots

7.5. A. 1.short time horizon 2.use of investment funds for speculation 3.high interest rates B. A lower current standard of living because of lower consumption spending, as evidenced by the high prices the Japanese must pay for food and housing.

7.6. A. research and development B. capital C. 1.the military 2.universities D. No. First of all, it earns only a normal profit and has no funds left over for R & D. Second, since there is perfect information, a firm could not profit by innovation.

7.7. A. employee empowerment B. more C. (Answers will vary.) 1.Employees at the pizza parlor may come up with new ideas for scheduling work time that would allow employees more flexibility. They could provide ideas about how to assemble the pizzas quicker or more efficiently. 2.Employees at the automobile manufacturing factory could also provide ideas about how to assemble the product more efficiently. They may have ideas about cross-training that could make it work better. For example, someone who installs windows in the automobile may be able to offer expertise about other specific tasks related to handling glass. 3.Employees at the bank could also offer ideas that would make cross-training more beneficial. They may have ideas about how to combine or separate various tasks into job assignments, too.

7.8. A. employee involvement B. 1.SM 2.SP 3.SM 4.PS C. the United States; Japan D. 1.unions 2.middle management

Case Application:

Dell Deals Direct

1. According to the information provided in the case, Dell has invested in capital equipment because their factory integration system requires a great deal of automation. They seem to have invested in training their employees to interact directly with customers (that is, building human capital), and their innovative processes suggest that they have invested in research and development. Given the company's performance in the market, the investments appear to be successful.

2. Since Dell builds the computer systems as each order comes in, the company does not have a huge inventory

from which it ships complete systems. The company manufactures and provides the product at the time the order is placed. If the system is set up so that the components and subassemblies are delivered by suppliers at the time they are needed, this is a just-in-time manufacturing system.

3. Dell's method seems cost-effective because the costs associated with the distributor or "middle man" are eliminated. Many customers also prefer to deal directly with the factory. However, some of Dell's competitors (e.g., Compaq) complain that customers who purchase Dell systems then require services from distributors that are located in the same geographic area. Therefore, Dell claims that its system eliminates distributors, when, in fact, Dell customers are relying on local distributors that sell other brands. Dell's increasing market share suggests that consumers prefer their system of dealing directly.

What Are the Effects of Industry Concentration on Performance?

7.9. A. 1.H 2.L 3.H 4.H 5.L 6.H 7.H or L 8.H 9.H 10.Answers will vary. 11.Answers will vary. B. monopoly and shared monopoly C. 1.40% 2.40% 3.12% D. industry Z

7.10. A. aggregate B. 1.AM 2.A 3.AM 4.A 5.AM

7.11. A. 1.mergers 2.economies of scale 3.predatory business practices B. predatory business practices. C. 1.high prices 2.inefficient resource allocation 3.higher costs 4.unnecessary product differentiation D. (answers may vary) 1.breakfast cereal 2.toothpaste 3.perfume

Case Application:

Rent-a-Kidney Business: Dialysis for Profit?

1. The home dialysis equipment industry is a shared monopoly. One firm sells almost 50% of all home equipment sold.

2. The hospital-based dialysis service industry does not have the same market structure as the home dialysis equipment industry. National Medical Care, the largest firm, has only 16% of the hospital-based business. Consequently, it can be concluded that the largest four firms have less than 50% of the industry sales.

3. Open answer. It could be argued that private firms provide dialysis service more economically than it would be provided directly by government agencies. Furthermore, it is not unusual for firms doing business under government programs to make high profits because such programs are frequently in new areas of technology and involve such business risks as on-and-off funding. Others would argue that government funding of programs provides excessive profits that would not exist in a purely free-enterprise market, and that such humanitarian programs should not be tainted with large profits being siphoned off by private industry. Also, high profits from government-funded programs may result in a misallocation of resources.

1.c 2.c 3.b 4.a 5.d 6.b 7.b 8.c 9.a 10.d 11.a 12.a 13.d 14.a 15.c 16.F 17.T 18.T 19.F 20.F

Chapter 8

How Does the Government Limit Monopoly Power?

8.1. A. 1.ICA 2.CKA 3.CA 4.CA 5.SA B. 1.monopolization 2.collusion 3.anticompetitive mergers C. There are too many firms for either effective collusion or attempted monopolization.

8.2. A. in order to promote international competitiveness B. the National Co-operative Research Act of 1984 C. There might be a duplication of effort. For example, three different firms may be independently working on the same brake problem. D. collusion between the two firms such as a price-fixing or market-sharing scheme

8.3. A. economies of scale B. Average costs (and prices) would be higher for each of the smaller firms. C. (answers will vary) 1.local electric company 2.local phone company 3.local cable television company D. There is difficulty agreeing on a "fair" price because regulators, consumers, and stockholders have conflicting objectives. It is difficult to reconcile adequate service at fair prices with a fair return to stockholders. Also, the fair-return principle of regulation discourages efficiency and innovation. A third reason that the industry may become competitive is that technological advances have reduced monopoly power in industries such as cable television.

8.4. A. government ownership and operation B. Answers will vary. C. 1.finding accurate cost information 2.determining a "fair" rate of return D. 1.probably not 2.probably so 3.firms E. a "normal profit"

8.5. A. competitive (either pure or differentiated competition) B. You should check 1, 3, and 4. C. Prices and profits fell.

Case Application:

Water, Water, Everywhere, and Not a Drop (That's Fit) to Drink

1. The trend in government policies in recent years has been to decrease the role of government in the business sector.

2. The fact that there was only one company supplying water to Dedham and Westwood meant that, even though the citizens were extremely unhappy with the water they were getting, they had no choice but to buy it. Since a water utility is a natural monopoly, there was no competition to force an improvement in the service.

3. Open answer. Water is essential to life, and the purity of our water supplies is important to us. We look to government to protect the interests of the public, especially where natural monopolies are concerned. On the other hand, we cannot afford absolute purity of water or practically anything else. (Besides, there is no such thing as completely pure water unless it is distilled, and distilled water is not recommended for drinking on a regular basis because it lacks the minerals our bodies need.) The market is a better regulator of business than the government. If people are dissatisfied with the water from the tap, they can purchase bottled water.

Why Does the Government Produce Goods and Services?

8.6. A. 1.CG 2.PS 3.CG 4.CG 5.PS 6.PS 7.PS 8.CG B. (answers will vary) 1.local schools 2.trash pick-up 3.libraries C. You could not exclude nonpayers. D. Determining how much the citizens value the good (the city cannot use the price mechanism to "force" people to reveal how much they value a service).

8.7. A. 1. EC 2. EC 3. EE 4. EE 5. EE 6. EC 7. EC 8. EC B. 1.

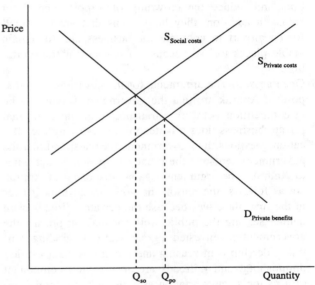

2.lower
C. 1.

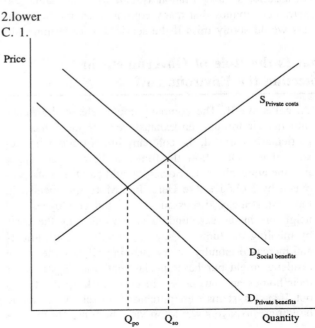

2.higher D. Too many goods are produced when external costs are present, and too few are produced when external economies are present. E. 1.less pollution 2.less congestion (or 3.less dependency on foreign energy sources)

Case Application:

Should the Government Be in the Railroad Business?

1. The government subsidy of Amtrak cannot be justified in terms of equity because it is not primarily lower-income people who take advantage of the government subsidies to rail passenger traffic.

2. There are external economies associated with rail passenger and freight traffic. Rail transportation is more energy efficient and less polluting than highway or air transportation. Railroads reduce congestion on the highways, reduce the need for petroleum, reduce air pollution, and reduce the crowding of airports and flight paths. In addition, they help towns that are too small for an airport to compete for business and to remain viable places to live because of convenient transportation.

3. Open answer. The arguments for the government to dispose of Amtrak are that the government should not be in competition with other transportation suppliers; that private business does a better job of resolving the allocation questions than government agencies; and that the government can save the money it spends on subsidies to Amtrak. The arguments against disposing of Amtrak are as follows: the reason the government took it over in the first place was because the private railroads were neither serving the public well nor making profits; the government has invested a great deal in upgrading Amtrak; ridership is increasing and the government subsidy diminishing; and railroads are an essential component of a nation's transportation system with substantial external economies that many communities and individuals would sorely miss if the services were terminated.

What Is the Role of Government in Protecting the Environment?

8.8. A. collective B. The company could release the fumes into the air through an exhaust vent. If the fumes are particularly harmful, the company might build a smokestack that would allow the fumes to be released higher into the atmosphere. C. Society would pay the costs generated by Holidays Are Here, Inc. More specifically, in the first strategy discussed above, the employees and neighbors in the surrounding area would pay the costs by inhaling the fumes. They might suffer health effects and increased laundry or dry cleaning bills. Some of the residents might purchase special ventilation systems for their homes and businesses in order to keep the fumes out. If such systems were purchased for schools or public buildings, taxpayers would provide the funds. In the sec-

ond strategy, the costs would be incurred by the same parties. The only difference is that the smokestack might possibly allow the fumes to travel farther before the most serious effects are evident. Therefore, residents, business owners, and taxpayers who live farther away would incur the costs. D. According to economists, the external costs should be internalized. The environmental protection authority can regulate the company's emissions to limit them, or they can impose an eco-tax on the emissions. If several companies in the area are polluting, a combination of regulation and emission permits could provide a cost-effective solution.

8.9. A. 1.command-and-control regulations 2.eco-taxes 3.the sale of emission allowances B. 1.100 tons for $750 2.Have firm X clean up 100 tons for only $500. 3.Firm X would be willing to clean up 100 tons if firm Y made it worth its while, and firm Y would be willing to pay up to $500. C. 1."third parties" 2.customers D. 1.higher electric prices 2.perhaps fewer jobs in the electric industry

Case Application:

Declaration of Air Pollution Emergency

1. The external costs associated with steel production in Allegheny County included air pollution, which resulted in many health problems, and decreased visibility, which interfered with traffic.

2. In order to internalize the external costs of its steel production operation, the U.S. Steel Corporation would have to install fabric filters for electric arcs, high-energy wet scrubbers for open-hearth and basic oxygen furnaces, and electrostatic precipitators for smokestacks. This would increase production costs, which would raise the price of steel and reduce the quantity of steel production. This can be shown on a demand-supply diagram by a shift of the supply curve to the left. The equilibrium price on the new supply curve is higher and the equilibrium quantity lower than on the previous supply curve.

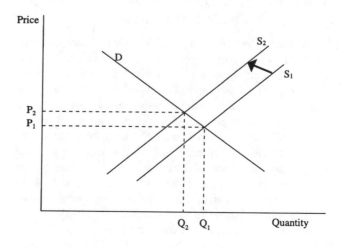

3. Open answer. Those who believe that reducing air pollution and the effects it has on health and safety are the most important considerations would favor forcing U.S. Steel to internalize its external costs. Those who believe that unemployment is the most important consideration would not.

Answers to Practice Test

1.d 2.d 3.c 4.b 5.d 6.b 7.b 8.a 9.a 10.d 11.a 12.a 13.c 14.d 15.a 16.T 17.F 18.T 19.F 20.T

Chapter 9

What Does the Government Do to Reduce Poverty?

9.1. A. income; size of family; whether it is a farm or non-farm household B. 1.$15,000 2.$25,000 3.The number of people under the poverty line would be greater if the correct share was 1/5 since there are more households earning less than $25,000 per year than there are earning less than $15,000 per year.

9.2. A. 1.3.7% 2.49.0% B. less C. 1.human capital 2.asset ownership 3.educational opportunities and motivation due to differences in gender, race, or ethnic group 4.ability to work and earn an income D. 1.4 2.3 3.1 4.1 5.4 6.2

9.3. A. computer B. skilled; non-skilled C. 1.education 2.training

9.4. A. 1.6 2.2 3.3 4.5 5.4 6.1 B. The government has passed legislation such as the Civil Rights Act of 1964, the Age Discrimination Act of 1967, and the Americans with Disabilities Act of 1990 to remove obstacles to economic opportunity based on gender, race, religion, ethnic background, age, or disability status.

Case Application:

The New Poor

1. The "old poor" were poverty-stricken because of such difficulties as lack of education, physical or mental disability, or exclusion from the workforce. The "new poor" are poverty-stricken because of declining demand in a number of industries, which has put many experienced workers out of a job.

2. The "new poor" will move out of poverty first when economic conditions improve because a rising number of job openings will be available to them, whereas the "old poor" are likely to still be excluded.

3. Open answer. Private welfare agencies should aid everyone in need of help regardless of the reason for their conditions. On the other hand, it could be argued that the "old poor" are more in need of assistance than the "new poor" because they have been in poverty longer, have fewer resources to fall back upon, and will continue to be in poverty after the "new poor" have found jobs.

What Is the Answer to Poverty?

9.5. A. 1.d 2.f 3.b 4.c 5.a 6.e B. 1.1,5,6 2.2,5,6 3.4,5,6 4.3 C.Those programs that provide increased education and opportunities to those in poverty to help themselves are the best long-run solutions for those who are able to work. 2.Those programs that provide immediate assistance through transfer payments to those in poverty are the best short-run solutions, as long as the programs are not structured in a way that provides incentives for recipients to remain dependent on public assistance.

Case Application:

Increased Opportunities for People with Disabilities

1. The number of people with disabilities who are poor has been reduced since 1973 by the enactment of federal and state legislation prohibiting employer discrimination against those with disabilities.

2. Affirmative action programs to employ people with disabilities are needed because there is a prejudice against hiring them. They frequently can be valuable employees, but fears on the part of employers about possible consequences prevent their being considered for jobs in the absence of affirmative action programs.

3. Open answer. Yes, the government should subsidize firms that hire people with disabilities because they can make a contribution to output, and income they earn reduces the need for government welfare payments and other assistance. No, the government should not subsidize firms to hire people with disabilities because it could result in less efficiency in the production process, and the market should determine resource allocation without government intervention.

What Does the Government Do to Help Older Americans?

9.6. A. public assistance; social insurance B. Answers may vary. 1.objective of the program—With public assistance, the objective is to help those who are in poverty while the objective of Social Security is to ensure that older Americans do not fall into poverty. 2.method of financing the program—Public assistance programs are financed through general tax revenues while Social Security is financed specifically through a payroll tax (FICA). 3.eligibility requirements—People are eligible for public assistance based on income levels while people are eligible for Social Security based on age and whether they have paid into the program for at least 10 years.

9.7. A. Medicaid; Medicare B.1.Medicaid 2.Medicare 3.eligibility requirements—Medicaid is specifically for low-income families while Medicare is specifically for older Americans.

9.8. A. The sector of the population that is nearing retirement (the "baby boomers") includes a large number of people. Once they retire, the dependency ratio (number of retirees to current workers) will increase significantly. If the program is not reformed, it could require payroll tax rates as high as 35% for the workers to support the retirees. B. People are living longer today due to advances in technology and health care. They are receiving Social Security benefits for many more years than people did in the past. C. The surplus that is generated today is used to buy government bonds. It is paying off debts in other areas of the budget. Once the money is needed again by the Social Security program, the government will have to raise taxes in order to pay it back.

9.9. A. 1.This money is invested in whichever funds Jasmine selects. 2.This money is used to pay benefits to current recipients of Social Security. 3.The money that she receives from the private pension plan will come from the actual funds that she invested in, plus the company's contributions, plus interest or dividends earned on the money. The money that she receives from Social Security will come from people who are working and paying money to the Social Security program at the time she retires. B. The basic difference is that money paid into the Social Security program today is paid out to those who receive Social Security benefits today while money paid into a private pension plan accumulates and is returned to the investor upon retirement.

9.10. A. payroll; current workers B. No. Payments made to the Social Security program are called "contributions," but it is a requirement that both employees and employers pay money into the Social Security trust funds. C. Roberto's "contributions" are used to pay benefits to today's recipients like his grandfather.

9.11. A. 1.Extend the retirement age. 2.Increase the payroll tax rate between 1 and 2 percentage points. B. defined benefits retirement plan; defined contributions retirement plan C. They are both private savings accounts that would be given special tax treatment as long as funds were not withdrawn before retirement. D. Open answer. If you favor government involvement in providing funds for retired persons, you would recommend keeping the program essentially the same and making minor changes like those described in exercise A. If you favor individuals providing for their own retirement without much gov-

ernment involvement, you would recommend changes that would privatize the Social Security program.

Case Application:

A Three-Legged Stool?

1. Social Security, private pensions, savings
2. Many people in today's society count on receiving Social Security when they retire. They consciously decide not to save as much for their own retirements because they know they will receive Social Security and since they have seen many retired people benefit from it. Many people in today's society also do not save money for, or make plans to accept responsibility for, supporting older members of their own families. They expect Social Security benefits to be available. There is a lot less planning for retirement in today's society.
3. Open answer. Yes, if you believe that most people are incapable of saving for their own retirements but deserve to have funds available to them. No, if you believe that people should be held accountable for their own actions and live in poverty if they did not save enough to support themselves in retirement.

What is the Role of Government in Protecting Consumers and Workers?

9.12. A. 1.SEC 2.DOT 3.CPSC 4.OSHA 5.FDA 6.FTC B. Most of us do not have the information to make informed decisions. C. Agriculture

Case Application:

Are Herbal Remedies Safe?

1. Food and Drug Administration (FDA)
2. They trust the claims they have read or heard about the herb's effectiveness, and they may not have heard any stories of awful side effects. They may also be frustrated at not finding a remedy for the problem and may be willing to try anything recommended. Some consumers may trust their own abilities to decide whether the herb is safe. They may gather information and consider themselves to be informed enough to make a good decision.
3. Open answer. Yes, if you believe that many citizens would benefit from taking the supplements and knowing more about their effectiveness, dosage requirements, and side effects so that the benefits gained from spending money on regulation of dietary supplements would outweigh the costs. No, if you believe that the benefits of more information about natural remedies would benefit a small enough group of the population that the costs of regulation would outweigh the benefits.

Answers to Practice Test

1.b 2.c 3.b 4.b 5.a 6.a 7.c 8.c 9.b 10.c 11.c 12.b 13.d 14.d 15.c 16.T 17.T 18.F 19.F 20.F

Crossword Puzzle for Chapters 5–9

Chapter 10

What Is Money?

10.1. A. (answers will vary) 1.sea shells 2.cows 3.cigarettes B. 17th; goldsmiths C. any privately owned bank that was chartered by a state or federal government D. the Federal Reserve System (Bank)

10.2. A. 1.currency (including coins) 2.checkable deposits 3.traveler's checks 4.ATS accounts B.checkable deposits C. only because people are willing to accept them as payment for goods and services

10.3. A. liquid B. ranking: 5, 2, 4, 1, 3 C. 1.commercial paper 2.savings bonds 3.short-term government bonds D. 1.M1, M2, M3, L 2.M2, M3, L 3.M1, M2, M3, L 4.L 5.M3, L 6.M1, M2, M3, L 7.M2, M3, L

Case Application:

What Isn't Money?

1. The expansion of money market mutual funds represented an increase in near money.

2. Money market mutual funds are more like money than are certificates of deposit because they are more liquid. Investments in money market mutual funds can be withdrawn immediately with no penalty, usually simply by writing a check. Investments in certificates of deposit, on the other hand, cannot be withdrawn by check and

cannot be withdrawn before maturity without a penalty being imposed.

3. Open answer. The advantages of deregulating financial institutions are that it increases competition in the financial services market and allows different types of financial institutions to compete on an equal basis. Disadvantages are that some financial institutions may not be able to survive and some types of loans, such as those for home mortgages, may be more difficult and costly to obtain because other types of lending are more profitable.

What Does Money Do?

10.4. A. 1.medium of exchange 2.unit of measurement 3.store of value B. (using the numbering from A) 1.3 2.2 3.1 4.1 5.2 6.2

10.5. A. 1.universally recognized 2.not easily reproduced 3.portable 4.durable 5.adequate but limited supply B. (using the numbering from A) 1.5 2.4 3.3,4 4.5 5.2 6.1 C. Credit cards do not serve as a "store of value" or a unit of measurement. Also, credit cards are not money; they are a means of borrowing money. D. It should be stable in value.

Case Application:

Primitive Money

1. When the price of slaves was quoted in cows and brass rods, those items were performing the function of a unit of account.

2. In the United States, money must be convertible from one denomination into another (for example, five $1 bills for a $5 bill) in order to serve as a universal means of exchange; shells could not have served this function among the Russell Islanders since shells were not convertible.

3. Open answer. Some possible ways in which it could be said that money performs social as well as economic functions in our society include the practices of lighting a cigar with a $100 bill to display affluence, leaving a very small tip for a rude waiter to show dissatisfaction, or leaving a quarter from the "tooth fairy" under the pillow of a child.

How Is Money Created?

10.6. A. 1.I 2.D 3.D 4.I 5.I 6.D B. a checking account (demand deposit) C. 1.Answers will vary. 2.usually none D. checking accounts E. 1.Yes, they usually have an increased balance in their checking accounts. 2.No. 3.It increases.

Case Application:

How the Government Creates Money

1. If the U.S. Treasury prints a $10,000 bond and you borrow the $10,000 from your bank to purchase the bond, the money supply is increased by $10,000. You are directly responsible for the expansion of the money supply

because it was your loan from the bank that increased it, not the printing of the bond by the Treasury.

2. If the government paid its bills by printing currency rather than by selling government securities, the result would be a greater increase in the money supply because some of the money paid for government securities represents a reduction in the privately held money stock.

3. Open answer. The lower interest rates paid on savings bonds can be called unfair to small investors because these investors do not have sufficient funds to purchase higher-denomination government securities. On the other hand, it could be argued that those who purchase U.S. savings bonds have the freedom to choose between those and other types of investments, and purchasing savings bonds may be considered patriotic.

How Is the Supply of Money Controlled?

10.7. A. Federal Reserve System B. 1. 12 2.Answers will vary. C. 1.acts as a banker's bank 2.serves the monetary needs of the federal government 3.controls the money supply (4.the Fed also "clears" checks for individuals and businesses.) D.control of the money supply E. 1.seven 2. 14 3.Because members of the Board of Governors have such long terms, they do not need to depend on the "kindness" of politicians in order to keep their jobs. This allows them to avoid political pressure.

10.8. A. 1.required reserves 2.excess reserves B. 1.$30,000 2.$15,000 3.$20,000 C. A commercial bank must have excess reserves on hand in order to make loans.

10.9. A. 1.changing the discount rate 2.changing the required reserve ratio 3.open market operations B. 1.from the Fed through discounting 2.from other banks in the Federal Funds market C. 1.I 2.D 3.D 4.D 5.I D. 1.$10,000 2.$90,000 3.$90,000 4.10 (1 ÷ 0.1) 5.$900,000 (10 × $90,000) 6.$70,000 7.$700,000 (10 × $70,000) E. 1.$20,000 2.$80,000 3.5 (1 ÷ 0.2) 4.$400,000 (5 × $80,000) 5.$40,000 6.$200,000 (5 × $40,000) F. 1.increases 2.increases 3.increases 4.decreases G. 1.increases 2.decreases 3.decreases 4.increases H. 1.I 2.I 3.D 4.D 5.I 6.I

I. 1, 2, and 3

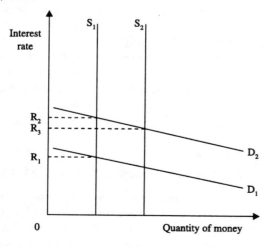

4.It might cause inflation.

Case Application:

Who's in Charge around Here?

1. The Depository Institutions Deregulation and Monetary Control Act of 1980 (the Monetary Control Act) expanded the authority of the Fed by making nonmember banks and other depository institutions subject to the same Fed regulations as those banks that are members of the system and by providing nonmember institutions with the Fed's services, for which they must pay a fee.

2. The principal regulatory power that the Fed needs in order to implement monetary policy is the power to mandate the required reserve ratio that the banks must maintain.

3. Open answer. The overlapping authority of the three bank regulatory agencies may result in duplication of activities and responsibilities. Especially in these times of widespread bank failures resulting from unsound lending practices, there should be clear regulatory responsibility by a single agency over a specific banking activity. On the other hand, the Federal Reserve has the primary responsibility for implementing a sound monetary policy and should have broad regulatory authority rather than being confined to a service and policy-making role.

Answers to Practice Test

1.c 2.b 3.d 4.b 5.c 6.d 7.d 8.c 9.b 10.a 11.c 12.a 13.b 14.d 15.c 16.F 17.F 18.F 19.T 20.T

Chapter 11

What Causes Unemployment?

11.1. A. 1.S 2.C 3.F 4.S 5.S 6.C 7.S B. 1.frictional 2.frictional 3.cyclical 4.frictional C. 1.F 2.C 3.S 4.S 5.F

11.2. A. actively seeking employment B. 1.N 2.N 3.C 4.N 5.N 6.N 7.N C. 1.nothing 2.It will increase. 3.understates 4.overstates

11.3. A. full employment; stable B. It will increase. C. 1.decrease 2.more 3.higher 4.higher; fewer 5.increase

Case Application:

Where the Jobs Went

1. The 100,000-plus jobs permanently lost in the automobile industry represented structural unemployment. They were lost by an increase in automation of automobile production methods and by an increase in the share of the U.S. automobile market accounted for by foreign car imports.

2. Women who lost their jobs because of the recession and did not try to find new jobs were not counted as unemployed because only those actively seeking jobs are con-

sidered unemployed. The women who did not seek new jobs represented hidden unemployment.

3. Open answer. A 40-year-old steelworker with a family who lost his job would have difficult alternatives. One possibility would be to try to scrape by on unemployment compensation, as long as it lasted, and then on savings in hopes the steel mill would reopen. Another possibility would be to move his family to a state with a lower unemployment rate than Pennsylvania in hopes of finding other work for which he was qualified. A third possibility would be for him to attempt to obtain retraining for a different type of work in an expanding industry. All of these choices involve difficulties and dangers for the economic security of his family.

What Causes Inflation?

11.4. A. Inflation is a continual increase in the general level of prices. 1.consumer price index (CPI) 2.market basket B. 1985: 100; 1986: 110; 1987: 115; 1988: 125; 1989: 130 C. 1985 to 1986 = 10%; 1986 to 1987 = 4.5%; 1987 to 1988 = 8.7%; 1988 to 1989 = 4.0%

11.5. A. product; factor B. 1.monetary 2.demand-pull 3.cost-push 4.demand-pull 5.cost-push

11.6. A. M = the money supply; V = the velocity of money; P = the average price level; T = the number of transactions. B. 1.M × V represents the number of dollars spent. 2.P × T represents the value of all goods and services bought. C. 1.Prices increase. 2.It stays the same. 3.The velocity of money must increase (each dollar must be spent more times). D. 1.S; I 2.I; S 3.I; I 4.during a recession

Case Application:

Talk about Inflation...

1. The restaurant dinner would have cost 47 shekels at the end of 1984. This is calculated by multiplying 10 shekels by 470% (= 370% + 100%). (Note that 470% of a number is 4.7 times the number, since the decimal point is moved two places to the right when expressing a percentage.)

2. The types of inflation described in this application are demand-pull and monetary inflation.

3. Open answer. Likely reasons why the inflation rates are so much greater in some other countries than in the United States are that other countries have smaller economies than the United States so that a monetary disturbance is not so easily absorbed as it is in the large U.S. economy; that they have had more severe economic problems, such as the Arab-Israeli conflict; and especially that they do not have a monetary control institution as effective as the Fed in the United States.

Is There a Trade-off between Unemployment and Inflation?

11.7. A. 1.D 2.I 3.D 4.D 5.I B. 5

C.

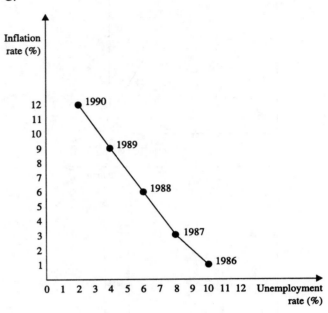

D.

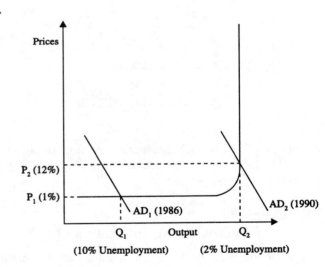

E. demand-pull F. 1.higher unemployment 2. higher inflation

11.8. A. directly; inconsistent B. 1.higher union wages 2.increased input prices 3.inflationary expectation

C.

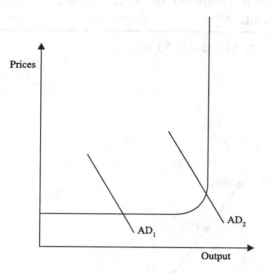

D.

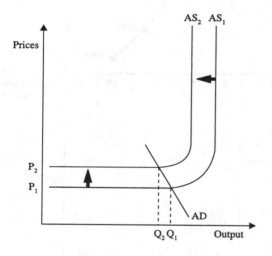

E. Question C; both prices and unemployment are higher. F. 1.P stays the same, T increases. 2.Both increase. 3.P increases, T stays the same.

Case Application:

Phillips Curve International

1. Prior to 1975, the European countries were operating more to the upper left on their Phillips curves, with higher inflation rates and lower unemployment rates than the United States.
2. The rise in energy costs in the 1970s made European production costs higher, which both raised the inflation rate and made their industries less competitive in the marketplace, thus slowing their economies and causing unemployment. The combination of higher prices and higher unemployment was represented by an upward shift in the Phillips curve.
3. Open answer. Answering this question is complicated and uncertain, depending on the assumptions and value judgments adopted. The upper-left portion of the Phil-

lips curve imposes the costs of inflation, such as possible declines in the efficiency and growth of the economy and other costs disproportionately borne by those with fixed incomes. On the other hand, it minimizes the human, social, and output costs of unemployment. The lower-right location on the Phillips curve increases those unemployment costs while minimizing the costs of inflation.

What Are the Consequences of Unemployment and Inflation?

11.9. A. 1.Real output decreases. 2.Real incomes decrease. 3.negative social effects B. (using the preceding numbering) 1.3 2.1 3.2 4.2 5.3 C. 1.B 2.L 3.L 4.L 5.L 6.B 7.B 8.B 9.B D. 1.A Business will benefit if the price of its product is increasing faster than the prices of its inputs. 2.A Business will suffer if the price of its inputs increases faster than the price of its output.

Case Application:

Disinflation Losers

1. The wealth and income of those who had purchased real assets such as houses, gold, precious gems, or commodities were negatively affected by an end to inflation. Debtors lose out when disinflation sets in, and the incomes of governments are also affected.
2. A decline in the price of gold and other commodities would be likely to affect the output of those commodities because of the law of supply. Unless the supply is perfectly inelastic, a price decline will result in reductions in their output.
3. Open answer. A severe disinflation could be worse than inflation. A collapse of prices such as that occurring in the early 1930s would cause many business failures and high unemployment. A disinflation resulting in a stable price level, however, would be better than inflation because it would benefit equity, efficiency, and growth.

Answers to Practice Test

1.b 2.d 3.a 4.c 5.b 6.a 7.d 8.d 9.c 10.a 11.c 12.b 13.b 14.c 15.d 16.T 17.F 18.T 19.F 20.F

Chapter 12

How Much Does the Economy Produce?

12.1. A. 1.spend. 2.earn. B. 1.product 2.factor (resource) C. The values added equal .30; .15; .20; .20; and .10. The addition to GDP equals .95. D. 1.I 2.N 3.N 4.I 5.I 6.I 7.I 8. 9.N E. 1.wages and salaries 2.profits 3.rent 4.interest income F. 1.indirect business taxes 2.capital consumption allowances (depreciation)

12.2. A. 1.G 2.X 3.X 4.I 5.C 6.I 7.I 8.C B. (answers will vary) 1.C: It becomes a second family vehicle. I: A landscaping company buys the truck. G: Your town buys the truck and uses it for hauling leaves. X: The truck is shipped to Russia. 2.C: You buy it and watch it. I: Your local news station buys it and uses it as a monitor. G: Your local school district buys it and uses it in class. X: The television is sold to China. C. 1.C 2.C 3.I 4.X 5.I 6.C 7.I 8.C

12.3. A. 1.price level 2.constant dollar; current dollar B. 1.Q 2.P × Q C. 1994: $2,000,000; 1995: $2,200,000; 1996: $2,400,000; 1997: $2,350,000; 1998: $2,500,000 D. 1997 E. Current dollar GDP will be greater because the prices of everything (on average) will be greater.

12.4. A. 1.B 2.neither 3.G 4.G 5.B 6.B B. 1. + 2. − 3.+ 4.− 5.+ 6.−

Case Application:

Helen's Gift City, Inc.

1. The contribution of Helen's Gift City to total output was $110,000. This was the value added by the firm to GDP, that is, its sales revenue minus its purchases from other firms.

2. The firm added $86,000 to National Income. The difference between its contribution to GDP and its contribution to NI is accounted for by the firm's capital-consumption allowance and business taxes.

3. Open answer. From the standpoint of the firm, the business accounting statement is the more useful organization of the information because it shows the total costs subtracted from sales to determine the firm's profit. The national income accounting statement is the more useful for determining the contributions of the firm to GDP.

What Determines Domestic Output From the Demand-Side Point of View?

12.5. A. aggregate demand. B. 1.It reduces aggregate demand. 2.It results in lower interest rates and greater investment demand. C. 1.D 2.G 3.G 4.D 5.G 6.G 7.D D. 1.budget deficit. 2.It will cause it to increase. E. 1.budget surplus. 2.It will cause it to decrease. F. additions to purchasing power from C, I, and G are just equal to the leakages from the income tank (C, S, and T). Thus, we must have I + G = S + T in order to have domestic output in equilibrium.

12.6. A. 1.leakage: consumption; addition: consumption 2.leakage: taxes; addition: government spending 3.leakage: savings; addition: investment 4.leakage: imports; addition: exports B. 1.nothing; consumption will always equal consumption 2.if the government does not spend all its tax receipts 3.if available savings are not borrowed C. 1.GDP falls 2.GDP rises 3.GDP remains the same D. 1.decrease 2.increase G 3.decrease T 4.It will develop a deficit 5.inflation 6.decrease G 7.increase T 8.It will develop a surplus.

Case Application:

Changes in Demand

1. The strongest GDP component in 1993 was business fixed investment, which grew 11.7%. The weakest component was net exports, falling by 132.4%. (The percentage changes tend to be larger for net exports than for other components because, since the net export figure is the difference between exports and imports, it is a smaller absolute number than the others, allowing a change to be a larger percentage.)

2. Imports grew much more rapidly than exports in 1993 principally because the U.S. economy was recovering from the worldwide recession more quickly than its trading partners.

3. Open answer. Most people attempt to maintain their lifestyle in spite of fluctuations in their income. Some, however, may be cautious and reduce their spending sharply if their income falls in order to have a savings cushion in case their income falls further.

What Determines Domestic Output from the Supply-Side Point of View?

12.7. A. aggregate supply or the level of income earned. B. 1.flexible wages and prices 2.There are powerful institutional forces that resist falling wages and prices. C. Wages and prices would have fallen.

12.8. A. 1.incentives to produce. 2.to lower taxes. B. 1.savings 2.investment 3.labor supplies C. 1.increased; increased 2.interest rates; decrease; decreased D. 1.D 2.S 3.S 4.S 5.D 6.S 7.S

Case Application:

Is War Good for the Economy?

1. The earlier, conventional view of the effect of war on the economy was a demand-side view because it was based on the results of adding the demand for goods and services for the war effort to existing demand, thus increasing total demand.

2. The anticipated effects were supply-side effects such as the additional supply costs due to higher energy prices and the crowding-out effect on investment resulting from larger government spending to pay for the war.

3. Open answer. One response might be that effects of war on the economy should be disregarded because moral, political, and security considerations are more important in deciding whether to go to war. The opposite opinion might be based on the positions that the government should consider the welfare of its own citizens above all, that the costs of war—material, financial, and personal— are too high, and that in the long run a healthy economy is the best security.

Answers to Practice Test

1.b 2.a 3.d 4.b 5.c 6.c 7.b 8.b 9.b 10.b 11.b 12.a 13.a 14.b 15.c 16.T 17.F 18.F 19.T 20.F

Chapter 13

On What Do Governments Spend Money?

13.1. A. 1. 32% 2. 18% B. 1.defense 2.transfer payments C. federal; state and local D. 1.roughly constant 2.nearly doubled

13.2. A. There is no production involved. The money is simply transferred from one sector of society to another. B. 1.28%, 2.72% C. 1.D 2.T 3.D 4.D 5.D 6.T

13.3. A. 1.defense 2.Social Security 3.income security B. 1.allocation of income 2.Transfer payments are a bigger part of the budget than direct payments. C. 1.CN 2.CN 3.CN 4.C 5.C 6.CN 7.C 8.C D. 1. 4, 5 2. 7, 8 3. 1, 2, 3 E. Answers will vary but could include defense, grants to local governments for transit, sewerage, or water projects, subsidies for education, and any transfers that a household may receive.

13.4. A. education. B. finance capital projects. C. 1.prisons 2.health care D. 1.SL 2.SL 3.SL 4.SL 5.F 6.F 7.F 8.F E. 1–3. Answers may vary, but just about every state was having serious problems as of 1995. Areas may include transportation (potholes, fuel for buses), education (low teacher salaries, understaffing, poor facilities), public safety (rising crime, inadequate number of prison cells), and underfunding of social service programs (health care, day care).

Case Application:

Renovating America

1. Federal spending on the renewal of the nation's public facilities would increase the pie slice labeled "Other direct," the slice that shows federal spending on nondefense goods and services.

2. The state and local government spending affected will be "Highways" and "Utilities."

3. Open answer. It could be argued that renewing America's infrastructure should constitute one of the highest priorities in government spending because continued deterioration of the nation's transportation system and other public facilities would lead to a decrease in economic efficiency and a slowdown of GDP growth, not to mention the dangers and inconveniences to the public. Those who oppose massive spending on the infrastructure might argue that we cannot afford the high cost it would entail because of more pressing needs such as an adequate national defense and adequate human services such as education, food programs for malnourished children, and medical care.

Where Do Governments Get the Money to Spend?

13.5. A. 1.F 2.S 3.F and S 4.S and L 5.F 6.L 7.F B. The federal tax system is more *progressive* than state and local tax systems. Therefore collecting taxes at the federal level results in more vertical equity. C. 1.income and payroll taxes 2.sales taxes, excise taxes 3.income taxes on earned interest and dividends, and corporate income taxes on a corporation *before* it pays the dividends. 4.property taxes D. 1.The supply of land would not change—it can't! 2.Taxes are a cost of production that must be paid, and removing the tax on buildings would make them less expensive to build. More (and bigger) buildings would therefore be built.

Case Application:

How to Pay for Schools

1. The pie slice showing the percentage of state and local revenues coming from property taxes would be reduced and the slice showing sales tax increased.

2. It is an illustration of the principle of fiscal federalism because a lower branch of government—the school district—is being financed by revenues collected at a higher level of government—the state.

3. Open answer. One of the arguments against shifting school funding to the state level is that control follows the money, and local control of schools will be lost in the process. Another argument, one that can be found in the following section of the chapter, is that sales taxes are especially regressive because the poor spend most of their income on goods that are taxed, although property taxes are also somewhat regressive. The arguments in favor of the shift are that property taxes have become very onerous, sometimes forcing the elderly to give up homes that were paid off long ago; and that basing school funding on property taxes is unfair to children in poor districts, and thus at least contrary to good public policy, if not a violation of the law.

Who Pays for Government Spending?

13.6. A. 1.horizontal equity. 2.vertical equity. B. 1.There would be less horizontal equity because two people with the same income could pay different taxes if one's income was from capital gains and the other's from wages. 2.There would be less vertical equity because wealthier households earning their incomes by buying and selling assets would pay a lower tax rate than lower-income wage earners. C. 1.whoever uses that service 2.Gasoline taxes are used to finance highway construction and maintenance. D. 1.collective goods (which cannot exclude nonpayers). 2.redistribution of income to the poor—if the poor could afford to pay for the services, they would not be poor! E. 1.E 2.B 3.B or E 4.E 5.E 6.E 7.B

13.7. A. 1.taxes on things considered "sins"—drinking and smoking. 2.Smokers and drinkers affect their own health and the health of others through secondhand smoke and accidents. Also, they often require public health assistance paid for by taxpayers. By paying extra taxes, they pay for some of these costs. B. 1.People may work less.

2.Fewer new buildings will be built. 3.Fewer people will invest in corporate stocks. 4.More people will buy and sell financial assets. 5.People will switch to blue pencils. 6.People will give less to charity.

13.8. A. If the demand is inelastic, the incidence will fall on the buyer. If demand is elastic, the incidence will fall on the seller, who must lower the price to keep people from switching to substitutes. B. 1.regressive 2.progressive 3.proportional C. regressive D. 1.P 2.R 3.R 4.R 5.Pr 6.R 7.R

Case Application:

A Look at the Flat-Rate Tax

1. A flat-rate income tax would eliminate the progressivity of the income tax structure and thereby change the vertical equity so that larger income earners would not pay higher percentages of their income in taxes.

2. A flat-rate tax could increase the efficiency of the tax system by eliminating the great complexity of income tax laws and regulations, thereby saving the enormous funds spent in the private sector to avoid taxes and the government expenditures on enforcing their collection. It might also reduce the degree to which income tax laws distort the pattern of capital and other resource allocations.

3. Open answer. Whether you favor a pure flat-rate tax, the modified flat-rate tax, or the progressive income tax system depends on your attitudes toward vertical equity in the tax system and your beliefs concerning the degree to which the progressive income tax system is more or less fair and efficient than a pure flat-rate tax system, or whether a compromise modified flat-rate system accomplishes the efficiency and equity objectives better.

Answers to Practice Test

1.b 2.d 3.c 4.a 5.c 6.c 7.d 8.c 9.b 10.a 11.d 12.d 13.d 14.a 15.d 16.F 17.F 18.T 19.F 20.T

Chapter 14

What Can the Government Do about Unemployment and Inflation?

14.1. A. 1.bonds or all bills 2.by taxing businesses and individuals 3.American citizens 4. American citizens are paying other American citizens. (We are paying ourselves.) B. 1.It increases. 2.private businesses 3.Private borrowing decreases. 4. private capital that is "crowded out." C. 1.Answers will vary. 2.Yes, because income and/or wealth would be much greater. 3.income 4.GDP D. The budget deficit is equal to annual tax revenues minus expenditures. When this is negative, the government's spending for that year has exceeded its revenues. The government borrows to make up this difference, and

that extra borrowing adds to the national debt. The national debt is the total amount that the U.S. government owes to its creditors.

14.2. A. 1.by decreasing personal taxes 2.by decreasing business taxes B. Increased military expenditures would require an increase in government expenditures. C. Keynesian fiscal policy recommends combating a recession by cutting taxes for households that spend all or most of their after-tax incomes (lower income households). The increase in aggregate demand will stimulate the economy. Keynesians would also recommend increases in government spending during a recession. Supply-side fiscal policy recommends combating a recession by cutting taxes for those with higher incomes and higher propensities to save. The increase in savings would increase output by making production and investment more profitable. Supply-side theorists recommend reductions in government spending during a recession so that government spending will not "crowd out" private investment.

14.3. A. Congress and the president; the Fed B. 1.d 2.c 3.a 4.b C. 1.increase 2.increasing 3.It will be ineffective. D. 1.F, Down 2.M, Up 3.M, Up 4.F,Up 5.F, Down

14.4. A. 1.Tax revenues decrease and expenditures increase. 2. Balancing the budget would require tax increases, less spending, or both. Either would reduce aggregate demand and make the recession worse. 3. Tax revenues increase and expenditures decrease. 4. Balancing the budget would require tax cuts, spending increases, or both. Either would increase aggregate demand and would be inflationary. B. surplus during expansions; deficit during recessions C. Surpluses require either less spending on things that constituents want, or higher taxes, or both. These are unpopular with voters. D. 1.C 2.F 3.A 4.A 5.C

Case Application:

The Balanced Budget Amendment

1. Congress could circumvent the requirement for a balanced budget by a vote of three-fifths of the whole number of both houses of Congress.

2. Passage of the Balanced Budget Amendment would virtually eliminate expansionary fiscal policy. If the government could not incur deficits when demand in the private sector was insufficient for full employment, there would be little it could do to combat recession or depression, since monetary policy may be ineffective at the bottom of a business cycle.

3. Open answer. Those in favor of the Balanced Budget Amendment believe that Congress and the administration do not have enough self-discipline to avoid budget deficits. They contend the political temptations to overspend are too great and, therefore, a balanced budget amendment to the Constitution is necessary. Those who oppose the Balanced Budget Amendment believe it would handcuff the federal government and prevent it

from serving the needs of the country (including the need to stabilize the economy and achieve full employment). If the restrictions of the amendment proved too hampering, Congress would simply override them.

How Can Fiscal Policy Help Stabilize the Economy?

14.5. A. 1.S 2.K 3.S 4.K 5.S 6.S 7.K B. Supply-side takes a longer view because it takes more time to increase the supply of productive resources than it does to increase spending. C. 1.Keynesian 2.Supply-side
14.6. A. 1. 10; $1,000 2. 5; $500 3. 3; $300 4. 2; $200 5. 1; $100 B. It would approach infinity. C. 1.inverse 2.Spending increases aggregate demand, and increased consumption rates increase the size of the multiplier. 3.It would cause it to increase. D. 1.$200,000,000 2.$250,000,000 3.$100,000,000
14.7. A. "cushion" downturns and upturns. B. 1.increase aggregate demand. 2.decrease aggregate demand. C. consumption D. You should check 1, 2, and 4.

Case Application:

What Happens to Tax-Cut Dollars?

1. The discretionary fiscal policy measure discussed in the application is the reduction of federal taxes in order to stimulate output, investment, income, and employment.
2. The multiplier effect works on tax-cut dollars as well as on government expenditure dollars. When taxpayers have additional after-tax income, they spend most of it on goods and services. The amounts they spend become income to other people, who in turn spend most of their new income on goods and services. The result is a multiplier effect that increases the total income generated by some multiple of the initial amount of tax reduction.
3. Open answer. The tax legislation passed in the 1980s was wise and effective fiscal policy to the extent that it helped the economy recover from the 1981–1982 recession. It was not wise and effective to the extent that it resulted in increased federal government deficits and a more unequal distribution of income.

How Can Monetary Policy Help Stabilize the Economy?

14.8. A. 1.MS up, R down, I up, AD up 2.MS up, R down, I up, AD up 3.MS down, R up, I down, AD down B. 1.interest rates 2.money supply 3.demand; savings

C. 1.

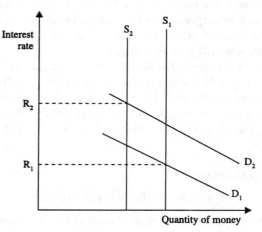

2. a. rise b. fall c. fall 3.They would hinder the government's efforts.
D. 1.

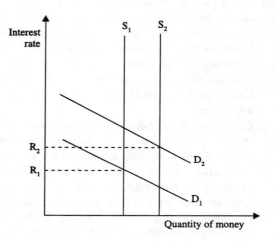

2.They stay about the same. 3.inflation 4.higher interest rates E. 1.a constant velocity of money 2.No. 3. During recessions, T will increase. Near the peak of the business cycle P will increase. In between the peaks and troughs, both will probably increase some.
14.9. A. 1.policymakers 2.the government or Fed 3.monetary or fiscal policy B. 1.D 2.I 3.R 4.I C. In order to be effective, the policies should be implemented just when the economy is entering a period of high inflation or recession. While economic activity is ongoing, it takes time to gather and analyze data describing the economy. The lags in recognizing the problem, deciding on a course of action, and experiencing the impacts of policies lead to problems in timing the implementation of fiscal and monetary policies. By the time policies are implemented, the economy may be at a different point in the business cycle.

Case Application:

The Interest Rate Yo-Yo

1. When the Federal Reserve sells government securities in the open market, it "sops up" excess bank reserves.

This restricts the banks' ability to expand credit to borrowers, which causes interest rates to rise.

2. The consequences of wide fluctuations in interest rates are to increase the amount of uncertainty for business firms, which may have formulated their plans on the basis of one interest rate and then find their plans defeated by large changes in the interest rates. This may lead to bankruptcy of the firms.

3. Open answer. Those who say that controlling the money supply necessitates wide swings in interest rates base their reasoning on the overriding importance of macroeconomic stability. They believe that the money supply is the key to putting an end to inflation, and interest rates are a secondary consideration. Those who are opposed to this policy believe that price stabilization can be achieved without the extreme swings in interest rates and that the costs that the policy imposes on individuals and businesses are too high to justify it.

How Can Economic Growth Be Increased?

14.10. A. 1.current consumption 2.a higher standard of living in the future B. decrease C. 1.quantity 2.quality D. 1.C 2.I 3.C 4.C 5.I 6.I 7.C 8.C E. (answers will vary) 1.highway improvements 2.water projects 3.human capital investment (education)

14.11. A. 1.quantity 2.quality B. 1."baby boomers" entering the labor force 2.more women working outside the home 3.more workers working longer years (retiring later). C. 1.formal education 2.on-the-job training D. 1.forgone wages while in school or lower wages during on-the-job training 2.The older someone is, the fewer remaining work years available to get the returns. E. 1.1 2.2 3.4 4.3

Case Application:

How to Grow

1. The factors discussed in this application that affect economic growth are expenditures on research and development and the number of years of education completed.

2. Spending on R & D would tend to increase in periods of rapid economic growth both because of rising demand for goods and services, causing producers to seek ways of increasing output to satisfy the market, and because of more revenues available to producers, enabling them to pay for increased R & D.

3. Open answer. Measures that might be taken to increase the rate of growth of GDP include encouraging research and development (for example, by government-sponsored research and development programs and subsidies) and encouraging youth to obtain more education (for example, by student loans).

Answers To Practice Test

1.c 2.c 3.a 4.b 5.b 6.b 7.d 8.b 9.b 10.b 11.b 12.d 13.a 14.a 15.c 16.F 17.T 18.T 19.T 20.F

Crossword Puzzle for Chapters 10–14

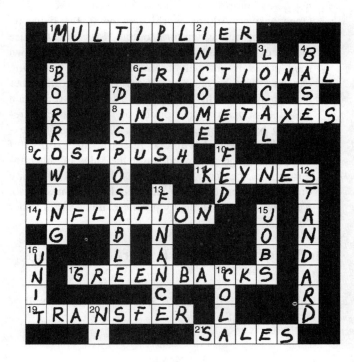

Chapter 15

Why Do We Trade With Other Countries?

15.1. A. 1.absolute 2.2 3.4 4.Mexico 5.1/2 6.1/4 7.Nigeria 8.Nigeria 9.Mexico 10. Mexico should trade textiles for Nigerian oil.

15.2. A. only when each country produces a good that is not produced in the other B. 1.A straight-line PPF implies that costs are constant. 2.increase as the output of a specific good increases 3.perfectly adaptable (mobile) to all uses 4.expensive 5.limited

15.3. A. 1.I 2.I 3.E 4.I 5.E 6.E B. from American purchases (imports) of their products C. capital (technology); labor

Case Application:

U.S. Farmers Selling Overseas

1. Judging from the data on U.S. exports as a percentage of world exports, the United States apparently had the largest efficiency advantage over the rest of the world in the production of corn, followed closely by soybeans. U.S. corn exports accounted for 69.7% of world exports of the crop, while U.S. soybean exports accounted for 66.3% of world exports.

2. The United States does not completely specialize in corn production because of increasing costs. If additional acreage planted in corn were not as productive or were located in areas of the country where the climate was not as suitable for growing corn, costs per bushel of corn produced would rise and the United States would not be as competitive in the world corn market.

3. Open answer. Adding world demand to the domestic demand for our agricultural output does tend to raise the prices for some food items at home. If holding down food prices is our only or main objective, restricting exports would be one way of doing that. On the other hand, policies in this country have for some time been aimed at supporting the prices of farm products, frequently by government subsidies. Restricting farm exports would hold down food prices at the expense of farmers' income and would hurt the sales of other industries to the farm communities. The cost of living might be lower, but so would people's incomes. Also, we would not be able to purchase much from other countries.

Who Benefits and Who Is Hurt By Foreign Trade?

15.4. A. 1. 1/2 unit of textiles 2. 2 units of oil 3. 1/4 unit of oil 4. 4 units of oil

5.

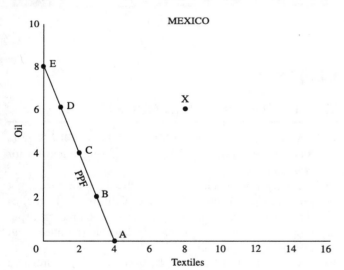

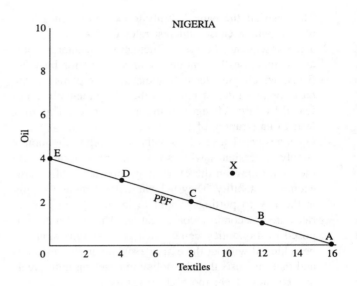

6. a. 5; 6 b. 3; 10 c. Both countries now have more of each good—they are better off after specialization and trade.

7.

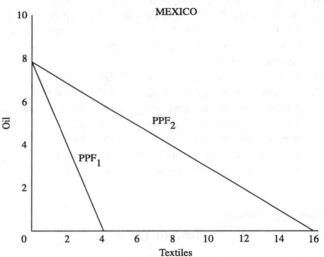

8.

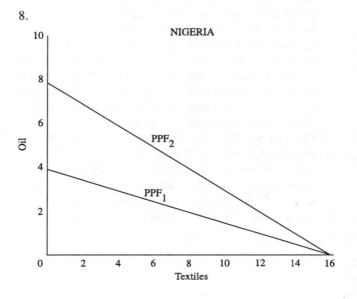

9. Trade moves the PPF to the right for both countries, allowing them to attain previously unattainable combinations of both goods.

15.5. A, B, and C. Answers will vary. D. consumers E. 1. American consumers; American auto workers 2. American farmers; American bread consumers 3. American shoe producers; American shoe buyers 4. American energy companies; American consumers F. structural G. (answers may vary) 1. autos 2. steel 3. textiles

Case Application:

NAFTA Winners and Losers

1. The petroleum and paper industries are hurt by U.S. Western Hemisphere trade.
2. The industrial machinery and electrical equipment industries benefit from U.S. Western Hemisphere trade because of large exports to Canada and Mexico. Other industries that benefit from the trade include those that use petroleum and paper because the imports of those commodities reduce production costs for the industries that use them.
3. Open answer. Some U.S. farm workers benefit from increased Western Hemisphere trade and some are injured by it. It could be argued that farm workers are equally well off, overall, as producers, but that as consumers, farm workers benefit from Western Hemisphere trade.

How Do We Restrict Foreign Trade?

15.6. A.

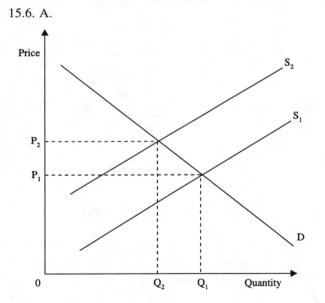

B.

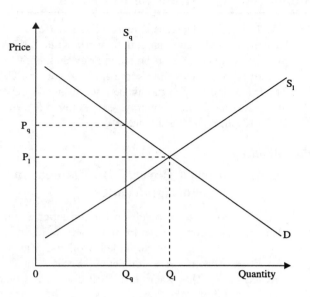

C. With quotas, because the supply curve will be vertical (perfectly inelastic), and the quantity supplied will be unable to increase to absorb some of the increased demand D. 1. politics (punishment) 2. to protect technological advantages (neomercantilism) 3. national security E. Answers will vary. F. 1. Smoot-Hawley 2. to reduce unemployment in the United States. 3. It reduced the trade, reduced the aggregate demand for U.S. goods, and resulted in increased unemployment in the United States.

15.7. A. multilateral B. 1. confusion resulting from different tariff rates with different countries on the same product 2. most-favored-nation clauses 3. They give the "favored" nation all tariff reductions that are negotiated with any other country.

Case Application:

Trade as an Instrument of Foreign Policy

1. Tariffs, quotas, and export embargoes have been used to implement foreign policy.
2. The effect of political embargoes is to nullify comparative advantage. As a result of an embargo, resources are not used to produce goods in which the United States has a comparative advantage.
3. Open answer. It might be argued that a nation must pursue those policies that protect its interests and its safety—including punishing its enemies and rewarding its friends—irrespective of the effects on trade and comparative advantage. On the other hand, trade restrictions hurt everyone, the countries imposing them as well as the countries against whom they are directed. And in an increasingly interdependent world, countries should not act unilaterally in violation of international agreements.

Should Foreign Trade Be Restricted?

15.8. A. 1.increase; decrease 2.increase; decrease B. 1.They have more and better capital to work with. 2.It would prevent the exporting of the technology that allows them to earn higher wages than some foreign workers. C. No. The infant industry argument applies to newly developing industries in an economy. The American steel and auto industries are hardly infants.

Case Application:

Can Increased Poverty Be Blamed on Foreign Trade?

1. This case focuses on the cheap foreign labor argument.
2. The increased competition from abroad would, in effect, increase the supply of unskilled workers with which American workers were competing. Because of the increased supply, U.S. wages of unskilled workers would be expected to drop. With lower wages, more of them would be hired. This would be shown on a diagram by a shift to the right of the labor supply curve. The employer would move to the new equilibrium point where demand equaled the new supply, hiring more workers at lower wages.

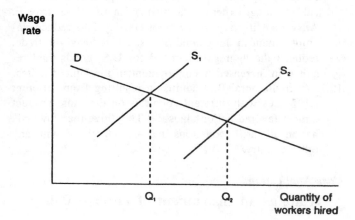

3. Open answer. On the one hand, it could be argued that the likelihood that technological changes within industries have overwhelmed the effects of trade on labor demand is no reason not to try and protect the wages of unskilled workers by restricting foreign competition. On the other hand, even if increased trade does worsen income inequality, the country's total real income ultimately benefits from freer trade. Part of those benefits can be transferred by government (through unemployment compensation, retraining programs, and direct subsidies) to the workers who suffer as a result of higher imports, leaving everyone better off.

Answers to Practice Test

1.d 2.b 3.b 4.b 5.c 6.a 7.a 8.d 9.d 10.c 11.d 12.c
13.c 14.b 15.c 16.F 17.T 18.T 19.F 20.F

Chapter 16

How Do We Pay for Imports?

16.1. A. foreign exchange B. 1. 0.20 or 1/5 (20 cents) 2. 0.25 or 1/4 (25 cents) 3. 0.10 or 1/10 (10 cents) C. 1. 5 francs 2.$20 3.$24 4.$25 D. 1.$0.20 2. 75 francs 3. 90 francs 4. 60 francs E. 1.more expensive 2.less expensive 3.more expensive F. 1.less expensive 2.more expensive 3.less expensive

16.2. A. 1.supply of dollars 2.supply of pounds
B.

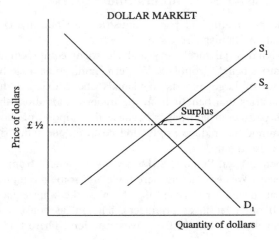

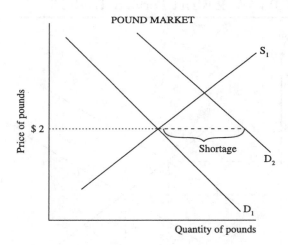

C. 1.shortage 2.The British government or central bank would need to provide pounds to the market at a rate of $2 = 1 pound. D. 1.surplus 2.The U.S. government or Federal Reserve would need to buy up the excess dollars with pounds that they keep in reserve.

E.

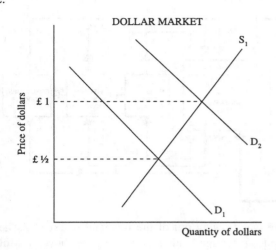

DOLLAR MARKET

Quantity of dollars

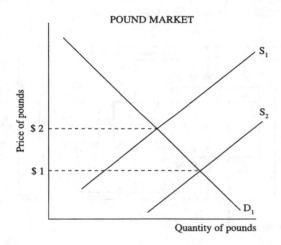

POUND MARKET

Quantity of pounds

F. Fixed exchange rates are legally set by the respective countries; therefore, a fixed exchange rate system is a *multilateral* agreement in which all of the participating countries agree to maintain the fixed exchange rates. Pegged exchange rates are not multilateral. A system of pegged exchange rates arises when the government of a smaller country attempts to reduce exchange rate risk for its currency by "pegging" its value to the value of a larger country's currency. In essence, the smaller country maintains a fixed exchange rate for its currency, but the larger country is not involved or affected.

16.3. A. 1.revalued 2.devalued B. 1.appreciates 2.depreciates C. 1.devaluing 2.exports 3.employment and GDP 4.Citizens of the country would be able to buy fewer imported goods. D. 1.Yes. A country can cause the value of its currency to appreciate by buying its own currency in exchange markets with foreign currencies that it has in reserve. It can cause its currency to depreciate by flooding the exchange markets with it. E. 1.D 2.A 3.A 4.D 5.A

16.4. A. 1.the chance that an investor in a foreign country may earn more or less than anticipated due to unanticipated changes in exchange rates. 2. Answers will vary.

Possibilities include Mexico, the countries that make up the former USSR, the countries that make up the former Yugoslavia. B. 1.350,000 2.455,000 3.130,000 4.350,000 5.53,846 6.The dollar value of Mr. Bing's investment decreased because the Mexican government abandoned the currency peg, and the currency depreciated. Mr. Bing lost his gamble on exchange rate risk. C.Charles' investment was harmed by the change in the exchange rates. When he converts his earnings back into U.S. dollars, the total will be reduced because the euro has depreciated.

Case Application:

The End of the World Credit Binge

1. Mexico was employing a fixed exchange rate system. The peso was officially devalued to 70 pesos to the dollar by government action rather than depreciating to that level as the result of demand and supply in the foreign exchange market.
2. When oil exporters receive payment for the petroleum that they sell, they leave a large amount of their receipts on deposit in New York and other Western nation banks because the stability in those countries provides security for their funds. Those funds thus become available for lending by the banks.
3. Open answer. The Mexican government believes that it must pursue the domestic policies that maximize the welfare of its citizens. It is committed to a high economic growth rate in order to improve its low living standards. The IMF and its industrialized members, however, believe that since it is largely their funds and those of their private banking institutions that are at stake, the IMF must require Mexico to adopt austerity measures to ensure that the loans can be repaid.

What Happens When Exports and Imports Do Not Balance?

16.5. A. 1.I, C 2.I, LT 3.E, ST 4.E, LT 5.E, C 6.E, ST 7.I, C B. 1.exports; imports 2.exporters and export workers 3.consumers 4.appreciate C. 1.imports; exports 2.exporters and export workers 3.consumers 4.depreciate D. 1.increasing. 2.increase. 3.decrease. 4.increase. 5.increase. 6.decrease. 7.disappear.

16.6. A. 1.outflows of gold or similar internationally accepted assets 2.borrowing funds from the IMF 3.It can sell its assets to other countries (or 4. It can allow its currency to depreciate). B. 1.Basic deficits are less likely to remain if rates can fluctuate because currency depreciation and/or appreciation automatically eliminate deficits and surpluses. C. 1.residual accounts. 2.gold; similar assets

16.7. A. 1.imports 2.surplus 3.falls; depreciates. 4.exports; imports. B. 1.exports 2.shortage 3.rises; appreciates. 4.imports; exports.

C. 1.

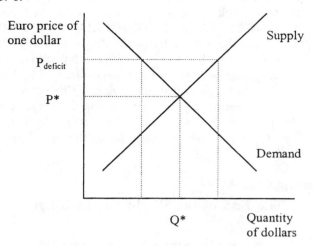

If there is a basic deficit in the balance of payments in the U.S. with a system of freely floating exchange rates, the exchange rate will be above the equilibrium level, and there will be a surplus of dollars in the foreign exchange market. 2.Since exchange rates are freely floating, market forces will cause the price of dollars to fall. In other words, the exchange rate will depreciate. 3.Now that dollars are cheaper, exports will increase and imports will decrease until the basic deficit is eliminated.

Case Application:

U.S. International Trade Position Takes a Nosedive

1. The balance-of-payments transactions not included in the data shown in the chart are long-term and short-term capital transactions and monetary gold transactions.
2. A recession causes a nation's consumption and investment demand to fall. As a result, imports decrease and the current account balance improves. If other countries fall into recession, their imports decline and exporting countries experience a deterioration of their balance of payments.
3. Open answer. One reason could be the decline in the competitiveness of U.S. producers in both the domestic market and world markets, as discussed in chapter 7. Another reason cited is the high consumption rate of U.S. consumers in the 1980s. A related reason is the large federal government deficits in the decade, inviting capital imports and postponing the normal adjustment mechanism to bring trade back into balance.

What Is the Relationship between International Finance and the National Economy?

16.8. A. G + I + X = T + S + M B. 1.T, S, M 2.inversely
C. 1.G, I, X 2.directly

D.

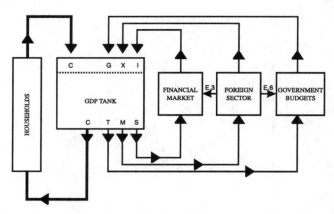

E. 1.More was flowing out of the financial markets. 2.They came from foreign lenders. 3. See Figure above. 4. More was flowing out of the government. 5.They came from foreign lenders. 6. See Figure above.

F. 1.

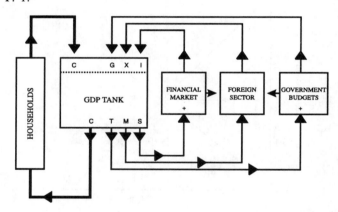

2.Lenders: government and financial markets; Borrowers: foreign sector. 3.It must be exporting more than it imports. 4.Japan

16.9. A. In the short run, Americans have increased their standard of living because they were able to consume more than they produced. B. to buy American real estate, businesses, and government bonds (to finance the government budget deficit) C. Eventually we will need to pay others back by consuming less than we produce—the balance will be exported for others to enjoy. Our standard of living will decrease. Post-1980s Americans will be the ones to pay this price.

16.10. A. 1.It would find it difficult to borrow and would need to cut back on spending or raise taxes. 2.It would decrease as G decreased (or T increased), and aggregate demand decreased. 3.The same as in the government sector—investment would fall. 4.The same—GDP would decrease as I decreased. 5.There would be less money available for consumers to spend. B. 1.exports 2.imports

Case Application:

A Penny Saved Is a Rare Occurrence

1. If the U.S. savings rate were greater, the consumption of domestic goods (C) and imported goods (I) would be less.
2. The low national savings rate in the United States contributes to an import surplus and balance of payments deficit, a fall in the dollar exchange rate, federal deficits that are partly financed by foreign capital, and a net debtor position in the world economy.
3. Open answer. It could be argued that the savings rate is the result of choices made by individuals and their representatives and that in a free-enterprise economy there should not be any interference with those choices. On the other side, it could be argued that when individual and national choices result in weakening the economy and reducing future standards of living, measures should be taken to change behaviors. Those measures might consist of tax incentives to increase personal and business savings and discourage consumption, reductions in federal deficits by cutting spending or raising taxes, and a campaign by the national leadership to change public attitudes.

Answers to Practice Test

1.b 2.d 3.b 4.b 5.a 6.c 7.b 8.b 9.c 10.a 11.e 12.d 13.c 14.b 15. 16.T 17.F 18.T 19.F 20.T

Chapter 17

How Is the Former Soviet Union's Economy Being Restructured?

17.1.
A. 1.

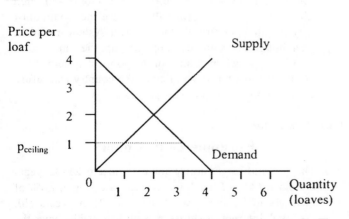

2.3 units 3.1 unit 4.There is a shortage of 2 units. B. The price would increase. If there is a shortage, market forces will drive the price up until equilibrium is reached. Once quantity demanded equals quantity supplied, the price is stable. C.$2

17.2. A. Organized crime has run rampant in Russia. Small businesses have had to pay for protection and make other payoffs to organized crime and government bureaucrats in order to stay in business. The nomenklatura have gained control of most of Russia's valuable resources. Rampant crime and political instability have discouraged potential foreign investors. B. nomenklatura C. Crony capitalism refers to an economic system that is based on allocating resources and goods according to favoritism rather than according to who can make the most productive use of the resources and goods.

17.3. A. Private banks are a new concept, and many Russians are afraid to trust them because many were initially poorly managed, unregulated, and subject to corruption. Russians convert their money into U.S. dollars (or euros) to protect themselves from inflation and depreciation of the ruble. B. 1.There are a number of stock markets in existence, and they are not linked by computers. 2.Full information about companies is not available for investors. (Other problems are that the markets are not well regulated so fraud is rampant, and Russians have little knowledge of stock markets and are reluctant to invest in the domestic markets.)

17.4. A. 1.Establish legal guidelines and regulations for the nation (including antitrust laws) and a system through which laws and regulations are enforced. 2.Provide public goods and services to citizens. 3.Establish a system by which taxes are collected. 4.Establish stabilization policies. B. 1.These institutions did not exist in the past, so the government has no experience in establishing or enforcing such laws. 2.Firms provided most of these services in the past, so the government has to learn what to provide and generate revenues (through taxes) to pay for the programs. 3.There was no national tax agency in the past, so workers must receive proper training, and they must learn how to catch evaders. 4.Again, they have no experience in setting these policies, so they are certain to make mistakes and learn from them (hopefully!).

17.5. A. rule of law; crony capitalism B. 1.C 2.R 3.R 4.C 5.R C. Markets work because of trust. Buyers must have confidence in sellers and know there is a system in place that protects their own rights, and the same holds for sellers. Everyone must have confidence that the legal system will work impartially in order to have confidence in the market.

Case Application:

Funding Business Activities in Russia

1. The financial markets in Russia have not developed efficiently on their own. Additional funds are needed to educate Russians about credit analysis, lending, and investing and to stimulate the financial markets there. The Russian people do not have confidence in financial markets; however, if they observe markets that work efficiently, they may develop such confidence.

2. Exchange rate risk due to political instability is a major problem facing potential investors. There is also rampant corruption in Russia, and the government has not yet created a stable system of laws and enforcement to curb it.

3. Open answer. This is a normative issue. Many economists would probably answer yes because there are overall gains from widespread capitalism and free trade. (See the Case Application in the textbook on page 525.) If countries produce according to comparative advantage and engage in free trade, total global output increases. However, countries such as Russia apparently need help developing a capitalist economy. There are also opportunities for risk-takers potentially to earn profits by investing in Russia. Arguments against giving aid to Russia for the development of financial markets would probably be based on the opinion that the money could be spent to help our own citizens.

How Are the Economies of Central and Eastern Europe Being Restructured?

17.6. A. 1.H 2.P 3.P 4.P 5.H B. 1.Instead of relying on vouchers to privatize industries as the Poles did, the Hungarians immediately sold them to the highest bidders, even if that meant selling them to foreigners. 2.The government in Hungary also provided tax incentives to foreign investors investing in Hungary.

17.7. A. 1.Unlike the Russians, the Poles were familiar with capitalism because they had a long history of it before they became communist. 2.The Poles also had more freedom to travel to the West during communism than the Russians did. They had observed that capitalism worked better than communism. 3.Many Polish emigrants sent money back to family members in Poland, and they used it to start small businesses. 4.Since Poland has a government that is more stable and a rule of law that is better established, foreign investors have been more willing to invest in Poland than in Russia. B.In Russia, the dinosaurs were subsidized so that they could continue to operate (until 1995) while in Poland, the dinosaurs were not protected so they failed right away. C.Unlike the Russians (and the Poles) the Hungarians did not have to use shock therapy because their economy was further along in the transformation to capitalism when communism fell. Also, unlike the Russians, the Hungarians opened up their economy to foreign investment right away, even allowing foreigners to own their telephone companies.

17.8. A. The CMEA was a formal international trade agreement among the USSR and the communist countries of CEE. B. They were able to purchase energy (oil and natural gas) and other natural resources at prices that were much lower than world prices. C. The CEE countries had to develop new markets for their goods in countries that had money to buy them, so they had to improve quality and lower prices.

Case Application:

Marketing Drugs in Hungary

1. In a communist economy, the government determines what to produce, how to produce, and how to distribute output. Thus, marketing and advertising are not necessary. Individual economic agents (consumers, firms) buy what is available for sale.

2. Currently, there is a large demand for medical representatives relative to the available supply because it is a new field with a lot of openings. Increases in demand increase the price. Doctors' salaries will increase more over time as they gain experience and a patient base.

3. Open answer. Medical representatives do not actually produce output, but they do provide important information to doctors. Whether they should earn more than doctors is debatable.

How Is the Chinese Economy Being Restructured?

17.9. A. self-interest; the good of China B. 1.This depends on your definition of fair. If you believe that dividing the money equally regardless of level of education or skill is fair, then the answer is yes. If you think Pat should earn more because she has earned a college degree, then the answer is no. 2.Many people would probably opt not to go to college if they were not going to earn more money as a result. There would be a lack of motivation to improve oneself through education. As a society, we would have a less-educated work force. Fewer investments in human capital would lead to lower standards of living, too. 3.Mao Zedong wanted the Chinese people to be motivated to work for the good of China instead of for individual financial gain. He had teachers, doctors, physicists, engineers, peasants, and everyone else working together in fields or in factories for equal pay. This is the same idea as the new plan for Winnie and Pat.

17.10. A. 1.C 2.R 3.C 4.P,R 5.R 6.H,P 7.H,C (some—through SEZs) 8.C B. This is primarily because the Communist Party is still in control of the political system in China. Even though the economy is opening up, the communists remain very much in control of the political system. They set the overall economy policy of the country and refuse to allow opposition political parties.

Case Application:

E-commerce in China

1. They should target single males who are 21–35 years old since 64% of the Internet users are single, 86% of them are male, and 80% of them are 21–35 years old. Potential Internet advertisers would probably have the most success in reaching this group. (Of course this could change as Internet use becomes more widespread

in China. Advertisers should certainly update the demographic statistics periodically.)

2. China is the most populous nation in the world; therefore, it provides a huge market for firms. The economy is also growing rapidly, and the country will have the world's largest economy by 2020 if current growth rates continue. The young people in China are also well-educated, highly motivated, and ready to accept free-market economics.

3. Open answer. It depends on how much you like risk. It is clear that China's economy is opening up. However, the pace is fairly slow because of the power of the Communist Party, so it may take time for your investment to pay off. There is also the possibility that your investment will not pay off. The government could always nationalize the industries again. As stated in the Case Application, invest at your own risk.

Answers to Practice Test

1.c 2.b 3.d 4.e 5.a 6.b 7.a 8.d 9.a 10.a 11.d 12.d 13.d 14.a 15.a 16.T 17.T 18.F 19.F 20.F

Chapter 18

What are the Characteristics of Less Developed Countries?

18.1. A. 1.less developed country 2.the process of increasing a country's income and improving the standard of living of its people B. 1.$21,168 2.$1,559 3.$7,045 4.$6,014 5.$8,859 6.$1,940 C. 1.Australia 2.Uruguay 3.Mexico

18.2. A. 1.per capita GDP or income 2.distribution of income B. 1.rate of child malnutrition 2.life expectancy at birth 3.child mortality rate 4.adult illiteracy rate C. (answers may vary) 1.television 2.personal computer 3.telephone 4.indoor plumbing

18.3. A. 1.Sub-Saharan Africa 2.South Asia B. (answers will vary) 1.Angola 2.Zimbabwe 3.Tanzania 4.Mozambique C. (answers will vary) 1.Pakistan 2.India 3.Cambodia 4.Vietnam

18.4. A. 1.differences in the buying power of a dollar 2.distributions of income are often highly skewed in LDCs B. purchasing power parity C. 1.E 2.B 3.A dollar has more purchasing power in Country E than in Country B. So, when adjustments for purchasing power parity are made, the per capita income in Country E buys more or has more purchasing power than the per capita income in Country B. D. We cannot tell for certain which country has more people living in poverty. If we look only at per capita income, Country ABC has a higher value. However, if we look at the distribution of income, Coun-

try ABC has a more skewed distribution of income. Therefore, it could be possible that there are fewer people living in poverty in Country XYZ with a lower per capita income and more equitable distribution of income. We don't know for certain from the information provided in the question. E. 1.land reform programs 2.industrialization 3.social programs such as universal education and health care

Case Application:

Capitalism versus Buddhism?

1. In 1996, 53 households per 1,000 in South Asia had televisions, and 1.5 households per 1,000 had personal computers. In 1996, 228 households per 1,000 in East Asia and the Pacific had televisions, and 4.5 households per 1,000 had personal computers.

2. Increases in income from development activities increase demand for labor, having a multiplier effect down the line. Income from inherited wealth does not create more jobs.

3. Open answer. It might be argued that the single-minded pursuit of profits that has characterized capitalistic development in the West and the transformation that modern industry entails are incompatible with the traditional social values and antimaterialistic philosophies of Asia. Countering this is the view that success in production and business activity is not incompatible with adherence to tradition and spirituality, as evidenced by the success of the Amana colonies in the United States.

What Makes Countries Poor?

18.5. A. environmental determination; cultural determination. B. 1.ED 2.CD 3.CD 4.ED 5.CD C. In today's society, there appears to be more evidence in support of the theory of cultural determination. There are certainly many contradictions to the theory of enviornmental determination, including economically rich but resource-poor countries such as Japan and Switzerland, and poor but resource-rich countries such as Russia and Nigeria. Some of the former USSR countries, in particular, are having difficulties adapting to capitalism because the people have a strong belief that making profits is "bad." It is difficult to impose a new economic system in a country where cultural attitudes and values are in opposition to the new institutional structures.

18.6. A. The economic surplus is anything left over after the people in a country take care of their basic needs. It is from this surplus that a country finances its investment spending. B. 1.overpopulation 2.low initial investment (the vicious circle of poverty) 3.little human capital (or the existence of external exploitation, which may have taken away any surplus to other countries) C. (order may vary) 1.increasing capital investment—This is missing in

LDCs. It was occurring in some of the richer developing countries until the recent Asian financial crisis. Now foreign investment in developing countries is declining (at least temporarily), and it is lacking in LDCs. 2.increasing capital efficiency—This is missing in LDCs. Many LDCs are labor abundant and use labor-intensive production methods. They do not have funds to invest in capital. 3.increasing labor-force participation—The labor-force participation rate is certainly lower in LDCs where women are expected to stay home and work there instead of obtaining a job outside of the home than in countries where men and women both participate in the labor force. This may be changing in LDCs that are becoming more urbanized. 4.increasing investment in human capital—Again, we know that illiteracy rates are high in many LDCs, so investment in human capital is low. But, it may be changing in LDCs that are becoming more urbanized. D. 1.producers and labor unions 2.Consumer choice is limited to high-priced, inferior local products.

Case Application:

Do You Like Company? How about 11 Billion?

1. Yes, Table 2 does show that, overall, poverty is associated with illiteracy. This is indicated by the fact that the male adult illiteracy rate for the low-income countries as a whole is 35%, whereas that for the middle-income countries is only 12% and that for high-income countries is generally less than 1%.
2. They are related because they are both part of the poverty syndrome—they occur together in the LDCs and each reinforces the other. They are different in that the vicious circle of poverty involves the relationship between poverty and economic productivity/growth while the population-education vicious circle involves the relationship among literacy, birthrates, and the perpetuation of poverty.
3. Open answer. Those who are concerned about the negative effects of high population growth rates in the LDCs on the world economy and environment might advocate such funding. Those who oppose the use of contraception and/or abortion to control population growth would likely be against the provision of funding.

What are the Prospects for the Economic Development of the LDCs?

18.7. A. 1.export-promotion 2.import-substitution B.1.import-substitution 2.export-promotion C. 1.IS 2.EP 3.EP 4.IS 5.IS D. Export-promotion policies have been more successful. They were used by the Asian tigers and tiger cubs and resulted in large increases in economic growth as the countries produced according to their comparative advantages.

18.8. A. 1.primary products. 2.increased. 3.loans 4.decreased. 5.interest 6.economic surplus. 7.vicious circle of poverty. 8.economic hardship B. 1.borrowers 2.Prices would have increased. 3.The LDCs would be in the enviable position of seeing their incomes increasing while their loan payments were decreasing in real terms. C. 1.a lack of future credit, future foreign aid, and/or future vital imports 2.The economic pressure on their populations may lead to social unrest and revolution. 3.Answers will vary but could include Poland, Hungary, Russia, and even the United States in 1776.

18.9 A. 1.geometric rate 2.arithmetic rate.

B.

Population	Ears of Corn	Ears per person
100	1,000	10.00
200	2,000	10.00
400	3,000	7.50
800	4,000	5.00
1,600	5,000	3.12

C. an inverse relationship D. 1.energy resources 2.the environment E. 1.starvation 2.high infant mortality rates (or low life expectancy rates)

Case Application:

A Learning Experience

1. Investment from private sources has declined as a result of the crisis; therefore, these sources are not available to cover current account deficits. If there are freely floating exchange rates, the deficits will lead to currency depreciations, which could cause other problems such as making debts more onerous and making imports more expensive for domestic buyers.
2. The objective of the World Bank is to have a world that is free of poverty. As stated in the textbook, its major role is to help finance development of LDCs. The reason it wants countries to experience economic development is because it will reduce poverty permanently. The Bank's primary interests are social concerns, and economic reform is a means to achieve social improvements.
3. Open answer. It depends on how accurate the World Bank's predictions are. If the LDCs promote globalization through industrialization, this will probably help reduce the gap. However, the LDCs still have to solve population, debt, and environmental problems described in the textbook. It will be a long time before the gap between living standards in industrialized countries and the poorest countries in sub-Saharan Africa is reduced.

Answers to Practice Test

1.a 2.c 3.b 4.d 5.d 6.d 7.d 8.d 9.c 10.b 11.c 12.b 13.c 14.a 15.d 16.F 17.F 18.T 19.T 20.F

Crossword Puzzle for Chapters 15–18